1. This book may be kept three weeks.
   It is to be returned on / before the last date
   stamped below.
2. A fine of 20p will be charged for every week
   or part of week a book is overdue.

THE COMPLETE WHO'S WHO OF IRISH INTERNATIONAL FOOTBALL 1945–96

THE COMPLETE WHO'S WHO OF
IRISH INTERNATIONAL FOOTBALL
1945-96

STEPHEN MCGARRIGLE

MAINSTREAM
PUBLISHING
EDINBURGH AND LONDON

Copyright © Stephen McGarrigle, 1996

First published in Great Britain in 1996 by
MAINSTREAM PUBLISHING COMPANY (EDINBURGH) LTD
7 Albany Street
Edinburgh EH1 3UG

ISBN 1 85158 894 9

A catalogue record for this book is available from the British Library

Designed by Jenny Haig

Typeset in Sabon
Printed and bound in Great Britain by Butler and Tanner Ltd, Frome

CONTENTS

ACKNOWLEDGEMENTS

Who's Who in Irish International Football 1945–96 is much more than the work of an individual. Numerous people and organisations have made vital contributions to the making of this book. Without their help, advice and contributions – whether in the form of photographs, provision of information, prose and so on – what is now a reality would have been an impossibility. My sincere thanks go to:

My editor Nigel Leese (but for whom it would have been finished in 1994); the *Irish Post*'s Peter Carbery for all his punctuation and photographs; the staff of the British Newspaper Library in Colindale; Ray Spiller, Association of Football Statisticians; Gerry Mackey; Michael Gannon; Tony Lewis; Seamus Dunne; Johnny Walsh; Dermot McCarthy; Edward Burke; Paul Harrison; Robert Goggins; Willie Cotter; Noel Hanley; Charlie Hurley, Drogheda United; Richard Kelly Photographs; Jeremy Makinson; Roy Bushby; Finbarr Callahan; *Belfast Telegraph*; Monitor Press Features; Ken Coton; Bill Smith; Chris Morris; Paul McGrath; David Kelly; John Aldridge; Tommy Coyne; Andy Townsend; Eddie McGoldrick; Mark Kennedy; Packie Bonner; Mike Milligan; Terry Phelan; Jeff Kenna; Alan Kernaghan; Liam O'Brien; David Greene; Cynthia Bateman; Mr and Mrs R. Lawlor; Mr and Mrs S. Given; Tim Carder; Tommy Dunne; Noel Hickey; Martin Sharkey; Shay Keogh; John McGowan; Malcolm Brodie MBE; Michael O'Flanagan; Ulrich Matheja, *Kiker-sportmagazin*; Leo Dunne; Elizabeth Duffy, Dundalk; Simon Marland, Bolton Wanderers; Rita Greenaway, Birmingham City; Tranmere Rovers FC; Norwich City FC; Graham Hughes, Wolverhampton Wanderers; Sunderland FC; Tony Hayes, Southend United; Spence Anderson, Dundee United FC; Blackburn Rovers FC; Gabriela Lang, Watford FC; James Galvin, Millwall FC; Motherwell FC; J. Ann Hough, Huddersfield Town; Oliver Byrne, Shelbourne; Garard Carmody, IRFU; Seamus Bellow, Dundalk FC; John O'Shaughnessy, *Limerick Leader*; J. Leo McMahon, *The Southern Star*; John Maddocks, Manchester City FC; Michael Parkinson; Charlie Stuart, *Irish Press*; Colin Benson, *Republic Programme*; Sean Creedon (Eire Managers); Nigel Clarke, *Daily Mirror*; Eric White, Brentford FC; Paul Gilligan, Doncaster Rovers FC; Michael Spinks, Barnsley FC; Lucy Pepper, *South London Press*; Miss K. Holdsworth, Blackburn Rovers FC; Ken Smales, Nottingham Forest FC; Graham Haynes, Brentford FC; Don Ardmore; Stephen Kelly (Johnny Carey); Chris Bethell, Millwall FC; Tony Reed, *Irish Press*; Phil Shaw, *The Independent*; Bill Nicholson; Jeff Powell, *Daily Mail*; Brian Granville, *The Sunday Times*; Ken Montgomery, *Sunday Mirror*; Hunter Davies; David Lacey, *The Guardian*; James Mossop, *Sunday Express*; Patrick Barclay, *The*

Independent; Reg Hayter, *Hayters Sports Reporting Service*; Jack Steggles, *Daily Mirror*; Shaun Curtis; John Doughry, *The Independent*; Andy Porter, Tottenham Hotspur FC; Ian Westbrook and Bob Hennessy, Brentford FC; Denis O'Hara, *Belfast News Letter*; Keith MacAlister, AFC Bournemouth; Ian Moat, Notts County FC; Sarah Carmichael, Southampton FC; Aston Villa FC; Brian Searl, Mansfield Town FC; K. R. Ashalley, Walsall FC; Sid Woodhead, Grimsby Town FC; Roger Walsh, Luton Town FC; Paul Mace; Dave Smith, Leicester City FC; Preston North End FC; Pat Redmond, *Irish Post*; Mike Cuerdon, Oxford United FC; Ray Simpson, Burnley FC; Falkirk FC; Bolton Wanderers FC; Kevin McKenna, *Irish Press*; Roger Harris, Brighton & Hove Albion FC; Bristol City FC; Cambridge United FC; Blackpool FC; M. Beck, *Peterborough Evening News*; Alastair MacLachlan, St Mirren FC; Ipswich Town FC; Kim Slaney, Peterborough United FC; Richard Lindsay, Millwall FC; Gordon Lawton, Oldham Athletic FC; Frank Grande, Northampton Town FC; Richard Owen, Portsmouth FC; West Ham United FC; David Batters, York City FC; Wade Martin, Stoke City FC; Frank Tweedle, Darlington FC; Jack Rollin, Editor *Rothmans Yearbook*; Aldershot FC; The Football Association of Ireland; Bill Acres, Ipswich Town FC; John Staff and A.D. Rowing, Scunthorpe United FC; Kathy Shea, Cardiff City FC; John Martin, Chester City FC; Newcastle United FC; Hull City AFC; Jim Blackstone, Exeter City FC; Mrs P. J. Hindson and Graham Hover, Coventry City FC; Rupert Metcalf, *The Independent*; Gordon Hanna.

FOREWORD

In June 1996 a Leeds United youngster, the Republic of Ireland's Ian Harte, became the 266th player since 1945 to achieve the honour of playing for the Republic of Ireland. This book is a tribute to all of those players who have shared that honour, past and present.

Whilst every effort has been made to ensure that the information contained here is as full and accurate as possible, it is perhaps inevitable that, with a volume of this size and nature, inaccuracies may creep in. I therefore apologise in advance.

DID YOU KNOW?

- Between 1888 and 1898 John Goodall, of Preston North End and Derby, won 14 England caps. His brother, Archie, of Derby and Glossop, was capped ten times, between 1899 and 1904, by Ireland!

- At the turn of the century goalkeepers were permitted to handle the ball outside the penalty area. Shelbourne's Irish international goalkeeper, Ginger Reilly, is the man deemed responsible for this practice being outlawed because he used to bounce the ball and avoid opponents, even as far as the halfway line.

- The oldest player to make his debut for Ireland was Shelbourne's Billy Lacey – he was 37 years, 7 months and 3 days old when he lined up against Italy in March 1926. He is also the oldest player to turn out for Ireland. He was 41 years, 7 months and 3 days when he played against Belgium in May 1930, in the last of his three Eire internationals.

- Ireland's Paddy Moore became the first player to score four goals in a World Cup game when he scored all of Ireland's goals in the 4–4 draw with Belgium, at Dalymount Park, in February 1934.

- The first time the Irish played under the title 'Republic of Ireland' (the title officially designated to them by FIFA) was against Norway in November 1954.

- Waterford-born Davy Walsh is the only player to have played World Cup games for both Irelands.

- Bill Gorman and Johnny Carey shared the unique experience of playing against England twice, within 48 hours, for two different countries. On 28 September 1946 they were in the Northern Ireland side thrashed 7–2 in Belfast, and two days later played for Eire in the 1–0 defeat in Dublin.

- The record for the longest gap between a first and second Irish cap is held by Alex Stevenson. He won his first cap in the 2–0 win over Holland in Amsterdam on 8 May 1932, but he had to wait another 14 years for his second call-up! It came in the 1–0 home defeat by England in September 1946. In his wait he had been capped 14 times by Northern Ireland and after 1946 he went on to play three more times for the North and win five more caps for the Republic.

- Of the six sets of brothers to appear for the Republic only the O'Flanagans, the O'Learys and the Dunnes have played together on the same team. Kevin and Mick O'Flanagan played just once together, against England in 1946. It was Mick's only international cap while Kevin was winning the eighth of his ten caps. They were both also capped for Ireland at rugby! Tony and Pat Dunne appeared in the same team just once, a 1–0 World Cup qualifying defeat by Spain in November 1965. Meanwhile the O'Learys, David and Pierce, played together three times and on one occasion one brother replaced the other. They played as central defenders against Bulgaria and Northern Ireland in 1979, and Holland in 1980. When David went off injured against England at Wembley in February 1980 he was replaced by Pierce. David won 67 caps and Pierce won seven before injury ended his career. The other sets of brothers to play for Ireland are: Ray and

Liam Brady; Con and George Moulson; and Fran and Ray O'Brien.

- Seven sets of fathers and sons have played for Ireland. They are the Fagans, Jack (1926) and Fionan (1954–61); the Dunnes, Jimmy (1930–39) and Tommy (1956); the Lawlors, John 'Kit' (1949–51) and Mick (1970–73); the Martins, Con (1946–56) and Mick (1971–1983); the Whelans, Ronnie (snr) (1963–64), and Ronnie (1981–95); the Donovans, Don (1954–57) and Terry (1979); and the Kellys, Alan (snr) (1956–73) and Alan (1993–95).

- The Dublin Bradys are the only known case of three brothers being sent off in League matches: Ray was sent off in October 1961 playing for Millwall v Colchester; Pat (ex-Millwall) for Gravesend v Wimbledon in 1965; and Liam three times for Arsenal in the 1970s.

- The last time the Republic fielded a team comprised wholly of players born in Ireland was in the 4–0 European Championship victory over Turkey in October 1975. The team on the day was: Roche, Dunne, Holmes, Mulligan, Hand, Martin, Brady, Giles, Heighway, Treacy, Givens. Subs: Conroy, Kinnear.

- The Republic's most frequent opponents have been Spain. They have met 21 times since 1945, and the last player to score a goal for the Republic in Spain was Andy McEvoy in October 1965 in the 4–1 defeat in Seville.

- In 1963 Stoke City had both Irish goalkeepers on their books: the Republic's Jimmy O'Neill and Northern Ireland's Bobby Irvine.

- Eamonn Dunphy scored a unique goal for Millwall in their 2–0 away victory over Blackburn Rovers in April 1971. At that time Blackburn's Development Association was raising funds by selling Golden Goal tickets. For the ticket-holder to win, a goal had to be scored by the player whose number appeared on the ticket and at the time stated. Dunphy purchased a ticket obligingly which he later found read: 'visitors, no. 10 – 88th minute'. The number was his own and at precisely that minute he flashed the second goal into the net.

- Ireland's Liam O'Brien holds the unwanted record for the fastest sending-off in the First Division: while playing for Manchester United v Southampton on 3 January 1987, he was shown the red card after just 85 seconds.

- Under Jack Charlton's managership of the Republic only two players were sent off: Liam Brady, against Bulgaria at Lansdowne Road in October 1987; and Packie Bonner, against Italy during World Cup USA in 1994. Prior to Brady's dismissal one has to go back ten years to June 1977 to find another Irish player sent off. That too was against Bulgaria but this time in Sofia when Mick Martin and Noel Campbell were both shown the red card in a stormy finish.

- Roy Keane was sent off against Russia in March 1996 in Mick McCarthy's first game as national team boss. McCarthy, Niall Quinn and Liam Daish were all shown the red card against Mexico in June 1996.

- In November 1951 Drumcondra's Irish international forward Dessie Glynn scored five goals against Transport. His fifth came from the penalty spot: it not only beat the goalkeeper but burst the net and knocked out a 17-year-old!

- John Aldridge became the first Eire player to miss a penalty in a Wembley FA Cup final when Wimbledon's Dave Beasant saved his spot kick in 1988.

- Aldridge holds the record for scoring in consecutive League matches. He scored in Liverpool's final game of the 1986–87 season and in their opening nine First Division games the following season.

• Aldridge's second-half penalty against Malta in November 1989 was the first penalty the Republic had been awarded in World Cup football in 55 years.

• Denis Irwin is the first Irish player to be capped at Under-21, Under-23, 'B' and full levels.

• Ireland's million-pound players are: S. Staunton, J. Aldridge, M. Milligan, A. Townsend, A. McLoughlin, A. Cascarino, F. Stapleton, T. Phelan, E. McGoldrick, R. Keane, A. Kernaghan, J. Kenna, J. McAteer, Mark Kennedy, P. Babb, L. Daish.

• Irishmen who have scored in the FA Cup final are: John Aldridge (1989, Liverpool v Everton) and Frank Stapleton (1983, Manchester United v Brighton and 1979, Arsenal v Manchester United).

• Stella Maris players who went on to achieve international distinction are: John Anderson, Joe Carolan, Jimmy Conway, Johnny Giles, Ashley Grimes, Eoin Hand, John Keogh, Liam O'Brien, Frank O'Neill and Ronnie Whelan (sen.).

• Two Irish internationals born on St Patrick's Day are: Paddy Mulligan and Gary Waddock.

• The Republic of Ireland team, with an average age of 29, was the oldest squad at Italia '90. When they competed in the 1996 US Cup in America under new boss Mick McCarthy, the average age of the team had dropped to 24.5.

• Alan Kelly (jun) made history on his debut for Sheffield United, against Spurs on 2 September 1992. Following Simon Tracey's dismissal Kelly became the first-ever substitute goalkeeper under new Premier League rules. He also kept his elder brother, Gary, the Bury goalkeeper, out of Ireland's Under-21 side, and played against him during the second half of Tony Gale's testimonial game between West Ham and Ireland (Gary was then on loan to West Ham).

IRISH INTERNATIONAL FOOTBALLERS 1945–96

Thomas Aherne (FULL-BACK)

Born: Limerick 26 January 1919
Debut for Eire: v Portugal June 1946

Thomas Aherne, known to everyone as 'Bud', played senior hurling for his native Limerick and played for Carrigaline in the South East Cork Junior Championship while stationed with the army at Fort Camden, Crosshaven. He began his senior soccer career in the League of Ireland with his hometown club Limerick before moving north to join Belfast Celtic in 1945.

A quick player with excellent positional sense which 'planted him in the right place at the right time', Bud was described as 'hard as nails'. He figured prominently in the closing chapters of the great Belfast side, winning an Irish League Championship medal in 1947–48 to add to the Irish Cup winners medal he'd won the previous season.

During his career Aherne played in some magnificent sides, including the Eire side which inflicted England's first home defeat by an overseas side, at Goodison Park in 1949. He was also a member of the Belfast Celtic team which the same year achieved an even more unexpected victory over Scotland, who had been dubbed the 'wonder team of 1949'. The Scots were Home International champions and believed they had little to fear from the Irish club side when they met in America's Triboro Stadium. The result was an astounding 2–0 victory to the Belfastmen.

In March 1949 Aherne was signed by Luton Town after they watched his performances at left-back for Belfast Celtic and for Northern Ireland against Wales. Bud's signing – for a fee believed to be over £6,000 – proved a shrewd piece of business for the Hatters. He claimed a first-team place immediately and over the next decade at Kenilworth Road he became a cult figure. The Luton faithful admired his tough tackling and his intelligent use of the ball from defence.

Luton was Aherne's only Football League club. He made a total of 267 League appearances for them and made a telling contribution to their 1954–55 promotion-winning season, after which they became a First Division club for the first time in their history. He left Luton in 1961 to become coach to the London Spartan League club Vauxhall Motors.

During his time in Belfast Bud was a regular in the Irish League representative side. He was also one of only a handful of players to represent both 'Irelands'. He made four appearances for the North, all at left-back, between September 1946 and March 1950, at a time when the North could choose players from the South for Home International fixtures.

Bud made his debut for Eire in their first post-war international, against Portugal, in an Irish team which contained ten debutants and Manchester United's Johnny Carey. Bud became his country's regular left-back in September 1949, playing in 13 consecutive games. He won his 16th and final Eire cap in a World Cup qualifier against France in Dublin in October 1953. France won 5–3.

John Aldridge (FORWARD)

Born: Liverpool 18 September 1958
Debut for Eire: v Wales March 1986

The man with the Midas touch in front of goal, John Aldridge has consistently found the net wherever he has gone, smashing records and collecting a glittering array of top

John Aldridge

honours during his 15 years in the game.

John won the Welsh Cup with Newport County in 1980, the League Cup with Oxford in 1986, and the FA Cup with Liverpool in 1989. He added an FA Cup runners-up medal to his collection following Liverpool's 1–0 defeat by Wimbledon in 1988.

Aldridge has defied the critics throughout his career, possessing a modern-day strike-rate second to none. In 1984–85 he won the Adidas Silver Boot award for being the Second Division's highest scorer – his 30 goals, a club record, contributed in no small measure to Oxford's championship success that season. He went one better in 1987–88, his first full season at Anfield, collecting the Adidas Golden Boot with 31 goals, and winning a League Championship medal.

He began his career playing part-time for non-League South Liverpool before joining Newport County for £3,500 in April 1979, after finishing his apprenticeship as a British Leyland toolmaker. After five seasons with the Welsh club (during which he scored an unmatched 69 goals in 170 games) Aldridge took his goalscoring boots to Oxford in March 1984 in a £78,000 deal. He helped the Manor Ground side win promotion from Division Three to One in successive seasons. John's tally in four seasons at the club was 72 goals in 114 games.

A Liverpool fan since childhood, John harboured an ambition to step down from the terraces of the Anfield Kop to play for his hometown club. After a trial as a 14-year-old, he was told they would be in touch – it took 14 years for the phone to ring!

When it became clear that Ian Rush was about to say *arrivederci* to Anfield and head for the sunnier climes of Juventus and the Stadio Comunale, the way was finally clear for Aldridge to realise his dream, and in January 1987 he joined Liverpool in a £750,000 deal.

Comparisons between the two hitmen were inevitable and went beyond their prowess on the park as their uncanny resemblance to each other added an extra dimension. Aldridge flourished at Anfield while Rush floundered in Italy, giving rise to tongue-in-cheek rumours that Juventus had been duped: that the real Rush remained at Anfield under the pseudonym of John Aldridge while Rush's twin brother had been sold to the Italians for £2.8 million.

Aldridge won a regular place at Anfield and had three highly successful seasons there scoring 50 goals in just 83 League games. But when Rush returned from Italy it became obvious that Anfield was not big enough for both of them. The writing was on the wall in September 1989 when Spanish club Real Sociedad offered £1.1 million for the 31-year-old striker – Liverpool and Aldridge had no option but to accept.

In signing Aldridge, Real broke with a fierce local tradition of playing only Basques from the small mountain-locked region at the western end of the Pyrenees. His exploits in Spain earned him the nickname El Zorro – quite appropriate considering his rapier-like thrusts in the goalmouth and his resemblance to the screen version of the Spanish hero. He became the first Real player to score in six consecutive matches, and in 76 games for the club his tally rose to 40.

In June 1991, after two years in Spain, John decided to return home, homesickness being a major factor. He returned to Merseyside, but this time he signed for John King's Tranmere Rovers for a bargain £250,000. Ironically, King had lost out to Newport 13 years earlier because he couldn't afford the player's £3,500 asking price.

At Prenton Park John became the linchpin of the side doing what he does best: scoring goals and breaking records. In 1991 he equalled the great Dixie Dean's 64-year-old record by notching up 20 League goals by the end of October. His 40 goals in 1991–92 matched the club's all-time record for a season set by Bunny Bell in 1933–34. Injury kept him out of action for a substantial part of 1992–93 but he still finished top of the club's scoring charts with 21 goals in just 30 games. He was top scorer again in 1993–94, again with 21 goals.

The following season, 1994–95, told a similar tale. But once again it was a bittersweet

year for Aldridge. He scored 24 goals in 33 games but for the third successive season Tranmere missed out on a place in the Premiership by failing in the Division One play-offs.

He was in familiar territory in 1995–96: he was top scorer with 27 goals in 44 games, which again confirmed him as the First Division hotshot. In April 1996 he was appointed player-manager at Prenton Park and ended the season in that role without having tasted defeat.

International honours eluded Aldridge until he was 27 years old, when Jack Charlton, who had just been appointed Republic manager, shook the player's family tree and out fell an Athlone-born great-grandmother!

John made his international debut in Charlton's first game in charge, against Wales in March 1986, and has been an integral part of the Irish set-up ever since. An unselfish worker who grafts hard for the rest of the team, he has been one of the mainstays of the Republic's great adventure which has taken them to two World Cup finals and a European Championship final. His relatively low strike-rate at international level – 19 goals in 69 games (including hat-tricks against Turkey in 1990 and Latvia in 1992) – must be largely because of the role he has been asked to perform for Ireland and his willingness to work, as their first line of defence. No one could put it down to any innate inability to score, as everyone knows what John is capable of in his preferred striker's position.

In May 1996 Liverpool's 1988 title-winning side played an Ireland XI in a benefit match for Aldridge.

Patrick Ambrose

(INSIDE/CENTRE-FORWARD)

Born: Dublin 17 October 1929
Debut for Eire: v Norway November 1954

Paddy Ambrose netted a hat-trick playing in

his first soccer game for junior club Clontarf, a performance witnessed by Shamrock Rovers' boss Jimmy Dunne, who was keen to have the player on his books. But Ambrose was a reluctant footballer; his first loves were Gaelic games and racing pigeons. It took Dunne a year to persuade Ambrose to agree to sign, and even then clauses about his hobbies of hurling and pigeon racing had to be incorporated into the contract.

Paddy signed for the Hoops in the summer of 1949 and remained on their books until 1973. A strong, determined and totally unselfish player, he began as an inside-forward but moved to centre-forward in 1953–54, after a season's absence through injury. He never looked back.

Ambrose scored 109 League goals for Rovers and won every domestic honour the Irish game has to offer. He won League Championship medals in 1953–54 (when he was top scorer), 1956–57, 1958–59 and 1963–64; FAI Cup winners medals in 1955, 1956, 1962 (when he scored twice in Rovers' 4–1 defeat of Shelbourne in the final) and 1964; and runners-up medals in 1957 and 1958.

A recurring ankle injury ended Paddy's playing career in 1964 but he continued to coach at Glenmalure Park until 1973.

Capped as an amateur against England in 1959, Ambrose won two 'B' caps and represented the League of Ireland seven times in the 1950s. He made his full debut in the 2–1 home victory over Norway in November 1954. He retained his place for Ireland's next game, against Holland. But despite another win he had to wait nine years for his next cap. That came against Poland in May 1964, a month in which he played in three consecutive internationals, taking his total to five caps.

John Anderson (DEFENDER)

Born: Dublin 7 November 1959
Debut for Eire: v Czechoslovakia
September 1979

John Anderson, like many of his contemporaries in his native Dublin, first learnt the basics of his trade with the city's famous soccer nursery, Stella Maris.

On leaving school John joined West Bromwich Albion as an apprentice and signed professionally for the club in November 1977. He wasn't, however, considered good enough for the first team; in August 1979 he was transferred to newly promoted Preston North End for £40,000. In three seasons at Deepdale John made 51 Second Division appearances. He was freed by the Lilywhites in September 1982 and joined Newcastle United.

John immediately claimed the right-back berth at St James' Park and in his second season there, 1983–84, he helped the Magpies with promotion to Division One, after a six-year absence. John proved a versatile defender, turning up in all back-four positions and in midfield during his nine seasons in the north-east. Towards the end of 1990 he experienced difficulty in holding down a regular first-team place and in March 1992 he was forced to retire because of an ankle injury. In all John made 299 League appearances for the Geordies and scored 14 goals.

In May 1992 he was appointed player-manager of Scottish Second Division club Berwick Rangers but resigned after just eight weeks in the job.

A former Eire Youth player, Anderson made 11 appearances at Under-21 level. Only Lee Power and David Greene have more at this level.

In a full international career spanning nine years John was not a regular. He made his debut as a substitute for Arsenal's John Devine in the 4–1 defeat by Czechoslovakia in Prague in September 1979. He was on the field for only four minutes but deflected the Czech's fourth goal past Gerry Peyton in the Irish goal. John replaced David O'Leary against the USA at home in October 1979 for his second cap. Three minutes after coming on he scored his only international goal to give Ireland a 3–2 victory. They had trailed 2–0 in the game. John won his 16th and final cap in the P.J. O'Driscoll testimonial against Tunisia in October 1988.

Philip Babb (CENTRE-HALF)

Born: Lambeth, London 30 November 1970
Debut for Eire: v Russia March 1994

Phil Babb had ambitions to become a journalist and had been accepted for a Media Studies course when he was spotted by Millwall, who took him on as a youth trainee and signed him professionally in April 1989.

Babb had spent two years at The Den when he incurred the wrath of Lions' boss Bruce Rioch because of his poor timekeeping on a pre-season tour. He left the club in July 1990 – without having made his League debut – to join Frank Stapleton's Bradford City. Babb prospered under the former Eire international at Valley Parade. He played in almost every position for the Bantams including left-back, centre-half, midfield and centre-forward, from where he scored ten League goals in 1990–91. In all, he made 80 appearances (14 goals) for Bradford.

Tall and quicksilver fast in the tackle, Babb was transferred to Coventry City in July 1992. He settled down well in the Premier League making 34 appearances, mostly at left-back, for Coventry to the end of the 1992–93 season, by which time he was captain at Highfield Road. He moved to centre-half in 1993–94 and was voted Coventry's 'Player of the Year' that season.

Mature beyond his years he plays with the unhurried assurance that marks out the most stylish players. Poised and purposeful he stands up to forwards rather than lunging at them and

Philip Babb

reads the game expertly. Such instinctive comprehension of opposition movements towards him, an understanding embellished by his association with the master craftsman Paul McGrath in the heart of Ireland's defence, made Babb one of the most sought-after defenders in Britain.

Following his exemplary performances for Ireland in the 1994 World Cup finals in the USA, Coventry knew they couldn't hang on to him any longer and in September 1994, having made a total of 81 League appearances for City, he was transferred to Liverpool for £3.6 million. The fee represented a club record for the Merseysiders and made Phil the most expensive defender in the domestic game.

In his first season at Anfield Phil collected his first major honour in the game – a League Cup winners medal – after Liverpool's final victory over Bolton Wanderers. In 1996 he was a losing Cup finalist when Liverpool were beaten 1–0 by Manchester United in the FA Cup final. To the end of that season he had made 62 League appearances for the Reds.

Raised with 'love, religion and all things

19

Irish' by his Carlow-born mother, Babb is once quoted as saying: 'My mother brought God and potatoes into the house.' As a 16-year-old apprentice at Millwall he wrote in the club's programme of his ambition to be 'the most capped black player in the Republic's history'. He is well on his way.

Phil first pulled on an Irish shirt in David O'Leary's testimonial against Hungary in 1994. He didn't play well then, but acquitted himself brilliantly in the pre-World Cup friendlies against Russia, Holland, Bolivia, Germany and the Czech Republic. He really sprang to prominence during the 1994 World Cup finals. Promoted to first-choice centre-half by Irish boss Jack Charlton, Phil played in all of the Republic's games in USA '94 and hardly put a foot wrong. Phil won his 20th cap in the 2–0 defeat by the Czech Republic in April 1996.

Edward Bailham (CENTRE-FORWARD)

Born: Dublin 1941
Debut for Eire: v England May 1964

Eddie Bailham was only 11 years old – the youngest ever player – when he won his first representative honour playing for the Boys' Brigade against Belfast. He later earned Youth and Junior international honours with Home Farm and nearly went to Manchester United, having spent his holidays at Old Trafford as a boy. Instead he joined Shamrock Rovers via Cork Hibs in 1960 and won all the honours the Irish game has to offer.

Eddie was the type of player who shot on sight. At Shamrock Rovers he teamed up with Jackie Mooney. 'Eddie Bailham and I made up a curious partnership. I was a fair header of the ball but couldn't shoot, while Eddie's explosive shot more than compensated for his lack of heading powers.'

A bustling, hard-hitting poacher and 'a menace when he gets room to swing his leg for a shot', he was top scorer with the Hoops in 1961–62 and in 1963–64 when Rovers won the Championship. He was an FAI Cup winner with Rovers in 1962 and in 1964 when he scored both goals in the replayed final – the winner being a magnificent left-foot drive.

A former League of Ireland player, Eddie had a 'glorious representative debut' in the 2–1 defeat of the English League in October 1963. He was a member of the Dublin City select team which played Arsenal in 1964. He won his one full cap in the 3–1 defeat by England at home in May that year.

Eddie's father Robert, who was caretaker of the Nelson Pillar in Dublin's O'Connell Street, was a centre-forward too; he played for YMCA in the League of Ireland in 1921 and later for Midland Athletic.

Eric Barber (CENTRE-FORWARD)

Born: Dublin 18 January 1942
Debut for Eire: v Spain October 1965

A forward with magnificent ability in front of goal, Eric Barber enjoyed a playing career spanning 15 seasons in Ireland, England, America and Austria, yet he represented his country just twice. He won his first cap in the 4–1 defeat by Spain in Seville in October 1965 and his second in the 3–2 victory over Belgium in Liège in May 1966.

Eric began playing with St Finbarr's in Dublin and in 1958 joined Shelbourne's junior team. He was a member of the Shels youth team – as was future Manchester United stalwart Tony Dunne – which won the FAI Youth Cup in 1959. Just 12 months later they won the senior Cup competition, repeating the feat in 1963.

Barber's main assets were an excellent first touch, two good feet, pace, control and bravery, and his greatest success came in 1961–62 when Shelbourne won the League Championship and he was the club's leading marksman.

In March 1966 Eric made an ill-fated move to First Division Birmingham City. He spent one unproductive and unhappy season at St Andrews getting his name on the first-team sheet only four times. Chicago Spurs (later Kansas) ended his nightmare when they paid Birmingham £12,000 to take him to the North American Soccer League in the summer of 1967.

Eric spent the 1969–70 season on loan to Shamrock Rovers, where he ended the campaign as the Hoops' leading scorer. Then he had two seasons – dogged by injury – in Austria with Wiener Sportclub.

He returned to Ireland and in 1972 rejoined Shelbourne. In 1973 he was one of only two survivors from Shelbourne's 1963 FAI Cup winning team to play in the 1973 Cup final, which they lost to Cork Hibs.

Eric, who was a former schoolboy boxer, played out the last three seasons of his career at Tolka Park where he proved he had lost none of his celebrated scoring skills by heading Shelbourne's scoring list on each occasion.

James Beglin (FULL-BACK)

Born: Waterford 29 July 1963
Debut for Eire: v China June 1984

A defender out of the top drawer, Jim Beglin moved from League of Ireland club Shamrock Rovers to Liverpool in May 1983, in a deal which cost the Merseysiders £25,000.

Jim made his League debut in November 1984, standing in for his Republic of Ireland colleague Ronnie Whelan, and earned a regular place the following season, as a replacement for veteran Alan Kennedy at left-back.

With his cool, unruffled style and long accurate passing out of defence, Beglin fitted perfectly into the 'Liverpool way'. He was duly rewarded with League Championship and FA Cup winners medals in 1985–86, Liverpool's historic double-winning year. He also collected a European Cup runners-up medal after Liverpool's ill-fated clash with Italian champions Juventus in the Heysel Stadium in 1985.

Jim had played just 64 League games for Liverpool when, in January 1987, he sustained a particularly serious broken leg, which brought his promising Liverpool and international careers to an end.

Jim won four Under-21 caps in 1982–83 and was a regular in the Republic's senior side for two years between November 1984 and November 1986, collecting 15 full caps. He added a 'B' cap to his international collection in March 1990 when the Irish second string defeated their English counterparts 4–1 in Cork.

Liverpool granted Beglin a free transfer, and in June 1989 he moved to Leeds United. Leeds' boss Howard Wilkinson regarded him as an important component in the club's major programme to rebuild the team in a bid to return to the First Division from which they had been relegated in 1981–82.

Leeds won the Second Division title in 1989–90, and although Jim played 19 League games that season, he failed to recapture the form which had made him a regular at Anfield, and when Leeds were crowned as the last First Division champions in 1991–92, the injury sustained five years earlier finally caught up with him. After loan spells to Plymouth in November 1989 (five games) and Blackburn Rovers in October 1990 (six games), he was forced to quit the game.

Jim is now a regular soccer reporter and expert assessor with both the BBC and RTE.

Patrick Bonner (GOALKEEPER)

Born: Keadue, Co. Donegal 24 May 1960
Debut for Eire: v Poland May 1981

Packie Bonner has been keeping goal for Ireland and Glasgow Celtic for a decade and more.

21

Patrick Bonner

Packie was Jock Stein's last signing before the great man's death in 1978, joining Celtic from Donegal junior side Keadue Rovers in that year. He became first-choice keeper at Parkhead in 1980 and, apart from a period in 1985–86 when he was injured, he remained first choice for the best part of a decade, clocking up 483 appearances in the Scottish League. Packie remains at his beloved Parkhead in a coaching capacity.

Medals are plentiful in the Bonner household. Packie was a Scottish League Championship winner in 1981, 1982, 1986 and 1988. He played in four Scottish League Cup finals with Celtic between 1983 and 1991. They faced their great Glasgow rivals Rangers in each of the showdowns, in 1983, 1984, 1987 and 1991, emerging victorious only in 1983. Bonner won Scottish Cup winners medals in 1985 and 1995 after victories over Dundee United and Airdrie. Scottish Cup runners-up medals in 1984 and 1990 complete Packie Bonner's impressive collection.

Bonner was dropped by Celtic manager Liam Brady in 1991–92 and was given a free transfer by Brady's successor Lou Macari in the summer of 1993. He subsequently joined his former Parkhead team-mate Tommy Burns at Kilmarnock. When Burns moved to Parkhead to take over from the dismissed Macari weeks later, he took Bonner back with him!

Packie, who stands 6ft 4in and weighs 14 stone, won four Under-21 caps with the Republic and was a Youth international. He won his first full cap against Poland on 24 May 1981 – his 21st birthday. However, it wasn't until Jack Charlton took charge of the Irish team in 1986 that he began to establish himself as first choice.

Renowned for his bravery, Bonner's confidence grew immeasurably under Charlton and he matured into one of the game's most respected keepers. Possessing good positional sense and agility, Packie's long kicks from goal were an important feature of Ireland's game under Charlton. He played in all of Ireland's games in Euro '88, Italia '90 and USA '94 and is Ireland's most capped goalkeeper, taking the record previously held by Alan Kelly senior. He guarded Ireland's goal on a total of 80 occasions and kept 44 clean sheets.

Bonner will be remembered for ever for two incidents in successive World Cup finals: his blunder which gifted Holland a second goal in the second-stage game in 1994 and all but ended Ireland's interest in that year's competition; and his brilliant penalty save from Romania's Daniel Timofte in Italy four years earlier which sent the Republic through to the quarter-finals of a World Cup for the first time in their history.

Packie is one of a family of seven, including five girls. His twin brother Dennis, who plays his soccer in the League of Ireland with Sligo Rovers, won an All-Ireland Championship medal with Donegal in 1992.

Synan Braddish (MIDFIELD)

Born: Dublin 27 January 1958
Debut for Eire: v Turkey April 1978

Born in the Dublin suburb of Finglas, Synan Braddish is a product of local junior club Rave Athletic. In the '70s the club was a nursery for League of Ireland club Dundalk; and so in 1976 Braddish was off to Oriel Park where he won an FAI Cup winners medal in 1977.

In April 1978 Liverpool stepped in to sign him, just as he was about to sign for the Los Angeles Skyhawks. But there was to be no English First Division glory. He returned to Dundalk the following year without having tasted League football in England.

He won a League Cup winners medal with Dundalk in 1981. The final was eventually decided by a penalty shoot-out after two legs and extra time failed to produce a goal.

At the start of the 1981–82 season Braddish joined St Patrick's Athletic, where he remained for five seasons, playing alongside Paul McGrath, later of Manchester United and Aston Villa. Then he turned out for Athlone (1986–90) and Kilkenny City (1990–91) before joining Longford Town in 1991.

Synan was honoured by the Republic at Schoolboy, Youth and Amateur levels and won five caps at Under-21 level. A particularly impressive showing in an Under-21 game against Northern Ireland in March 1978 helped earn him a call-up to the senior ranks a month later when he won two full caps against Turkey and Poland in one week.

Liam Brady (MIDFIELD)

Born: Dublin 13 February 1956
Debut for Eire: v USSR October 1974

The seventh son of a Dublin docker, Liam Brady is arguably the most talented footballer ever produced by the Republic of Ireland. As

Liam Brady

a youngster he was Ireland's wonder boy, his class crystal clear from an early age. Unlike elder brother Ray, who knocked on Millwall's door seeking a trial, the world beat a path to Liam's door.

At 13 he signed for Arsenal, at 15 he left Dublin for north London; at 17 he was in the Gunners' first team.

The outstanding player of his generation, he was the most creative of midfielders with an ever so educated left foot. He could pass over any distance, take on markers and leave them for dead, and lash spectacular goals from 30 yards. A player of the highest order, his vision and imagination touched heights most players only dream of.

When Arsenal boss Terry Neill sold Alan Ball to Southampton in December 1976, Brady became the club's midfield general and in seven seasons as a Gunner he made 235 League appearances and scored 43 goals.

His golden display in the 1979 FA Cup final earned Brady the only winners medal of his Arsenal career. He was the general who plotted Manchester United's downfall in that final, dancing a merry Irish jig on the famous sward, in the most exciting climax to a Cup final this century. Arsenal somehow managed to lose a two-goal cushion in the dying minutes of the tie, only to snatch the game with a Brady-inspired winner in the last seconds to run out 3–2 winners.

Brady collected runners-up medals in the same competition either side of the 1979 triumph. He wasn't fully fit in 1978 when he was substituted in the Gunners' 1–0 defeat by Ipswich Town. Arsenal also lost the 1980 final 1–0, this time to West Ham.

His final 'big game' for Arsenal was the 1980 European Cup-Winners' Cup final against Valencia, which they lost on penalties to the Spanish club.

During the close season, Liam turned down Manchester United's £1.5 million bid – which would have smashed the British transfer record. He moved to Italian giants Juventus for £600,000. Few foreign players can have settled so glamorously into the goldfish bowl of Italian football. He won the Italian League Championship in each of his two seasons with the club. Towards the end of his second season Liam was replaced by French international Michel Platini whereupon he moved to newly promoted Sampdoria, having scored 13 goals in 57 games for Juventus.

In June 1984, after six goals in 57 games for Sampdoria, Liam switched to up-and-coming Internazionale in a £1.75 million transfer deal. He played 58 games (five goals) for Inter. Lastly, he made 17 appearances for Ascoli, whom he joined for £500,000, completing seven years in Italian football – only class players last that long in the Lega Nazionale.

On his return to England in March 1987 Brady joined West Ham United and before long he was showing he hadn't lost any of the skills which had made him a superstar at Arsenal.

In February 1987 he sustained badly torn ligaments, which kept him out for the rest of the season. At the end of the next campaign, after eight goals in 89 games for the Hammers, he announced his retirement from the game.

In June 1991 Brady became the first manager of Celtic who had not played for the Glasgow giants. He brought his own aesthetic, free-flowing style of football to Parkhead; but it wasn't enough. In October 1993, after a string of poor results, he resigned.

In January 1994 he was appointed manager of Second Division strugglers Brighton. He resigned from the post in November 1995 and in May 1996 headed a consortium in an attempt to buy out the club. He withdrew from the consortium the following August to return to Arsenal as head of their youth development programme.

Liam Brady won the admiration of his peers the world over and became a living legend in London and Dublin. He was voted Arsenal's 'Player of the Year' three times, Ireland's 'Player of the Year' in 1976 and the PFA 'Player of the Year' in 1979.

A former Irish Schoolboy captain, he won 11 Youth caps and a record 72 full caps. He also scored nine goals for Ireland and captained his country on a dozen occasions.

Liam made his full debut in the 3–0 defeat of the USSR in Dublin in October 1974 and immediately became a regular in the side – the jewel in the Irish crown for 13 years.

Liam was sent off once at this level, in the European Championship qualifier against Bulgaria in October 1987. The dismissal had far-reaching consequences, however. That red card, combined with injury, forced him to miss the European Championship finals in Germany in 1988 and restricted him to just five more caps before his retirement.

He was awarded an international testimonial in May 1990 when Ireland entertained Finland.

Raymond Brady (DEFENDER)

Born: Dublin 3 June 1937
Debut for Eire: v Austria September 1963

The brother of Pat Brady of Millwall and QPR and Liam Brady of Arsenal and Juventus, Ray Brady left local League of Ireland club Transport FC in 1957 and moved to London. There he sought a trial at Millwall; was accepted into the Lions' Den; and in July of that year signed for the Division Three (South) club. He then said: 'I've got a brother, Pat. He's not bad, take a look at him.' They did, liked what they saw and signed him too!

Almost immediately Ray claimed a regular place in the Lions' League side and, although he joined the club as a full-back, his build and height – he was 6ft tall – made him ideally suited for a position in the centre of the defence, the position he made his own towards the end of 1960–61.

Ray made a total of 165 League appearances (four goals) in a Millwall shirt and in 1961–62 won a Fourth Division Championship medal. He missed just two League games that season and his rugged, uncompromising defending and fearless tackling proved an inspiration to his team-mates.

At the close of 1962–63 Ray and brother Pat moved together across London to Queen's Park Rangers. During his two seasons at Loftus Road, Ray appeared in 89 Third Division games, before joining Southern League club Hastings United. Soon after his debut for QPR Ray made his first international appearance for Ireland, in the scoreless draw with Austria in September 1963. The first man from Transport to win international honours, Ray played at right-half and was named 'Man of the Match'. 'He slotted perfectly into the defensive set-up, tackling furiously, using his height splendidly and showing real constructive skill as he moved upfield to rat-a-tat a stream of smooth passes,' said one commentator at the time. He appeared in Ireland's next five games, winning his sixth and final cap in the 4–1 defeat of Norway in May 1964.

Ray now runs a pub in Kent and Pat is an economics lecturer.

Gary Breen (DEFENDER)

Born: London 12 December 1973
Debut for Eire: v Portugal May 1996

Gary Breen made his League debut for Maidstone United, then a Division Three club, in January 1992. At the end of that season – when Maidstone dropped out of League football – having made 19 League appearances for the Stones, Gary moved to Gillingham.

He made 51 Third Division appearances for the Gills before his £50,000 transfer to Peterborough United in August 1994. In February 1996, after 69 Second Division appearances for Peterborough, Breen was taken to Birmingham City as a replacement for Liam Daish, who had transferred to Coventry City. To the end of 1995–96 he had made 18 League appearances for Birmingham.

Ambitious but level-headed, and with obvious leadership qualities, Gary is a distinctly exciting prospect. There are shades of David O'Leary and Alan Hansen in his play; he likes to caress the ball rather than hoof it away.

Breen won his first Eire Under-21 cap against Denmark in October 1992 and for over three seasons was regarded as the outstanding player in Ireland's Under-21 side. In May 1996 he was an 89th-minute substitute for Alan Kernaghan in the Republic's 1–0 defeat by Portugal at Lansdowne Road. He won five more caps in Mick McCarthy's friendly summer of 1996 and scored his first international goal in the 3–1 defeat by Holland in June 1996. Gary collected his eighth cap in the 3–0 win over Macedonia in October 1996.

Thomas Breen (GOALKEEPER)

Born: Belfast 27 April 1917
Debut for Eire: v Switzerland May 1937

Tommy Breen, who joined Belfast Celtic from Newry with defender Johnny Feehan in the early 1930s, was 'undoubtedly one of the most outstanding players to appear for the legendary Belfast club'. A splendid and fearless keeper, he originally played Gaelic football from which he developed the art of safe handling and long kicking.

Tommy won Irish League Championship medals with Celtic in 1932–33 and 1935–36. Towards the end of that 1935–36 season he left Celtic Park for Manchester United.

He helped United win promotion to Division One in 1937–38 (after a season in Division Two), and had made 67 League appearances for the Old Trafford club by September 1939 when League football was abandoned because of the war.

Tommy immediately returned to Belfast, having been given permission by United to resume his career at Celtic Park. When the war ended Tommy ventured south to join Dublin club Shamrock Rovers.

Before the war Breen had won nine caps as Northern Ireland keeper in the old Home International series.

He made his debut for Eire in the 1–0 defeat of Switzerland in May 1937 and kept another clean sheet for his second cap the following week when the Irish beat France 2–0 in Paris. Thereafter Ireland's goalkeeping responsibilities were handled by Southend United's keeper George McKenzie, and Tommy had to wait until September 1946 for his third cap. His fifth and final call-up for Eire came, almost exactly ten years after his first, against Portugal in May 1947.

Francis Brennan (DEFENDER)

Born: Dublin
Debut for Eire: v Belgium March 1965

Red-headed Fran Brennan was an adventurous and commanding full-back or centre-half. He won a League Championship medal with Drumcondra in 1964–65 before moving to Co. Louth to continue his career with Dundalk.

The 1966–67 season was one of the most successful in the Lilywhites' history, for they won the League Championship, the Shield, the Top 4 Trophy and the Donegan Cup, and Fran played his part in the club's successes. 'His mobility was never more in evidence, he streaked up into attack and back to defence in a manner which suggests he's at the peak of his physical fitness.' He was even caught offside once – a feat in itself for a full-back!

The following season he was a member of the Dundalk side which beat DOS Utrecht in the first round of the Fairs Cup.

Fran, who played once for the inter-League team, won his one full cap, against Belgium in March 1965, as a replacement for the injured Charlie Hurley. Although Brennan 'did a commendable job and went about his work with tremendous zest', he was given a baptism of fire as a weakened home side went down 2–0 to the Belgians.

Seamus (Shay) Brennan (FULL-BACK)

Born: Manchester 6 May 1937
Debut for Eire: v Spain May 1965

In 1966 Mancunian Shay Brennan became the first of a long line of second-generation Irishmen to benefit from FIFA's ruling that a player could turn out for the country of his parents. He made his first appearance for Ireland in the World Cup qualifier against Spain in Dublin in May 1965; over the next six years he collected a total of 19 full caps and led the national team five times.

Shay Brennan joined Manchester United as a junior in December 1953, graduating to professional status in April 1955. A member of United's all-conquering Youth team of the late 1950s, Shay was thrown into the first team long before he or anyone else would ever have imagined, after the Munich Air Disaster of 1958 in which eight United first-team players died. Brennan was one of the Busby Babes who took the field in front of 60,000 spectators at an eerie and emotional Old Trafford in what was the first game after the crash: the FA Cup game against Sheffield Wednesday. Playing out of position at outside-left, Shay overcame the intensity of the occasion and, scoring twice in United's unexpected 3–0 victory, was the overwhelming choice as 'Man of the Match'.

It wasn't until 1959–60, however, that Brennan laid serious claim to a first-team place. Initially he was preferred at wing-half then, a couple of seasons later, he was moved to full-back where he soon established himself as a cool, constructive and cultured defender.

An attacking full-back with good ball control, Shay was something of an unsung hero. He was a regular at right-back when United won the League Championship in 1964–65 and collected another Championship medal in 1966–67. The following season he won a European Cup winners medal after United's 4–1 defeat of Portuguese champions Benfica in the Wembley final.

In 1972, after 292 League appearances for United, his only Football League club, Brennan joined League of Ireland club Waterford United. He continued his winning ways in Ireland, collecting two more Championship medals, in 1972 and 1973. Shay experienced the sweet smell of success once again in October 1973 when Waterford defeated Finn Harps 2–1 to lift Ireland's inaugural League Cup competition.

William Browne (RIGHT-BACK)

Born: Longford
Debut for Eire: v Austria September 1963

A brilliant amateur, Willie Browne played soccer for University College Dublin, refusing offers to join any of the big Irish clubs. On completion of his studies he joined amateur side Bohemians. The big Longford man, who went on to captain the Gypsies, spent five seasons with Bohs between 1961 and 1966. He won President's and Leinster Cup winners medals with the club and was their top scorer in 1962–63 with five goals.

A former captain of the Irish amateur XI, Willie won seven inter-League caps and one 'B' cap, against South Africa in October 1958, when he was still a student.

Browne played a 'noble part' in two nights of glory for Irish soccer in the last week of September 1963. He made his international debut against Austria in Vienna in a European Nations Cup game on 25 September in what became known as the 'battle' when Ireland recorded their first-ever scoreless draw. 'There must be the greatest of praise for Willie Browne, for he did nothing wrong in this game which proved a tough international baptism,' said one commentator. A week later he was a member of the League of Ireland XI which recorded a sensational 2–1 victory over the English League at Dalymount Park. His performance on that day made him the target of many cross-channel clubs, but again he resisted the offers. Browne won two more full caps, against Spain in April 1964, and against England the following month. He actually delayed his retirement, scheduled for the end of 1965–66, so that he could lead the Irish in the European Amateur Tournament that summer.

Liam Buckley (FORWARD)

Born: Dublin 14 April 1960
Debut for Eire: v Poland May 1984

Strong and stylish, Liam Buckley was one of the trickiest forwards in the Irish game in the mid-1980s.

Buckley was just 18 when he broke into Shelbourne's first team in 1978. The following year he transferred to Shamrock Rovers where his courageous qualities, sharp and fast anticipation and superb heading prowess helped

Florrie Burke

him to become the club's leading scorer in successive seasons from 1980–81 to 1982–83.

His progress was halted in February 1984 by a broken collar bone. Only seven weeks later, however, he was back in the fray and scored the goal against his former club Shelbourne which took Rovers into the 1984 FAI Cup final and – with the Championship already won – gave them a chance to do the double.

Rovers lost 2–1 to University College Dublin in the replay, and soon after Buckley left for Belgian club KSV Waregem. He later returned to Rovers and in 1992 signed for St Patrick's Athletic where he is now assistant manager.

Capped once at Under-21 level, against England in February 1981, Liam won a call-up to the full squad in 1984. He was a 79th minute replacement for Frank Stapleton in the 0–0 draw with Poland in May 1984 and won his second cap in the goalless draw against Mexico three months later.

Florence Burke (CENTRE-HALF)

Born: Ballintemple, Co. Cork 1921
Debut for Eire: v West Germany October 1951

Florrie Burke played minor and junior hurling for Blackrock. He was just 17 when he played for Blackrock against Brian Dillons in the City Division Cup final, and great things were predicted for him after an outstanding performance that day. And he did achieve great things – by becoming one of the towering personalities of Irish soccer!

Burke began his soccer career with Rockwell Minors and Blackrock Juniors from where he joined Cork United in 1941. At inside-right in his first full season, 1941–42, Florrie helped United retain the title they had won the previous season and reach the FAI Cup final. He won a further five Championship medals with Cork United (later Cork Athletic) in 1942–43, 1944–45, 1945–46, 1949–50, and 1950–51 when as club captain he led Athletic to the League and FAI Cup double. He also played in the 1947 and 1950 Cup finals, emerging as a winner and a runner-up respectively.

Soon after, he was in dispute with Athletic, but they were reluctant to let a player of his calibre go. In a curious arrangement under the rules of the time he was farmed out to city neighbours Evergreen United, but as a retained player of Cork Athletic, could not play for the Turner's Cross side in the League. The Cup, however, was a different matter. And in 1953 he faced his employers in the Cup final, which Athletic won 2–1 in the replay.

The week before that final Burke played for an FAI XI which beat Glasgow Celtic 3–2.

A commanding centre-half and a popular, sporting player, 'who rarely had an off day', Florrie captained the League of Ireland side against the English, Scottish and German Leagues, and was 'Man of the Match' when he won his one full cap in the 3–2 defeat of West Germany in October 1951.

Following the 1953 Cup final, Florrie left Ireland to live in Pyle in Wales, where he died in July 1995.

Anthony Byrne (DEFENDER)

Born: Rathdowney, Co. Laois 2 February 1946
Debut for Eire: v Denmark October 1969

Tony Byrne was 12 years old when his family left Ireland to live in England. He joined Millwall as a junior and signed professional terms with the club in August 1963. Exactly a year later, with just one Third Division appearance to his credit, he was transferred to Southampton.

Byrne was learning the ropes in the Saints' reserves in April 1966 when he broke his leg. Having resumed his budding career, he made

his debut against Manchester United – and the likes of Best, Charlton and Law – at a packed Old Trafford in April 1967, at the end of Southampton's first season in Division One.

Tony was slightly built for a defender (standing just 5ft 7in and weighing less than 10st), but he was keen, nimble and alert. He spent exactly a decade at the Dell, and although he did not command a regular first-team place, he made 93 First Division appearances and, between October 1969 and October 1973, collected 14 full caps with the Republic.

In August 1974 Byrne joined Hereford United, who were embarking on just their third season of League football. He made 55 League appearances for United and in 1975–76 won a Third Division Championship medal. Tony ended his League career with 80 appearances for Fourth Division Newport County whom he joined in March 1977.

In July 1979 he was appointed player-coach at Trowbridge Town; two years later he became a foreman at Hereford Golf Course.

John Byrne (FORWARD)

Born: Manchester 1 February 1961
Debut for Eire: v Italy February 1985

There is a touch of Hollywood in the story of how John Byrne's football career began. The young Byrne was enjoying a kick-about with his mates during the holidays when a car drew up. The driver stopped to watch and then approached Byrne and asked if he would like a trial for York. The driver was Mike Walker, a taxi driver and part-time scout for York City. John signed schoolboy forms with York, became an apprentice in July 1977 and became a fully fledged 'Minsterman' in January 1979.

A strong and powerful front man, John scored 55 goals in 175 League games for York. He scored 27 goals in 1983–84, York's Fourth Division Championship winning season, and

John Byrne

was voted Fourth Division 'Player of the Year'.

John's elegant skills and effective finishing attracted the attention of First Division Queen's Park Rangers, who in the close season paid York £115,000 for their hitman, thereby making Byrne Mike Walker's most expensive 'fare'!

John scored 30 times in 116 League games for QPR and collected a League Cup runners-up medal in 1986 after Rangers went down 3–0 in the final to unfancied Oxford. When Jim Smith took over from Allan Mullery as Rangers' boss in 1985, Byrne found himself in and out of the team. In May 1988 he left England for French club Le Havre in a £150,000 transfer deal.

Byrne finished the 1988–89 season as Le Havre's top scorer despite breaking his leg after just three months in France. After two years he wanted to return home. Le Havre's

management, however, had other ideas and made life so difficult for him that at one point he was on the verge of packing in the game. Brighton saved the day when their £125,000 offer for him was accepted in September 1990.

Byrne enjoyed a brief spell at the Goldstone ground, scoring 14 goals in 51 games. But once again he was on the losing side at Wembley when the Seagulls went down 3–1 to Notts County in the Division Two play-offs in 1990–91.

In October 1991 John was on his travels once again. Sunderland boss Dennis Smith, who had been at York at the same time as Byrne, signed him for £225,000, as a replacement for Marco Gabbiadini. John became the idol of the Roker crowd; he helped the club all the way to the 1992 FA Cup final with a goal in every round. But his attempt to emulate northern legends Nat Lofthouse, Stan Mortenson and Jackie Milburn by scoring in every round was thwarted; the Rokerites went down 2–0 to Liverpool – making Byrne a three-times Wembley runner-up.

In October 1992 after eight goals in 33 League games for Sunderland, John joined Mick McCarthy's Millwall in a £250,000 deal. Unfortunately he was hampered by injury and his career in London barely got off the ground. In March he was farmed out to Brighton on loan for the remainder of the season during which he scored twice in seven League outings.

After just 17 games for Millwall John was allowed to leave the Den and in November 1993 he joined Millwall's First Division rivals Oxford. The 'U's were relegated at the end of 1993–94 and in January 1995, after 18 goals in 55 games, Byrne moved to Liam Brady's Brighton where he was released at the end of 1995–96, having scored six goals in 39 League games. In August 1996 he joined non-league Crawley Town.

A deep-lying and skilful striker who is also adaptable to midfield, John qualified to represent the Republic because his father was born in Carlow. He represented Ireland in 23 internationals and scored four goals. Former Ireland manager Jack Charlton used him in his familiar front running role but also as cover for Ray Houghton down the right side of midfield.

Patrick Byrne (MIDFIELD)

Born: Dublin 15 May 1956
Debut for Eire: v Poland May 1984

The 5ft 7in, 11st 3lb Pat Byrne was a skilful and energetic wide midfielder – one of the most influential players in Irish football in the 1980s. In a career spanning two decades, he won every honour the Irish game has to offer.

He collected his first medal with Bohemians when they beat Finn Harps in the 1975 League Cup final. A year later he collected an FAI Cup winners medal. Bohs were crowned League of Ireland champions in 1977–78, but shortly before the end of the campaign – in March 1978 – Byrne, with his Dalymount Park colleagues Eddie Byrne and Fran O'Brien, left the club to join Philadelphia Fury.

Pat returned to Dublin after his American summer and joined Shelbourne before signing for Leicester City in June 1979. He made his debut for City against Watford at Filbert Street on the opening day of 1979–80, the club's Second Division Championship winning season. He was released at the end of 1980–81 after 31 League appearances.

Pat spent the next two seasons in Scotland with Hearts before returning to Dublin in 1983, this time to don the famous green and white hoops of Shamrock Rovers. In 1984 he was a member of the Hoops side which won the League title and were runners-up in the FAI Cup. His contribution to Rovers' success that season was recognised by the PFAI when they voted him 'Player of the Year'. Pat went on to help Rovers win the League and Cup three years in a row from 1985 to 1987, and reach the 1987 League Cup final, which they lost 1–0 to Dundalk.

Soon after, Byrne departed for Shelbourne. He joined Cobh Ramblers in December 1993 and in February 1994 was appointed player-manager at St James's Gate.

Pat's success at domestic level was recognised at international level and he was awarded eight full caps between May 1984 and May 1986. He played at right- and left-back for Ireland as well as in his usual midfield role.

Alan Campbell (CENTRE-FORWARD)

Born: Dublin
Debut for Eire: v Italy February 1985

'His first goal was a gem, characteristic of a forward on the same footing as Ian Rush or Nico Claessen' was the lavish praise heaped upon Shamrock Rovers' Alan Campbell after a League game in April 1984. Campbell may not have been a Rush or a Claessen but in League of Ireland terms he was a top-drawer player.

Exceptionally quick and a prolific scorer, Campbell was the Hoops' leading scorer in 1979–80 (his first full season with the club) with 22 goals and was the deserved winner of the Soccer Reporters Award.

His style was somewhat cramped by the arrival of Liam Buckley at Rovers towards the end of 1979–80. During the next three seasons Buckley was the Hoops' main hitman, although Alan weighed in with 23 goals in that period.

Buckley's departure for Belgium in 1984 acted as a spur to Campbell. In 1983–84 he was again the League's top scorer with 24 goals and helped Rovers to their first League Championship in 20 years. Rovers missed the double by losing to University College Dublin in the 1984 FAI Cup final, and Alan collected his second runners-up medal. His first had come after the 1982 League Cup final defeat by Athlone.

Campbell's League form didn't go unnoticed abroad, and in September 1984 he joined Belgian club RC Santander.

He made 'splendid progress' in Belgium and in February 1985 made his international debut for Ireland as a substitute against Italy. Three weeks later he played alongside Frank Stapleton against Israel in Tel Aviv. He won his third and final cap in May 1985 against Spain; the game, like his previous one, ended in a 0–0 draw.

Noel Campbell (INSIDE-FORWARD)

Born: Dublin 11 December 1949
Debut for Eire: v Austria May 1971

Noel Campbell's playing days began as a 17-year-old in the League of Ireland with St Patrick's Athletic. He was an FA Cup runner-up in 1967 when St Pat's lost the final in a 3–2 thriller against Shamrock Rovers; then he was St Pat's top scorer in 1968–69 and 1969–70. The following season he left Ireland for West German Second Division side Fortuna Cologne.

A red-haired inside-forward dynamo, Campbell was a skilful ball player and settled quickly in his new surroundings to the delight of his new boss Hans Loring. From 1971 to 1973 he made 51 appearances (nine goals) in the Regionalliga West (Regional Division Two); he also played five games and scored two goals in the promotion play-off to the Bundesliga. In 1973–74 he played 29 Bundesliga matches and from 1974 to 1979 he scored 16 goals in 110 Bundesliga Division Two games.

Noel later returned to Ireland and became assistant manager to Johnny Giles at Shamrock Rovers. When Giles went back to Vancouver Whitecaps in March 1982 Campbell stepped up to become manager of Rovers.

Noel made his full international debut as a half-time substitute for Eamonn Dunphy in the 4–1 defeat by Austria in Dublin in May 1971. When he lined up for his sixth cap, against the USSR in October 1972, he became Ireland's

first continental player to appear in the World Cup.

In June 1977, just over six years after his debut, Noel won his 11th and final cap in a World Cup qualifier against Bulgaria in Sofia, which Ireland lost 2–1. Noel came on as 79th-minute substitute for Gerry Daly. A minute later he was heading back to the tunnel, one of four players dismissed after a brawl ignited by Tzetkov's reckless challenge on Frank Stapleton.

Noel Cantwell (LEFT-BACK)

Born: Cork 28 February 1932
Debut for Eire: v Luxembourg October 1953

Noel Cantwell was one of the many players Manchester United drafted into Old Trafford as part of the painful process of rebuilding the team after the Munich air crash in 1958.

Cork-born Cantwell made his way to Manchester via local junior side Western United, League of Ireland club Cork Athletic and finally West Ham United from whom he joined Manchester United for £29,000 in November 1960. The fee was a record for a defender at the time.

Noel signed for West Ham from Cork Athletic in August 1952. He became captain at Upton Park and in seven seasons there made 248 League appearances (11 goals) and led the Hammers to the Second Division title in 1957–58. His achievements in London were recognised in his native land when he was voted Ireland's 'Footballer of the Year' for 1958–59.

A solid, stylish and thoughtful performer, Cantwell became a key figure at Manchester United after his move to Old Trafford in 1960. His versatility meant he could be deployed in positions as varied as centre-half and centre-forward, in addition to his more familiar position in the left-back berth. Noel's natural leadership qualities, honed and nurtured in London, were recognised at Old Trafford and he was appointed United's captain.

In seven seasons at Old Trafford Cantwell made 123 League appearances (six goals) and led United to their first trophy since Munich when they beat Leicester City 3–1 to lift the FA Cup in 1963. Towards the end of his United career he concentrated on coaching, and when the League Championship returned to Old Trafford in 1965, he was only an occasional player.

An articulate and pleasant man, Noel succeeded Jimmy Hill as Chairman of the PFA in 1966, relinquishing the post in October 1967 to become manager of Coventry City.

He led the Sky Blues to their best ever position of sixth in Division One in 1969–70 but was sacked in March 1972, shortly after a Cup defeat by Hull.

He became manager of Peterborough in October 1972, leading the club to the Fourth Division Championship in 1973–74, before departing for a spell as manager of New England Tea Men in the North American Soccer League in 1977. In 1986 he returned to Peterborough; and then retired as manager in March 1988, though continuing as general manager. He now runs a pub in the Cambridgeshire town and is also a director of a prestigious club.

A man of many and varied talents, Noel gained his FA coaching badge during his time in Manchester.

A double international, he represented Ireland twice at Schoolboy level and 36 times at full level, and played international cricket for Ireland as a teenager.

In 23 of his 36 games for the Republic, Cantwell was captain. He played in a more attacking role at this level and scored a creditable 14 goals, the last of them coming in the 89th minute of his final game, against Turkey in February 1967.

Brian Carey (CENTRE-HALF)

Born: Cork 31 May 1968
Debut for Eire: v USA April 1992

Born in the city which produced former Manchester United captain Noel Cantwell, Brian Carey came near to forming a modern-day trio of Corkonians at Old Trafford.

A gritty 6ft 3in centre-back, Brian learnt his trade in his native Cork with Albert Rovers, before progressing to League of Ireland club Cork City. Four months after starring in the Cork team which lost the 1989 FAI Cup final to Derry City, he was on his way to Manchester United in a £100,000 transfer deal.

Carey, who holds a Diploma in Construction Economics, was joined at Old Trafford by fellow-citizens Denis Irwin, who arrived in June 1990, and Roy Keane, in June 1993. Irwin and Keane claimed first-team places upon arrival; but Carey, despite spending almost four years at the club, made it only as far as the substitute's bench and failed to make the breakthrough, even when established centre-backs Steve Bruce and Gary Pallister were injured.

In January and December 1991 Brian was loaned to Fourth Division Wrexham for whom he made 16 League appearances. He was a member of the Wrexham team which knocked Arsenal out of the 1992 FA Cup. After the game Brian was commended for containing Arsenal forward Alan Smith.

In the summer of 1993 Carey's contract with United expired, and in July he was transferred to First Division Leicester City; an independent tribunal set the fee at £250,000. He was a member of the Foxes' team which won promotion, via the play-offs, to the Premiership in 1993–94 and which were relegated after just one season in the top flight.

When Martin O'Neill took over from Brian Little as Leicester boss, Carey found himself out in the cold. He didn't feature in the club's success in the 1996 play-offs which took them back to the Premiership once again.

To the end of 1995–96 Brian had made 58 League appearances for Leicester.

Capped once by the Republic at Under 21-level, against Switzerland in March 1992, Brian has appeared in three full internationals, all of them friendlies.

John Carey (DEFENDER)

Born: Dublin 23 February 1919
Debut for Eire: v Norway November 1937

Gentleman Johnny Carey, the quiet pipe-smoking Dubliner, was one of the finest players of his day. He was tall, assured and as elegant a footballer as any in the Football League. His manager at Manchester United, Matt Busby, believed he was the finest defender of his generation – a player to rank alongside any of United's all-time greats such as George Best and Bobby Charlton.

He was busy, yet calm and always in control; tenacious but polite and unruffled; thinning on top but as fresh and fit as a youth underneath; and always making the game look easy, using his brain to the full and playing the game sportingly at all times.

Carey was a mere 17-year-old in October 1936 when he left his native Dublin for Manchester. The story goes that Louis Rocca, United's celebrated Dublin scout, went to watch other players and spotted Carey, playing in only his third game of soccer for League of Ireland club St James's Gate. Rocca couldn't believe his eyes and before Carey had even unlaced his boots after the match Rocca had signed him for Manchester United. Six weeks later Carey was on his way to Old Trafford for £250 after United had seen off a late bid from Celtic.

A year later Johnny was in United's first team and in his first season, 1937–38, helped the club win promotion to the top flight. His rapidly developing genius made him a magnet for other First Division clubs, several of whom made tentative offers. All were refused, and

Johnny went on to become one of United's longest-serving players, remaining on the club's books for 17 years.

The 1939–45 war carved a huge chunk out of Johnny's career. He volunteered for service and was posted to Italy where he played for several clubs. Fortunately he was young enough to resume his career when League football began again after the war.

United's new manager Matt Busby handed Carey the captaincy. Busby knew about Johnny's leadership qualities, his on-the-field authority and above all his professionalism. In 1948 Carey became the first Manchester United captain for almost 40 years to hold aloft the FA Cup, after United's 4–2 win over Blackpool in the final.

Carey became Busby's mouthpiece on the pitch. Under the pair of them United were transformed from a middle-of-the-table side to Championship challengers: they were four times runners-up between 1947 and 1951, and finally League champions in 1951–52 – their first title since 1911.

One of the most complete and versatile players in the history of the game, Johnny was primarily a full-back, who could fill either berth, though he was more recognised as one of the finest right-backs of his era. He was equally happy at half-back and even fancied himself as an attacker. In all he played in nine positions for United. He also appeared in seven positions for Ireland.

Johnny retired at the end of 1952–53, after 304 League outings (16 goals) for United. By then he'd won every honour in the game: 'Footballer of the Year' in 1949; captain of the Rest of Europe v Britain at Hampden in 1947, in the 'Match of the Century', and, fittingly, 'Sportsman of the Year' in 1950.

When he was offered the manager's position at Blackburn Rovers in 1953, Carey accepted – though with 'great diffidence and misgivings' and despite United's efforts to dissuade him. Immediately after restoring Rovers to Division One in 1958, he became manager at Everton, only to be sacked three years later for no apparent reason.

He later had managerial spells at Leyton Orient (1961–63) taking the Londoners into Division One for the first time in their history in his first season. After Orient's relegation the following season Carey left to take over at Nottingham Forest (1963–68).

His managerial career ended where it had started, at Ewood Park, where he became general manager in 1970 before drifting, disillusioned, out of the game a year later.

Johnny became an Irish international within six weeks of arriving in Manchester. He made his debut for Eire against Norway in November 1937 and played in Ireland's next 23 games. He went on to win a total of 29 Eire caps, turning out in various positions for his country and captaining the Irish on 19 occasions, including the historic 2–0 win over England at Goodison Park in September 1949.

Carey also won seven Northern Ireland caps between September 1946 and March 1949, appearing at left- and right-back, right-half and inside-right for the North.

Johnny Carey died in August 1995.

Joseph Carolan (FULL-BACK)

Born: Dublin 8 September 1937
Debut for Eire: v Sweden November 1959

The motto of League of Ireland club Home Farm could well be: 'Suppliers of quality footballers to the Football League'. Joe Carolan was one of the first in a long line of illustrious players to tumble off the production line at Tolka Park; they included Liverpool's Ronnie Whelan and Ken DeMange and Manchester United's Billy Whelan, Johnny Giles and Mick Martin.

Carolan joined Manchester United in February 1956. A strong and industrious left-back, he spent almost five years at Old Trafford but had to wait nearly three years for a run out in the first team. Once in the side he

proved difficult to shift and in the next two seasons he made 66 League appearances for United.

Early in 1960–61 Joe lost his first-team place to his Republic of Ireland colleague Shay Brennan and in December 1960 was sold to Second Division Brighton for £8,000. He made 33 League appearances for Brighton before returning to Ireland in the summer of 1962.

Joe was chosen to play for Ireland on two occasions, in friendlies against Sweden in November 1959 and Chile in March 1960. Both games were staged in Dublin and ended in victories for the home side.

Brendan Carroll (CENTRE-FORWARD)

Born: Bray, Co. Wicklow
Debut for Eire: v Belgium April 1949

In the late 1940s Brendan Carroll was regarded in some quarters as potentially the best centre-forward in the League of Ireland. He possessed 'great speed from a standing start and clever and delightful anticipation and control'. On the downside, Carroll suffered the curse of many of his fellow tradesmen – he was one-footed. 'If only he could improve on his shooting and make better use of his left foot.'

Brendan joined Shelbourne in 1947 from his local club Bray Wanderers. In three seasons with the Reds he scored 23 League goals and was the club's top scorer in 1947–48 and 1948–49.

He was a League of Ireland representative player in 1949 and the same year helped Shels to the FAI Cup final, which they lost 3–0 to Dundalk.

Carroll, who spent 1950–51 with Transport, 'did well on his international debut' in the defeat by Belgium in April 1949. His second run out for his country came in the 3–0 World Cup qualifying victory over Finland in September 1949; he was injured after 25 minutes and was replaced by Shamrock Rovers' player Paddy Daly.

35

Thomas Carroll (DEFENDER)

Born: Dublin 18 August 1942
Debut for Eire: v Poland May 1968

Tommy Carroll was just six months past his 15th birthday when he joined his elder brother Eddie in Shelbourne's League of Ireland side.

During seven years at Tolka Park Tommy won a League of Ireland Championship medal, an FAI Cup winners medal and a President's Cup winners medal. He popped up in every position for the club, including goalkeeper, though he was an experienced 20-year-old before he appeared in the right-back position in which he was to make his name in the Football League.

Carroll left his native Dublin to join Cambridge City in August 1964. He had two seasons with the club and had the rare distinction of winning an Ireland Under-23 cap while playing Southern League football when he played at right-back in the 0–0 draw with France in June 1966.

In July 1966 Tommy left Cambridge for Ipswich Town. During seven seasons at Portman Road he made 117 League appearances and won a Second Division Championship medal in 1967–68. Competition for defensive places at the club became acute in the late 1960s and Tommy had to vie with England international full-backs Mick Mills and Michael McNeill as well as home-grown defender Colin Harper, for his place. In the end Carroll lost out, and in November 1971, after impressing on a month's trial, he signed for Birmingham City.

He claimed a regular first-team place immediately and helped the Blues win promotion to Division One in his first season at St Andrews. Having made just 38 League appearances for City, however, he was forced out of the game through injury.

A former League of Ireland representative player, Tommy won three Amateur caps. In a 17-cap full international career he appeared in all of the defensive positions for the Republic and scored his only goal at this level from the penalty spot in the 1–1 draw with Sweden in October 1970.

Anthony Cascarino (FORWARD)

Born: St Paul's Cray, Kent 1 September 1962
Debut for Eire: v Switzerland September 1985

The man who was once sold for a set of football jerseys and was later bought for £1.5 million, Tony Cascarino has had his fair share of criticism over the years but has invariably bounced back and let his football do the talking.

Standing 6ft 3in and weighing 14st, Cascarino possesses an aerial power and strength which defenders find intimidating; he is regarded as one of the foremost headers of the ball in the game.

Third Division Gillingham introduced Tony to League football when they signed him from junior club Crockenhill in January 1982. In four of his six seasons at the Priestfield Stadium he was the club's leading scorer, netting 78 goals in 219 League appearances.

In June 1987 he was transferred to Second Division Millwall for a £250,000 fee. For a player who had supported the Lions from the terraces as a youngster, it was a dream come true.

At the Den, Cascarino linked up with Teddy Sheringham to form the most feared and prolific strike force in the Division. The partnership paid dividends immediately: in his first season Cascarino netted 20 goals in 39 games compared to Sheringham's 22 in 43 games; and the Lions were Division Two champions, moving into the top flight for the first time in their history. Tony spent a further two seasons at Millwall, scoring 22 more goals in a further 66 games.

Towards the end of 1990–91 Aston Villa

were in a championship dogfight with Liverpool. Villa manager Graham Taylor wanted a player to beef up his forward line and was convinced of Cascarino's pedigree. Taylor hoped that Tony could do for Villa what he'd done for Millwall three seasons earlier and push his club to championship success – and he was prepared to pay for it. In March 1990 he smashed the club transfer record by paying Millwall £1.5 million for the player.

It wasn't to be. Cascarino had no time to acclimatise and didn't find the target until the final two games of the season as Villa were pipped to the post. At the close of the following season, after 11 goals in 46 games, he was sold to Celtic at a cut price £1.1 million.

He also failed to hit form with the famous Glasgow club, spending most of 1991–92 on the subs bench, playing second fiddle to Charlie Nicholas and Tommy Coyne. Eleven of his 24 appearances were as a substitute and he managed just four goals.

In January 1992 Tony joined Chelsea in a straight swap deal which took Scottish full-back Tommy Boyd to Parkhead. But if Cascarino expected some respite for his rapidly ailing career, he was mistaken.

Initially his fortunes took a turn for the better when he opened his account on his debut for Chelsea. But it turned out to be a false dawn and he scored just once more in ten further outings in 1991–92. The following season was a disaster for the big man as he was laid low by two cartilage operations and found injury piling upon injury. When the season ended he had managed just nine appearances and two goals.

Tony was a playing substitute when Chelsea lost the 1994 FA Cup final to Manchester United. In August 1994, after a total of eight goals in 40 League appearances, Cascarino was freed by Chelsea and subsequently joined French Second Division club Marseille.

His career took an upward swing in France: he began scoring regularly and became

Anthony Cascarino

something of a cult hero at the club. He ended his first season at Marseille as top scorer in France, with 38 League goals.

Tony became eligible to pull on the green shirt of Ireland when FIFA altered their rules to allow a mother's origins to be taken into account: his maternal grandfather came from Westport in Co. Mayo.

He won his first cap under Eoin Hand, then was passed over for the first 17 games of Jack Charlton's reign. Big Jack, who refers to Cascarino as the 'Ice Cream Man', later brought him in from the cold. He became a regular in Charlton's side and in October 1996 won his 65th cap, 33 of which started from the substitute's bench.

He played in the 1988 European Championships and the 1990 World Cup finals, but injury limited him to a token 17 minutes of play in the 1994 World Cup finals in the USA.

Cascarino has scored 14 international goals, including Ireland's opener in their 2–0 defeat of world champions Germany in Hanover in May 1994.

Jeffrey Chandler (OUTSIDE-LEFT)

Born: Hammersmith, London 19 June 1959
Debut for Eire: v Czechoslovakia
September 1979

A player who did the rounds of the divisions, Jeff Chandler swapped employers six times in his 13-year Football League career.

He began as an apprentice at Second Division Blackpool, whom he joined professionally in August 1976. He scored seven times in 37 League games for Rovers before joining First Division Leeds United in September 1979.

He managed just 26 League games (two goals) for Leeds before joining Bolton Wanderers for £40,000 in October 1981. Jeff found his feet at Burnden Park. He was a devastating wing wizard, providing pin-point crosses for others to score and scoring himself – 36 goals in 157 games.

In July 1985 Chandler moved to Derby County, with a tribunal fixing his transfer fee at £38,000. He made quite an impact at the Baseball Ground contributing significantly to the club's promotion from Division Three in 1985–86. Derby were Second Division champions the following season, but Chandler lost his place to Graham Harbey in October 1986. He was loaned to Mansfield Town in November (six appearances) and in July 1987, after 46 games for Derby, he was on his way back to Burnden Park.

During his second spell at Bolton Jeff suffered knee ligament damage, and after just 24 League games (four goals) he joined Cardiff City in November 1989. He appeared in 25 League games for the Welsh club before his contract was cancelled in 1990.

Capped once by the Republic at Under-21 level, against Poland in 1979–80, Jeff won the first of his two full caps as a substitute in a patchwork Irish side which contained five other debutants, against Czechoslovakia in September 1979. His second call-up came the following month when Ireland, despite falling 2–0 behind, defeated the USA 3–2 in a friendly in Dublin.

Jerome Clarke (FORWARD)

Born: Drogheda, Co. Louth 15 July 1951
Debut for Eire: v Poland April 1978

At 15 Jerome Clarke joined his local club Drogheda United. He spent 12 seasons with the club, winning an FAI Cup runners-up medal as a substitute in 1976 when United went down 1–0 to Bohemians in the final.

In July 1980 Clarke joined Co. Louth rivals Dundalk in a player-exchange deal; he was valued at £2,000. He spent two eventful seasons at Oriel Park, winning a League Championship medal in 1981–82. Although known to possess a 'lethal drive', Clarke missed Dundalk's first penalty in the 1981 League Cup final shoot-out, after two legs and extra time failed to produce a goal between Dundalk and Galway Rovers. Nevertheless, the Louthmen went on to win the shoot-out 3–2.

Clarke represented the League of Ireland on five occasions, once playing opposite Diego Maradona in Argentina in 1978. In April that year he joined his Drogheda colleague Cathal Muckian in the full Irish side which lost 3–0 to Poland in Lodz. It was both players' only cap, and Jerome was on the pitch for just 12 minutes, replacing captain/player-manager Johnny Giles.

Kevin Clarke (HALF-BACK)

Born: Dublin 3 December 1921
Debut for Eire: v Portugal May 1948

A cool, stylish half-back from the Dublin suburb of Santry, Kevin Clarke began his senior career with local club Drumcondra.

Kevin played in three FAI Cup finals with the Drums. He was a winner in 1943, playing at left-back, when Drumcondra beat Cork United. In 1946 and 1948 the Drums lined up against Dublin rivals Shamrock Rovers. They won 2–1 in 1946, when Kevin played at centre-half, but lost to the Hoops two years later when the scoreline was reversed. After helping Drumcondra to the League Championship in 1947–48 Clarke left Irish shores for Swansea Town in November 1948.

The Welsh club won the Third Division (South) Championship in 1948–49 but Kevin managed just ten League appearances before leaving Wales to join non-League Kent side Gravesend and Northfleet, with whom he spent two seasons. His son Charlie played for the club in 1965–66, one of the rare occasions of father and son playing for Fleet.

Kevin, who was a steeplejack by trade, represented the League of Ireland six times in his Drumcondra days and won two caps in away defeats by Portugal and Spain in May 1948.

Matthew Clarke (FULL-BACK)

Born: Dublin
Debut for Eire: v Belgium May 1950

Although remembered as one of the League of Ireland's outstanding defenders of the 1940s, Mattie Clarke joined Shamrock Rovers in 1938 as a centre-forward and scored a hat-trick in one of his first games for the club in that position.

Mattie spent 12 seasons at Rovers, playing as a reserve for two seasons before gaining his place in the League team. A stalwart in defence, playing at right- or left-back, Mattie was a resolute and consistent operator with tremendous enthusiasm and a 'never-say-die attitude'. By the time he left the capital for Dundalk in 1950 he was Rovers' longest-serving player. The club made him a special presentation for his loyalty.

He won a League Championship medal in 1938–39 with Rovers and played in five FAI Cup finals (1940, 1944, 1945, 1946 and 1948). He was captain in the 1946 final – the only one of his five appearances when he did not pick up a winners medal.

Clarke played in his last Cup final in 1952 when he led Dundalk to victory after a replay in which he had 'the game of his life' playing at centre-half.

Mattie, who was an employee of Guinness Brewery, was a juvenile international. After an almost unbroken run of appearances for the League side for whom he 'rarely had a poor game', he was called up to the full international side to face Belgium in May 1950. Though at the veteran stage, he had been 'amazingly consistent' and in his only full international he played right-back in place of Johnny Carey.

Mattie Clarke, who has passed away, was described as one of the greatest sportsmen and soccer players in the country. The terror of wingers on the park, he was an 'almost shy, unassuming gentleman off the field'.

Thomas Clinton (FULL-BACK)

Born: Dublin 13 April 1926
Debut for Eire: v Norway May 1951

Tommy Clinton left his native Dublin at 18 to work in the office at Dundalk railway station. He was playing local football when he was invited to join the town's League of Ireland side.

Whilst playing for Dundalk Tommy was spotted by scouts from Everton, who sent their secretary, Theo Kelly, to the town in March 1948 to sign the player. The business was concluded in dramatic style: Clinton signed the terms that would take him to Merseyside as Kelly's train was pulling out of the station and he had to push the hastily signed contract through the window of the moving train.

Tommy joined Everton as a wing-half but was soon converted to full-back, the position in which he made most of his 73 League appearances for the club.

In April 1955 Tommy signed for Johnny Carey's Blackburn Rovers, but after just half a dozen League appearances, he returned to Merseyside in June 1956 to join Tranmere Rovers. He spent a year with Rovers and made nine League appearances before joining Runcorn in the Cheshire League.

Tommy is often reminded of the penalty he missed for Everton against Bolton in the 1953 FA Cup semi-final. Everton had been awarded a penalty just before half-time. Tommy blasted the spot kick wide, though it didn't seem to matter because they were 4–0 down at the time. However, thoughts turned to what might have been, for Everton reduced the deficit to 4–3 in the second half. Bolton went through to face Blackpool in the famous 1953 'Matthews' Final'.

Tommy won three full caps for the Republic between May 1951 and March 1954 when he played at right-back in the games against Norway, France and Luxembourg.

Patrick Coad (WING-HALF/FORWARD)

Born: Waterford 1920
Debut for Eire: v England September 1946

In 1983 Paddy Coad was awarded the PFA of Ireland Merit Award for services to the game in Ireland. Few deserved it more. His records

of 126 League of Ireland goals and 41 goals in the FAI Cup competition are testimony to his ability on the field.

Coad joined Waterford from Corinthians in 1937, moving north to Lurgan club Glenavon the following year. He had been there only a few weeks when war erupted, whereupon he returned to Waterford.

Controversy entered his career in 1941. In a dispute over bonuses, Coad – with his Waterford colleagues – refused to play in a 'test match' against Cork United which would have decided the winner of that year's League Championship. They also lost that year's FAI Cup final to Cork after a replay.

Paddy signed for Shamrock Rovers in January 1942 and remained at the club until 1959. A magnificent midfield general and wonderful long passer, Paddy became such an influential player at Milltown that the team in the '50s earned the nickname Coad's Colts.

He played in seven FAI Cup finals with Rovers, emerging as winner in 1944, 1945, 1948 and 1956 and as a runner-up in 1946, 1957 and 1958. As club captain in the '50s, he also skippered them to three League of Ireland Championships in 1953–54, (when he was player-manager), 1956–57 and 1958–59, after which he returned to his hometown club Waterford.

Paddy won junior international honours in 1938 when the FAI entertained the Birmingham FA; and he was a regular inter-League player from 1943.

In September 1946 he cut short his honeymoon to make his debut in the full Irish squad to face England in Dublin. He won ten more full caps over the next five years during which he scored three goals. Each time he scored, Ireland won. He netted in the 3–2 defeat of Spain in Dublin in March 1947, scored the only goal of the game against Portugal in May 1949 and hit an 82nd-minute winner in the 3–2 defeat of Norway in Oslo in May 1951.

Timothy Coffey (LEFT-HALF)

Born: Dublin
Debut for Eire: v Finland October 1949

Timmy Coffey spent his best years in the League of Ireland with Drumcondra in the late 1940s and the early 1950s. He was a League Championship winner in 1948–49, and in 1954 he won an FAI Cup winners medal, courtesy of St Pat's Athletic own goal – the only goal of the match

Coffey was a member of the Irish team to face Finland in Helsinki in a World Cup qualifier in October 1949. He came into the reckoning because Willie Walsh of Manchester City was injured. His selection was considered by some to be a useful and promising player. He was played out of position at right-half in what turned out to be his only full international match. Nevertheless, he put in a solid performance and supplied the pass from which Peter Farrell scored Ireland's goal in the 1–1 draw.

The following month Timmy was back in his own position of left-half as the League of Ireland took on their Scottish counterparts.

Martin Colfer (CENTRE-FORWARD)

Born: Dublin
Debut for Eire: v Belgium May 1950

'An amazingly clever centre-forward opportunist, Martin Colfer has those extra artful touches that distinguish the champion from the craftsman.'

The former St James's Gate outside-right went to Shelbourne during the 1948–49 season. The first FAI Cup tie he played in that season was the final, which Shels lost 3–0 to Dundalk, though he found himself in the starting XI only because of an injury to Mattser Cranley.

Once described as 'the man who can hit the ball with the goal stamp', Colfer was Shels' top scorer in the next two seasons and in 1951 he played in another losing Cup-final side when Cork Athletic overcame the Dubliners by a single goal in the replay.

Martin helped the Reds win the League Championship in 1952–53. Moreover, he was the club's top scorer in three of his seven seasons there and scored a total of 40 League goals.

In May 1950 Colfer was called up for his first cap even though: 'he hasn't been a model of consistency this season . . . but on form can be a match winner. He is earnest and he roams at will. It is then that the Shelbourne leader is seen at his best.'

That first cap came in the 5–1 defeat by Belgium in Brussels. He won his second cap a year later in a 3–2 victory over Norway in Oslo.

Oliver Conmy (WINGER)

Born: Mulrany, Co. Mayo 13 November 1939
Debut for Eire: v Belgium March 1965

Oliver Conmy was nine years old when his parents left Mayo to live in Dewsbury, Yorkshire. There he played football for the local school's team. Three years after leaving school Oliver was playing for St Paulinus YC in Dewsbury when he was noticed by Huddersfield Town, who signed him professionally in May 1959.

Conmy became a regular in Town's Central League side, playing mainly on the right wing, and made his first-team debut against Liverpool in October 1960. He managed just two further senior appearances before new Peterborough boss Gordon Clarke – who began his managerial career with Waterford – took him to London Road in May 1964 for £2,000.

Conmy spent the rest of his senior career with Peterborough and in eight years at the club he scored 34 goals in 262 League games. He

Oliver Conmy

David Connolly (FORWARD)

Born: London 6 June 1977
Debut for Eire: v Portugal May 1996

From Willesden Green, north-west London, David Connolly is one of Mick McCarthy's youngsters for whom a bright future is predicted.

Connolly signed professionally for Watford in November 1994 after completing two years with the club as a trainee. He had been the Hornets' top scorer at schoolboy, youth and reserve team levels.

David made a couple of appearances as substitute for Watford in 1994–95 and featured in the club's first XI at the beginning of the next season. He was laid low for six months, however, after an ankle operation. At the end of 1995–96, with Watford involved in a relegation dogfight, David burst on to the scene again, with eight goals in six games, including two hat-tricks. But it was too late to save Graham Taylor's club from dropping into the Second Division.

In May 1996 he played for Ireland in Mick McCarthy's testimonial game against Glasgow Celtic when he scored in the 3–0 victory. That was enough to earn him his first full cap three days later when Portugal were the visitors to Lansdowne Road.

'It's every player's ambition to play for his country. This is a dream come true,' said Connolly after hearing he was in the team. 'I was lucky to get a game and a goal against Celtic, but this is even better.'

An impish livewire with an eye for goal, he showed some deft touches on his debut and is an exciting prospect. He won his fourth cap in the US Cup game against Mexico in June 1996, a game in which he scored his second international goal.

was freed by the Fourth Division club (although they finished ninth in Division Three in 1967–68 they were relegated for illegal payments) in 1972 and later played non-League football with Cambridge City, Ely City and March Town.

Oliver still lives in Peterborough, and his son Ben plays for the club's youth team.

Although Conmy had spent his school holidays in Mayo, he had never seen Ireland play. He got his first opportunity to do that in March 1965 when he received a surprise call-up to the Irish squad to face Belgium in Dublin. He played in three successive Irish fixtures between May 1967 and May 1968, and completed his collection of five full caps in October 1969, against Czechoslovakia, whom he had lined up against twice before.

Gerard Conroy (FORWARD)

Born: Dublin 2 October 1946
Debut for Eire: v Czechoslovakia October 1969

A ginger-haired, fair-skinned Dubliner, Terry – as he was known, but Gerard as he was christened – Conroy played hurling and Gaelic football before turning to Association football. He played his early soccer for local club Home Farm, turning out for the Under-13s to the Under-17s, and described himself as a 'regular midget' in those days.

Terry shot up in his late teens and was soon snapped up by Belfast club Glentoran in the Irish League. In March 1967 George Eastham (sen.), seeing off competition from Newcastle and Fulham, signed Conroy for First Division Stoke City.

Although he scored on his League debut against Leicester City, Terry took two years to settle and claim a regular first-team place.

His free-running style exposed his rather slim frame to mistimed tackles and associated knocks, but, apart from a couple of cartilage operations, Terry never looked back. In 11 seasons at the Victoria Ground he made 271 League appearances and scored 49 goals, exciting supporters with his lissom performances.

Stoke appeared in a major final for the first time in their 105-year history in 1972 when they faced Chelsea in the League Cup final. Conroy headed the opening goal after just 4½ minutes and George Eastham (jun.) sealed the tie for the Potters to run out 2–1 winners over the much-fancied Londoners.

Stoke were relegated to Division Two at the end of 1976–77 and the following season Terry headed off for a spell in Hong Kong.

Terry made a fleeting return to the Football League in January 1980 when he signed for Fourth Division Crewe Alexandra. He ended his League career with five goals in 37 games for the Railwaymen.

Terry made his debut for the Republic

Gerard Conroy

against Czechoslovakia in October 1969 and immediately became a regular, playing in nine consecutive games to December 1970. After an absence from international football of almost two years, he returned with a bang in October 1972, scoring in successive games against USSR and France. He reclaimed his place in the side, and won his 27th and final cap against Poland in April 1977.

James Conway (HALF-BACK)

Born: Dublin 10 August 1946
Debut for Eire: v Spain October 1966

One of a family of 17, Jimmy Conway had unsuccessful trials as a 15-year-old with

James Conway

to fitness and in 1975 walked out at Wembley to face West Ham United in the FA Cup final; the Cottagers went down 2–0 to their fellow Londoners.

In August 1976, after 316 League games and 67 goals for Fulham Jimmy signed for First Division Manchester City. He spent less than four months with City, playing only 13 League games before packing his bags to play in America.

Capped at Schoolboy, Youth and Amateur levels for Eire, Jimmy won his first cap in the goalless draw with Spain in October 1966. Almost ten years later, in April 1977, he won his 20th and final cap in another goalless draw, this time with Poland. Jimmy scored three international goals including the 89th-minute winner against West Germany 'B' in March 1975.

Manchester United and Leeds United before returning to Ireland to continue playing for Stella Maris and serve his apprenticeship as a carpenter. In 1964 he joined Bohemians in the League of Ireland and in May 1966 signed for Fulham.

Jimmy became one of the enduring links in Fulham's trials and tribulations of the '60s and '70s, surviving the west London club's relegation from Division One to Division Three in successive seasons between 1968 and 1970.

Jimmy had a total of ten seasons at Craven Cottage during which he appeared in almost every position for the club. A thoroughbred midfielder, he was equally at home as a striker, the position he appeared in during 1969–70. He left no one in any doubt about his all-round ability when he ended that season as Fulham's leading scorer with 23 goals. In 1970–71 he finally found his niche, at his own request, down the right flank where he used his pace to unsettle defenders, and he had the satisfaction of helping Fulham win promotion to Division Two that season.

Jimmy was dogged by injuries in the following two seasons but fought his way back

Peter Corr (OUTSIDE-RIGHT)

Born: Dundalk, Co. Louth 26 June 1923
Debut for Eire: v Portugal May 1949

A former Co. Louth Gaelic player, Peter Corr joined Preston North End, then a force in the First Division, from League of Ireland club Dundalk in April 1947. He was understudy to the great Tom Finney at Deepdale and was unlucky with injuries during his time there. As a result he managed just three League appearances for the Lilywhites before his transfer to Everton in the summer of 1948.

At Everton he linked up with fellow countrymen Alex Stevenson, Tom Eglington and Peter Farrell and together they constituted a formidable attacking quartet bursting with ability and flair. A player with an extensive repertoire of slick skills, Corr possessed a great turn of speed which enabled him to lose his marker and provide the accurate crosses which became something of a hallmark. Despite his undoubted ability Peter was no more than an occasional player in the Blues' First Division side. He made 24 appearances (two goals) in his two seasons with the club before leaving for Bangor in 1949.

A full international between May and November 1949, Peter won four full caps. He made his debut in the 1–0 victory over Portugal in Dublin in May 1949 and was a member of the historic Irish side which beat England 2–0 at Goodison Park in September of that year to become the first foreign side to defeat England at home.

Edward Courtney (GOALKEEPER)

Born: Dublin
Debut for Eire: v Portugal June 1946

Edward 'Ned' Courtney was a Gaelic player from Dublin who joined the army and settled in Cork. A reliable and gallant goalminder, the army captain played in goal for the Cork Gaelic team before signing for League club Cork United in 1945.

Ned won a League Championship medal with United in 1945–46 but enjoyed his best years with Cork Athletic, who took over from United in the late 1940s.

He won back-to-back League Championship medals in 1949–50 and 1950–51, and played in three successive FAI Cup finals between 1951 and 1953. He was a Cup winner in 1951; he played in the 1–1 draw with Dundalk in the 1952 final but missed the replay, which his team lost 3–0; he spent most of 1952–53 in retirement, having been deposed by Cork keepers Healy and Waters; 'but he springs up like a mushroom', and he got his place back in the 1953 final win, in which England and Sunderland legend Raich Carter played at inside-right for Cork.

In June 1946 Courtney made his international debut in dramatic fashion: he was driven by army lorry from Cork to Dublin in an emergency when Shamrock Rovers' keeper Tommy Breen cried off the

international side to face Portugal. It was Ned's only cap. But he became part of Ireland's footballing history. When he was injured after 30 minutes attempting to prevent Portugal's third goal, he was replaced in goal by Con Martin who thus became Ireland's first-ever substitute goalkeeper.

Owen Coyle (FORWARD)

Born: Glasgow 14 July 1966
Debut for Eire: v Holland April 1994

Owen Coyle played his junior football in Scotland with Renfrew YM. In 1984 he joined Dumbarton where his two older brothers, Joseph and Thomas, were professionals at the time.

Coyle made his League debut for Dumbarton in February 1986 and over the next four seasons netted 36 goals in 103 League outings. In September 1988 he departed for Clydebank where in a season and a half he scored 33 times in 63 games.

In February 1990 Airdrie boss Jimmy Bone took him to Broomfield Park for a record £175,000. 'He will score goals at any level because he's a natural. He has the priceless gift of being able to find space in the six-yard box and remains cool under pressure,' was Bone's assessment of his new acquisition.

Owen didn't disappoint him. He led Airdrie's scoring charts in each of his four seasons at the club and had scored an incredible 17 goals in just seven League games at the beginning of 1990–91 when a training ground injury put him out of action for four months. He had scored a total of 50 League goals in 123 games for the Diamonds before his £250,000 transfer to Bolton Wanderers in June 1993.

Coyle played a leading role in First Division Bolton's magnificent FA Cup run in 1993–94 when they disposed of Premiership giants Everton, Arsenal and Aston Villa on their way to the quarter-finals.

The following season, 1994–95, he helped Bolton win their way into the FA Premiership, scoring in the dramatic 4–3 defeat of Reading in the Division One play-offs. He didn't play in Bolton's League Cup final defeat by Liverpool that season and in October 1995 he was transferred to Dundee United for £280,000 after 12 goals in 54 League games for the club.

He scored five times in 28 games for Dundee United in 1995–96. In May 1996 his extra-time goal gave United a 2–1 win over Partick Thistle, thereby putting them into the Premiership by an aggregate score of 4–3.

Coyle, though Glasgow born and bred, is the son of Donegal-born parents and since childhood has harboured a burning ambition to play for Ireland. In fact, during his time at Airdrie he declined the opportunity of playing for Scotland's Under-21 side.

Capped twice by Eire at Under-21 level,

Thomas Coyne

once at Under-23 and twice at 'B' level, Owen won his one full cap to date as a substitute in the 1–0 victory over Holland in April 1994.

Thomas Coyne (FORWARD)

Born: Glasgow 14 November 1962
Debut for Eire: v Switzerland March 1992

The man with the most lethal boot in Scottish football in the '80s, Tommy Coyne was a latecomer to the international scene: he was 29 when he won his first cap in March 1992, scoring in that 2–1 victory over Switzerland in Dublin.

He played in three out of Ireland's four World Cup games in the USA in 1994 when he ran himself to exhaustion ploughing a lonely furrow as Ireland's solitary striker.

In a total of 21 outings with the Republic, eleven of which have been as a substitute, Coyne has scored six goals, the most memorable of which was the winner against Holland in Tilburg in April 1994.

His goal ratio in ten seasons in the Scottish Premier League was such that when he became eligible to represent Ireland because of his Irish-born grandparents, he had no hesitation in doing so and Ireland were only too glad to avail themselves of his services.

Coyne played his junior football with Hillwood BC and began his Scottish League career with Clydebank, for whom he scored 38 goals in 80 League games. His ten goals in 11 outings at the beginning of 1983–84, which confirmed him as Clydebank's leading scorer for the whole season, attracted a lot of attention and in October 1983 he joined Dundee United.

Coyne's three seasons at Tannadice were difficult ones. The goal machine began to creak a little, and he managed just eight goals in 52 League games.

At the beginning of 1986–87 he moved to United's neighbours and arch rivals Dundee. It was at Dens Park that his career really took off. In four seasons he took in 89 League games and

51 goals. The total included an incredible 33 in 43 games in 1987–88, which put him in contention for the coveted Adidas Golden Boot award; it was eventually won by Turkish player Tanja Colak.

In March 1989 Celtic moved in and signed Tommy for a 'large fee'. In four seasons at Parkhead he scored 43 goals in 105 games and in 1990 collected a Scottish Cup runners-up medal, as a substitute, after Celtic's penalties defeat by Aberdeen. Despite his success he found himself edged out of the Parkhead picture by Gerry Creaney and Charlie Nicholas. He refused the offer of a new contract and in March 1993 moved to Tranmere Rovers in a £400,000 deal.

His rival at Tranmere for the main striking role was John Aldridge, the man who more than any other is responsible for Coyne's bit-part role in the Irish set-up. Aldridge's brilliance in front of goal meant that Tommy managed just nine full League appearances plus three as a substitute for Rovers in 1992–93.

After the sudden death of his wife Alison, Tommy returned to Scotland in October 1993 to look after his three young sons. He refused offers from several Scottish clubs until November 1993 when he finally agreed to join Motherwell for £110,000.

Tommy was the Well's top scorer in his first two seasons at the club, helping them to runners-up spot in the Scottish Premier Division in 1994–95. He missed most of the 1995–96 season through injury. The team suffered as a consequence of his absence, finishing third from bottom of the League. To the end of that season Tommy had scored 32 goals in 73 games for Motherwell.

George Cummins (INSIDE-FORWARD)

Born: Dublin 12 March 1931
Debut for Eire: v Luxembourg October 1953

An inside-forward with plenty of ability, George Cummins began his Football League career with Everton, whom he joined from St Patrick's Athletic in November 1950.

Just over a year later he joined fellow Irishmen Jimmy O'Neill, Don Donovan, Peter Farrell and Tommy Clinton in the Blues' first team. He failed, however, to hold down a regular first-team place and in August 1953 he was transferred to Second Division Luton Town for £12,000.

After only two games in Luton's first XI George was dropped – it seems he had difficulty coming to terms with 'the cramped conditions at Kenilworth Road having become accustomed to the wide open spaces of Goodison Park'.

Noted for his high workrate, Cummins wasn't long in winning back his first-team place, which he kept, injuries excepted, until 1960. Overall George made 186 League appearances for the Hatters, scoring 21 goals in one of the most productive eras in the club's history.

In 1954–55 he helped Luton win promotion to the top flight for the first time and in 1959 he picked up an FA Cup runners-up medal after the Hatters went down 2–1 to Nottingham Forest in the only FA Cup final they have contested.

The latest in a series of knee injuries at the beginning of 1960–61 sidelined Cummins for most of the season, and he failed to show sufficient signs of recovery in the reserves to justify a regular first-team place. To compound matters, when he refused to change position during the match against Leeds on Easter Saturday, he was fined £10 and ostracised by the first XI; at the end of that season, he was given a free transfer.

In July 1961 he joined non-League Cambridge City in a £3,500 transfer deal, after turning down the chance to join three League clubs.

He returned to League football in November 1962, joining Third Division Hull City where he ended his League career with 21 appearances (two goals) in 1962–63.

George made his international debut in the 4–0 defeat of Luxembourg in a World Cup qualifier in October 1953. In the return leg in Luxembourg he scored his first international goal, which proved to be enough to take all the points on the day. Over the next seven years at Kenilworth Road George took his international record to five goals in 19 games.

Timothy Cuneen (INSIDE-RIGHT)

Born: Limerick 1924
Debut for Eire: v Norway May 1951

Tim Cuneen played for Pike Rovers in the Munster Senior League and turned out for Limerick in the League of Ireland in the 1939–40 season, before he had celebrated his 15th birthday!

A right-winger of great talent, Cuneen joined Irish League club Coleraine during the 1950–51 season. He later returned to his home-town and again turned out for Pike and Limerick.

With Limerick colleague Sean Cusack, Timmy 'shone brilliantly' for the League of Ireland representative side against the English League in April 1951. 'An artiste with the ball at his feet, he manipulated it with the wizardry of any [Wilf] Mannion.'

Cuneen won his one full cap the following month when he played for Ireland against Norway. Unfortunately he suffered a hip injury in the 42nd minute and was replaced by Paddy Coad of Shamrock Rovers, who netted Ireland's winner in a five-goal thriller.

Kenneth Cunningham (RIGHT-BACK)

Born: Dublin 26 June 1971
Debut for Eire: v Czech Republic April 1996

Ken Cunningham played in the Dublin and District Schoolboys League with Tolka Rovers and Home Farm. His manager at Farm had contacts with Millwall which led to Ken getting a trial with the Lions and ultimately signing as a professional for the London club. He made his League debut in a 1–1 draw with Norwich in March 1990, but the end of that season saw Millwall relegated to the old Division Two.

After securing the right-back berth in 1992, the stylish and versatile Glasnevin defender built up a band of admirers at the Den, not least of whom was Millwall and the future Ireland boss Mick McCarthy, who described him as 'intelligent, comfortable on either foot, dependable and quick enough'. After 136 League appearances (one goal) for Millwall, McCarthy cashed in on Ken's growing reputation in November 1994 by accepting Wimbledon's offer of £1.3 million in a joint deal which also took Jon Goodman to Selhurst Park.

Thoughtful, articulate and mannerly, Ken has been described as the antithesis of the public image of the madcap Dons. The Irishman immediately staked his claim to the right-back position at Wimbledon, although he was used as a midfield marker, a position some at the club believe is his best. By the end of the 1995–96, he had made 61 League appearances for the Dons.

Capped by the Republic at Under-21 and 'B' levels, Kenny's natural ability as a right-back put him in position in Ireland's senior side. But, following wholesale withdrawals from the national side for the game against the Czech Republic in April 1996, Mick McCarthy had sometimes used Cunningham as a centre-half, and it was in this position alongside Paul McGrath and Phil Babb, that Ken made his international debut. He remained in the side for the series of friendlies in the summer of 1996, taking his caps tally to six against Bolivia in June.

Dermot Curtis (CENTRE-FORWARD)

Born: Dublin 26 August 1932
Debut for Eire: v Denmark October 1956

Dermot Curtis started his Football League career with Second Division Bristol City, who signed him from Dublin club Shelbourne in September 1956.

After one season, 26 appearances and 16 goals at Ashton Gate, Curtis was transferred to Second Division Ipswich Town where he successfully deputised in either inside-forward berths. However, he was unable to secure a regular first-team place at Portman Road and made just 41 League appearances (17 goals) in four seasons. In August 1963 he was transferred to Fourth Division Exeter City.

Dermot had three seasons at St James Park where, for the first time in his career, he got regular first-team football. In 1963–64 he helped the Grecians claw their way out of Division Four, but when they slipped back into the bottom division at the end of 1965–66, Dermot decided to move on. Thus in the close season, with 98 League outings and 23 goals under his belt, he joined Torquay United, who'd just won promotion to Division Three. After just a dozen games for the Devon club, he was back at Exeter where he ended his League career with 10 goals in 67 League appearances.

Dermot had already been capped twice by the time he arrived in England in 1956 and, although he played most of his football in the lower divisions, he became a regular in the Ireland set-up in the late 1950s.

He marked his international debut with Ireland's first goal in the 2–1 home victory over Denmark in a World Cup qualifying game in October 1956 and eventually took his international tally to eight goals in 17 appearances.

When Dermot won his 17th and final cap, against Austria in September 1963, he became the first Exeter City player to achieve full international honours.

Sean Cusack (DEFENDER)

Born: Limerick
Debut for Eire: v France November 1952

A versatile player, Sean Cusack's senior career began in 1947 when he joined his hometown club Limerick – his one and only League club. In nine seasons Sean scored 30 League goals; moreover, he was the club's top scorer in 1948–49, with six goals. His only honour at domestic level came in 1953 when Limerick won the Shield.

Sean 'tackled well and went about his work in a businesslike manner and was thorough in all he did'. In April 1951 he and his Limerick colleague Timmy Cuneen earned lavish praise for their performances for the League of Ireland representative side against the English League.

'Words cannot describe the brilliance of the Limerick pair. Cusack showed that his versatility is of a rare kind. He was at left-half, playing the game of his life as he thwarted the might of the right flank of the English side. Florrie Burke's injury caused a reshuffle, with the Thomondgate man reverting to the left-back berth. Again he was the shining light.'

In November 1952 Sean was one of three Limerick-born players in the Ireland side which lined up against France at Dalymount Park; the other two were John Gavin of Spurs and Norwich, and Luton Town stalwart Bud Aherne. It was Cusack's only cap. He played left-half in the game, which finished 1–1.

Liam Daish (CENTRE-HALF)

Born: Portsmouth 23 September 1968
Debut for Eire: v Wales February 1992

The son of a Dublin-born sailor, Liam Daish progressed to the Republic of Ireland's senior squad in February 1992 after five appearances at Under-21 level. He made his full international debut partnering David O'Leary in the centre of the Irish defence, in the 1–0 defeat by Wales in Dublin in February 1992.

His future looked secure; he had recovered from a back operation the previous summer and won back his place at the heart of Cambridge United's defence.

A run of injuries in 1992–93, however, put his career on hold for most of that season. A broken leg kept him out for three months at the outset. Then, just 17 games after his return, he sustained knee ligament damage in March and spent the summer on a rehabilitation course at Lilleshall.

Liam began his career as an apprentice with his hometown club Portsmouth, signing as a professional in September 1986. He was released after just one League game and joined Fourth Division Cambridge in July 1988.

A 6ft 2in stopper renowned for his aerial ability, Liam became captain at the Abbey Stadium and helped his club win promotion from the Fourth to the Second Division in successive seasons, winning the Third Division Championship in 1990–91.

United just missed out on promotion to the new Premier League, losing to Leicester in the 1991–92 Second Division play-offs. As a result of that near miss, Daish and several colleagues incurred the wrath of their controversial and disciplinarian manager John Beck who told the players they were finished with the club. Things went from bad to worse at the Abbey and at the end of the following season they were relegated to the new Division Two.

In February 1994, after 139 League appearances for Cambridge, Liam signed for Birmingham City in a £50,000 transfer deal, having spent the previous month on loan at St Andrews. Liam made an immediate impact at City. He captained them to the Second Division title in 1994–95 and to victory in the Auto Windscreens Shield the same season. When Bolton bid £1.5 million for him in July 1994, Blues' boss Barry Fry was unimpressed: 'Liam is one of our major assets, a leader of the team and someone we want to help us into the Premiership. He's got to be worth £3.5

million the way prices are nowadays and if he has another season like last, it will be even more.' In fact, in February 1996 he was transferred to Coventry City for £1.75 million, having made 72 League appearances for the club.

Liam made 11 appearances for Coventry in 1995–96 and gained much of the credit for keeping the club in the Premiership.

His international career, dormant since his debut in 1992, was revived by new national team boss Mick McCarthy in 1996. With Niall Quinn and McCarthy, Daish was sent off in an ill-tempered affair against Mexico in June. He now has four full caps.

Gerard Daly (MIDFIELD)

Born: Dublin 30 April 1954
Debut for Eire: v Poland May 1973

Midfielder Gerry Daly was one of the bright young stars in Tommy Docherty's Manchester United side after his arrival from Dublin club Bohemians for £12,500 in April 1973.

Daly's time at Old Trafford was a mixture of joy and despair: he was on the fringes of the 1973–74 relegation side; an integral part of the team which won the Second Division Championship the following season; and a losing Wembley finalist in 1976 when United went down 1–0 to Southampton in the FA Cup final.

United's spot king of the period, Gerry had netted 23 goals in 111 League games for the club when a disagreement with the manager brought his United career to an abrupt end. In March 1977 Derby County boss Colin Murphy stepped in and secured his services for £190,000, making him Ireland's most expensive player at the time.

Daly had an immediate impact on the struggling Derby side. His hard work and battling qualities helped the club to a position of safety in the First Division. However, when

Tommy Docherty arrived from Old Trafford in 1977 to take over from Colin Murphy, Daly asked for a transfer. The request was later withdrawn, but the two men had an uneasy relationship. In August 1980, after 112 League games and 31 goals, Daly was sold by Colin Addison, who had replaced Docherty in the Derby hotseat.

Daly went to First Division rivals Coventry City for £300,000. In four years at Highfield Road he scored 19 goals in 84 League appearances. He also scored once in 17 games on loan to Leicester City, contributing to Leicester's promotion to the top flight that season.

In August 1984 Gerry transferred to Birmingham City for a meagre £10,000 – set by a tribunal. Exactly a decade after helping Manchester United win the Second Division title, Daly helped the Bluebirds to second place in Division Two. He had 32 League outings (one goal) for Birmingham, before joining Second Division Shrewsbury Town in October 1985. His record at Gay Meadow was eight goals in 55 games.

Gerry joined Stoke City for £15,000 in March 1987. He made 22 First Division appearances (one goal) for Stoke before signing for his final League club, Fourth Division Doncaster Rovers, whom he joined in July 1988 and for whom he made 39 League appearances (four goals) before calling it a day in League football.

Not content with donning the colours of eight Football League clubs, Gerry also spent May 1973 and May 1979 with New England Tea Men in the North American Soccer League.

At the beginning of 1990–91 he became player-manager at Vauxhall Conference club Telford United, a post from which he was dismissed in October 1993.

It has been said that Gerry Daly had few equals as a midfielder. At his best he was a delightful player. A full international for 12 years, he won 48 full Ireland caps and scored 13 goals. Daly took three spot kicks for his country, converting all of them.

Gerry was capped once at Under 21-level, against Belgium in September 1986, as an over-age player. He was 32 years old.

Maurice Daly (LEFT-BACK)

Born: Dublin 28 November 1955
Debut for Eire: v Turkey April 1978

Seventeen-year-old Maurice Daly transferred from junior club Home Farm to Wolverhampton Wanderers in July 1973.

A player who brought 'skill, pace and not least a good positional sense to the left-back berth', Daly was nevertheless a slow developer at Molineux and didn't make his League debut until November 1975. He made four appearances in that 1975–76 season but did not feature in the first team the following season.

He was a regular in Wolves' First Division side in 1977–78, playing in 28 League games. That season was the most significant in Daly's career, both domestically (Wolves cancelled his contract in August 1978) and internationally.

In March 1978 he had a successful international debut in the Republic's Under-21 game against Northern Ireland. It proved a stepping-stone to full honours, for the following month he had a promising full debut in the 4–2 defeat of Turkey. He played in his traditional left-back role in that game, 'performing competently in dealing with Turkish winger Ali Kemal', but was switched to a wide midfield role the following week when Ireland went down 3–0 to Poland in Lodz. Although that was his last full cap, he won three more Under-21 caps in the Toulon Tournament in May 1978.

Patrick Daly (CENTRE-HALF)

Born: Dublin 4 December 1927
Debut for Eire: v Finland September 1949

Paddy Daly came to Shamrock Rovers from Jacobs in 1949. On 2 November of that year, he was a member of the Rovers side which played Aston Villa at Villa Park. Daly impressed that day and subsequently became the subject of many transfer enquiries from English clubs. As it happened, he ended up at Villa Park. The Birmingham club secured the signatures of Daly and his Rovers colleague Ossie Higgins at a total cost of £15,000. Paddy spent most of his time at the club in the reserves, however, and only managed to make a total of three League appearances for Villa before dropping out of League football.

At the zenith of his career, Paddy was regarded as the best centre-half in League of Ireland football and won many representative honours in that position. 'Daly has played in many fine games. He is always in position with head or foot and effectively gets the ball out of the danger zone,' was one typical opinion.

He won his only full cap when he replaced the injured Brendan Carroll after 25 minutes in the 3–0 defeat of Finland in a World Cup qualifier in September 1949. Daly's appearance on the pitch at Dalymount Park that day was shrouded in controversy, however. The FAI had unwittingly infringed the rules of the World Cup tournament by bringing on a subtitute, which, at the time, prohibited players being replaced.

Eamonn Deacy (FULL-BACK)

Born: Galway 1 October 1958
Debut for Eire: v Algeria April 1982

Eamonn 'Chick' Deacy was one of the pioneers in Galway Rovers' first season as a League of Ireland club, 1977–78.

In March 1979 Chick transferred to First Division Aston Villa. In four seasons at Villa Park he was limited to just 33 First Division appearances due to the consistently fine form of the club's established left-back, Colin Gibson; and he had only nine games in 1980–81, when Villa won their first League Championship since 1909–10.

Deacy impressed on a month's loan to Derby County in October 1983, during which he made five Second Division appearances. He rejected the offer of a permanent move, however, preferring to return to his hometown League of Ireland club, who by then had changed their name to Galway United.

Once again, Chick became a part of Galwegian history. He was a member of the first Terryland Park side to contest a major Cup final; unfortunately they lost the 1985 FAI Cup final to Shamrock Rovers.

A former Eire Amateur player, Chick won his first full cap as a substitute for Kevin Moran in the 2–0 defeat by Algeria in Algiers in April 1982. His next three caps came in the disastrous South American tour the following month when Ireland lost to Chile, Brazil, and Trinidad and Tobago.

Kenneth De Mange (MIDFIELD)

Born: Dublin 3 September 1964
Debut for Eire: v Brazil May 1987

Former Eire Youth international Ken De Mange joined Liverpool in August 1983, having headed Home Farm's scoring charts the previous season with seven goals.

DeMange spent four seasons at Anfield, but the only time he experienced League football in that time was during a spell on loan to Fourth Division Scunthorpe in December 1986 when he scored twice in three games.

In September 1987 Ken was transferred to Leeds United for £75,000. He made 15 Second Division appearances for the club before moving to Second Division Hull City in March 1988, in a transfer deal which gave Leeds a £10,000 profit.

During his time at Boothferry Park De Mange made 68 League appearances, 20 of which were as a substitute. He also had two loan spells with Fourth Division strugglers Cardiff City in November 1990 and March 1991, adding a further 15 games to his League appearance tally.

Hull cancelled his contract at the end of 1991–92 whereupon he returned to Ireland and joined Limerick. A year later he joined Newtonards club in the Irish League for a 'huge fee'.

A strong and talented midfielder who packs a powerful shot, Ken is a former Eire Youth international. He won five Under-21 caps while at Anfield, one Under-23 cap as a Hull City player and made one 'B' international appearance, against England in 1989–90.

His first full cap came on a famous day in Dublin in May 1987 when, as a substitute for captain Mick McCarthy, he helped the Republic record a 1–0 victory over Brazil. He made his second and final appearance in a green shirt, again as a substitute, in the 4–0 home victory over Tunisia in October 1988.

John Dempsey (CENTRE-HALF)

Born: Hampstead 15 March 1946
Debut for Eire: v Spain December 1966

London-born John Dempsey didn't stray far from home in his career as a professional footballer. A solid, strong and powerful defender, he worked as a car insurance salesman before joining Fulham as an apprentice in October 1962. In March 1964 he turned professional and was an instant success, earning a regular place in Fulham's rearguard in 1963–66.

In five seasons with Fulham Dempsey made 149 League appearances, playing at centre-forward for a brief period in his first full season during which he scored a League Cup hat-trick against Northampton Town. After the Cottagers were relegated from the First to the Third Division in successive seasons (1967–1968 and 1968–1969), Dempsey

John Dempsey

seemed destined to see out his playing days with the club; however, in January 1969 Fulham's West London neighbours Chelsea offered £70,000 for his services and Fulham accepted.

John played a leading role in the halcyon days of Stamford Bridge. The Chelsea of Osgood, Hollins, Webb, McCreadie, Cooke and Harris won the FA Cup in 1970, the European Cup-Winners' Cup the following year – in which Dempsey scored Chelsea's first goal in the replayed final against Real Madrid – and were runners-up in the League Cup in 1972.

A broken toe sustained at the end of the 1972–73 season, which required an operation to untie the bones and ultimately a specially built boot, kept him out for much of the new season. He returned to the fray, however, and in nine seasons with the Blues made over 200 first-team appearances before joining Philadelphia Fury of the North American Soccer League in March 1978.

The son of Irish parents – his mother hailed from Kildare, his father from Waterford – Dempsey was regarded as something of an oddity in the 1960s: an Englishman playing for Ireland! The opportunity to represent the country of his parents came about when Irish selectors visiting Craven Cottage to watch Jimmy Conway were told of Dempsey's credentials. He was offered the chance to play for Ireland, accepted it and in December 1966 won his first cap in the 2–0 defeat by Spain in Valencia.

The number one figured prominently in Dempsey's international career. He scored one goal, against Poland in May 1968; netted one own goal, against Czechoslovakia in November 1967; was sent off once, against Hungary in November 1969; and in May 1969 captained the national side for the only time, against Denmark!

John made a return to English football in the late 1980s as manager of non-League clubs Maidenhead United and Egham Town.

He is now a PE instructor at the Broadfields Centre for the physically and mentally handicapped in Edgware, London.

Jeremiah Dennehy (WINGER)

Born: Cork 29 March 1950
Debut for Eire: v Ecuador June 1972

Jeremiah Dennehy

Christened Jeremiah but known as Miah, Dennehy helped Cork Hibs win the League of Ireland Championship in 1970–71. In 1972 his hat-trick against Waterford in the FAI Cup final secured the Cup for Cork. Nine months later, in January 1973, Nottingham Forest manager Dave Mackay paid Cork £20,000 to take the player to the City Ground.

A ball-playing inside-forward, Dennehy settled in well at Forest, and by the time Brian Clough arrived as manager in January 1975, Miah was a regular first-teamer. Almost immediately, however, he was inexplicably dropped by Clough and in July 1975, after 41 Second Division appearances (four goals), he was transferred to Third Division Walsall. In exactly three years at Fellows Park Miah made 128 League appearances and scored 22 goals.

In July 1978 Dennehy moved to Bristol Rovers. He made 52 Second Division appearances (six goals) for them. He was given a free transfer at the end of 1978–79 whereupon he joined Cardiff City. He hadn't managed to make the Welsh club's first team when his contract was cancelled in September 1980.

Miah then had a spell in non-League and League of Ireland football before returning to his native city, where he works in the Gurranebraher district of Cork where he grew up. These days he concentrates on junior soccer and plays hurley with the local St Vincent's GAA club.

When he was in England Miah played Gaelic football in Leicester and represented Warwickshire with whom he won a Provincial Championship medal in 1976, lining up in the 1976 final against a London side which included future Ireland captain Tony Grealish.

On his day Miah Dennehy could be quite exceptional, his play down the flanks combining graceful artistry with probing penetration. He won the first of his 11 full caps for the Republic (seven of which were as a substitute) in the 3–2 victory over Ecuador in the Brazilian Independence Cup in June 1972.

Miah scored twice for his country: his first goal earned a 1–1 draw with Norway in June 1973; and his second was the only goal in the 1–0 defeat of Poland at home in October 1973 – Johnny Giles' first game in charge of the national side.

He was a substitute in the historic All-Ireland XI which played Brazil in 1973, a game in which he played nursing a broken toe.

Peter Desmond (INSIDE-FORWARD)

Born: Cork 23 November 1926
Debut for Eire: v Finland September 1949

Peter Desmond was an Irish soldier when he began his League of Ireland career with Waterford in 1947–48. A tremendous worker with a powerful shot, he spent the next season with Shelbourne and was a member of the Shels' side beaten 3–0 by Dundalk in the 1949 FAI Cup final. Just weeks after that Cup final Desmond, with Shels' colleague Arthur Fitzsimons, joined First Division Middlesbrough.

The cross-channel move improved Desmond's play significantly. Already known in Ireland for his pace, he speeded up his play after his transfer to Boro and he could 'riddle a defence with his quick bursts'.

It was after Ireland's shock 2–0 win over England at Goodison Park in September 1949 that Peter finally made Boro's First Division side, and although he was promoted to the first XI immediately after the victory, he managed only two League games before his transfer to Southport in August 1950.

After a dozen appearances (two goals) for Southport, Peter joined York City in December 1951. He made just one League appearance for York soon after signing and spent the next 20 months at Bootham Crescent playing in the Midland League where he regularly found the net. Peter was freed by York in August 1953 whereupon he joined Hartlepool United where he ended his League career with just one League outing.

A former League of Ireland representative player, Peter won four full caps for Eire in consecutive internationals between September and November 1949. His run in the international team included the 2–0 defeat of England at Goodison Park in September 1949 when Ireland became the first non-British team to defeat the English at home.

Peter Desmond died in 1990.

John Devine (RIGHT-BACK)

Born: Dublin 11 November 1958
Debut for Eire: v Czechoslovakia September 1979

Nicknamed 'Joker' because of his happy-go-lucky nature, John Devine spent most of his formative years with Arsenal.

An attacking right-back of genuine quality, Devine played his junior football with the St John Bosco club in Dublin. He became an amateur at Arsenal in January 1974, an apprentice ten months later and in October 1976 was confirmed as a fully fledged Gunner.

John spent most of his seven years as a professional in north London attempting to oust Northern Ireland international Pat Rice from the right-back position in the Arsenal first team. Towards the end of 1977–78 an injury to Rice gave Devine the chance to shine in the first XI, but when Rice returned from injury, Devine was again reduced to the role of understudy. He began the 1980–81 season, however, as first-choice right-back and the sale of Rice to Watford in November 1980 left the way clear for him to make the position his own.

But it wasn't to be. Rice's departure did little for John's competitive spirit: his game deteriorated so much that in August 1983 he was given a free transfer. He had made 89 First Division appearances for Arsenal and collected an FA Cup runners-up medal (in the 1–0 defeat by West Ham in 1980) when he joined First Division Norwich City that summer of 1983.

In just over a season at Carrow Road John made 53 League appearances (three goals) before embarking on an ill-fated spell at Stoke City in November 1985. He had played just 15 First Division games for Stoke when he suffered a badly broken leg, playing against Brighton in March 1986. The injury all but ended Devine's top-flight career. He later spent 18 months in Norway with IK Start and in the summer of 1989 joined League of Ireland club Shamrock Rovers.

John, who won two Republic of Ireland Under-21 caps, was in the full international reckoning for five years but didn't become a regular. He played in both full-back berths for his country and collected a dozen caps.

Donald Donovan (FULL-BACK)

Born: Cork 23 December 1920
Debut for Eire: v Norway November 1954

An extremely versatile performer, Don Donovan appeared regularly at right-half in his junior days with Maymount Rovers in his native Cork and with Dalymount Rovers in Dublin. On joining First Division Everton in May 1949, however, he played first in midfield and then at centre-half before finally settling down at right-back for most of his 178 appearances for the club.

In 1950–51 Everton were relegated for only the second time in their history; but they bounced back three seasons later. Donovan was a regular in that 1953–54 promotion-winning line-up and had a total of six seasons with Everton. In August 1958 he was back in the Second Division, having been signed by Grimsby Town for £10,000 as a replacement for the newly retired Bill Brown.

Donovan lined up for Grimsby in a number of positions including right-half and left-half and in both full-back berths. He soon became the club's captain and missed only half a dozen games in his first four seasons at Blundell Park. But he couldn't prevent the east-coast club from dropping into Division Three at the end of 1958–59. He was on hand two seasons later, however, to haul them back up the ladder: in 1962–63 the Mariners were once again sailing in the calmer waters of Division Two, having finished runners-up in Division Three the previous season.

Don made 236 League appearance for Grimsby before leaving to become player-manager of Boston United in May 1965.

A former Eire Schoolboy international, Don made his full debut at right-back in the 2–1 home victory over Norway in November 1954. He retained that position for Ireland's next three games, which were wins over Holland and Norway and a 2–1 defeat by West Germany in Hamburg in May 1955. Two years later he won his fifth and final cap in the World

Cup qualifier against England at Wembley.

Terence Donovan (FORWARD)

Born: Liverpool 27 February 1958
Debut for Eire: v Czechoslovakia September 1979

Terry is the son of former Eire international defender Don Donovan. A former pupil at Clee Grammar School, Terry played his junior football with Louth United in Lincolnshire and in August 1976 joined his father's old club, Grimsby Town.

Donovan had three seasons at Blundell Park in which he scored 23 goals in 74 League games. The Mariners were relegated to Division Four in his first season at the club, 1976–77, but won promotion in his last, 1978–79.

In September 1979 Terry was transferred to Aston Villa for £75,000 – a record receipt for Grimsby at the time. Undaunted by the leap from Division Three to Division One, he scored in the 3–0 defeat of Coventry City on his Villa Park debut in December 1979. Terry spent the summer of 1982 on loan to Portland Timbers in the North American Soccer League and played three games on loan to Oxford in February 1983. That month, after just 17 League games (six goals) for Villa, he was transferred to Second Division strugglers Burnley for £25,000.

Burnley were relegated that season and in September 1983, after six goals in 15 games, Donovan was transferred to Rotherham United for £25,000. After 13 Second Division appearances with the Merry Millers plus two on loan to Blackpool in October 1984, Terry was forced to quit the game because of a knee injury.

A former England Schoolboy international, Terry was capped once by Ireland at Under-21 level, against England in 1980–81. He won his one full cap against Czechoslovakia in Prague in September 1979 as one of six Irish players making their international debuts. He was substituted after 83 minutes and the under-strength side lost heavily, going down 4–1 to the Czechs.

Christopher Doyle (FORWARD)

Born: Dublin
Debut for Eire: v Czechoslovakia April 1959

Former Alton hitman, Christy 'Kit' Doyle exploded on to the League of Ireland scene with Shelbourne in 1957. He spent just over three seasons with the club and was their top scorer on each occasion between 1957–58 and 1959–1960, netting 34 League goals in that period.

Doyle was a member of the Reds side which overcame Cork Hibernians 2–0 in the 1960 FAI Cup final to lift the Cup for only the second time in the club's history; the first was in 1939.

Christy, who was a nephew of Jimmy 'Snowy' Dunne, won his one full cap against Czechoslovakia in April 1959 in a preliminary round game for the first European Nations Cup. The Irish won that game in Dublin 2–0 but lost the return leg 4–0.

Robert Duffy (CENTRE-FORWARD)

Born: Dublin
Debut for Eire: v Belgium May 1950

Bobby Duffy was a dashing centre-forward. He played for St James's Gate before entering League of Ireland football with Shamrock Rovers in 1949. He was promoted from Rovers' reserves after Ossie Higgins was transferred to Aston Villa in November 1949, and he finished the 1949–50 season as the Hoops' top League scorer with 11 goals.

By 1953–54, however, Bobby was playing for Drumcondra, though he spent most of that

Anthony Dunne

season playing junior football and was 'lucky' to find himself playing in Drumcondra's 1954 FAI Cup final victory over St Patrick's Athletic.

Duffy played for the inter-League side against the Irish League in March and April 1950 and, after barely six months in League of Ireland football, he deposed the more experienced Davy Walsh of West Bromwich Albion in the Irish side to face Belgium in May 1950. It was Bobby's only cap and proved a bittersweet experience: Bobby headed Ireland's consolation goal 18 minutes from time after Belgium had scored five.

Anthony Dunne (LEFT-BACK)

Born: Dublin 24 July 1941
Debut for Eire: v Austria April 1962

Just weeks after winning an FAI Cup winners

medal with Shelbourne in April 1960, Tony Dunne was on his way to Manchester United at a giveaway £5,000.

A centre-forward during his junior days in Dublin with St Finbarr's and Tara United, Tony was allowed to mature in United's reserves before claiming a regular first-team place halfway through the 1961–62 season, replacing his international colleague Noel Cantwell in the left-back position.

That breakthrough signalled the beginning of the career of one of the greatest full-backs ever seen in the game. Small, compact and tenacious, Dunne was deceptively fast and his defensive covering was described by his former Old Trafford team-mate Bill Foulkes as 'unbelievable'.

Tony had 13 seasons at Old Trafford during which he turned out for the Reds in League combat 414 times. He picked up League Championship medals in 1964–65 and 1966–67 (he missed just two games during those seasons); an FA Cup winners medal after United's 3–1 victory over Leicester City in the 1963 final; and a European Cup winners medal in 1968.

It was in that epic European Cup final, in which United defeated Portuguese champions Benfica 4–1, that the football pundits reckon Dunne gave one of the greatest displays of his career: he frustrated the Benfica attackers with resolute defending, moved forward at will and curved long accurate passes into the paths of the front men. His contribution was officially recognised in Ireland when he was voted 'Footballer of the Year' for 1969.

In April 1973 Tony – with six other United players, including Denis Law – was freed by United boss Tommy Docherty and in August, over 13 years after arriving in Manchester, Dunne was transferred to Third Division Champions Bolton Wanderers. In five seasons at Burnden Park Dunne played 170 League games and in his final season in the Football League, 1977–78 – before jetting off to the USA – he won a Second Division Championship medal with Bolton.

Tony, who still follows the fortunes of the Trotters, now manages the golf driving range he built in Altrincham.

A former Eire Amateur international, Tony made his full international debut in the 3–2 home defeat by Austria in April 1962. Over 13 years he took his tally to 33 full caps, appearing in both full-back positions and at centre-half. Tony, who played alongside his brother Pat in the Irish side in the mid-1960s, captained the national side on four occasions.

James C. Dunne (DEFENDER)

**Born: Dublin 1 December 1947
Debut for Eire: v Austria May 1971**

A temperamental and sometimes unorthodox player, Jimmy Dunne's Football League career got off to a rather slow start. In February 1966 Millwall paid League of Ireland club Shelbourne £1,500 to take the big centre-half to the Den. But first-team football eluded Dunne at Millwall, and in July 1967 he joined Third Division Torquay United.

He got his chance of first-team football with the Devon club and must have impressed: in July 1970, after 13 goals in 126 League games for the Gulls, Dunne was transferred to Fulham, who paid Torquay £15,000 to take him to Craven Cottage as part of their drive to regain Second Division status. It was money well spent: Jimmy missed only one League game in 1970–71 and the Cottagers got their promotion. He retained his place in the Fulham rearguard, clocking up 143 League appearances, until 1974 when he emigrated to South Africa.

Less than a year later he was back in London playing with Fulham reserves; he remained there until April 1976 when he returned to the club which had given him his first taste of League football – Torquay United – for a £4,000 fee. In his second spell with Torquay, who by then were firmly rooted in the bottom division, Jimmy made 121 League appearances before calling it a day in League football.

A whole-hearted player who became known for his accurate passing out of defence, Jimmy was called upon to represent Ireland on one occasion. That was in the home European Championship game against Austria in May 1971. It was not a happy debut: Jimmy deflected a cross into his own net to give the Austrians their third goal in a 4–1 defeat for Ireland.

Patrick Dunne (GOALKEEPER)

**Born: Dublin 9 February 1943
Debut for Eire: v Spain May 1965**

The younger brother of former Ireland and Manchester United stalwart Tony Dunne, Pat joined Everton as an apprentice in May 1960, having previously not made the grade as a junior with Manchester United.

Pat failed to get his name on the first-team sheet at Goodison and, disillusioned, he returned to his native Dublin to play for Shamrock Rovers. He won an FAI Cup winners medal with Rovers in 1964 after the Hoops' 2–1 victory over Cork Celtic in the replayed final. In May 1964 Manchester United, in the middle of a minor goalkeeping crisis, paid Rovers £10,500 to take Dunne back to Old Trafford.

His second visit to the north-west was much more productive and fulfilling than the first. In three seasons with United he made 45 appearances, plus 13 in Europe, and collected a League Championship medal in 1965–66, before eventually losing his place to Northern Ireland's Harry Gregg. (Pat's Championship medal was stolen in a burglary at his home in 1992.)

Pat was transferred to Second Division Portsmouth in February 1967 and during his four years at Fratton Park he made 152 League appearances.

59

On the international front Pat made one Under-23 appearance for the Republic, against France in 1965–66. He joined brother Tony in the senior side in May 1965 when he won his first full cap in a World Cup qualifying game against Spain. Pat won a total of five full caps, three of which were against Spain, and kept one clean sheet.

Seamus Dunne (FULL-BACK)

Born: Wicklow 13 April 1930
Debut for Eire: v France November 1952

Like many of his compatriots, Seamus Dunne was schooled in the art of Ireland's national code. He turned out at minor and junior level for the Co. Wicklow Gaelic football team before

Seamus Dunne

turning his attention to Association rules.

He was a junior at Drogheda United and in 1949 joined League club Shelbourne from Wicklow Town. After less than a season at Milltown, Dunne was transferred to Luton Town. For over a decade since he signed for Luton Town from Shelbourne in July 1950, Seamus formed a formidable all Irish full-back pairing with Bud Aherne in Luton's defence.

Seamus helped make history at Kenilworth Road. He was a member of the Hatters' promotion-winning side which saw Luton gain entry to Division One for the first time in their history. In 1959 he missed the club's solitary appearance in an FA Cup final (they lost 2–1 to Nottingham Forest).

After 300 League appearances for Luton, Dunne joined Yiewsley of the Southern League who, at the time, were under the managership of the former Newcastle and England legend, Jackie Milburn. In 1964, after three seasons at Yiewsley, he signed for Dunstable Town, helping them gain entry to the Southern League. Seamus was captain of the FAI Youths (for whom he won seven caps) when they participated in the World Youth Tournament in London in 1948. He also won three Junior caps during his time at Drogheda.

Seamus kicked off his full international career with a 1–1 draw against France in November 1952 and went on to collect a total of 15 caps. He was captain of Ireland when they beat Denmark 2–1 in a World Cup qualifier in Dublin in October 1956.

He retired from playing in 1968 and in 1971 returned to his native Wicklow. He is now a retired design draughtsman

Thomas Dunne (RIGHT-HALF)

Born: Dublin 1932
Debut for Eire: v Holland May 1956

A clever, attack-conscious wing-half, capable of taking a firm grip on the middle of the field,

Tommy Dunne had 15 successful seasons as a League of Ireland player after he completed his apprenticeship with Johnville.

Tommy began his senior career as an inside-forward with Shamrock Rovers in 1951. When Rovers were League champions in 1953–54, Tommy was playing in the Leinster Senior League; though retained as a player at Rovers. At the end of that season he departed for St Patrick's Athletic. His transfer to Inchicore for a small fee was one of the best deals done by St Pat's.

In his first season, 1954–55, Tommy helped St Pat's wrest the Championship crown from Rovers and retain it the following season. As captain he led the club to success in two FAI Cup finals, in 1959 and 1961.

Dunne left St Pat's for Sligo Rovers in 1964 and joined Dundalk in 1966, helping the Louthmen win the Championship in 1966–67, before retiring.

Tommy is the son of Jimmy Dunne who played for Arsenal in the '30s and brother of Jimmy who represented Ireland at Schoolboy level; Jimmy junior wasn't eligible to play for Ireland at senior level because he was born in Liverpool.

One of the few 'home-based players' to receive full honours before inter-League honours, Tommy played in three successive winning Irish sides between May and November 1956 when Ireland defeated Holland, Denmark and West Germany. He went on to represent the League of Ireland 11 times and was capped twice by the Republic at 'B' level, against South Africa and Iceland.

Patrick Dunning (CENTRE-HALF)

Born: Dublin 1951
Debut for Eire: v Sweden October 1970

When centre-back Paddy Dunning left Shelbourne for Dundalk in 1977, all he had to show for eight seasons at Tolka Park were two FAI Cup runners-up medals which he won in 1973 when he was a substitute in the replay defeat by Cork Hibs and in 1975 when Shels lost to Home Farm. His luck improved, however, upon arrival at Oriel Park.

Dunning won his first winners medal after Dundalk's League Cup-final defeat of Cork Albion in 1978. The following season, 1978–79, he enjoyed the greatest success of his domestic career: he helped Dundalk win the League Championship and FAI Cup double; in the final month of the season he was voted 'Player of the Month' by the Soccer Writers' Association; and he was centre-half in the same association's 'Team of the Year' for 1978–79.

'Never a flamboyant player, Paddy has been a model of consistency and dependability and while principally a defender, he hasn't allowed himself to be anchored in defence and was invariably seen up in the opposing area for free kicks and corners where his height and skill in the air brought Dundalk some valuable goals.'

With his Dundalk colleagues Michael Lawlor and Cathal Muckian, Dunning was a member of the League of Ireland squad which toured Italy and Switzerland at Easter time 1979; then as he'd done the previous summer, he went to America to play for Los Angeles Skyhawks in the close season.

Dunning won more domestic honour with Dundalk in the 1980s: League Cup and FAI Cup winners medals in 1981; another Championship medal in 1981–82; and a League Cup runners-up medal in 1983.

After six years of 'yeoman service' to Dundalk Paddy returned to Dublin to join University College Dublin. He played a role in The Students' finest hour when in 1984, against all the odds, they defeated their more illustrious neighbours Shamrock Rovers to lift the FAI Cup – the only major honour in the club's history.

In September 1970, as a 19-year-old, Paddy played for the League of Ireland against the Scottish League. The game was witnessed by national team boss Mick Meagan, who was so impressed that he awarded the youngster two full caps against Sweden and Italy in October and December 1970. In May 1973 Paddy collected an Under-23 cap against France.

Eamonn Dunphy (INSIDE-LEFT)

Born: Dublin 3 August 1945
Debut for Eire: v Spain November 1965

Eamonn Dunphy packed a lot of footballing skill into a very light frame. He weighed barely 9st when, as a 15-year-old in 1960, he joined Manchester United as an apprentice. Two years later, in August 1962, he was upgraded to professional status.

Although his light frame belied an inner strength of character, Dunphy was unable to break into the United first team and in August 1965 moved to Third Division newcomers York City. He made just 22 League appearances (three goals) for York before signing for

Eamonn Dunphy

Millwall the following January for £8,000.

Dunphy turned out to be one of the 'best buys and brilliant footballers ever to pull on a Millwall shirt. A master schemer, whose final pass into the box often proved lethal, he used his huge skill rather than brute strength to turn many matches Millwall's way during his seven years at the Den.'

Eamonn helped the Lions win promotion to Division Two in his first season and became a fixture in the side, clocking up 274 League appearances.

His ability didn't go unnoticed by the selectors and in November 1965, when still at York City, he won his first Eire cap in the World Cup play-off against Spain in Paris. Over the next five years he won 23 full caps, plus one at Under-23 level, against France in June 1966.

Eamonn remains Millwall's most capped player, winning 22 of his 23 caps while at the club.

He spent two seasons in the Third Division with Charlton Athletic, whom he joined in November 1973 for £20,000. He made 42 League appearances for the Londoners and helped Charlton win promotion at the end of 1974–75 before moving to Reading in July 1975.

He helped Reading win promotion to Division Three in 1975–76, but when they dropped back to Division Four the following season, he hung up his boots for a full-time career as an author and journalist.

Eamonn had already written *Only A Game?*, a book which chronicled a season in the life of Millwall FC, during his early playing days. At Reading he wrote the Eamonn Dunphy column in the local *Evening Post* for two years. He went on to achieve considerable success as Sir Matt Busby's official biographer and as the best-selling author of the story of U2, the world-famous Irish rock band

He also appears on Irish television as a knowledgeble and articulate, if somewhat controversial, soccer pundit and writes a weekly column in Ireland's *Sunday Independent*.

Noel Dwyer (GOALKEEPER)

Born: Dublin 30 October 1934
Debut for Eire: v Sweden November 1959

Wolverhampton Wanderers signed Noel Dwyer from Dublin junior club Ormeau in August 1953, at the start of their first Championship-winning year. However, as understudy to established Molineux keepers Malcolm Finlayson and Bert Williams (who was also an England keeper), Dwyer's contribution to Wolves' success was negligible. He got little opportunity to demonstrate his skills and in December 1958 left the club for West Ham United after just five League games.

Although Noel won a Second Division Championship medal in his first season in east London, he experienced similar difficulties there to the ones he'd had in Wolverhampton and was restricted to 36 League appearances in two seasons.

Second Division Swansea signed him in August 1960, and it was there that he established his reputation as a more than competent goalminder and booked his place as Eire's international goalkeeper, collecting a total of 14 caps in the early 1960s.

An acrobatic and stylish keeper, Dwyer made 140 League appearances for the Welsh club; then he had 26 games for Second Division Plymouth in 1965 and half a dozen for Second Division Charlton Athletic in 1966, before injury ended his League career. Upon retirement Noel took over a public house in Plymouth.

Capped once at 'B' level, Noel won the first of his 14 full caps in the 3–2 home victory over Sweden in November 1959; but he made his mark on the game in his third international outing, against West Germany in Dusseldorf in May 1960. After the Republic's shock 1–0 victory over the Germans, the West German FA used Dwyer's performance between the posts to illustrate a film on the art of goalkeeping!

Noel played in ten consecutive internationals for the Republic between November 1959 and October 1961 before losing his place to the up-and-coming Alan Kelly of Preston after the 7–1 away defeat by Czechoslovakia in October 1961.

Noel Dwyer died in January 1993, at the age of 58, after a long battle against cancer. He left a wife, one son and three daughters, one of whom is married to former England international Frank Worthington.

Peter Eccles (CENTRE-HALF)

Born: Dublin 24 August 1962
Debut for Eire: v Uruguay April 1986

Classy defender Peter Eccles began his League of Ireland career with Shamrock Rovers, whom he joined from St Brendan's in 1981. When he departed for Leicester City in October 1988, it was with a pocketful of medals.

He was a League winner in successive seasons from 1983–84 to 1986–87 and won FAI Cup winners medals in 1986 and 1987. He also collected runners-up medals in the League Cup finals of 1982 and 1988.

Peter's flirtation with English football was a brief one; in April 1989 he lined up for Leicester City for his one League game, in the 0–0 draw with Blackburn Rovers.

He returned to Shamrock Rovers in 1991 and was a member of the Hoops side beaten 1–0 by Galway in that year's FAI Cup final. He captained Rovers to the League Championship in 1993–94, after which he moved north to join Belfast club Crusaders.

A service attendant with the Department of Marine in Dublin, Eccles broke his leg in only his fourth game for Crusaders. He returned to the fray a year later, in September 1995. His manager at Seaview, Roy Walker, was clearly pleased to have him back: 'There's not much better than a fit Peter Eccles. He's unbeatable in the air and a natural leader.'

Peter holds the record for the shortest international career of any Eire player. He came on as a substitute for Ray Houghton in the 80th minute of Jack Charlton's second game in charge of the national team – a 1–1 draw with Uruguay in April 1986.

Thomas Eglington (OUTSIDE-LEFT)

Born: Dublin 15 January 1923
Debut for Eire: v Portugal June 1946

Tommy Eglington stands out as one of the early giants of Irish football. Like many of his contemporaries, 'Eggo' excelled at hurling and Gaelic football in his schoolboy days. In the late '40s and early '50s the mere mention of his name sent shivers down the spines of First Division defenders.

Poised and graceful; head down; fast; haring straight for the corner flag before firing off pin-point crosses; Tommy was a winger of the old school – a latter-day Andrei Kanchelskis.

Tommy joined Everton in July 1946 in a double transfer deal involving that other post-war great, Peter Farrell. The double deal, which cost Everton just £10,000, has been described as the best piece of business in the club's history.

Elegant and unruffled, with an explosive burst of pace and a thundering shot, Tommy had been with Shamrock Rovers for just one full season, 1945–46, ending the campaign as the Hoops' top scorer with 11 goals, before he departed for Goodison Park.

Eglington came to be regarded as one of the finest match-winning left-wingers in the game. He claimed a regular place in Everton's first XI almost immediately and kept it for 11 seasons, all but three of which were spent in the top flight. The Blues were relegated at the end of 1950–51, but were promoted back to Division One at the end of 1953–54, having finished runners-up to Leicester City on goal difference.

Eglington's personal record at Goodison Park was an impressive one. He was top scorer in 1952–53 with 14 goals; his tally included five goals netted in Everton's 7–1 victory over

Doncaster Rovers in September 1952. By June 1957, when Tommy made the short trip across the Mersey to join Tranmere Rovers, he had scored 76 times in 394 League games.

For three seasons he gave the Birkenhead club the same whole-hearted service that he had given their illustrious neighbours, scoring 36 goals in 172 outings in Division Three (North). When he finally hung up his boots Tommy returned to his native Dublin, where he now runs a butcher's shop.

Tommy is one of the handful of players who appeared for both Northern Ireland and the Republic. He was Eire's regular outside-right for a decade in the immediate post-war era. During that time he won 24 caps, scored two goals and was national team captain twice.

He was a member of the Irish side which recorded that historic 2–0 victory over an England side – appropriately enough at Goodison Park – in 1949 when they became the first overseas side to defeat England on English soil. He also appeared in the outside-right position in half a dozen consecutive matches for the North between November 1946 and October 1948.

Eamonn Fagan (DEFENDER)

Born: Dublin
Debut for Eire: v Norway June 1973

Eamonn Fagan began his League of Ireland career in the early 1970s with Shamrock Rovers. He moved to Amby Fogarty's Athlone Town in 1975. Town had just rejoined the League in 1969 and Fagan was introduced to provide generalship and experience. He was said to be able to 'keep composure within the side even in the most adverse situations'. Unfortunately, however, his career at St Mel's Park was seriously disrupted by injury and didn't really get going.

In November 1972 and May 1973 Fagan won two Under-23 caps (both of which were draws with France). Sean Thomas managed those Under-23 sides and became 'national team manager for a day', between the reigns of Tuohy and Giles, he picked Fagan for his side to face Norway in June 1973. Although a defender, Fagan was named as a midfielder in the team. Eamonn had the shortest career of them all. He came on as a 79th-minute substitution for Ray Treacy in the 1–1 draw.

Fionan Fagan (WING-FORWARD)

Born: Dublin 7 June 1930
Debut for Eire: v Norway November 1954

Second Division Hull City secured the services of Fionan Fagan from Dublin junior club Transport in March 1951. He scored twice in 25 League outings for the Boothferry Park club before his transfer to First Division Manchester City in December 1953.

Seven seasons on Manchester's Moss Side saw Fagan wear the blue of City in 153 League duels in which he found the net 34 times. In 1955 he collected the only medal of his League career, an FA Cup runners-up medal, after City's 3–1 defeat by Newcastle United.

In March 1960 Fionan was transferred to Second Division Derby County for £7,500. The following season, 1960–61, he was voted the Republic's 'Player of the Year', despite playing his football in Derby's second XI for most of the season.

In June 1961, after six goals in 24 League outings, Fionan left Derby to take up the post of player-manager of non-League Altrincham. Thereafter he had spells with Northwich Victoria and Ashton United.

Capped once by the Republic at 'B' level, against Romania in October 1957, Fionan won the first of his eight full caps in the 2–1 victory over Norway in November 1954, thereby becoming the first player to follow his father into the Irish team. His father Jack 'Kruger' played against Italy in 1926.

Five years later, in November 1959, Fionan won his second cap in the 3–2 defeat of Sweden. He kept his place in the side until May 1961 by which time he had scored in four consecutive internationals, including the only goal of the game against West Germany in Dusseldorf in May 1960.

Michael Fairclough (FORWARD)

Born: Drogheda 21 October 1952
Debut for Eire: v Chile May 1982

In the early 1970s – especially when he led the Drogheda Under-18 side to their first FAI Youth Cup victory – Mick Fairclough was hailed as the best young forward in Ireland. His cavalier attacking style of forward play made him a folk hero on the banks of the Boyne.

Mick was the only local player in the Drogheda side which contested the FAI Cup final in 1971 – the club's first senior final; after a drawn first game they lost 3–0 to Limerick in the replay.

Fairclough joined Huddersfield Town in August 1971 and broke into Town's First Division side just three months after signing, following stints in the Under-19s and reserves.

Mick's time at Leeds Road was far from happy. He saw Huddersfield slump to Division Four in as many seasons and he received a serious knee injury, which caused his retirement from the game in 1975. He had made just 36 League appearances, 11 of which started from the substitutes bench.

He returned to Ireland and didn't play football for five years, until 1980 when he joined Dundalk where he enjoyed five successful seasons.

Mick was Dundalk's top scorer in three successive seasons, including the club's Championship winning season, 1981–82. He scored in the 2–0 victory over Sligo in the 1981 FAI Cup final; collected a League Cup winners medal the same year; and was voted Dundalk's

'Player of the Year', for 1980–81, having won the Co. Louth Sports Personality award the previous season.

In 1984 he left Dundalk and spent brief spells with Sligo Rovers and Newry Town before a recurrence of knee problems forced his retirement from the game.

Mick, who is currently employed by Lotus Development as European Information Systems manager, is a former League of Ireland representative player. He was capped once at Under-23 level, against France in May 1973, when still at Huddersfield and won two full caps as a substitute in May 1982 against Chile and Trinidad and Tobago.

Sean Fallon

(DEFENDER/CENTRE-FORWARD)

Born: Sligo 31 July 1922
Debut for Eire: v Norway November 1950

Sean Fallon's name is synonymous with Glasgow Celtic. He learnt his trade in the junior soccer circles in and around his native Sligo, turning out for Sligo St Mary's juniors, Longford Town, McArthurs FC and Sligo Distillery. He had a season with Sligo Rovers in the League of Ireland (1947–48) and spent the 1948–49 season in the Irish League with Lurgan club Glenavon before joining Glasgow Celtic in March 1950. His association with the Glasgow giants lasted almost 30 years.

Described as a big-hearted player, Sean was 'as rugged as his native Sligo shore', and became Celtic's iron man of the '50s. In eight seasons as a player at Parkhead he made 177 League appearances and played in five Cup finals.

He was a runner-up in the Scottish Cup in 1955 and a winner in 1951 and 1954. He missed most of the Bhoys' 1953–54 double-winning season owing to a broken collar bone but recovered in time to play in the Cup final against Aberdeen. He also won Scottish League

Cup winners medals in 1957 and in 1958 when Celtic thrashed their deadly Glasgow rivals Rangers 7–1 in the final.

After his retirement due to a knee injury in 1958, the former Celtic captain held a variety of posts at Parkhead, including that of first-team coach, (1959–61), assistant manager, acting manager and chief scout. He left Glasgow to become assistant manager at Dumbarton in 1978; he later managed Dumbarton and in 1986 became a Director at Clyde.

Sean played Gaelic football in Ireland with Craobh Ruadh GAA and Coolers GAA, and won the McHenry Cup for long-distance swimming in Sligo in 1957. Sean, who was fiercely proud of his Celtic connections, was awarded a testimonial dinner by the club in October 1993.

Between November 1950 and May 1955 Sean played eight times for Eire, five as a defender and three as a centre-forward. He scored twice: in the 1–1 draw with France in November 1952 and in his final game against West Germany in May 1955.

Peter Farrell (WING-HALF)

Born: Dublin 16 August 1922
Debut for Eire: v Portugal June 1946

Peter Farrell played for Shamrock Rovers' first team as a schoolboy. In August 1946, with his Rovers' team-mate Tom Eglington, Farrell joined Everton in a combined deal which cost the Merseysiders just £10,000 spread over two years. Considering that the transaction was regarded by many as one of Everton's most successful transfer deals, it is ironic that club scouts had actually gone to Dublin to see another player in an Inter City Cup final!

Of medium height, stocky and curly haired, he was an archetypal wing-half: a tireless worker who thrived on one-to-one situations and never shirked a tackle. Peter, like his close friend Eglington, had 11 seasons with Everton during which he became something of a living legend on Merseyside. In fact he is one of the few footballers to have a street named after him – Farrell Close.

In 1950–51 he was team captain when Everton dropped down to Division Two, for only the second time in their history. Their fall from grace, however, was short-lived because they found their way back to Division One three seasons later.

Peter's debut for Everton was postponed until late November 1946 owing to an injury he sustained whilst playing tennis! He was never dropped thereafter and went on to make 421 League appearances. On a Saturday in September 1956 Everton decided to give Farrell a well-earned rest, affording one local scribe the opportunity to pay tribute to one of the 'most loyal servants the Goodison Park club has ever seen in its long history . . . Personally I think his inspiration and experience will be missed . . . as captain there have been few as good and none better, always giving his last ounce to the cause.'

In October 1957, less than six months after Eglington left Everton for Tranmere, Peter Farrell embarked on the same short journey across the Mersey to link up yet again with his close friend and colleague.

He immediately became captain at Prenton Park and in three seasons with the club he made 114 League appearances, playing as enthusiastically as ever and more than justifying Tranmere's £2,500 investment in a player in the autumn of his playing career. He became manager of Rovers in 1957, leaving at the end of 1960 to join Welsh non-League side Hdyhist Town as player-manager.

Peter was blessed with a saintly air, on and off the field of play; indeed at one stage he was forced to make a formal announcement denying rumours that he was joining the priesthood!

On the international scene Peter scored one of the goals in Ireland's epic 2–0 defeat of England at – appropriately enough – Goodison Park in September 1949, making them the first overseas team to beat England on English soil. Peter was a regular in the Irish XI from 1946 to 1957, making a total of 28 appearances. He achieved the unusual honour of captaining his country in his first international. He was national team captain on a further 11 occasions and scored three goals. Peter won his final cap in the 7–1 World Cup qualifier defeat by Czechoslovakia in Prague in October 1961.

Peter appeared at left-half for Northern Ireland in seven internationals between September 1946 and March 1949.

Gareth Farrelly (MIDFIELD)

Born: Dublin 28 August 1975
Debut for Eire: v Portugal May 1996

Gareth Farrelly had to overcome serious injury to reach the dizzy heights of international football.

A former Home Farm player, Gareth was taken to Aston Villa by Villa boss Ron Atkinson as a 17-year-old. Unfortunately he spent a year and a half on the sidelines with a serious back injury.

Farrelly recovered and made his League debut in March 1995, whilst on loan to Second Division Rotherham United. He scored twice in ten League games for the Merry Millers before returning to his employers at the end of the season.

Naturally left-footed, Gareth could be a candidate to succeed Andy Townsend at both club and national level. He made his senior debut for Villa against Liverpool in March 1996 and had made five League appearances for the club by the end of 1995–96.

A former Youth and Schoolboy international, Farrelly made his first appearance for the Under-21 side against England in March 1995. He impressed on his full debut, the 1–0 defeat by Portugal in May 1996, before injury halted his progress. He won three caps in the friendly summer of 1996.

Al Finucane (CENTRE-HALF)

Born: Limerick 1943
Debut for Eire: v Turkey February 1967

Al Finucane played with Reds United as a schoolboy, then joined local League of Ireland club Limerick as a junior in 1960.

Finucane played regularly as a right-half in his early days at the club until Limerick boss Ewan Fenton decided to play him in the centre of defence. Subsequent events proved him right.

Over the next two decades Finucane developed into one of the soundest centre-halves in the country. His immaculate style, positional play, steadiness under pressure and ability to move forward won plaudits from friend and opponent alike. He developed into a 'personality player' who was 'a credit not only to his own club but to Irish football, his all-round sportsmanship being on a par with his footballing ability'.

Al was a runner-up in the FAI Cup finals of 1965 and 1966 when the Shannonsiders lost both finals to Shamrock Rovers. In 1971 he captained Limerick to their first FAI Cup success when they beat Drogheda in the final.

Al moved to Waterford in the early '70s; he became a fixture in the heart of Waterford's defence and added to his collection of medals. He was a League Cup winner in 1973 when Waterford beat Finn Harps to win the inaugural competition. In 1979 he was again a runner-up in the FAI Cup, and the following year he captained Waterford to victory in the competition. On the same day that he skippered Waterford to the Cup, Limerick clinched the League title for the first time in 43 years. It was a wonderful double for Limerickman Finucane, who described it as 'the greatest moment of my career'.

That same year, 1980, was his testimonial year and champions Limerick entertained Cup winners Waterford in his honour.

One of Limerick's favourite sons, Al returned home in 1981. The following year he ran out at Dalymount Park in his sixth FAI Cup final, emerging with his third winners medal.

'A quietly spoken, extremely modest and likeable man, Al exerted a profound influence off the field, particularly for the young ones growing up around him.'

Finucane captained the League of Ireland in their Golden Jubilee match and was capped once at Under-23 level, against France in June 1966. He won 11 full caps while at Limerick in the '70s. In October 1971, in his 11th international – Liam Tuohy's first game in charge of the national team – Al was honoured with the captaincy of the Irish squad, 'a richly deserved tribute to the Limerick man, who has yet to have had a bad game for his country'.

Jack Fitzgerald (CENTRE-FORWARD)

Born: Waterford 3 April 1930
Debut for Eire: v Holland May 1955

Jack Fitzgerald was a right-half with Waterford junior club Bohemians when they won the FAI Youth Cup in 1947.

It was as a centre-forward, however, that the man from Munster's most famous footballing family made an indelible mark in Waterford soccer history. Jack's brothers, Denny, Peter Tom, Ned and Paul all turned out for Waterford and other clubs, and their father was an international selector.

Jack first appeared for Waterford in 1949–50 after which he went to work in England for a year. His career took off when he returned to the club in 1951–52 where an injury crisis saw him switched to centre-forward. The following season he was a member of Waterford's Shield-winning side.

As a centre-forward, Jack made the most of his pace, heading ability and two good feet, and chased everything; the tall blond hitman became the terror of League of Ireland defences throughout the '50s and beyond. In 13 seasons with the Blues he was top scorer in eight seasons, scoring 122 League goals.

Arguably the most surprising feature of Fitzgerald's career was his lack of domestic honours. An FAI Cup runners-up medal, gained after a replay against St Patrick's Athletic in the 1959 final, was his only 'major honour'.

At the end of 1963–64 Waterford had to seek re-election to the League, and Fitzgerald was released. He played one more season in the League, 1964–65, with Cork Hibs, in which he topped the club's scoring charts with nine goals, then he retired.

A former milkman, Jack is a past League and Amateur player. He scored the only goal of the game in his full international debut against Holland in May 1955. He was injured when Ireland next played but was back for his second cap in the return game with the Dutch in Holland in May 1956, helping Ireland do the double over the Dutch with an emphatic 4–1 victory.

Peter Fitzgerald (FORWARD)

Born: Waterford 17 June 1937
Debut for Eire: v Wales September 1960

Peter Fitzgerald began his career with local League of Ireland side, Waterford United. In 1958–59, his second season with the club, Peter scored 17 League goals and netted the Blues' consolation goal when they went down 2–1 to St Patrick's Athletic in the 1959 FAI Cup final.

Soon after that Cup final, in April 1959, Fitzgerald was transferred to the famous Sparta Club of Rotterdam where he spent just over a year.

Meanwhile Football League club Leeds United, who had been relegated to Division Two at the end of the 1959–60 season and were looking for a quick return to the top flight, paid £50,000 for new players, including £7,000 to take Peter Fitzgerald to

Elland Road. The move was unsuccessful. Leeds failed to return to Division One the next season, and Fitzgerald played just eight League games before he was transferred to Chester City in July 1961.

Peter played on the left wing for the Sealand Road club and is remembered there for his speed down the flank. He scored a dozen goals in 80 Fourth Division games for Chester before returning to Waterford in 1963 where he won a League of Ireland Championship medal in 1965–66.

A former League of Ireland representative player, Peter was a full Irish international for just over a year, between September 1960 and October 1961, during which he played in five international fixtures for the Republic.

He made his debut in the 3–2 defeat by Wales in September 1960. Wales were on their first visit to Ireland and their victory ended Ireland's eight-match unbeaten run at home. The highlight of Fitzgerald's international career came in his second international, against Norway in Dublin in November 1960, when he scored twice in the Republic's 3–1 victory.

Kevin Fitzpatrick (GOALKEEPER)

Born: Limerick 1943
Debut for Eire: v Czechoslovakia October 1969

Kevin Fitzpatrick, a 5ft 11in and 11st goalminder, was one of the finest sportsmen and longest serving characters in League of Ireland soccer in the 1960s and 1970s.

A one-club man, Fitzy joined local club Limerick and first wore the club jersey in August 1959 against Glasgow Celtic. It was the beginning of a relationship between player and club which spanned more than two decades. He was a member of the Limerick CBS team which won the Munster Colleges Senior Football Championships in 1960. After

Kevin Fitzpatrick

serving his time in the Limerick 'B' team, Kevin became the club's regular senior keeper in 1962–63.

Despite attracting the attention of several big cross-channel clubs, Kevin remained loyal to his hometown club, and when Limerick struck a bad patch he had the courage and spirit to take the manager's chair. He won Munster Cup medals with the club in 1963 and 1977; was a League Cup winner in 1975; and appeared in five FAI Cup finals, picking up winners medals in 1971 and 1982. He also won a League Championship medal in 1979–80 when the national team boss Eoin Hand was in charge of the side.

Kevin won one full cap, against Czechoslovakia in October 1969, when Ireland were felled by three first-half goals.

Arthur Fitzsimons (INSIDE-FORWARD)

Born: Dublin 16 December 1929
Debut for Eire: v Finland September 1949

'Arthur Fitzsimons was marked for greatness from the start, with a quick footballing brain and the feet to obey it.'

A product of the great football nursery at Johnville, for whom he played at centre-forward, Arthur was described as 'one of the craftiest inside-forwards to blossom forth from the junior ranks'. He was honoured by the Irish minors as an outside-right and became an inside-right when he joined Shelbourne in 1946.

Just weeks after playing in the Shelbourne side beaten 3–0 by Dundalk in the 1949 FAI Cup final, he was transferred to First Division Middlesbrough with club colleague Peter Desmond in an £18,000 joint deal. Arthur had a total of ten seasons at Boro, five in Division One and five in Division Two, after the club was relegated at the end of 1953–54.

Lightly built, skilful and pacey, Arthur could weave around several defenders on the edge of the penalty area; but he would often blast his shot over the bar. This trait caused his centre-forward colleague Brian Clough to bellow: 'You make the bloody goals and I'll score them.' Nevertheless Fitzsimons scored 49 League goals in 223 League games for the club.

In March 1959 he transferred to Lincoln City for whom he made seven appearances in Division Three (North) before transferring to his final League club, Mansfield Town, five months later. Fitzsimons scored 23 goals in 62 appearances for Mansfield but couldn't prevent the club from being relegated to Division Four in his first season, 1959–60. He retired from the game soon after.

A former League of Ireland representative player, Arthur later managed the representative side.

He was a regular in the Irish senior XI in the '50s, winning 26 full caps and scoring seven goals. His international goals helped Ireland sit comfortably among Europe's finest at the time. He netted in the victory over West Germany in 1951, in the 2–2 draw with Spain in 1955 and twice in Ireland's 4–1 win over Holland in 1956.

Curtis Fleming (FULL-BACK)

Born: Manchester 8 October 1968
Debut for Eire: v Czech Republic April 1996

'One of the most popular players to surface in Irish football for years', the Manchester-born, Dublin-reared Curtis Fleming learned his trade in the League of Ireland with St Pat's Athletic.

Fleming spent a period with Swindon Town in 1988–89 but returned to St Pat's (where he won a Championship medal in 1989–90) without having made his League debut. Nevertheless he made another crack at the English game. He was rejected by several clubs and was told by people in Ireland that he wouldn't make the grade in England. However, with the help and encouragement of St Pat's boss Brian Kerr (the same man who'd taken him to the club as a youngster), Fleming was Middlesbrough's regular right-back by 1991–92.

The arrival in August 1992 of Republic international Chris Morris from Celtic put the Dubliner's position in jeopardy. Morris took over at right-back unchallenged as Fleming was out with a torn muscle at the time. An injury to the former Celtic player let Fleming back in, however, and when Boro won the Division One Championship in 1994–95, he played all his 21 games that season at left-back! To the end of 1995–96 he had notched up 126 League games for the club.

Curtis, whose ambition is 'to play for my country at Lansdowne Road', was capped at Under-21 and Under-23 level whilst at St Pat's. He won his first full cap as a half-time replacement for Denis Irwin in the 2–0 away

defeat by the Czech Republic in April 1996. He didn't look out of place as a right-sided wing-back, and won a total of six caps in the summer of 1996.

Ambrose Fogarty (INSIDE-LEFT)

Born: Dublin 11 September 1933
Debut for Eire: v West Germany May 1960

A goalscoring inside-forward, Amby Fogarty was in his second season of League of Ireland football with Bohemians in 1955 when he moved north to join Irish League club Glentoran.

He became a great favourite at the Oval and was a member of the Glentoran side which lost to Distillery in the 1956 Irish Cup final after a three-match marathon.

In September 1957 Fogarty seemed to be on his way back south; negotiations for his transfer to Cork Hibernians were at an advanced stage. Sunderland, however, stepped in with a £5,000 bid. No contest. And so in October 1957 the unemployed Dublin carpenter joined the Football League's 'Bank of England' club.

Fogarty immediately joined his Eire international colleague Charlie Hurley in Sunderland's First Division side. In his first season, 1957–58, the once-great club were relegated for the first time in their history. It was the beginning of a decline from which they have never recovered.

Amby had a total of six seasons at Roker Park during which he turned up in both inside-forward positions and also on either wing. He scored 37 goals in 152 League games for the club.

In November 1963 Amby was transferred to Fourth Division Hartlepool United for a 'substantial fee'. He ended his League career with 22 goals in 128 League games for the Pool before returning to Ireland as player-manager of Cork Hibernians in 1966.

Amby joined Cork Celtic in 1969 and in 1970 returned to his native Dublin to join Drumcondra.

He made his international debut in the 1–0 victory over West Germany in Dusseldorf in May 1960 and collected a total of 11 full caps over the next three years, scoring three goals.

Theodore Foley (RIGHT-BACK)

Born: Dublin 2 April 1937
Debut for Eire: v Spain March 1964

Exeter City, then playing in Division Three (South), recruited Theo Foley from Dublin junior club Home Farm in March 1955.

A fast-moving, tough and honest full-back,

Theodore Foley

Theo made 154 League appearances for the Devon club before being transferred to Northampton Town in May 1961.

Theo's six seasons at the County Ground coincided with the most successful era in the club's history. They had just won promotion to Division Three when he joined and two seasons later moved up another rung as Division Three champions. In 1964–65 they again won promotion and for the first time ever Northampton became a First Division club. Unfortunately the club's downfall was just as dramatic as their rise had been, and after just one season in the top flight, they dropped to Division Three in successive seasons.

In August 1967, shortly after the Cobblers had lost their battle for Second Division survival, Theo moved to Second Division Charlton Athletic, having made 205 League appearances in a Northampton shirt.

After half a dozen appearances for Charlton, he become chief scout at the club. Thereafter he had spells as George Graham's assistant at Millwall, QPR and Arsenal.

In May 1990, after three very successful seasons, Theo left Highbury to return to Northampton, this time as club manager. He was sacked in April 1992 when the club was taken over by new administrators.

He later became youth team manager at Fulham and in July 1994 was appointed assistant manager at Southend United.

A player who never lost his enthusiasm for the game, Theo was capped nine times by the Republic of Ireland between 1964 and 1967. Theo recalls how he learned of his international call-ups. Incredibly the FAI did not contact him. Instead he would be called at home by the secretary of Northampton's fan club, who had heard of his inclusion on the radio.

He also had the honour of leading his country when, in the absence of regular skipper, Manchester United's Noel Cantwell, he captained the side against Belgium in March 1965.

John Fullam (WING-HALF)

Born: Dublin 22 March 1940
Debut for Eire: v Norway November 1960

Johnny Fullam, who was one of the game's great tacticians, started out as an 11-year-old with Carrow Celtic in the Park League. A solid defender, he progressed to Castleville in Ringsend at 14 before joining the greatest nursery of them all – Home Farm – at 16.

Fullam moved on to First Division Preston North End in October 1958; in three seasons he made 49 First Division appearances, mostly at inside-left, before returning to Ireland in 1961 to join Shamrock Rovers and work with Associated Engineering (Sales).

At Rovers he and Frank O'Neill struck up one of the game's great partnerships – the 'Hope and Crosby' of Irish football. Fullam sprayed the passes with timing and perfection; O'Neill, with his burst of speed over 20 yards, dribbling and accurate crosses, made full-backs' lives a '90-minute nightmare'.

Fullam won five FAI Cup winners medals with the Hoops – scoring the winner in the 1965 replayed final against Limerick – and one League Championship medal in 1963–64.

He missed the 1962 and 1969 Cup finals due to knee problems. His career indeed seemed over in 1969 until he was snapped up by Bohemians, who discarded their amateur status and opened their doors to professionals.

A calm player and polished performer 'who epitomises the general leading a battalion into battle', he captained Bohs when they won the FAI Cup in 1976, collecting his seventh FAI Cup winners medal – his second with Bohs. He also won a Championship medal with the club in 1974–75.

Johnny appeared in three League Cup finals. He scored for Bohemians in the victory over Finn Harps in 1975; in 1977 he was on the winning side again, but for Shamrock Rovers, with whom he was a runner-up in the competition in March 1979. It was the only occasion in major competition in which he finished on the losing side. The opponents in that game were none other than Bohemians.

In November 1979, just four months before his 40th birthday and ten years after he'd been written off, Fullam helped Athlone Town to victory in the competition.

Twice winner of the Irish Soccer Writers' 'Personality of the Year' award, Johnny played for the Dublin City select against Arsenal in 1964. He played Schoolboy, minor and full internationals and won Inter-League honours. Although not a regular in the Irish senior XI, Fullam did collect 11 full caps between November 1960 and October 1969. He scored one goal for Ireland, which was a 68th-minute winner in the 3–2 defeat of Belgium in Liège in May 1966.

At 36 Johnny was running two successful companies, a motor factors company and an industrial supply company, as well as playing football.

Charles Gallagher (INSIDE-FORWARD)

Born: Glasgow 3 November 1940
Debut for Eire: v Turkey February 1967

Charlie Gallagher played his schoolboy football with St John's Boys' Guild in Glasgow's Gorbals and with Holyrood Senior Secondary. At 15 he joined Kilmarnock Amateurs and at 18 he moved to Yoker Athletic.

A cousin of former Manchester United and Scotland player Paddy Crerand, Charlie signed professionally for Glasgow Celtic in March 1959, having been on their books provisionally the previous September.

A deep-lying inside-forward, adept at creating space, Gallagher was a 'player's player'. He possessed a thundering shot, scoring many goals from up to 35 yards, and provided inch-perfect passes. 'Corner kicks were executed with venom and accuracy.'

In February 1968 Gallagher took over

Bertie Auld's job of controlling the Bhoys' midfield, winning balls and feeding the wingers. Described as the 'Glenn Hoddle of the '60s', he helped Celtic to their fourth successive Championship in that 1967–68 season.

In June 1970 Gallagher left Parkhead for Dumbarton on a free transfer, having donned the famous green and white hoops 106 times in League encounters and scored 17 goals. He masterminded Dumbarton's Second Division Championship success in 1972 before retiring the following year.

Charlie was a scout for Celtic between April 1976 and April 1978.

Charlie had already been capped at Under-18 level for Scotland when, in 1967, he opted to play for the Republic; both his parents came from Donegal. His decision to play for Eire was a source of great joy among the Parkhead faithful. And so in 1967 he became the first Scottish-born player to be capped by Eire, winning two full caps against Turkey and Czechoslovakia.

Michael Gallagher (HALF-BACK)

Born: Donegal
Debut for Eire: v Luxembourg March 1954

A native of Arranmore, Mick Gallagher played with Rosses GAA club and began his soccer career in junior circles in Glasgow. He later joined Alloa Athletic, from whom he was transferred to Hibernian in 1951 for a fee of £5,000.

Gallagher was an unlikely-looking professional footballer, with thick-set legs and very long shorts. Nevertheless, he formed part of the unsung half-back line that supported Hibs' 'famous five' forward line of the early 1950s. Two successive Scottish League Championships in 1950–51 and 1951–52 could have been three but for Rangers pipping them by a superior goal difference of one in 1952–53.

Mick's domestic success brought him to the attention of the Irish selectors and in March 1954 he became the first Scotland-based player to be picked for Ireland since Joe O'Reilly and the legendary Paddy Moore 20 years earlier.

Described as a fine half-back, the big Donegalman was one of half a dozen Irish debutants in the side which beat Luxembourg 1–0 in a World Cup qualifier in Luxembourg in March 1954. It was to be his only cap.

Anthony Galvin (WINGER)

Born: Huddersfield 12 July 1956
Debut for Eire: v Holland September 1982

A model professional and a multi-talented player, Tony Galvin's career – like those of many other professional footballers – had humble beginnings. A former Russian language student at Hull University, Tony was playing non-League football with Goole Town in January 1978 when he was snapped up by Tottenham Hotspur for £30,000. Spurs actually spotted Galvin playing for Goole against Buxton on an icy windswept moor, 1,000 feet up in the Peak District.

The younger brother of Chris Galvin, the former Leeds, Hull, York and Stockport midfielder, Tony made his full debut for Spurs in 1979 and over the next nine seasons at White Hart Lane he made a total of 201 First Division appearances and scored 20 goals.

Tony's tireless running style and skilful ball distribution played a major role in Tottenham's cup successes in the early 1980s, the highlight of which was the UEFA Cup final victory over RCS Anderlecht in 1984. Galvin picked up an FA Cup winners medal in 1981 when Spurs overcame Manchester City 3–2 in the replayed final, and a second one the following year when Spurs disposed of QPR 1–0 in the replayed final. He also won a League Cup runners-up medal in 1982 after Spurs lost 3–1 to Liverpool in the final.

In August 1987 Sheffield Wednesday paid Spurs £200,000 to take Galvin to Hillsborough. He made 36 appearances for Wednesday before joining Swindon Town in August 1989. He played 11 times for the Robins at the start of 1989–90 but was sidelined by a back injury in September.

Tony played an important role as manager Ossie Ardiles' right-hand man in Swindon's bid for Second Division promotion that year. The Wiltshire club won their way into Division One for the first time in their history, only to be condemned back to the Second after a scandal over illegal payments to players.

Both men found themselves out of work for a period, but when Ardiles became manager of Newcastle (1991–92) and West Bromwich Albion (1992–93), he took Galvin with him as his assistant.

Certainly not one of the 'sick as a parrot' breed of players, Galvin squeezed in a three-year part-time management degree in the late 1980s and gained his FA coaching badge. He later took up a position as sports lecturer at Ware College.

An Eire international for eight years, Tony won a total of 29 full caps. He was something of an unsung hero in Jack Charlton's side of the late '80s as the man who provided the crosses on which the Irish players such as Cascarino and Quinn thrived.

Tony scored one international goal in the 2–0 defeat of Luxembourg in a European Championship qualifier in May 1987.

Always held in high regard by Charlton, he went to the World Cup finals in Italy in 1990 as part of the Irish manager's team of spies.

Edward Gannon (WING-HALF)

Born: Dublin 3 January 1921
Debut for Eire: v Switzerland December 1948

Eddie Gannon was a famous junior, starting out with Creighton Rovers from Dublin's Pearse Street. He then had spells at Hammond Lane, Shelbourne and Belfast club Distillery before returning to Shelbourne.

He was a League of Ireland Championship winner with Shels in 1943–44 when they narrowly failed to do the double, losing the FAI Cup final 3–2 to local rivals Shamrock Rovers.

Eddie was introduced to English League football by Notts County, who took him to Meadow Lane in August 1946. In three seasons at the club Gannon made 106 appearances in Division Three (South). In March 1949 Sheffield Wednesday boss Eric Taylor took him to Hillsborough in a £15,000 transfer deal.

Eddie had the best years of his career at Wednesday. An attacking wing-half of genuine quality, he scored few goals himself but created plenty for those around him. He played a major role in the Owls' promotion from Division Two in 1949–50 and – after they were relegated the next season – in their Second Division Championship-winning season in 1951–52. When Wednesday reached the FA Cup semi-finals in 1954 Eddie was once again the main driving force.

In 1955, after 204 League games for the Owls, Eddie returned to his former club, Shelbourne, as player-manager. He later managed Dublin junior club Bolton Athletic.

Eddie made his international debut for Eire in the 1–0 home defeat by Switzerland in December 1948. He appeared in Ireland's next five games but was a bit-part player thereafter, collecting just eight more caps over a seven-year period and taking his final tally to 14 against West Germany in May 1955.

Eddie Gannon died on 31 July 1989, aged 68.

Michael Gannon (RIGHT-BACK)

Born: Dublin 2 February 1947
Debut for Eire: v Austria October 1971

A model of consistency, Mick Gannon nicknamed ('Mousey' because he did not say much) was one of the finest defenders to grace League of Ireland football.

Gannon played his schoolboy football with the esteemed Ringsend junior club, Bolton Athletics, before joining Shelbourne as a 19-year-old. He reached two FAI Cup finals with the Reds, losing to Cork Hibs in 1973 in the replay and going down 1–0 to Home Farm two years later.

Mick joined Shamrock Rovers in 1977. He had three years at Milltown under Johnny Giles, who preferred him in midfield. He won an FAI Cup winners medal with Rovers in 1978, when he was carried off injured with 20 minutes remaining, and a League Cup runners-up medal the following year. As he also won a Leinster Senior Cup medal and a Shield medal, his spell at Rovers was the most successful of his career.

He returned to Shelbourne in 1980, where he ended his League career. He was coach at north Dublin schoolboy club Whitehorn Celtic, before signing for Aer Lingus in the Leinster Senior League.

Diminutive but highly effective, Mick hails from a family of strong footballing traditions. His son Karl is a current Shamrock Rovers player and his uncle Eddie played for Ireland while at Notts County and Sheffield Wednesday in the late 1940s and 1950s.

Mick played in an Irish friendly against Argentina in Buenos Aires and represented the League of Ireland against Northern Ireland. He won one full cap, against Austria in October 1971, owing to the absence of Chelsea's John Dempsey.

John Gavin (OUTSIDE-RIGHT)

Born: Limerick 20 April 1928
Debut for Eire: v Finland September 1949

John Gavin joined Division Three (South) Norwich City from his hometown League of Ireland club, Limerick City, in August 1948 for £1,500.

At Carrow Road Johnny gained a reputation as a high-scoring winger. His tally of 122 goals in 312 League games in two spells for Norwich still stands as a club record. In October 1954 he left Carrow Road for First Division Tottenham Hotspur.

Gavin had already won four Eire caps before arriving at Spurs, scoring on his debut in the 3–0 defeat of Finland in September 1949. He gained two more caps during his 13-month sojourn in north London, becoming the first Spurs player to represent the Republic of Ireland.

Johnny's 15 goals in 32 League games for Spurs were the only interruption to a ten-year stint with Norwich, for he returned to Carrow Road in November 1955.

Johnny won his seventh and final cap during his second spell at Norwich before departing for the Canaries' divisional rivals Watford in July 1958. He had scored 12 goals in 43 League appearances for Watford when he transferred to Fourth Division Crystal Palace in May 1959.

He ended his League career with 15 goals in 66 League appearances for Palace; and then he spent some time in non-League football with Cambridge City and Newmarket Town.

Johnny became a publican and later went into the painting and decorating business. He now lives in Cambridge.

Seamus Gibbons (CENTRE-FORWARD)

Born: Dublin 19 May 1929
Debut for Eire: v West Germany May 1952

Shay Gibbons had a glittering career ahead of him as a Gaelic midfielder before he opted for Association football. He captained Parnell's in a Dublin junior final, was in the Parnell's team beaten by St Vincents in the 1950 Dublin senior final and even sat on the subs' bench for the Dublin senior team when he was 17. He began his soccer career as a centre-half with Dublin City Under-14s, then Home Farm Under-16s and Bohemians Youth team.

A youth trial game against the Liverpool FA was the catalyst for Shay's career. He played as a centre-forward for the first time and went on to become the League of Ireland's most prolific hitman in the '50s.

He shunned League football for a period, preferring to turn out for Whitehall Rangers in the Athletic Union League and helping them win the Leinster Junior Cup.

Shay played for Bohemians a few times in the absence of Mick O'Flanagan, but he made his name with St Patrick's Athletic, whom he joined in 1950. In 1950–51 St Pat's were Leinster Senior League winners and the following season, 1951–52, they were elected to the League of Ireland, which they won at a canter in their first League season.

Gibbons was an ideal target man, a big burly centre-forward, noted for his unselfish play and thunderous shots from outside the box. His contribution to St Pat's championship success came in the form of 26 goals in 22 games. The next season, 1952–53, he was again the League's top gun, with 22 goals. That tally included five against Raich Carter's Cork Athletic – he had one ruled out – as St Pat's ran out 6–2 winners. Not bad for a player described as 'palpably one-footed'.

In four more seasons with the Saints, Gibbons topped the club's scoring charts three times; in two of those seasons, 1954–55 and 1955–56, he was the League's top scorer and St Pat's were League champions. In fact he set a club scoring record of 28 goals in 1954–55.

After a few months with Holyhead Town at the end of 1956–57, Shay joined League new boys Cork Hibs in 1957–58 and spent 1958–59 with Dundalk, topping the club's scoring charts with 11 goals. Shay quit League of Ireland football in 1959, at the age of 30, having scored 120 League goals.

A former Junior international, Shay won representative inter-League honours and between May 1952 and November 1955 he won four full caps.

Robert Gilbert (CENTRE-FORWARD)

Born: Dublin
Debut for Eire: v West Germany May 1966

Bobby Gilbert joined Shamrock Rovers from Derry City during 1965–66 and that season was the Hoops' top scorer, with 14 League goals.

The big Dubliner, whose strength was in the air, played in three successive FAI Cup finals with Rovers. They won the lot, beating Limerick in 1966 and St Pat's in 1967; and in 1968, in front of a record crowd of over 39,000, they beat Waterford.

Gilbert joined Drumcondra in 1968 where he again became his club's top scorer, with nine goals in 1968–69. He spent the 1970–71 season with Dundalk.

In May 1966 Bobby was drafted into the Irish team to face West Germany in Dublin. The selectors decided to move Ray Treacy from centre-forward to inside-forward to replace the injured Andy McEvoy, and brought Gilbert in to lead the attack. It turned out to be a forgettable experience for Bobby as Beckenbauer and company recorded West Germany's first ever victory in Dublin, winning easily by a four-goal margin. It was to be his only cap.

Christopher Giles (OUTSIDE-RIGHT)

Born: Dublin 17 July 1928
Debut for Eire: v Norway November 1950

A lightly built and nippy outside-right, Christy Giles joined League of Ireland club Drumcondra in 1947.

In his first season at the club, 1947–48, Christy narrowly missed out on the League and Cup double; for the Drums claimed the Championship only to lose the 1948 FAI Cup final 2–1 to fellow Dubliners Shamrock Rovers. The Drums retained their

Championship title the following season, 1948–49, and just missed out on a unique treble by finishing second a year later.

At the end of that 1949–50 season, English Division Three (North) champions Doncaster Rovers – whose manager then was Northern Ireland international Peter Doherty – were touring Ireland and were so impressed by Giles that they signed him that summer.

Christy made 11 League appearances (two goals) for the Belle Vue club in 1951–52. He fell foul of the club's authorities, however, in November when he failed to turn up for a game against Coventry. He had left Doncaster to visit his sick wife although the club had refused him permission to do so. He returned to Belle Vue in December and later regained his place in the side, making 16 more League appearances and scoring another two goals. At the end of 1951–52 Giles left again, and this time he did not return.

Doncaster retained his registration, and in August 1953 Christy was transferred to Aldershot. A week later he returned to Ireland, without having played for the Shots. He played in the Irish League with Portadown and in March 1954 was transferred to Belfast club Distillery for 'around £1,000'.

Christy won one full Irish cap, in the 2–2 draw with Norway at Dalymount Park in November 1950.

John Giles (MIDFIELD)

Born: Dublin 6 January 1940
Debut for Eire: v Sweden November 1959

Another product of the famous Dublin football nursery Home Farm, Johnny Giles left Dublin when he was just 15 to join Manchester United. He signed professionally for the club in November 1957, rose through the junior sides at Old Trafford and graduated to the senior team in September 1959. Giles made 98 League appearances for United and won an FA Cup winners medal in 1963 after the 3–1 victory over Leicester City, and then was surprisingly sold to arch-rivals Leeds United for a mere £32,000 the following August. Indeed it has been said on many occasions that the worst decision the Old Trafford club ever made was to release Giles to Leeds.

A brilliant tactician with one of football's shrewdest brains, Giles took over the role of Leeds' midfield general from Bobby Collins. The former winger was transformed by Leeds' boss Don Revie into one of the greatest midfield dynamos of the '60's and '70s. Linking magnificently with Billy Bremner in the Leeds' engine room, the pair drove the Yorkshire club to unprecedented glory.

In his first season at the club Giles assisted Leeds to the Second Division Championship which marked the beginning of the most successful era in the club's history. In the following ten seasons with the Yorkshire giant, Giles won a host of honours including League Championship medals in 1969 and 1974; an FA Cup winners medal after the 1–0 victory over Arsenal in 1972; a League Cup winners medal in 1968 after defeating Arsenal again by the same margin; and Fairs Cup winners medals in 1968 and 1971 following victories over Ferencvaros and Juventus.

Johnny's last game for Leeds was in the 1975 European Cup final, which they lost 2–0 to German champions Bayern Munich. The runners-up medal he collected after that game was only the second of his career; the other came when Leeds lost the 1965 FA Cup final to Liverpool. His record in cup competitions is remarkable when one considers that he played in eight finals, and won six of them.

In June 1975 after 383 League games for Leeds, Giles moved to West Bromwich Albion for £48,000 to play out the autumn of a highly meritorious career. As player-manager at the Hawthorns, he took the Baggies into Division One at the end of his first season.

Johnny made 75 League appearances in two seasons at the Hawthorns before returning to

Ireland to play for and manage Shamrock Rovers. In 1978 he guided Rovers to victory in the 1978 FAI Cup – their 21st success in the competition.

It is said that Johnny Giles – nicknamed Mr Availability – hit two kinds of passes; good passes and great passes. A dedicated professional with concentration bordering on the frightening, the former Eire Schoolboy international was an automatic choice for Ireland for almost two decades, accumulating 59 full caps.

He captained the Republic a record 30 times and became the youngest player to score for Ireland when he scored the first of his five international goals, just 16 minutes into his debut against Sweden in November 1959, two months short of his 20th birthday. That record stands to day.

Giles was appointed player-manager of the Republic in October 1973. He continued playing until 1979, winning his last cap at 39 in May of that year, and quit as manager the following March. Thereafter he had brief spells in management with Vancouver Whitecaps in 1983 and again at West Brom from 1984–85.

Seamus Given (GOALKEEPER)

Born: Lifford, Co. Donegal 20 April 1976
Debut for Eire: v Russia March 1996

A teenage goalkeeping sensation, Shay Given's rise from reserve team obscurity to the pinnacle of First Division and international football in the space of a few months has been breathtaking.

Given was a midfielder in the St Columba's College (Stranorler) Under-14 team which lost the 1989 All-Ireland final. By the time the school contested the following year's final, Shay had move to goalkeeper – the position which would soon earn him many plaudits.

Given later kept goal for Lifford Celtic

John Giles

before signing a two-year apprenticeship with Glasgow Celtic in September 1992. At Parkhead he was a Scottish Youth League and Cup winner. He played in 46 youth games, 22 reserve team games and made it to the substitutes bench five times before being snapped up by Blackburn Rovers in August 1994.

After a spell on loan to Swindon Town in August 1995, during which he made five appearances for the 1995–96 Second Division champions, he joined Sunderland on loan in January 1996.

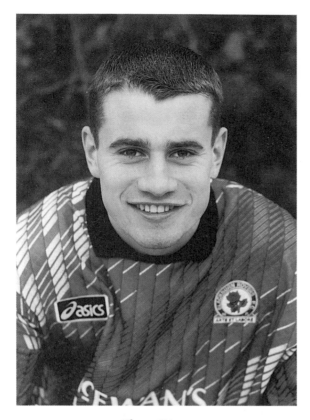

Shay Given

His form for the Rokerites was brilliant. His 12 clean sheets in 17 starts saw Sunderland storm from seventh place to the top of the First Division and ultimately the First Division Championship.

Shay, who has been favourably compared to Peter Shilton, earned rave reviews for his displays for Sunderland including one from *The Times*' Louise Taylor: 'Boasting positional sense, judgement of angles and robust physical maturity to belie his youth, Given looks poised for a highly promising future. Sunderland should make every endeavour to sign him permanently.'

Sunderland boss Peter Reid offered Blackburn £2 million to keep Shay at Roker Park permanently. Blackburn, however, firmly nailed the 'Not for Sale' sign to the Ewood Park gates and in April 1996 Shay returned to Rovers.

Given, who had already represented Ireland at Under-16, Under-18 and Under-21 level, was elevated to the senior squad from the Under-21s for the game against Russia in Dublin in March 1996, after Alan Kelly's withdrawal.

Despite Ireland's 2–0 defeat in Mick McCarthy's first game in charge of the national team, Shay had a 'nerveless debut'. He was the Republic's number 1 in the summer of 1996, taking his caps total to eight with a series of 'eye-popping' displays. His ambition is to emulate his boyhood idol and fellow Donegalman, Packie Bonner, and become Ireland's regular number 1.

Donald Givens (FORWARD)

Born: Limerick 9 August 1949
Debut for Eire: v Denmark May 1969

Don Givens made his international debut for Eire in a World Cup qualifier against Denmark in May 1969. It marked the beginning of a colourful and action-packed international career which spanned 12 years and brought him 56 full caps.

Don holds the record for scoring Ireland's quickest hat-trick. It came in the 4–0 defeat of Turkey in October 1975 and took him just nine minutes. And, for good measure, he scored Ireland's fourth goal in that game. Givens was also the Republic's leading goalscorer, with 19 goals in 56 games, from 1980 to 1990 when he lost his record to Frank Stapleton.

Don was sent off twice while playing for Ireland – against Ecuador in June 1972 and Chile in May 1974. He played his final game for his country in the epic 3–2 defeat of France in Dublin in October 1981.

Givens started out in the Football League initially with Manchester United, whom he joined as a teenager in 1966, signing as a professional in December of that year. He didn't managed to hold down a regular first-team place at Old Trafford, however, and when he was transferred to Second Division Luton Town for £15,000 in April 1970, he had played just eight League games for United, though he was already an established international.

Don had netted 19 times in 83 League games for Luton when, in July 1972, Queen's Park Rangers secured his services for £40,000.

A potent, intelligent and dangerous hitman, Givens spent over six seasons at Loftus Road during which he hit the target 76 times in 242 League games, helping Rangers win promotion as runners-up to Burnley in Division Two in 1972–73 and sending his own value soaring to £165,000 – the fee Birmingham City paid QPR to take him to the Midlands in March 1980.

In two and a half seasons with Birmingham Don scored ten goals in 59 League games and helped the Blues win promotion from Division Two in 1979–80, just one season after they were relegated from the top flight. During his time at St Andrews he was briefly loaned to Bournemouth for whom he scored four times in five games.

Givens ended his League career with three goals in 11 games for Sheffield United, whom he joined in March 1981.

His last kick in the English game, before joining Swiss club Xamax Neuchatel in the summer of 1981, was a missed penalty in the relegation dogfight with Walsall in May of that year. Walsall had a one-point lead before the game, but United had a vastly superior goal difference which meant that a point would be sufficient to keep them up . . . United lost the game 1–0 and Givens's missed spot kick condemned United to Fourth Division football the following season.

Desmond Glynn (CENTRE-FORWARD)

Born: Dublin 7 June 1928
Debut for Eire: v West Germany October 1951

Dessie Glynn was a fast, direct, all-purpose player. He won a host of medals with Dublin junior club Johnville, including an FAI Youth Cup winners medal in 1946.

Glynn joined League of Ireland club Drumcondra from Clifton United in January 1949 and won a Championship medal in his first season. He appeared in virtually every position bar that of keeper and played in two FAI Cup finals with Drumcondra, collecting a winners medal in 1954 and a runners-up medal the following season. Small but deadly in front of goal, he scored 96 League goals in eight seasons with Drumcondra and was the club's top scorer in six seasons.

He moved to Shelbourne for the 1956–57 season where he again finished top scorer with 12 League goals.

In October 1951 Glynn was a member of the League of Ireland XI crushed 9–1 by their English counterparts. The following week he was the only member of that team asked to make the step up to full international level.

In order to make the line-up for his international debut, against West Germany in October 1951, Glynn was forced to cancel his honeymoon. It was worth it. He scored the winning goal in the historic 3–2 home victory over the side which three years later would be crowned world champions. He won his second cap in the 3–1 victory over Norway in Oslo in May 1955.

Dessie spent nine months in hospital in 1958, suffering from tuberculosis – a condition which effectively ended his playing career. He later coached in New York.

Thomas Godwin (GOALKEEPER)

Born: Dublin 20 August 1927
Debut for Eire: v Portugal May 1949

A sound custodian who excelled at plucking high balls out of the air, Tommy Godwin played junior football with Reds United Under-14s and began his senior career in the League of

Ireland with Home Farm, and then Shamrock Rovers. He was earning a living as a carpenter and keeping goal for Rovers when he starred in Ireland's shock 2–0 victory over England at Goodison Park in September 1949. That international was the turning-point in his career. Within days he was transferred to Second Division Leicester City.

During his time at Filbert Street Tommy was constantly under pressure from Scottish international keeper John Anderson to hand over the Foxes' number 1 shirt. Anderson, who was two years younger than Godwin, eventually won the day, and in four seasons at Filbert Street Godwin made just 45 League appearances.

In June 1952 he was transferred to Bournemouth and Boscombe, later AFC Bournemouth. He had ten seasons at Dean Court during which he made 357 League appearances, all in Division Three (South) and in Division Three from 1958.

On retirement in 1962 Tommy didn't stray far from Dean Court. He settled near the ground and worked for Bournemouth Council as a parks supervisor in King's Park, where AFC Bournemouth is situated.

A keeper 'in the traditional mould of unspectacular soundness', Tommy represented the League of Ireland during his Shamrock Rovers days. While at Rovers he also played in the semi-final of the 1948 FAI Cup, only to break his leg during the tie, which ruled him out of that year's final.

Tommy won his first Eire cap against Portugal in May 1949, and kept his place in the side for the next 18 months. He was ousted from pole position by Shamrock Rovers' custodian Fred Kiernan in 1951, but his 'brilliant form' at Bournemouth earned him an international recall in May 1956. Tommy, who kept two clean sheets in his international career, took his final tally to 13 caps when he guarded the Irish goal against Poland in May 1958.

He died in August 1969 at the age of 69.

William Gorman (FULL-BACK)

Born: Sligo 13 July 1911
Debut for Eire: v Switzerland March 1936

The prematurely bald head of this none-too-tall Irish-Scot-turned-Londoner was one of the familiar sights in the game just before and after the Second World War.

His speed off the mark and enthusiasm combined to make Bill Gorman one of the finest defenders in the game and earned him 13 full caps for Eire and four for Northern Ireland. Bill's qualification for both the North and the South came about by chance: he had made a premature entry into the world while his parents – dad was Scottish, mum was English – were on holiday in Sligo.

Gorman's international career straddled the Second World War. He made his debut for the Republic in the 1–0 victory over Switzerland in March 1936 and was a regular in the Irish rearguard when war broke out in 1939. He was 35 years old when he won his last Eire cap, against Portugal in May 1947.

He played at right-back for Northern Ireland against England, Scotland and Wales in the first post-war Home Internationals in 1946–47 and won his fourth cap for the North as a left-back in the 0–2 defeat by Wales in Wrexham in March 1948.

Bill was brought up on Clydebank and moved south to play for Second Division Bury, making 52 appearances before joining Brentford for £7,000 December 1938. Those were halcyon days at Griffin Park; the Bees were enjoying the only period of First Division football in their history and, by signing players of the calibre of Bill Gorman, they hoped to keep it that way. It wasn't to be, however, and in 1946–47 they slipped back into Division Two.

The war carved a huge chunk out of Bill's career, as it did for many other players, and when he departed from Griffin Park in October 1950 to take over as player-manager of Kent League Deal Town, his total League appearances for Brentford amounted to just 125.

Bill Gorman died in December 1978, aged 67.

Anthony Grealish (MIDFIELD)

Born: Paddington, London 21 September 1956
Debut for Eire: v Norway March 1976

Tony Grealish was a schoolboy footballer with Leyton Orient before joining the club as an apprentice in June 1972. He signed professional terms in July 1974 and was the O's 'Young Player of the Year' in 1976.

A 5ft 7in, bearded, tigerish midfielder with a powerful shot, Tony had five seasons as a pro with Orient during which he made 171 Second Division appearances (ten goals).

In August 1979 Tony was transferred to the 'O's divisional rivals, Luton Town. Orient had wanted £350,000 for the player, but Luton boss David Pleat had refused to meet their asking price. Luton eventually paid £150,000, the fee agreed by the Transfer Appeals Board, and just beat Tommy Docherty at QPR for Grealish's signature.

In two seasons with the Hatters, Tony made 78 appearances before joining Brighton and Hove Albion for £100,000 in July 1981. He was captain of the Brighton side which drew 2–2 with Manchester United in the 1983 FA Cup final and then lost the replay 4–0. That season, 1982–83, the Seagulls were relegated to Division Two.

When former Eire international Johnny Giles took over as manager of West Bromwich Albion in 1984, he targeted Grealish as the man to be his midfield general. In March that year Grealish became Giles's first major signing in a £75,000 transfer deal. In one and a half seasons at the Hawthorns Tony made 65 First Division appearances before Jimmy Frizzell took him to Manchester City for £20,000 in October 1986.

Anthony Grealish

Grealish made his City debut against Manchester United the same month, and on the same day as former United defender John Gidman played his first game for City. Grealish, by all accounts, had an outstanding game in the 1–1 draw. However, he managed just ten further League games in a City jersey. At the end of the season City were relegated to Division Two, and Tony was granted a free transfer. Thus, in August 1987, he joined Third Division Rotherham.

In three seasons at Millmoor, which included a loan spell in Portugal with Salgueros, he made 110 League appearances and won a Fourth Division Championship medal in 1988–89 (Rotherham had been relegated the previous season).

Tony wound down his League career with 36 Fourth Division appearances for Walsall, whom he joined in August 1990. He parted

83

company with Walsall in May 1992 and soon after joined non-League Bromsgrove Rovers. In July 1993 he was appointed player-coach at Halesowen Harriers.

A former junior Gaelic footballer and Republic of Ireland Youth cap, Grealish was one of Ireland's greatest servants in the '70s and '80s. He made his full debut, as a defender, against Norway in March 1976. At the start of his international career he played at full-back before reverting to his normal midfield role in 1978 when he became a regular in the national side.

Tony was an integral part of the Irish set-up during Eoin Hand's period as manager, indeed he was Hand's first captain in Liam Brady's absence. He won 45 full caps, scored eight goals and captained his country on 17 occasions. Hand's departure from the manager's post in 1986 coincided with the demise of Grealish's international career. Player's and manager's international careers ended simultaneously after a 4–1 home defeat by Denmark in a World Cup qualifier in November 1985.

Eamonn Gregg (RIGHT-BACK)

Born: Dublin 1953
Debut for Eire: v Poland April 1978

Eamonn Gregg has been involved in League of Ireland football, both as a player and a manager, for over a quarter of a century.

A resourceful full-back, Gregg joined Bohemians in 1973, after a season with Shamrock Rovers. His time at Bohs coincided with the most successful era in the club's history. They won the League Championship in 1974–75 and 1977–78, the FAI Cup in 1976 and the League Cup in 1975 and 1979.

Gregg won another Championship medal with Dundalk in 1981–82. After spells with St Patrick's Athletic and again with Shamrock Rovers in the late 1980s, he became player-

manager at Kilkenny City in 1989. In May 1990 he was appointed manager of Bohemians. He led the Gypsies to success in the 1992 FAI Cup before vacating the post in December 1993. A month later he became manager of Shelbourne.

A former inter-League player, Gregg won one Under-23 cap as a substitute against France in May 1973. He won his first full cap against Poland in April 1978. 'On his debut the 25-year-old Bohs defender was like a man inspired and probably reached heights even greater than his talents have already shown in League of Ireland football. He really excelled himself.'

That display ensured him further international honours; over the next 17 months he took his tally to eight caps.

Ashley Grimes (MIDFIELD/DEFENCE)

Born: Dublin 2 August 1957
Debut for Eire: v Turkey April 1978

Although later regarded as one of the finest left-footed players in the League – on a par with fellow Irish internationals Liam Brady and Kevin Sheedy – Ashley Grimes had unsuccessful trials with Manchester United as a schoolboy. But he returned to Old Trafford in March 1977, having served his apprenticeship in Dublin with Stella Maris and League of Ireland club Bohemians, whom United paid £35,000 for their man.

The footballer with a powerful voice, Ashley could always take comfort from the fact that, if his playing career didn't work out, he could quite easily earn a living as a ballad singer!

Just before his transfer to Old Trafford, Ashley had in fact agreed terms with QPR manager Dave Sexton; but when Manchester United's name appeared in the frame, it was a no-contest for the lifelong Reds fan. Ironically it was Dave Sexton who later nurtured and developed Grimes at Old Trafford.

Mobile and intelligent, with good pace and a good left-foot shot, Grimes' long-striding style earned him the nickname 'Spiderman' during his early days at United. Versatility was added to his wide repertoire of skill: in 90 First Division games for United he turned up in midfield, on both flanks and in defence.

The 1982–83 season sounded the death-knell of Ashley's United career. It seemed an omen when he was sent off at West Ham in October for allegedly manhandling the referee. As a result he was charged with bringing the game into disrepute and fined £750. And illness and injury kept him out of the reckoning for most of the season. During the close season he was transferred to First Division Coventry City for £275,000.

Grimes spent exactly a year at Highfield Road playing in 32 League games before moving to Luton Town in a player exchange deal with right-back Kirk Stephens.

In five seasons at Kenilworth Road, where, for the most part, he was preferred at left-back, Ashley made 87 League appearances and went to Wembley with the Hatters to contest the 1988 and 1989 League Cup finals. In the showdown with Arsenal he came off the bench to supply the cross for Brian Stein's winning goal in the surprise 3–2 victory. A year later the trophy was wrested from the club by Nottingham Forest who won 3–1 in the final.

In August 1989 Grimes joined Spanish club Ossasuna where he became an instant hit with the local fans.

Grimes returned to the Football League in January 1991 to join Second Division Stoke City on a non-contract basis and in 1991–92 made 20 League appearances for the club, all but one of them at right-back. He later became Lou Macari's assistant at the Victoria Ground, and when Macari left Stoke to became manager of Celtic in November 1993, he took Grimes with him as youth team coach.

Grimes was capped six times by the Republic at Under-21 level and scored two penalty goals. He won 17 full caps between 1978 and 1988 and was a member of the Irish squad for the 1988 European Championships in Germany. And he scored one goal for the Republic in a pulsating European Championship game against Spain in November 1982 when the Irish pulled back from 3–1 down to level the score.

Alfred Hale (INSIDE-FORWARD)

Born: Waterford 28 August 1939
Debut for Eire: v Austria April 1962

Alfie Hale was one of six members of his family to turn out for League of Ireland club Waterford. The other five were his father Alfie (sen.), his uncles John, Thomas and George and his brother Richard (Dixie).

A sharp, quick player with an explosive turn of speed and a natural instinct for goals, Alfie played his schoolboy football with St Joseph's before joining Waterford in 1957. He had a brief spell with Cork Hibernians the following season and then returned to his hometown club in 1958 where he ended the 1958–59 season as the club's top scorer, with 18 goals.

As a Waterford player, Hale won inter-League honours and was in the Irish Olympic side which defeated Holland 6–3 in 1960. That Olympic qualifying game turned out to be Hale's passport to League football. His contribution to Ireland's success – a hat-trick – was witnessed by Aston Villa boss Joe Mercer, who signed Hale for £4,500 in June 1960.

Alfie had been brought in as a replacement for Italy-bound Gerry Hitchens, but his progress was hampered by injuries and he scored just once in five League games before his £3,500 transfer to Doncaster Rovers in July 1962.

He scored 42 goals in 119 League appearances for Rovers before moving to their Fourth Division rivals Newport County in a straight swap deal for Lawrie Sheffield in August 1965.

Alfie had just one season at Newport, missing three months of it through injury, though he managed to score 21 goals in 34 games. In 1966 he left Newport to return to Waterford in a £3,500 deal.

Hale helped the Blues to five League of Ireland titles, and though he missed most of the 1969–70 season through injury, he returned to score 12 goals in 13 games to help the club secure their third successive League Championship.

In 1973 he moved to Cork Celtic for a £3,000 fee, winning another Championship medal in his first season. Thereafter he had spells with St Patrick's Athletic and Limerick before retiring. He made a brief comeback in 1981–82 when, as manager of Thurles Town, he scored once to earn the distinction of having scored in four decades – the '50s, '60s, '70s and '80s.

In January 1990 he became manager of Waterford United, the club which replaced Waterford FC in the League of Ireland.

A player who scored persistently with his head – no mean feat for a man of just 5ft 6in – Alfie was a former Eire Amateur international. He was capped 13 times at senior level in a nine and a half year full international career which began against Austria in April 1962 and ended against the same opposition in October 1971.

His two international goals were both late strikes which earned Ireland draws against Poland in May 1968 (he scored in the 89th minute) and against Austria in November 1968 when he equalised with just five minutes remaining.

Tommy had seven successful seasons as a Shamrock Rovers player. His career at Milltown got off to a blistering start in 1955–56 when he was an FAI Cup winner, scoring in Rovers' 3–2 final victory over Cork Athletic. The next season, 1956–57, the Hoops won the League Championship, and Hamilton topped the club's scoring charts with 15 goals. He netted a further four goals when Rovers won the title again in 1958–59.

In 1962, just before that season's FAI Cup semi-final, he was dropped from the team, but an injury to Tony Byrne let him back in and he helped bring about Rovers' Cup success, scoring twice in the 4–1 defeat of Shelbourne in the final. For his efforts he was presented with the 'Soccer Personality of the Year' award.

He played in the 1963 Cup final, again lining up against Shelbourne, but this time he was wearing the colours of Cork Hibs and finished on the losing side. He had three seasons with the Cork club before transferring to their Munster rivals Limerick in 1965.

As with his previous two clubs Hamilton reached the FAI Cup final. In 1966 he lined up for Limerick against his former employers, Shamrock Rovers. Once again the trophy found its way to the capital as Rovers won the tie 2–0.

Tommy won two full caps for Eire, both European Championship games against Czechoslovakia, in April and May 1959, which resulted in wins for the home sides in Dublin and Bratislava. In September 1960 he scored both Irish goals in the Irish 'B' team's 2–1 defeat of Iceland at Dalymount Park.

Thomas Hamilton (MIDFIELD)

Born: Dublin
Debut for Eire: v Czechoslovakia April 1959

A cool player who could control the pace of a game, Tommy Hamilton's style was effortless yet masterful.

Eoin Hand (DEFENDER)

Born: Dublin 30 March 1946
Debut for Eire: v Czechoslovakia October 1969

Eoin Hand was one of the many players who played their junior football with Dublin's Stella

Maris club before going on to achieve international honours.

Hand signed for Swindon Town shortly after his 17th birthday but was released a year later without getting a first-team game and returned to Ireland.

He turned out initially for Dundalk, and then for Drumcondra in his native Dublin. He was the Drums' leading scorer in each of his two seasons with the club.

During his time in Ireland Eoin was chosen to represent the League of Ireland against the Scottish League. It was his inclusion in the Irish side as a defender, and not in his normal striking role, that signalled a dramatic change in his fortunes. In October 1968 Portsmouth paid Drumcondra £5,000 to take him back to England.

He had two spells with Pompey: from 1968 to 1975 and – after a stint in South Africa – in 1977–78. Although performing in various roles for the Fratton Park club during his 277 League appearances, Hand was generally recognised as a strong and determined defender who gave everything for 90 minutes.

Hand returned to Ireland in 1973 and took over as player-manager of Limerick United. Reverting to his former forward role, he scored 11 goals in Limerick's League Championship success in 1979–80. He was a winner again in 1982 when Limerick won the FAI Cup for the only time in their history.

Thereafter he coached in Saudi Arabia and managed St Patrick's Athletic. In June 1988 he was appointed manager of Third Division Huddersfield, a post he vacated 'by mutual consent' in March 1992.

While a Portsmouth player, Eoin was capped 20 times by the Republic. He scored two goals for Ireland and left the international arena after Ireland's 4–0 European Championship victory over Turkey in Dublin in October 1975. He was appointed national team boss in 1980, a post he vacated in 1985 to make way for Jack Charlton.

Eoin Hand

Ian Harte (MIDFIELD)

Born: Drogheda, Co. Louth 31 August 1977
Debut for Eire: v Croatia June 1996

Mature beyond his years, Ian Harte has huge potential as a player. He was a regular in Ireland's Under-16 side before his transfer from St Kevin's to Leeds United. And he can play as a defender, wing-back or even in midfield.

Ian made his senior debut for Leeds in the League Cup tie against Reading in January 1996 and had made just four League appearances for Leeds to the end of 1995–96.

In June 1996 he became the tenth new player to be capped in Mick McCarthy's first four games as national team manager. Harte was a half-time replacement for Terry Phelan in the 2–2 draw with Croatia in June 1996. He was the 'baby' in McCarthy's side in the summer friendlies of 1996, as his uncle Gary Kelly was in the World Cup finals in the USA two years earlier. Harte has won six caps and has scored two international goals – in the 3–0 defeat of Bolivia in June 1996, Ireland's first victory under new boss Mick McCarthy and in the 5–0 demolition of Liechtenstein in August 1996.

James Hartnett (OUTSIDE-LEFT)

Born: Dublin 21 March 1927
Debut for Eire: v Spain June 1949

An agile, exceptionally fast and eager player, Jim Hartnett 'overcame a lack of inches with delightful ball skills and perfect timing'.

He began his career in the League of Ireland with Dundalk and soon showed signs that he had the makings of a top class pro. After spending time in the club's reserves, he replaced Joe O'Brien in the first XI.

Hartnett spent less than a season at Oriel Park. In June 1948 he became the fifth Dundalk player to cross the Channel within 15 months, when he signed for First Division Middlesbrough for a 'substantial' fee.

In half a dozen seasons at Ayresome Park, James managed just 48 League games (eight goals). He dropped out of the League game in 1954 and joined Welsh club Barry Town.

Hartlepool United gave him another chance at League level when they signed him in September 1957. But he scored just once in seven League games for the Division Three (North) club, and then was transferred to his final League club York City in August 1958.

James spent most of his one season at Bootham Crescent in the reserves, and when he was released at the end of it, he had made just two League appearances and scored one goal.

There was some surprise in April 1948 when Hartnett was chosen at outside-left in the League of Ireland side to face the Scottish League: he was thought to be on the small side and lacking experience. Nevertheless he showed up well in the game and won his first full cap in the 1–4 defeat by Spain at home in June 1949.

Almost five years later, in March 1954, he got his second and final call-up, for the World Cup qualifier against Luxembourg at the Municipal Stadium in Luxembourg. An inexperienced Irish side, containing six debutants, won the game 1–0.

Joseph Haverty (OUTSIDE-LEFT)

Born: Dublin 17 February 1936
Debut for Eire: v Holland May 1956

Standing only 5ft 3in and weighing under 10st, Joe Haverty was one of the smallest players in the Football League in the '50s and '60s. The little man with the big heart learnt his trade with Home Farm and St Patrick's Athletic in the League of Ireland. He was introduced to the Football League by Arsenal in July 1954, two months after collecting an FAI Cup runners-up medal with St Pat's.

A rapid whippet of an outside-left, Joe delighted in twisting, turning and leaving defenders – who invariably towered over him – in his wake. Some, however, did not appreciate his nifty footwork, and Joe often paid for his cheeky skills with long spells on the treatment table, which kept him out of the frame for long periods. Consequently his six seasons at Highbury produced only 114 League games (25 goals) before his £17,500 transfer to Arsenal's First Division adversaries Blackburn Rovers in July 1961.

Haverty was at Ewood Park for less than a season when he lost his place to Michael Harrison, who had just arrived from Chelsea. Thus, in September 1963, after just 27 games (one goal) Joe was on his way back to the capital to play for Division Four champions Millwall.

Joe enjoyed his time at the Den. He had lost none of his intricate skills and ran rings around the Third Division defences. In two seasons there, he represented Millwall 68 times in League duels.

December 1964 saw Haverty on his way to his fourth and final League club – Third Division Bristol Rovers for whom he appeared on only 13 occasions – before joining Glasgow Celtic for one game, and then returning to Ireland to play for Shelbourne in the summer of 1965.

Joe's reputation as one of football's great nomads was increased with his move to American club Chicago Spurs after just two years with Shelbourne.

One of the most popular figures in the game in the '60s, Joe Haverty was capped at every club he played with and was Ireland's regular outside-left between 1956 and 1966.

The perfect inheritor of Tommy Eglington's number 11 shirt, Joe made his international debut in the 4–1 victory over Holland in Rotterdam in May 1956, marking the event with a spectacular scissors-kick goal. Joe made 32 appearances (three goals) for Ireland, the last one in the 2–0 defeat by Spain in Valencia in December 1966.

He now helps Arsenal's chief Irish scout Bill Darby in the search for new talent for Highbury.

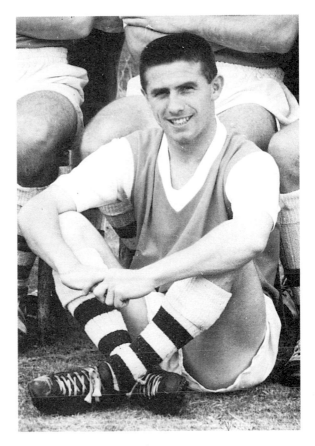

Joseph Haverty

Austin Hayes (WINGER)

Born: Hammersmith, London 15 July 1958
Debut for Eire: v Denmark May 1979

Described as a tricky, but sometimes frustrating flanksman, Austin Hayes could conjure up a goal out of nothing.

Hayes was an apprentice at Southampton and agreed professional terms with the Second Division club in July 1976. He was not a regular in the team and in four seasons at the Dell he managed just 31 League games (five goals). But he will be remembered at the club – he swung on a crossbar and broke it, which caused a reserve team game to be abandoned.

In February 1981 he was transferred to Millwall for £25,000. He was a popular player at the Den and in two seasons there he scored five goals in 47 Third Division games.

Austin joined Northampton Town on a free transfer in August 1983. He was a regular in his two seasons at the club and had made 63 Fourth Division appearances (13 goals) when he was released, with seven other players, after Graham Carr became manager in 1985.

When his League career ended, Austin spent brief spells with Barnet and in Swedish soccer.

Capped five times by the Republic at Under-21 level between 1978 and 1980,

Austin won one full cap. It came in the 2–0 European Championship qualifier victory over Denmark in Dublin in May 1979. He received a booking in the game and was substituted after an hour.

Austin Hayes was just 28 when he lost his battle against lung cancer in a London hospital on 2 February 1986.

William E. Hayes (FULL-BACK)

Born: Cork 7 November 1915
Debut for Eire: v England September 1946

Cork born but Sheffield raised, Billy Hayes represented England Schoolboys as a youngster. He was turning out for Sheffield St Vincents in June 1932, when Huddersfield Town took him on as an amateur.

Hayes signed professional terms with Huddersfield in April 1933 and made his League debut in August of that year. He went on to become the club's longest-serving player, spending 18 years at Leeds Road, in a career which straddled the war.

He had made 181 First Division appearances and had scored five goals by January 1950 when he suffered an injury, which allowed fellow Irishman Charlie Gallogly into the side. Hayes didn't play for Town's first team again. He was transfer-listed in August 1949, but was given a new contract the following month.

While at Huddersfield, Billy was living in Accrington and training at Burnley's Turf Moor ground and so it was no surprise when, in February 1950, he signed for the First Division club. At 34, however, his career was all but over, and he was released by Burnley in May 1952 after a dozen League outings.

Billy played four times for Northern Ireland in the 1937–1938 and 1938–1939 Home International Championships and played twice for Eire in defeats by England in September 1946 and Portugal in May 1947.

The winner of the Professional Footballers' Golf Tournament in 1949, Billy went into business in Accrington, running his own garage when his playing days ended.

He died on 22 April 1987.

William J. Hayes (GOALKEEPER)

Born: Limerick 30 March 1928
Debut for Eire: v Belgium April 1949

Bill Hayes joined Wrexham from Limerick in July 1950. He made just 14 appearances in Division Three (North) before dropping out of League football.

He was playing for non-League Ellesmere Port in August 1952 when Third Division (South) club Torquay United gave him another chance at League level.

Hayes made his debut for the Gulls against Coventry City in December 1952 and had the unenviable task of retrieving the ball seven times from his own net in the 7–2 away defeat. He did not play again until the last 12 games of that 1952–53 season when he established himself as a first-team regular.

A brave and athletic keeper, if somewhat small at 5ft 9in, Bill held the number 1 slot for most of the following season. He remained at the club for a further two seasons but played few games. His final game for the club was in March 1956.

Bill later played for local West Country non-League sides before retiring. He still lives in Torquay.

A former League of Ireland representative player, Bill won Amateur international honours and became Ireland's fifth post-war keeper when he took his position between the sticks for his one full cap in the 2–0 defeat by Belgium in Dublin in April 1949.

Ronald Healey (GOALKEEPER)

Born: Manchester 30 August 1952
Debut for Eire: v Poland April 1977

A former Manchester Boys' representative player, Ron Healey joined Manchester City as an amateur in November 1966, he became an apprentice two years later and signed full professional terms with the club in October 1969.

Ron, who stood just under 6ft, was understudy to England international goalkeeper Joe Corrigan at Maine Road. Opportunities for the Irishman to demonstrate his skills were thus limited and in almost four seasons at the club he played in only 30 First Division fixtures.

Healey gained valuable experience, however, during several loan spells in the period. In October 1969 he was loaned to non-League Altrincham; Coventry City (December 1971, three appearances) and Preston North End (December 1973, six appearances).

In March 1974 he was loaned to Cardiff City, a move made permanent in a £15,000 transfer deal two months later. He became the Welsh club's first-choice custodian for five seasons – after Bill Irwin retired in 1977 – during which he made 216 League appearances and helped them win promotion back to Division Two in 1975–76 following their relegation the previous year.

Injury cut short his career and he retired in 1982 whereupon he moved back to Manchester and worked at the local airport.

While a Cardiff player, Ron won two full Eire caps. Although he kept a clean sheet on his debut against Poland in April 1977, it was three years before he guarded the Irish goal again. In February 1980 he replaced the injured Gerry Peyton in the European Championship qualifier against England for his final 30 minutes of international football.

Steven Heighway (WINGER)

Born: Dublin 25 November 1947
Debut for Eire: v Poland September 1970

One of the most bemedalled players in Irish football history (only Ronnie Whelan could hope to compete), Steve Heighway picked up practically every honour the game has to offer in ten glittering years at Anfield.

The mercurial wing wizard helped Liverpool to European Cup success in 1977 and 1978 after victories over Moenchengladbach and FC Bruges respectively. The same teams provided the opposition in 1973 and 1976 when Liverpool won the UEFA Cup. Four First Division winners medals were added to Steve's collection in 1973, 1976, 1977 and 1979; an FA Cup

Steven Heighway

winners medal in 1974 when he scored in the 3–0 defeat of Newcastle United; and FA Cup runners-up medals in 1971, when he scored Liverpool's only goal in the 2–1 defeat by Arsenal, and 1977, after a similar defeat by Manchester United. He collected another runners-up medal in 1978 after Liverpool lost the League Cup final to Nottingham Forest.

A one-club player, Heighway joined the playing staff at Anfield as an amateur in early 1970, turning professional in May of that year, having previously been an amateur at Manchester City and Skelmersdale United.

Renowned for his athleticism, electrifying speed and intelligent football, Steve, who became known as 'Big Bamber' at Anfield, played a major role in Liverpool's emergence under Bill Shankly in the '70s as the dominant force in not only British but also European football. He proved a match-winner with his lightning forays down the flank, side-stepping tackles and swerving every which way to provide ample ammunition for the Liverpool forwards of the day, as well as knocking in 50 League goals himself.

In 1981, after 329 League appearances, he jetted off to America to join Minnesota Kicks where he shimmied, darted and dashed in his own inimitable style for three seasons before becoming a coach and guiding the American Under-19 team to the last 16 of the Junior World Cup.

When the position of youth development officer at Anfield became available in 1988, Steve jumped at the chance to return to his spiritual home. His experience with the youngsters in the USA and his inside knowledge of the 'Liverpool way' made him the obvious choice for the job. He later became youth team manager and led his young charges to success in the FA Youth Cup in 1996.

Steve, who was born in Dublin, did not see a game of football until he moved to England with his English parents at the age of ten. A BA (Econs) graduate from Warwick University, Steve represented Cheshire, England Grammar Schools and the English Universities as a junior.

But then he rejected the country of his parents to play his international football for the country of his birth.

He became idolised in Ireland as the South's George Best and won his first full cap in the 2–0 home defeat by Poland in September 1970 before he made his League debut for Liverpool. He went on to represent Ireland a further 33 times. His 34-cap total would have been much higher had it not been for Liverpool's immense success at home and abroad, which meant he wasn't always available for international fixtures.

Steve, who made his last appearance for Ireland in the 2–2 draw with Holland in September 1981 while on the books of Minnesota Kicks, incredibly never managed to find the net at international level.

Bernard Henderson (OUTSIDE-RIGHT)

Born: Dublin
Debut for Eire: v Portugal May 1948

In ten seasons with Drumcondra, from 1945 to 1955, the enigmatic Benny Henderson scored 46 League goals, won two League of Ireland Championship medals (1947–48 and 1948–49) and played in four FAI Cup finals.

Reputedly the tallest winger in the League of Ireland, Henderson played with St Paul's, Bohemians, Transport and Ierne before moving to Drumcondra. A former employee of Messrs Alex Findlater and Co., he was equally at home on either wing and possessed one of the strongest shots in the League.

Benny was described as unpredictable – 'no one ever knows what he'll do with the ball when he gets it'. But he was one of the greatest match-winners Dublin has known: 'The parts he played in four Cup finals are known the countryside over.'

In 1946 he scored the winner in Drums' 2–1 FAI Cup final victory over Shamrock Rovers. Two years later he netted the consolation goal but missed a last-minute penalty as Rovers reversed the 1946 scoreline. In 1954 he was a winner again when Drums beat St Patrick's Athletic. Old acquaintances were renewed the following year, for Drumcondra and Shamrock Rovers lined up for the final: Rovers won 1–0.

Henderson, who later played for Dundalk, was a League of Ireland player. 'For everyone who agrees with the selection of Henderson for the League at outside left another will be found to disagree.'

In May 1948 he scored twice and made two goals in the League of Ireland's 5–2 defeat of the Defence Forces, and was voted 'Man of the Match'. The following day he was named in the Irish squad for the Iberian tour of May 1948 on which he won caps against Portugal and Spain.

John (Jackie) Hennessy

(WING-HALF/INSIDE-FORWARD)

Born: Dublin
Debut for Eire: v Poland October 1964

The description 'appears to be a defensively minded player but has a great flair for attacking when he puts his mind to it' captures the essence of Jackie Hennessy.

In nine seasons with Shelbourne, wing-half Hennessy scored 39 goals, won FAI Cup winners medals in 1960 and 1963 (beating Cork Hibs on both occasions), a runners-up medal in 1962 and a League Championship medal in 1961–62. He was at St Patrick's Athletic when he won his second FAI Cup runners-up medal in 1967 (losing to Shamrock Rovers).

Jackie had a brief spell in 1966 in the Irish League with Derry City, but when he became unsettled, his old Shelbourne mentor and then St Pat's boss Gerry Doyle stepped in and signed him. And Hennessy became the rock on which the opposition perished.

Although Jackie preferred an orthodox wing-half role, he had the attributes of a sweeper: moving forward and setting up attacks. 'Most wing halves love the opportunity to attack, to flow with sudden power through the opposition defences. It's eye-catching crowd-pleasing stuff but there is always someone who must stay at "home" to mind the "house". And Jackie has always been at his best playing back.' After a few runs at inside-forward, Jackie was sent 'home' and was put into a sweeper role. His calm, unhurried approach and pin-point passing were credited with bringing glamour to the role of sweeper.

In September 1960, again playing a forward role, Hennessy scored both Irish goals in the 2–1 defeat of Iceland in a 'B' international. He won his first full cap, once more as a forward, in the 3–2 home victory over Poland in October 1964. Four years later, in November 1968, he won his fifth and final cap in the 2–2 draw with Austria.

John Herrick (DEFENDER)

Born: Cork 1947
Debut for Eire: v Austria October 1971

John Herrick joined his local League of Ireland side Cork Hibernians from junior club Glasheen when he was 17.

The 'iron hard yet poised defender' became a full-time pro in 1970–71. He said, 'It really paid dividends.' It certainly did, for Hibs won the League of Ireland Championship that year. He returned to part-time status in 1971–72 when he took up employment with the Cork sports firm of B.J. Roche. At the end of that season he won an FAI Cup winners medal when Miah Dennehy's hat-trick saw off the challenge of Waterford in the final.

John was lost to the game for a period, but in November 1976 he was persuaded to return by Limerick boss Frank Johnson. He contributed in a big way to the Shannonsiders' revival. In April 1977 he was an FAI Cup runner-up with Limerick and became the first Limerick player to be selected as the Irish Soccer Writers' 'Player of the Month'.

Herrick produced a 'brilliant display' in the League of Ireland Golden Jubilee game in 1971 and was a member of the All-Ireland select which played Leeds United the same year.

After just two games for the inter-League team, his 'long overdue' call-up to the full international scene came in October 1971 when he was selected for the game against Austria. He became the first Hibs player to be capped; several players had been capped before or after they had played for the club but none whilst they were actually in Hibs' colours. John took his international appearance tally to three against Chile and France in June and November 1972, replacing Birmingham's Tommy Carroll on both occasions.

James Higgins (FORWARD)

Born: Dublin 3 February 1926
Debut for Eire: v Argentina May 1951

Jim Higgins started out as a junior with Home Farm in his native Dublin. His reputation as a prolific striker was such that he was called upon sometimes to play on both Saturday and Sunday for the club's 'A' and 'B' sides.

Higgins joined Dundalk in 1947, and though he wasn't a regular in the club's League side in his first season, he made an impression. 'In his first season in the League of Ireland, Higgins has shown in his few matches that in addition to being a clever player he is an opportunist and a goal scorer.' In November 1949, with his Dundalk team-mate Eddie O'Hara, Higgins was transferred to Birmingham City.

Described as 'something of a tearaway with a bustling style', Higgins was drafted straight into the Blues' First Division side. But his

arrival came too late to prevent the club's relegation at the end of that 1949–50 season.

Jim scored a dozen goals in 50 League outings with Birmingham but will be best remembered for his 45th-minute second goal against Manchester United in the quarter-final of the FA Cup in February 1951, which took the Blues into the semi-final.

He departed for non-League Hereford United in July 1953 but returned to Dundalk a year later.

Jim won his only Eire cap while at Birmingham, in the 1–0 defeat by Argentina in Dublin in May 1951.

James Holmes (DEFENDER)

Born: Dublin 11 November 1953
Debut for Eire: v Austria May 1971

A former Eire Youth international, Jimmy Holmes became the Republic's youngest full international when he took the field as a substitute in the European Championship match against Austria in May 1971. He was just 17 years and 200 days old and had yet to feature in the first team at Coventry City, the club he had joined as an apprentice in November 1970 in preference to several other Division One clubs.

It was to be 18 months before he pulled on the green shirt again. He held on to it this time and over the next nine years he took his total to 30 caps.

Jimmy would surely have added to that tally had he not suffered a particularly badly broken leg against Bulgaria in May 1979, in his 29th – and 21st consecutive – appearance for Ireland. The injury all but wrecked his career and he won just one more international call-up. In August 1985 he was rewarded with a testimonial in which an Irish XI took on and beat Glenn Hoddle's International XI 2–1 at Dalymount Park.

Soon after his first international appearance,

Coventry gave Jimmy his first taste of League football. In the following five years at Highfield Road, he turned out for the Sky Blues on 130 occasions in the First Division.

Jimmy left Coventry for Spurs in a £100,000 transfer deal towards the end of the 1976–77 League campaign, a season in which the north Londoners were relegated to Division Two. Holmes was on hand the following season, however, to help Spurs regain their place among the élite.

After 81 appearances in a Spurs jersey Jimmy left White Hart Lane for Vancouver Whitecaps in the North American Soccer League. He subsequently played for Leicester City (twice) and made four appearances for Brentford in the early part of 1983. From Griffin Park he moved to Torquay United where in two seasons he made 25 League appearances. Then, he departed for Peterborough where he was assistant manager until his contract was cancelled in November 1985 after 49 League appearances.

Thereafter he managed Beazer Homes League side Bedford United and now serves in the police force in the Midlands.

Raymond Houghton (MIDFIELD)

Born: Glasgow 9 January 1962
Debut for Eire: v Wales March 1986

When Ray Houghton joined Aston Villa from Liverpool for £900,000 in July 1992, Villa boss Ron Atkinson described him as 'the best right-sided midfielder in the country'. Houghton had come a long way since being rejected at 17 by Scotland manager Andy Roxbrough as not good enough to make the grade at international level and by West Ham boss John Lyall, who gave him a free transfer after just one game in 1982.

In the intervening years Ray won every honour the domestic game has to offer, went to the finals of three major championships with

the Republic of Ireland – the country of his father's birth – and has so far won 67 full caps . . . Not bad for a double reject.

Born in Glasgow, Ray moved with his family to London in 1972 when he was ten. He joined West Ham United as a junior, signing professionally for the club in July 1979. Exactly three years later, and with just one substitute appearance to his credit, he was released. Malcolm McDonald, then manager at Second Division Fulham, snapped him up immediately.

In three seasons at Craven Cottage, Houghton made 129 League appearances and scored 16 goals. In September 1985 he moved to ambitious Oxford United for £125,000. In the previous two seasons Oxford had won the Third and Second Division titles.

He played 83 League games for Oxford and helped them win the first major trophy in their 24-year League history by scoring in the 3–0 League Cup final victory over QPR in 1986.

Ray's move to Oxford had a profound effect on his career. At the Manor Ground he linked up with his future Irish international colleague John Aldridge – the man whom Jack Charlton had come to check out when he spotted the quick, aggressive, skilful and competitive Glasgow-born midfielder with a Co. Donegal-born father. Ray was immediately recruited to the Irish cause. With every appearance for Ireland his value soared on the transfer market until it peaked at £900,000 – the fee Villa paid Liverpool in 1992.

In October 1987 Houghton moved from Oxford to Liverpool for £825,000. He had five glittering seasons on Merseyside during which he made 153 League appearances and scored 28 goals. He appeared in three FA Cup finals with Liverpool, losing 1–0 to Wimbledon in 1988 and collecting winners medals after beating Everton in 1989 and Sunderland in 1992. He added League Championship winners medals to his collection in 1987–88 and 1989–90, and runners-up medals in 1988–89 and 1990–91.

In 1992–93 Ray was a League Championship runner-up once again but by then he had swapped the red of Liverpool for the claret and blue of Aston Villa. He was a non-playing substitute when Villa beat Manchester United in the 1994 League Cup final. Ray had scored six goals in 95 Premiership games for Villa when he was transferred to Crystal Palace for £300,000 in March 1995. He was signed too late, however, to halt the club's drop into Division One.

Houghton did his best to earn the Eagles a quick return to the top flight in 1995–96. He scored the goal against Charlton which booked Palace a place in the Division One play-off. A Leicester City winner seconds from the end of extra time in the final condemned the Londoners to another season in Division One. To the end of the 1995–96 season Ray had scored six goals in 51 League games for the Eagles.

Ray is a fine all-round midfielder who can dribble, pass accurately and shoot powerfully, and whose consistency and commitment are unquestionable. A player who seems to get stronger as the game progresses, he has become a valuable asset to the Irish team and fitted well into Jack Charlton's scheme of things.

He made his debut in Charlton's first game in charge and has been a regular on the right side of the Republic's midfield ever since. Ray has scored five times for Ireland, two of which rank as the most important goals in Irish football history. His dramatic winners against England in the 1988 European Championship finals and against Italy in the 1994 World Cup finals gave the Republic their only outright victories in the finals of major championships.

Gary Howlett (MIDFIELD)

Born: Dublin 2 April 1963
Debut for Eire: v China June 1984

Gary Howlett began his career in the League of Ireland with Home Farm before crossing the channel to serve his apprenticeship with Coventry City. He signed professionally for the Sky Blues in November 1980. Having failed to break into Coventry's League side, he was transferred to Brighton and Hove Albion 19 months later.

Gary scored for Brighton on his First Division debut against Liverpool in March 1983 and a few months later was in the Seagulls' sides which drew 2–2 with Manchester United in the FA Cup final but lost the replay 4–0. To make matters worse they were relegated at the end of that 1982–83 season.

In December 1984, after 32 League games for the Seagulls, Howlett was transferred to AFC Bournemouth, for whom he played 60 League games and won a Third Division Championship medal in 1986–87.

He joined York City in January 1988 after loan spells with Aldershot (August 1987, one appearance) and Chester City (December 1987, six appearances).

After initial injury problems, Gary established himself in York's Fourth Division side. He had scored 13 goals in 101 games for the club when his contract was cancelled in February 1991 whereupon he returned to the League of Ireland to join Dublin club Shelbourne.

In the summer of 1992 he had a delicate operation to rebuild his ankle and he was in pain for weeks. He missed Shelbourne's victory over Dundalk in the 1993 FAI Cup final after another operation on the same ankle and was left out of the side which lost to Derry in the 1995 decider. The jinx struck again in 1996 when he missed the Cup final through an ankle injury. The irony of the situation was not lost on Howlett. He had got into the Brighton side for the 1983 FA Cup run only after former Bohemians player Gerry Ryan had broken his leg.

An intelligent and skilful midfielder, Gary represented Ireland at Under-15 and Youth levels. He won four Under-21 caps in 1982–83 and one full cap in the 1–0 victory over China in the semi-final of the Japan Cup in Sapporo in June 1984.

Christopher Hughton (LEFT-BACK)

Born: London 11 December 1958
Debut for Eire: v USA October 1979

A credit to both club and country, Chris Hughton is widely respected as one of the game's most articulate and finest ambassadors.

Chris joined Tottenham Hotspur when he was 13 years old, in 1972. It was the beginning of a relationship between player and club which spanned more than two decades.

The diminutive defender became a part-time professional at White Hart Lane in June 1977 after completing a four-year apprenticeship as a lift engineer, and made his League debut two years later, in September 1979. Over the next ten years Chris took his League appearance tally with Spurs to 297.

Hughton was a cup winner with Spurs on three occasions in the early 1980s. He picked up FA Cup winners medals in 1981 and 1982 after victories in replayed finals over Manchester City and Queen's Park Rangers. He added another winners medal to his collection when Spurs beat Anderlecht on penalties in the 1984 UEFA Cup final. The only runners-up medal of his career came in 1982 when Tottenham lost that year's League Cup final 3–1 to Liverpool.

Hughton lost his place in the Spurs side in 1989 after a hernia operation. A year later, in October 1990, he returned to his roots in London's East End by joining Second Division West Ham United on loan. Two months later he joined the Upton Park club permanently.

He made 33 League appearances for the Hammers and played a key role in the club's 1990–91 promotion-winning season, before joining Brentford on a free transfer in February 1992.

He played 13 games in the Bees' Third Division Championship winning season in 1991–92 and had made a total of 32 League appearances for the Griffin Park club before leaving the game in April 1992, at the age of 34, because of recurrent knee problems.

Christopher Hughton

Chris, who holds an FA coaching badge, returned to his Alma Mater in June 1993, when new Spurs boss Ossie Ardiles appointed him youth team coach. He is now reserve team manager at the club.

Hughton qualified to represent Ireland through his Limerick-born mother and made history in 1979 by becoming the first black player to represent Ireland.

His pace, competitiveness and resolute defensive qualities endeared him to the Irish fans and he became an integral part of the Irish set-up for over ten years, claiming the Irish number 3 shirt for his own and winning 53 full caps.

He played in all of Ireland's European Championship games in Germany in 1988 and scored his only international goal in

Ireland's 6–0 rout of Cyprus in November 1980. Chris still maintains the link with Ireland as the patron of the London branch of the Republic of Ireland Supporters' Club. He was given a testimonial in June 1995 in which a Premiership XI played the Republic of Ireland.

Charles Hurley (CENTRE-HALF)

Born: Cork 4 October 1936
Debut for Eire: v England May 1957

A typical old-style, dominating centre-back, Charlie Hurley gained a reputation for getting among the goals. Good in the air and comfortable in possession, he relished getting forward and at his peak in the early 1960s he was reckoned by many football writers to be the best centre-half in Britain.

Indeed the Charlie Hurley legend is alive and well today in the minds of many who witnessed his unique style. One renowned pundit of the modern era, Michael Parkinson, had this to say of the great man: 'Remember Charlie Hurley of Sunderland? He could play a bit. He used to give his supporters and team-mates palpitations by dribbling the ball out of the tightest situations. I saw him at Barnsley beat three attackers in his own penalty area and then float a perfect pass out of defence, but not before he first flicked the ball on to his head and down to his instep as if he was centre stage at the London Palladium.'

Charlie was born in Cork and moved to Rainham in Essex when he was ten. He was spotted by Millwall scout Bill Voisey whilst playing with Rainham Youth Centre and signed amateur forms with the club. He had also played for West Ham's colts team and had trials with Arsenal, but neither club took him on.

In October 1953, Charlie signed as a professional for Millwall, who were playing in Division Three (South). He made his League debut in 1954 when he was 17, ousting fellow Irishman Gerry Bowler from the side. He held on to his place in the team for four seasons, during which he became something of a folk hero at the Den. He made a total of 105 League appearances for the Lions, and then, in September 1957, Sunderland paid £20,000 to entice him to Roker Park.

At the end of Hurley's first season at Roker Park, Sunderland were relegated from Division One for the first time in their 79-year history. Over the next six seasons Ireland's Charlie Hurley became the bedrock on which Sunderland rebuilt their team for their return to the top flight; their goal was finally achieved in 1963–64.

In June 1969, after 11 seasons and a record 356 League games for the Rokerites, Charlie joined Second Division Bolton Wanderers as player-manager. He made 42 League appearances for Bolton before his appointment as manager of Fourth Division Reading in 1972, a post he held until 1977.

Charlie – a Sunderland man through and through – was held in high regard by the Roker Park faithful and that sentiment has not been diluted by the passing years, as is aptly illustrated by the following quote from the recently published *Sunderland Greats*: 'constructed entirely from pre-cast concrete, Charlie Hurley is without doubt the greatest human being to have ever lived. . . . He often played when fatally injured with his head missing!'

A commanding figure in every way, Charlie made his international debut in the 1–1 draw with England in May 1957. He was chosen to represent his country in a further 39 internationals over the next 12 years.

He scored twice for Ireland and was captain in 21 games. For his final three internationals in 1968–69, he combined the positions of captain and coach until Mick Meagan was appointed Ireland's first official manager in September 1969.

Denis Irwin (FULL-BACK)

Born: Cork 31 October 1965
Debut for Eire: v Morocco September 1990

The only Irishman in Manchester United's Premier League-winning side in 1992–93, Denis Irwin has become one of the finest full-backs in the game and has collected a host of major honours since being freed by Leeds United in 1986.

Denis began his League career as an apprentice with Second Division Leeds, turning professional in October 1983. He had made 92 League appearances for the Elland Road club before being released. Leeds thought Irwin wasn't aggressive enough: Oldham Athletic thought differently. In May 1986 Oldham manager Joe Royle stepped in to sign Irwin, ahead of Chesterfield.

At Oldham, under the guidance of Royle, Irwin matured into a cool and classy full-back. 'Because he's so quiet people assume he's a soft touch – but Denis can stand his corner with any opponent,' said Royle.

Denis made 167 League appearances for the Latics; moreover, his outstanding performances in Oldham's epic FA Cup semi-final battles with Manchester United in 1990 were the turning-point in his career.

Just three months after those games Irwin made the short journey down the M1 to Old Trafford in a £700,000 deal. Signed initially as a right-back, Denis was moved to left-back to make room for newcomer and England international right-back Paul Parker.

Irwin responded magnificently and his strong attacking instincts, allied to pin-point crossing, played no small part in Manchester United's elevation to the 'most successful club in the country' in the '90s.

In his first season at the club Denis collected a European Cup-Winners' Cup winners medal after United overcame Barcelona 2–1 in the 1991 final. The same year he was in the United side which defeated European Cup holders Red Star Belgrade 1–0

Denis Irwin

to lift the European Super Cup.

In 1992 Irwin appeared in his third successive League Cup final. He had been on the losing side of 1–0 defeats in 1990 for Oldham against Nottingham Forest and in 1991 for United against Sheffield Wednesday. It all came right in 1992, however, as another 1–0 victory, against Forest, was enough for United to lift the trophy for the first time in their history.

That impressive array of honours paled into relative insignificance, as United pursued their Holy Grail – the League Championship. They finally achieved the goal that had eluded them for so long when they lifted the inaugural FA Premier League title in 1993.

Denis Irwin's role in that success must not be underestimated. He missed just two League games all season and, as well as fulfilling his defensive duties manfully, he doubled as a flying winger, supplying sufficient ammunition for the forward line to feed off. His performances in the crucial run in after Easter earned him lavish praise from those around him, players and fans alike; the tougher the going became, the better Irwin performed. Furthermore he weighed in with some spectacular goals. The one at Coventry in April was both spectacular and crucial: a 30-yard piledriver which earned the three points and blasted United into pole position from which they never looked back.

1993–94 proved to be another glittering season for Irwin and Co: United were League Cup runners-up, after losing 3–1 to Aston Villa in the final: moreover they retained their Premiership title and thrashed Chelsea 4–0 in the FA Cup final to become only the fourth side this century to complete the double.

Denis was some people's United 'Player of the Season' in that epic 1993–94 season. As one of the most accomplished defenders in the game, his name was the first, after the keeper, on Alex Ferguson's teamsheet. 'Defensively he's sound, he gets forward superbly to link play, strikes a tremendous ball and delivers crosses that forwards dream about. He's got the lot,' was the manager's assessment of his defender.

The 1994–95 season promised more success, but United slipped up in the title race, finishing second, and were defeated in the Cup final by Everton by a single goal.

Amends were made a year later, for United became the first team in history to achieve the Double double. The Premiership title was secured for the third time in four seasons and Liverpool were beaten 1–0 in the FA Cup final.

To the end of 1995–96 Irwin had accumulated 225 League appearances in a United shirt and scored 14 goals.

Just weeks after his United debut, Denis made his international debut, thereby becoming the first Irishman to achieve the 'full set' of international honours: Schoolboy, Youth, Under-21 (three appearances), Under-23 (one appearance), 'B' (one appearance) and full caps. He became a regular in the international set-up almost immediately,

earning his old club Oldham a £75,000 bonus.

A regular and integral part of the senior Irish side – where he was preferred at right-back until young Gary Kelly burst on to the scene in 1994, whereupon he moved to left-back – Denis won his 42th cap against Macedonia in October 1996.

Rory Keane (FULL-BACK)

Born: Limerick 31 August 1922
Debut for Eire: v Switzerland December 1948

Rory Keane was a tough, traditional defender. His defensive tackles were 'whole-hearted, strong and rugged' and his clearances from defence 'sure, strong and snappy'.

He began his career with his hometown club Limerick in the early 1940s and in June 1947 he was transferred to Swansea Town. Rory was injured in his debut for the Welsh club against Leyton Orient but made a full recovery and was a 'near ever-present' in the team that won promotion to Division Two at the end of 1948–49, as Division Three (South) champions.

In early April 1950 Rory badly fractured his leg. He recovered, but the injury marked the beginning of the end of his League career. Between 1947 and 1954 Rory made a total of 164 League appearances for Swansea.

Keane's full international debut was for Northern Ireland in November 1948 when he partnered Johnny Carey in defence in the 3–2 defeat by Scotland in Glasgow.

He made his Eire debut against Switzerland that December; he came of age in his second outing for the Republic, a 1–0 defeat of Portugal in Dublin in May 1949. One match reporter observed: 'For once in a while Johnny Carey had a very serious rival for the title of "better full-back" and that's not taking away from Carey's ability to say that Keane was outstanding at left-back. He did everything in fine style and on this display will have many more caps coming his way.'

He won two more caps to be exact, against Sweden and Spain in June 1949, bringing his total to four before being succeeded in the team by Luton Town's Bud Aherne.

Roy Keane (MIDFIELD)

Born: Cork 10 August 1971
Debut for Eire: v Chile May 1991

'It's a long time since I've been excited by a young man . . . I'd quite happily have paid £500,000 for him.' That was Nottingham Forest manager Brian Clough's reaction after watching Irish wonder boy Roy Keane play in a reserve team game, just weeks after signing him from Cobh Ramblers for a mere £25,000. Three years later Forest's relegation from the Premier League signalled Keane's availability on the transfer market, which sparked off a scramble for his signature among the country's top clubs, the likes of which was never seen before. The months of speculation ended in June 1993 when he joined Manchester United in a £3.75 million deal.

Keane's rise from the backwoods of Irish soccer to the pinnacle of the English game has been meteoric – forget Roy of the Rovers, Roy of the Ramblers is the stuff that real heroes are made of.

From the Cork suburb of Mayfield, a hotbed of Gaelic football, Roy played the national game as a corner-forward. He also holds the proud record of never having lost a fight as an amateur boxer.

He began his soccer career playing with Ballinderry Park in the local street leagues, later joining Rockmount. There he played as a centre-forward but was forced back into midfield when he stopped growing and was considered too small to lead the attack. His lack of inches also caused difficulty for him at international level: he was selected for Ireland's Under-15, Under-16 and Youth squads but couldn't get into the team because he was too small!

After Rockmount, Keane moved to League of Ireland club Cobh Ramblers where he was spotted by Nottingham Forest's Irish scout Noel McCabe. He was immediately shipped off to the City Ground for a trial, after which he was offered terms.

Just days after performing in front of just over 200 spectators in his last game in Ireland, and after only ten minutes of reserve team football in England, Keane made his debut for Forest against Liverpool at Anfield.

With the lungs of a marathon runner, the guile of a midfield architect in the mould of a Liam Brady, and an instinctive attacking flair from which he conjures up priceless goals in the style of Bryan Robson, Keane took the First Division by storm with his brilliant midfield performances. 'Keane's from a different planet, his runs can be devastating,' was Oldham boss Joe Royle's assessment after watching him play.

In three seasons at the City Ground, Roy made 144 League appearances (22 goals) and went to Wembley three times in less than a year. In 1991 Forest lost the FA Cup final 2–1 to Tottenham Hotspur. They won the ZDS trophy the following March by overcoming Southampton 3–2 in the final tie. And a month later lost the League Cup final 1–0 to Keane's future employers, Manchester United.

Roy's skill, vision, tackling and pace have prompted observers to describe him as the 'best player between the penalty areas in today's game'. Roy Keane most certainly has the world at his feet. A midfield metronome, he combines athleticism with resourceful distribution: he quickly fitted into Manchester United's team and is seen as the ideal replacement for Bryan Robson.

In three seasons at Old Trafford to the end of 1995–96 Keane made 91 League appearances and scored 13 goals.

He was a member of the United side beaten 3–1 by Aston Villa in the 1994 League Cup final, a defeat for which there was adequate compensation in the form of a League and FA Cup double that season.

In 1995 Keane added another runners-up

medal to his collection after the Reds' 1–0 defeat by Everton in the FA Cup final.

In 1995–96 United made history by becoming the first side to win the double of FA Cup and League Championship twice. Keane secured his second Championship medal and was 'Man of the Match' when United beat Liverpool 1–0 in the Cup final.

The Barclay's Young Eagle of the Year for 1991–92, Roy is a former captain of Ireland's Under-21 team for whom he made four appearances.

He made the step up to the senior squad in the 1–1 draw with Chile in May 1991 and has since been an integral component in the Republic's engine-room.

One of only five players to appear in all four of the Republic's World Cup games in the USA, Roy was Ireland's captain for the second half of his 30th international against Russia in March 1996. Ireland lost 2–0 and Keane was sent off. He was appointed captain for Ireland's USA tour in June 1996 but went AWOL and subsequently missed the entire tour.

Michael Kearin (LEFT-HALF)

Born: Dublin
Debut for Eire: Austria October 1971

At his first senior club, Bohemians, Mick Kearin was a centre-forward. But when he became a professional with his move to Shamrock Rovers in 1966, he found himself playing in turn not only in all five forward positions, but also at right- and left-half. No one could say he wasn't adaptable.

He was an industrious little player – 'when he gets a job to do he does it well, always battling to the end'. Be that as it may, the change from amateur to professional status was fraught with difficulties for Kearin and it seemed as if he wasn't fitting in at his new club; that was until he was moved to left-half.

His touch returned; his tigerish tackling and shadowing of an opponent proved invaluable. After a month of trying Kearin had found his niche at Milltown and went on to captain the club.

Kearin was a tremendous success in his new role and helped the Hoops to FAI Cup successes in three successive seasons between 1967 and 1969, scoring in the 4–1 replay victory over Cork Celtic in 1969.

At the end of 1972–73 Mick returned to Bohs briefly before joining Athlone Town the same season.

Mick, who had a 'brilliant display' in the League of Ireland Golden Jubilee game in 1971, had a 'frustrating wait' on the reserves bench for his first international honour. It came in Liam Tuohy's first game in charge of the national team against Austria in October 1971, when the new gaffer's League of Ireland experiment went disastrously wrong; a team

Michael Kearin

consisting of League of Ireland players bar one, were thrashed 6–0 by Austria in Linz. It was to be Kearin's only cap.

Frederick Kearns (CENTRE-FORWARD)

Born: Cork 8 November 1927
Debut for Eire: v Luxembourg March 1954

Ben Ives, West Ham United's chief scout, went to Ireland in May 1949 to sign Shamrock Rovers' player Fred Kearns and Shelbourne's Danny McGowan, having been impressed by the style of both players the previous January.

West Ham at the time were keen to increase the ever growing Irish 'colony' at Upton Park, having viewed with some satisfaction the way that their previous Irish signings – John Carroll, Tommy Moroney and Frank O'Farrell – had adapted to the English game. Furthermore, unlike their English contemporaries, the Irishmen were exempt from national service and were thus able to devote their whole career to the game.

Kearns had been just two seasons at Shamrock Rovers before joining the Hammers as a raw 20-year-old. A player 'with a fine physique', he went to Upton Park with a very good reputation. Fred had half a dozen seasons with the East End club during which he scored 14 goals in 43 Second Division outings.

He was transferred to Norwich City in June 1954 and scored 11 times in 24 games in Division Three (South) for the Canaries before dropping out of the League game.

Fred won one Irish cap in March 1954 when a patchwork Irish side, containing five other debutants, beat Luxembourg 1–0 in a World Cup qualifier.

Michael Kearns (GOALKEEPER)

Born: Banbury 26 November 1950
Debut for Eire: v Poland September 1970

Mick Kearns began his career at Oxford as an apprentice, signing as a professional for the 1967–68 Third Division champions in July 1968. The gangling 6ft 4in goalkeeper spent a difficult five years at the Manor Ground during which he made 67 Second Division appearances.

In October 1972 he was loaned to Third Division Plymouth (one appearance) and was about to sign for the club when he broke his leg in a training accident. The fracture put his career on hold for four months. When he was fully recovered, he spent a brief period on loan to Charlton (February 1973, four appearances) before being sold to Walsall for £12,000 in July 1973.

For six years Mick was fairly much a regular between the sticks for the Saddlers, clocking up a total of 249 League appearances. At the end of 1978–79 Walsall were relegated to Division Four and during the close season lost their keeper to First Division Wolverhampton Wanderers.

Mick's three years at Molineux were spent in the shadow of first-choice keeper Paul Bradshaw, and in the summer of 1982, he was allowed to leave the club, having made just nine League appearances.

He immediately returned to Walsall, who by then were back in Division Three, and concluded his League career with 26 League outings for the club.

During his early days at Oxford Mick attended England training sessions, although nothing came of it. His club manager at the time, Gerry Summers, pointed out that as both Kearns' parents hailed from Mayo, he was eligible to play for Ireland.

When Mick won his first full cap – as a substitute for Preston's Alan Kelly – in the 2–0 home defeat by Poland in September 1970, he became the youngest goalkeeper to play for

Ireland. He was 19 years, nine months and 28 days old. He was Ireland's first-choice keeper between 1976 and 1978, keeping at bay the claims of other capable goalminders such as Alan Kelly, Manchester United's Paddy Roche and Waterford's Peter Thomas before finally succumbing to those of Fulham's Gerry Peyton.

From 1973 to 1979 Mick heroically bridged the gulf between Third Division football with Walsall and international duty with Ireland. He played his 18th and final game for his country, having kept seven clean sheets, in the 1–0 defeat by Northern Ireland in November 1979.

A keen golfer and cricketer, Mick, who coaches at non-League Worcester City, recently scooped an international hat-trick by holing-in-one in courses in England, Ireland and Scotland.

Alan Kelly

Alan Kelly (GOALKEEPER)

Born: Dublin 5 July 1936
Debut for Eire: v West Germany
November 1956

Alan Kelly (sen.) is the Republic of Ireland's second most capped goalkeeper after Celtic's Packie Bonner. Only a serious injury in September 1973, in a game against Bristol City, prevented him from winning more caps.

At the time of his injury, Alan had made 48 full international appearances for Ireland. He kept five clean sheets in international football and, until recently, was the only keeper to have captained Ireland, a role he performed against the USSR in October 1972. He also took over the international managerial reins for one game, against Switzerland in April 1980.

Alan would certainly have added to his cap tally. But the shoulder injury he sustained led to serious complications: he lost the power in his right hand and had to learn to write with his left.

A glorious career was over after 417 League games for Preston. It was a sad end for a man once described by Bobby Charlton as 'a truly great goalkeeper' for whom 'no cause was a lost one'. Charlton was manager of Preston at the time of Alan's injury and the former Manchester United and England international went on to say that Kelly's name would be synonymous with Preston North End, as is that of the club's brilliant and legendary Tom Finney.

The father of Alan Kelly, the current Republic of Ireland and Sheffield United goalkeeper, and of Bury's custodian Gary Kelly, Alan grew up in Bray, Co. Wicklow, where he attended the local St Peter's School. His early promise was noted by the scouts attending schoolboy matches and he was snapped up by League of Ireland club Drumcondra. He won an FAI Cup winners medal with the Drums when they defeated Shamrock Rovers 2–0 in the 1957 final. A year later, in April 1958, Alan moved to Preston.

Kelly had already made his international debut against West Germany when he suffered the traumatic experience of losing 5–1 to England in a World Cup tie at Wembley in May 1957. The goals against Ireland were less the fault of Kelly and more that of several outfield players who 'seized up' on the big occasion. Alan had to wait almost five years, however, for his next cap. From then on, his inspired displays made him a regular in the international side.

Alan played his first League game for Preston in February 1961 and went on to establish a League appearance record which stands today. His consistency can be seen by the fact that in five successive seasons from 1966 he missed just five out of a possible 214 League games and he was never dropped, after waiting almost three seasons to succeed long-standing keeper Fred Else as first-choice keeper at the club.

In 13 seasons as a player at Deepdale, Alan experienced all the traumas, exaltations and drama normally associated with a top-flight club. He saw the club sliding from a peak of second place in Division One in 1957–58 to Division Three, for the first time in the club's history at the end of 1969–70. On the other hand they won the Third Division Championship title the following season and were narrowly defeated 3–2 by West Ham United in the 1964 FA Cup final.

When he was forced to retire, Kelly remained loyal to Preston. He became assistant manager and in 1983 became manager. He resigned the post in February 1985 and was later attached to the coaching staff at Everton.

Alan now runs goalkeeping clinics in Washington DC.

Alan T. Kelly (GOALKEEPER)

Born: Preston 11 August 1968
Debut for Eire: v Wales February 1993

Kelly is the name; goalkeeping is the game.

Alan Kelly is the son of Alan Kelly (sen), the former Republic of Ireland keeper who holds the Preston North End League appearance record. He is also the brother of Bury keeper Gary Kelly.

Alan (jun.), who has inherited his father's bravery and agility, was Sheffield United's joint 'Player of the Year' for 1992–93, sharing the award with Blades' centre-back Paul Beesley. He has also recently stepped into Packie Bonner's boots as Ireland's number 1.

But it has been a rocky road to the top for the former British Leyland electrician. Alan followed in his father's footsteps by joining Preston, where he played at right-back in the club's junior teams until just before his 16th birthday. He then joined as a youth trainee before becoming a professional in September 1985.

Things had been going well when, in 1988, he stepped off a pavement and was hit by a motorcycle. He couldn't walk for five months and didn't play for a year. Then, in a comeback testimonial game, he challenged for a ball and broke his leg again. It took another six months to heal. Such setbacks would have finished lesser men, but Alan returned to Preston to resume his career.

Alan helped the Lilywhites win promotion from Division Three in 1986–87. In the summer of 1991 bargain-hunter supreme Dave Bassett excelled himself when he paid Preston just £150,000 to take Kelly to Bramall Lane. Kelly had made 142 League appearances for Preston.

Alan won rave reviews playing for Sheffield United but lost his place owing to injury. When United were relegated on the last day of 1993–94 he was playing second fiddle to Simon Tracey. The following summer he ended a long contractual dispute by signing a new three-year contract which made him one of the highest-paid players in Division One.

Towards the end of 1995–96, after 136 League appearances for the Blades, Kelly suffered a back injury, which kept him out of Ireland's summer of friendly internationals.

A former Republic Youth and Under-21

player, Alan made his debut against Wales at home in February 1993. The Welsh were a goal up when Kelly took over from Bonner in the Irish goal. Ireland went on to win 2–1. It was the first of six matches in which Kelly kept clean sheets and included a 2–0 victory over Germany in Hanover – the first German defeat in that city for 40 years. Now established as Ireland's number 1, though facing fierce competition from the up-and-coming Shay Given, Alan won his 15th cap against Macedonia in October 1996.

David Kelly (FORWARD)

Born: Birmingham 25 November 1965
Debut for Eire: v Israel November 1987

The son of a Dublin-born lorry driver, David Kelly's 11 goals in 1991–92 proved crucial, for Newcastle narrowly avoided relegation to Division Three. The following season he shot the Geordies into the Premier League with 24 goals.

The fact that David became a professional footballer is a minor miracle. When he was four, he fell out of a tree, fractured a leg and was diagnosed as having Perthes' Disease. Neither bone nor muscle was growing in his upper left thigh, and when he was discharged from hospital, his left leg was four inches shorter than his right.

Initially David had to wear a brace, and he couldn't walk easily without the aid of crutches until he was ten. Not until he was 18 did he stop attending hospital for bi-annual check-ups.

Despite his disability, David signed schoolboy forms with West Bromwich Albion when he was 15. The Hawthorns' boss Ron Atkinson didn't take up an option to sign him professionally; and so David took up employment in the office at Cadbury's Bourneville factory and played non-League football with Alvechurch. There he was spotted by Walsall boss Alan Buckley, who signed him for the Saddlers in December 1983.

An industrious and energetic performer, David had five seasons at Fellows Park. He went on to score 63 League goals in 147 appearances for the club, including five in five games in the Division Three play-offs in 1987–88, which shot Walsall into Division Two.

In August 1988, in the face of attractive offers from Spurs, Paris St Germain and Bayern Munich, Kelly joined West Ham United for £600,000. He was viewed as the new goal machine to fill the vacuum created by Tony Cottee's departure to Everton. Not only did he have to step up two divisions in class but he also had to justify that price tag with instant success.

It didn't happen for David. Playing in a far from fluent Hammers side he failed to find the form which made him a magnet for the big clubs at home and abroad. He was substituted, dropped and harshly barracked by the Upton Park fans. To make matters worse the Hammers were relegated in his first season at Upton Park. Consequently he was grateful when a £300,000 move to Leicester City materialised in March 1990 after 41 League games (seven goals) for the Hammers.

At Filbert Street his old confidence and eagerness returned and he recaptured the form of a few years earlier. Five goals in his first four games for the Foxes endeared him to the home fans. Once again, however, it all turned sour. In 1990–91 Leicester narrowly avoided relegation from Division Two and in October 1991, after 22 goals in 66 League games, Kelly was dropped from the team and was the subject, once again, of much transfer speculation, which ended when he joined Newcastle in December for £250,000.

Confident and eager with a terrific turn of pace, David had just one and a half seasons at St James' Park during which he netted 35 goals in 70 League games. At the end of 1992–93 he was again transferred, this time to Wolverhampton Wanderers for £750,000, thus remaining in the First Division instead of sampling the Premier League with Newcastle.

In just over two seasons at Molineux, David has scored 26 goals in 83 games. Although he was the only regular in 1994–95, he was placed on the transfer list by manager Graham Taylor, a casualty of the club's failed bid to reach the Premiership.

In September 1995 he was transferred to Sunderland for a £900,000 fee. Before losing his place through injury, Kelly scored twice in ten games in the Rokerites' 1995–96 Division One Championship-winning season.

David won his international chance as a Third Division player with Walsall. He made a sensational full debut for the Republic, scoring a hat-trick in the 5–0 defeat of Israel in Dublin in November 1987. Ironically on the night of his debut he was actually pencilled-in to play for England Under-21s against Yugoslavia – his name actually appeared on the squad list distributed by the FA. His lively and aggressive dovetailing with Niall Quinn and success in front of goal in the Irish 'B' team earned him a seat on the plane to Italy for the 1990 World Cup finals. Although proving himself to be a prolific goal-getter in friendlies for Ireland, David has yet really to stake his claim in competitive representative games. To date he has scored eight goals in 20 internationals.

the Premiership by his fellow professionals in the PFA, and in the summer he went with Ireland to the World Cup finals in America – tremendous achievements for a youngster after just one season of first-class football.

Gary began his career as a striker before being converted to a defensive role by Leeds boss Howard Wilkinson. But he has not lost the knack of going forward and now provides an excellent example of the new breed of 'wing-backs'. A will-o'-the-wisp defender, his blistering pace can unlock the tightest defences and enable him to sprint back quickly to close players down and win the ball.

Before his first Premiership season was over Kelly was called up for his first Eire cap, against Russia in March 1994. He had an outstanding international debut and added Ireland boss Jack Charlton to his ever-growing list of admirers.

He strengthened his claim for a place in the 1994 World Cup squad after excellent performances in victories in friendlies against Holland and Germany. His first senior goal came in the 2–0 defeat of the Germans – their first defeat in Hanover since 1954.

The youngest player in the Irish World Cup squad in the USA, Gary played at right-back against Norway in New York in place of the suspended Denis Irwin, but he won his seventh cap in the next game, against Holland, on merit. He now has 18 full caps.

Gary Kelly (RIGHT-BACK)

Born: Drogheda, Co. Louth 9 July 1974
Debut for Eire: v Russia March 1994

Leeds United signed Gary Kelly from Dublin club Home Farm in 1992. His progress since then has been remarkable. He broke into Leeds' Premiership side in 1993–94, making the right-back berth his own, and to the end of 1994–95 he hadn't missed a League game, appearing in 86 consecutive League encounters. He added another 34 appearances to his tally in 1995–96.

In 1994 he was voted the best right-back in

Mark Kelly (WINGER)

Born: Sutton, Surrey 27 November 1969
Debut for Eire: v Yugoslavia April 1988

Mark Kelly was a youth trainee apprentice with Portsmouth before joining the club as a professional on his 17th birthday, in November 1986. He made his senior debut for the club against West Ham in February 1988 and began the 1988–89 season as a regular first-teamer. He even scored a brilliant winning goal against

Shrewsbury on the first day of that season.

But Kelly's stay at Fratton Park was littered with false dawns. A serious injury to his right knee resulted in the joint having to be rebuilt. And each time he attempted to make a comeback in reserve team football, he was knocked back by other injuries.

Mark, who spent a brief period on loan to Spurs in November 1990, played his last senior game for Portsmouth in September 1990. He had made 49 League appearances, 24 of them as a substitute, when he was given a free transfer in May 1994. His persistent injury difficulties prevent him from playing professional football again.

Capped by England at Youth international level, Mark won two Republic of Ireland 'B' caps, two Under-23 caps and three Under-21 caps. He came into the Irish senior side for the first time in April 1988 when he helped the Republic to a 2–0 victory over Yugoslavia in Dublin. It was a bittersweet experience for the youngster, for he had to leave the fray in the 89th minute due to injury. Mark played three more times for Eire and finished a winner each time: against Poland in May 1988; Tunisia in October 1988 and Morocco in September 1990.

Noel Kelly (INSIDE-FORWARD)

Born: Dublin 28 December 1921
Debut for Eire: v Luxembourg March 1954

Noel Kelly was an inventive little inside-forward who learnt his trade in his native Dublin with Bohemians and Shamrock Rovers. He was turning out for Belfast club Glentoran in the Irish League in September 1947 when he agreed to join Arsenal for £650.

Three seasons at Highbury saw Kelly in the Gunners' first team just once and in March 1950 he was transferred to Crystal Palace in Division Three (South) for £8,000. Noel had just one season at Selhurst Park, scoring five

goals in 42 League appearances before moving to Second Division Nottingham Forest in August 1951.

By late 1953 Noel, who had been kicking his heels at the City Ground, had given up hope of making the first team. Then, on 12 December, he was brought on against Everton. It was his big break. The newspaper critics were lavish in their praise of him: 'Kelly gave the finest inside–forward display I've seen in Division Two for a long time. There hasn't been a finer exhibition of star inside-forward than that provided by Noel Kelly.' Noel netted 11 times for Forest in 48 games.

He won one Irish cap, in a World Cup qualifier against Luxembourg in March 1954, playing in an experimental Irish side which included six new caps.

In July 1955 Noel became player-manager of Tranmere Rovers. From then until 1957 he scored six goals in 52 outings in Division Three (North). In 1957 he became player-manager of Ellesmere Port and later managed Holyhead Town and Northwich Victoria.

Philip Kelly (FULL-BACK)

Born: Dublin 10 July 1939
Debut for Eire: v Wales September 1960

Phil Kelly was brought up in Birmingham and used to attend evening training at Birmingham City's ground. But he slipped through the club's net and in September 1957 Wolverhampton Wanderers signed him from local junior club Sheldon Town.

When Kelly joined Wolves he was regarded as a centre-back but he was converted into a full-back by the club. He made his senior debut for Wolves in 1958–59 (Wolves' second successive League Championship-winning season), but was unable to establish a regular first-team place at Molineux.

Despite his inability to gain a regular place in Wolves' first XI, Phil was called up as Eire's right-back five times between September 1960 and October 1961 before losing the position to Manchester United's 20-year-old full-back Tony Dunne.

He was transfer-listed by Wolves in 1967, having made just 16 League appearances, and joined Norwich City in August of that year.

A cousin of former Everton and Ireland star Peter Farrell, Kelly became a regular in Second Division Canaries' side and in four seasons at Carrow Road he made 115 League appearances (two goals) before dropping out of League football.

Jeffrey Kenna (DEFENDER/MIDFIELD)

Born: Dublin 27 August 1970
Debut for Eire: v Portugal April 1995

Jeff Kenna joined Southampton from Dublin junior club Palmerstown Rangers, aged 17. A versatile, all-purpose player, Kenna made his way through the ranks at the Dell and, after a period on loan to Wigan Athletic in 1991–92, he made his League debut for the Saints against Spurs in January 1992.

From then until his £1.5 million transfer to Blackburn Rovers less than three years later, Kenna made the right-back position in the Saints Premiership side his own, playing in 114 League games for the club. In March 1992 Jeff played in front of almost 68,000 people at Wembley which Southampton lost 2–3 to Nottingham Forest in the Zenith Data Systems Cup final after extra time.

Following his transfer to Rovers in March 1995, Jeff joined his former Southampton colleagues Alan Shearer and Tim Flowers in Blackburn's first XI. At Ewood Park he is preferred on the right side of midfield, where he made nine League appearances in Rovers' Championship-winning season – their first since 1914. He took his appearance tally to 41 by the end of 1995–96.

Jeff, a former Eire 'B' cap, has eight Under-

21 caps. He made his full debut in the 1–0 defeat of Portugal in Dublin in April 1995, when he replaced Ray Houghton after 84 minutes. He became a regular in the senior side towards the end of Jack Charlton's reign and has 14 full caps to date.

One of a family of five brothers and one sister, Jeff's father is former Irish snooker international Liam Kenna.

Mark Kennedy

(LEFT-WINGER/FORWARD)

Born: Dublin 15 May 1976
Debut for Eire: v Austria September 1995

The 'proudest moment' in Mark Kennedy's young life was in February 1995 when he became the most expensive 18-year-old in soccer history, joining his idols Liverpool from Millwall for £2 million.

A left-winger or forward, Kennedy has many attributes: he is comfortable receiving the ball, can go past people and is a good passer and finisher. Not dissimilar to another Dubliner who lit up a previous Liverpool side – Steve Heighway.

When he was eight, Mark wore the goalkeeper's jersey at Belvedere Boys in his native Dublin – no doubt intending to follow in the footsteps of his dad Brendan who had been a Junior international keeper. But he moved outfield after five years between the sticks and was 15 when Millwall's chief scout Alan Batsford watched him smash in four goals for Belvedere against Stella Maris. He scored 66 goals that season and Millwall offered him a contract, which he signed on his 16th birthday, in May 1992.

Kennedy was three weeks short of his 17th birthday when, as a result of his phenomenal scoring rate in the Millwall youth team, Lions boss Mick McCarthy gave him his full debut against Charlton in April 1993.

At Millwall Mark was widely regarded as

Mark Kennedy

the most exciting talent to emerge at the club since Teddy Sheringham.

When the move to Liverpool materialised, Mark had scored nine times in 43 League outings for the Lions. Although Liverpool boss Roy Evans described his transfer as a 'buy for the future', Mark broke into the first XI at the end of 1994–95 and made half a dozen League appearances. He added a further four appearances to his tally at the end of the following season.

The boy from Blanchardstown, who has seven Eire Youth caps, was promoted from the Under-21 squad to the full Eire team as a replacement for the injured Steve Staunton for the European Championship qualifier against Austria in September 1995. It was a bittersweet experience: Ireland went down 3–1 but Kennedy acquitted himself magnificently, playing with the confidence of a veteran.

He won his tenth cap, against Bolivia in June 1996.

Michael Kennedy (MIDFIELD)

Born: Salford 9 April 1961
Debut for Eire: v Iceland May 1986

Mick Kennedy joined Halifax Town as an apprentice and was upgraded to full-time professional status in January 1979.

An aggressive, industrious midfielder, his performances in Town's engine room quickly caught the attention of the likes of Liverpool, Everton and Tottenham, all of whom checked out the 17-year-old. Mick was 'not for sale' according to the club's board but, after 76 Fourth Division games for the Shaymen, Kennedy refused the offer of a new contract and in August 1980 moved to Fourth Division Champions Huddersfield Town for a club record £50,000.

Mick had exactly two years at Leeds Road (81 League outings) before joining Middlesbrough in August 1982 for £100,000. He played 68 League games for Boro and in June 1984 swapped his red and white yoke shirt for the blue of Boro's Second Division rivals Portsmouth in another £100,000 deal.

A Republic of Ireland Under-21 international on four occasions, Mick came under the full international spotlight for the only time in his career during his time at Portsmouth, when he won two caps in victories over Iceland and Czechoslovakia in the Reykjavik 200 Tournament in 1986.

In 1986–87 Kennedy helped Pompey into Division One; they were relegated after just one season. In January 1988, after 129 League games, he transferred to Bradford City. Just over a year and 45 League outings later, in March 1989, Mick left Valley Parade for Bradford's Second Division rivals Leicester City.

He appeared for Leicester on just nine occasions before moving to Luton Town in a player exchange deal which took Luton's full-back Rob Johnson to Filbert Street. Once again Kennedy's sojourn lasted only a year. He made 32 First Division appearances for the Hatters before joining Third Division Stoke City for £250,000 in August 1990.

Stoke freed Mick in August 1992 after 52 games, whereupon he joined Chesterfield in the new Division Three. Mick had made 27 League appearances for the Blues before dropping out of League football at the end of 1992–93.

John Keogh (RIGHT-BACK)

Born: Dublin 1942
Debut for Eire: v West Germany May 1966

John Keogh arrived at Shamrock Rovers' Glenmalure Park from Stella Maris as a 16-year-old in 1958, just as the Dublin giants were embarking on their ninth Championship-winning campaign.

A highly reliable defender, Keogh won a League Championship medal with the Hoops in 1963–64 and five FAI Cup winners medals. The first Cup medal arrived after the 4–1 demolition of Shelbourne in the 1962 final. Then came four successive victories between 1964 and 1967. Incredibly Keogh was injured before the finals of 1964, 1965 and 1966 and was unable to train before the big day each time.

His run of bad luck seemed to have ended before the 1967 decider against St Patrick's Athletic. But he was having minor cuts to his legs treated in hospital when he fainted, fell, hit his head and needed four stitches in a wound. Nevertheless he recovered once again to play his role at right-back for Rovers.

John departed for Cork Celtic in 1968 and lined up for them in the 1969 FAI Cup final against none other than Shamrock Rovers. But it was a sad last Cup-final appearance for Keogh. The 28-year-old milk salesman scored the own goal which gave his former club a 1–1 draw. Rovers won the replay 4–1.

John, who is a former League of Ireland player, won Schoolboy Minor and Junior international caps and won his only full honour

as a substitute for the injured Theo Foley in the 4–0 home defeat by West Germany in May 1966.

Shay Keogh (FULL-BACK)

Born: Dublin
Debut for Eire: v Poland October 1958

A strong, quiet, but capable full-back or centre-half, Shay Keogh was one of the mainstays of Shamrock Rovers' successful side of the late 1950s.

He began playing as an under-14 with St Joseph's and actually won his first medal playing for the club against Stella Maris in the curtain-raiser to the 1948 FAI Cup final between Shamrock Rovers and Drumcondra.

He had quite a chequered career as a centre-half with Rovers, after he joined them in 1952. He began brilliantly and was honoured by the League of Ireland. Following an injury, however, he lost his place to Gerry Mackey, who got the international honours which might otherwise have come Keogh's way. In the meantime, Shay laboured to make a success of the left-back position without ever rising above mediocrity. He won his favoused centre-half position back at the end of 1957–58 and the following term was back to his brilliant best.

He won League Championships medals in 1953–54, 1957–58 and 1958–59 and played in two FAI Cup finals, 1955 and 1957, collecting a winner's medal as team captain in 1955. His Rovers career was ended through injury in 1962. A year later he became player-coach of St Patrick's Athletic.

Honoured 15 times by the League of Ireland, 'he played a captain's part' when the League side produced one of their best ever away performances against the Scottish League at Ibrox in September 1963.

Capped against England at Schoolboy and Youth level, Shay won a couple of 'B' caps against Romania in October 1957 and Iceland in August 1958. His one full cap came against Poland in October 1958. Despite being a 'very popular choice', Shay only managed to get into the side because regular centre-half Charlie Hurley couldn't make it to Dublin in time.

The game itself, despite ending 2–2, was described as a 'drab draw'. The only success on the Irish side was Keogh himself, the sole home-based player on the starting XI. He came through his debut in 'sparkling fashion as pivot, quietly but efficiently tackling his job. He made no mistakes and looked every bit as good as his "big-time" team mates', claimed one report at the time.

Alan Kernaghan (CENTRE-HALF)

Born: Otley 25 April 1967
Debut for Eire: v Latvia September 1992

The player who more than any other brings sharply into focus the inconsistencies and inadequacies of football's parentage qualifications rulings. Manchester City's big centre-half, who grew up in Bangor, Co. Down, offered his services to the Republic after being turned down by Northern Ireland.

He won six Northern Ireland Schoolboy caps and spent most of his adult life in Bangor, where his parents still live. But he was born in England where his family was living before returning to Northern Ireland four years later. As his parents were also born in England, the IFA – in line with the other home countries – scuppered Alan's lifetime ambition to play senior soccer for the North by refusing to consider eligibility further up the family tree.

The FAI are less strict: grandparents will do. As Kernaghan's late grandparents were born in Ireland before partition, he qualified for the Republic. He was a regular in Ireland's defence before the arrival of Phil Babb on the scene. He was Ireland's skipper for the US Cup games in June 1996, having got into the squad due to

Roy Keane's absence. Alan has so far collected 22 full caps.

Alan, who began his career as a centre-forward, was an apprentice at Middlesbrough. He rose through the ranks and signed professionally in March 1985. Although he earned the nickname 'The Judge', after 35 games in one season on the bench, he persevered and became first-choice centre-back and captain.

In January 1991 he played 13 games on loan to Charlton and was about to sign for the Second Division club when their manager, Lennie Lawrence, moved to Boro in July 1991 and took Alan back north with him.

Kernaghan played 212 League games (17 goals) and helped Boro win promotion to the new Premier League in 1991–92, but after their relegation the following season, he decided to move on and during the summer wrote to all the Premiership clubs offering his services. Although a young, strong and steady centre-back, touted as the best defender outside the Premiership, Kernaghan had to wait until September before he had a reply. Then new Manchester City supremo Brian Horton moved in to make Kernaghan his first signing – the fee was a massive £1.5 million.

Kernaghan immediately linked up with his Eire colleagues Niall Quinn and Terry Phelan in City's first team. But he experienced some difficulty in adapting to the game at the higher level and in August 1994 he went to Bolton on loan amid claims that he was hounded out by City fans. Two months earlier, in June 1994, he publicly revealed that he suffers from diabetes, which was diagnosed in 1989.

He made 11 appearances in Bolton's 1994–95 promotion-winning season and spent most of 1995–96 (at the end of which City were relegated to Division One) playing reserve team football. He made just six League appearances for City that season, taking his League appearance tally with the club to 52. He also played five games whilst on loan to Bradford City that season.

Frederick Kiernan (GOALKEEPER)

Born: Dublin 7 July 1919
Debut for Eire: v Argentina May 1951

Standing just 5ft 8in, Fred Kiernan was one of the smallest goalkeepers ever to appear in the Football League. Undeterred by his lack of inches, Fred was a solid and dependable goalminder who possessed cat-like agility.

Fred won a League of Ireland Championship medal and an FAI Cup runners-up medal with Shelbourne in 1944 and later served Dundalk and Shamrock Rovers.

In October 1951 he transferred from Shamrock Rovers to Second Division Southampton and spent the next five seasons vying with John Christie for the Saints' number 1 shirt. The former Ayr United custodian, who had arrived at the Dell just eight months before Kiernan, eventually won the tussle. In 1956, after 132 League appearances for the Saints, Fred departed for non-League Yeovil.

Fred succeeded Leicester City's Tommy Godwin as the Republic of Ireland's number 1 in 1951. He made his international debut in the 1–0 defeat by Argentina in May of that year. He kept his place for Ireland's next three games, one of which ended in defeat. His fifth and final game for his country came almost exactly a year after his debut. Ireland were thrashed 6–0 by Austria in Vienna and Fred was replaced in the Irish goal by Everton's Jimmy O'Neill for their match against Spain the following month.

Fred Kiernan died in 1981.

Joseph Kinnear (RIGHT-BACK)

Born: Dublin 27 December 1946
Debut for Eire: v Turkey February 1967

Joe Kinnear joined Tottenham from St Albans in February 1965 and spent ten years at White Hart Lane during which he made the right-back berth his own. He was part of the marvellous Spurs team of the '60s and '70s which included Martin Peters, Martin Chivers, Mike England, Alan Gilzean and Ralph Coates and which had the purists drooling.

A tigerish defender, Kinnear could attack on the wing when the opportunity presented itself. Noted for his intelligent distribution of the ball, he made 196 League appearances for Spurs. At 21 he was an FA Cup winner when Spurs beat Chelsea 2–1 in the 1967 final. He also won League Cup winners medals in 1971 and 1973, and a UEFA Cup winners medal in 1972.

In August 1975 Kinnear was transferred to Third Division Brighton where he made 16 appearances before calling it a day in senior football.

Armed with his FA coaching badge, Joe had a spell as player-manager of non-League Woodford Town before heading for Dubai to take charge of a team owned by the immensely rich Maktoum family. He later linked up with

Joseph Kinnear

former Spurs favourite Dave Mackay running the Dubai national team.

Thereafter he had a three-year spell as coach to the Indian national squad before returning to England as Mackay's right-hand man at Doncaster Rovers. He led Rovers to the FA Youth Cup final in 1988, the first time a Fourth Division club achieved that distinction. Joe lost his job at Doncaster in 1989 after Mackay's departure from the club.

In 1990 he became reserve team coach at Wimbledon. He was appointed first-team manager after the sacking of Peter Withe in February 1992 and took the credit for a rapid upturn in the fortunes of the club, saving them from almost certain relegation to win a precious place in the newly established Premier League. His success was rewarded with a new three-year contract in May 1992.

Kinnear claimed a place in the history books when he became the Republic's first-ever substitute in European Championship football when he replaced Ipswich's Tommy Carroll in the 1–1 home draw with Sweden in October 1970.

He became the Republic's regular right-back soon after Shay Brennan's departure from Manchester United to Waterford in 1970. Previously Joe had vied with Brennan and Ipswich's Tommy Carroll for the right-back berth and on one occasion had to be content with a place in the Irish engine-room. In an international career spanning ten years, he won 26 full caps.

David Langan (RIGHT-BACK)

Born: Dublin 15 February 1957
Debut for Eire: v Turkey April 1978

As a youngster Dave Langan had trials with Birmingham City and Manchester United but joined Derby County straight from school, initially as an apprentice and then as a professional in February 1975.

Langan had been a purposeful midfielder in the Rams' reserves when he was promoted to the first XI in February 1977. Although playing out of position at right-back, he was an instant success.

He had a good turn of speed, tackling ability and pressed forward with gusto. He made such an impact that he retained his place in the side and over the next four seasons he missed just four League games, accumulating 143 Division One appearances.

Things turned sour for Langan in 1979–80, however. The spectre of relegation cast a dark cloud over the Baseball Ground, and in January 1980 Langan earned himself a £750 fine and a severe reprimand for refusing to travel to Bristol City for an FA Cup tie. Six months later, in July 1980, cash-strapped Derby cashed in on the player by selling him to newly promoted Birmingham for £350,000.

In two seasons at St Andrews (92 First Division appearances), Dave's world collapsed. A knee injury signalled the start of his troubles, and he had been on crutches after a fourth operation when he cracked a vertebra and was forced to sit out the 1983–84 season. At the end of that season he was freed by Birmingham and in the summer Jim Smith, who had originally taken him to St Andrews, came to the rescue by signing him for Oxford United.

Dave not only proved his fitness at the Manor Ground but ended his first season there with a Second Division Championship medal. Furthermore his Irish international career, which had remained on 15 caps since the 3–2 defeat of France in Dublin in October 1981, resumed for the World Cup qualifier against Norway in May 1985, and Dave went on to take his tally to 25 caps.

In 1986 he won a League Cup winners medal as Oxford trounced QPR 3–0 to lift the first major trophy in the club's history.

In October 1987 Dave played five games on loan to Leicester City before transferring to Second Division rivals Bournemouth in December of that year.

After just 20 League appearances for the

Cherries, Dave joined his sixth and final club, Fourth Division Peterborough, for whom he made 19 League appearances before bowing out of League football.

Joseph Lawler (LEFT-BACK)

Born: Dublin 28 August 1925
Debut for Eire: v Austria March 1953

Christened Joseph but known as Robin, Lawler was one of the many Irish internationals who were reared in the Gaelic code. He was in his school's first XV at 12, playing centre-field. He spent his formative soccer years with the famous Home Farm club in Dublin, where he played at wing half-back before spending five years at half-back.

He moved north to Belfast as an 18-year-old in 1943 to join Irish League club Distillery; he spent 18 months there, and then returned to his native city where he turned out for Transport FC and Drumcondra.

Lawler signed for the famous Belfast Celtic in 1945 and then, with Celtic colleagues Johnny Campbell and Hugh Kelly, signed for Fulham in a £30,000 transfer deal in March 1949.

Although registered as Fulham players, he and Johnny Campbell were permitted by the club to take part in Belfast Celtic's American tour of 1949. They played in Celtic's famous 2–0 defeat of the Scotland side – the first time that a club side had beaten a national team.

Robin spent three years in Fulham's reserves before becoming the club's regular left-back in 1952. He also turned up at right-back before moving to left-half in 1958.

The blond-haired defender became one of Fulham's most consistent players of the 1950s. He had an excellent footballing brain and combined sharp anticipation with thoughtful and accurate passing. He helped the Cottagers win promotion from Division Two in 1958–59 and in 13 seasons at the club he made 281 League appearances.

But an unfortunate run of injuries cost Robin his place in Fulham's First Division side in the early '60s, and in the summer of 1962 he left the club for southern League side Yiewsley, with whom he played for one season. Thereafter he became a salesman for Dean's Blinds of Putney.

A former Eire Junior international and Irish League representative player, Robin became the first Fulham player to achieve international honours when he took his place at left-back in the Republic side which beat Austria 4–0 in Dublin in March 1953. He became the Republic's regular left-back over the next 30 months before losing out to West Ham's Noel Cantwell. Robin won his eighth and final cap in the 4–1 home defeat by Yugoslavia in September 1955.

John 'Kit' Lawlor (FORWARD)

Born: Dublin 3 December 1922
Debut for Eire: v Belgium April 1949

'A pestering pimpernel with unquenchable spirit', John Christopher 'Kit' Lawlor followed in the footsteps of his father, who was a goal-getting centre-forward with Talbot United and Mullingar. A former employee of O'Rourke's bakery, John played in the Bakery league and for Bradmola. He moved to Drumcondra from Dublin rivals Shamrock Rovers in 1946. He had two successful spells with Drumcondra in between which he spent a stint in England with Doncaster Rovers. He was 'a crafty player with a tendency to slow up the game and with the ability to score from long range'.

His first spell with Drumcondra, from 1946 to June 1950, when he moved to Division Three (North) champions Doncaster, yielded two League of Ireland Championship medals (1947–48 and 1948–49). He was the club's leading scorer in both campaigns. He also won an FAI Cup winners medal in 1946 when Drumcondra overcame Dublin rivals

Shamrock Rovers 2–1. The same teams lined up for the 1948 showdown, but this time the scores were reversed.

In five seasons at Doncaster, before his return to Drumcondra in 1955, Kit scored 46 goals in 128 Second Division games.

In 1957 he played in his third FAI Cup final and again Shamrock Rovers provided the Drums' opposition. On this occasion Drumcondra exacted revenge for their defeat nine years earlier, winning 2–0. Another League of Ireland Championship medal was added to his collection in 1957–58, and in 1959 he moved to Dundalk.

Kit, whose son Mick also played for the international XI, won three full caps in friendly internationals for the Republic between April 1949 and May 1951.

Michael Lawlor (MIDFIELD/FORWARD)

Born: Dublin 1948
Debut for Eire: v Poland September 1970

In over two decades of League of Ireland football Mick Lawlor won the lot. A hard-grafting midfielder, he started his medal collection in grand style in 1967–68 when he scored for Shamrock Rovers in every round of the FAI Cup, including the 3–0 defeat of Waterford in the final. He was also in the side which retained the trophy the following season.

After nine seasons with the Hoops Mick spent 1974–75 and 1975–76 with Dublin rivals Shelbourne. He was joint top scorer in 1974–75 and top scorer the following season; and he was an FAI Cup finalist in 1975 when Shels lost 1–0 to Home Farm.

The most successful era of Lawlor's career was spent in Co. Louth with Dundalk between 1976 and 1981, where for a time he was assistant manager.

In his first season with the club, 1976–77, he was again an FAI Cup-winner. He also won a League Cup winners medal in April 1978. Next season, 1978–79, he helped the Lilywhites win the League Championship and FAI Cup double for the first time in their history.

Lawlor returned to Shelbourne for a spell before becoming player-manager at Home Farm in March 1984.

The son of 'Kit' Lawlor, who played for Ireland in the late '40s and '50s, Mick played in four successive Ireland games between September and December 1970. His fifth and final cap came against Poland in May 1973. The opposition and result was the same as in his debut game: a 2–0 victory for the Poles. He also won one Under-23 cap, against France in November 1972.

Mark Lawrenson (DEFENDER)

Born: Preston 2 June 1957
Debut for Eire: v Poland April 1977

Mark Lawrenson was one of the most stylish and polished defenders of the modern era, winning virtually every honour in the book with Liverpool in the 1980s.

On the field Mark was calmness personified. His anticipation, the essence of a skilled performer, allowed him time and he was simple and deliberate with the shortest of passes. A good tackler, he could also break down a raid and immediately seize upon the chance to launch a counterattack.

Born just 200 yards from Preston North End's Deepdale Ground, he first represented Preston Schoolboys. Later he followed in his father Tommy's footsteps by joining the once proud Preston, having ditched his 'A' levels and rejected the opportunity to pursue a cricketing career with Lancashire.

He agreed professional terms with Preston in August 1974. Mark started in the reserves as a winger and then played mainly in a central defensive role at the club. As he later showed at Anfield, he could perform with equal aplomb anywhere along the back four and also in midfield.

Lawrenson played for Ireland owing to a chance conversation with former Deepdale favourite Alan Kelly, who was then coach to both Preston and the Republic of Ireland. The young Lawrenson happened to mention that his mother was born in Waterford. Kelly followed it up, and in April 1977 Mark won the first of his 39 Irish caps. He remained a regular in the green shirt until his retirement in 1988, turning up at full-back, centre-back and in midfield.

Mark scored five international goals, including a couple in the record 8–0 home victory over Malta in November 1983, but his most memorable contribution was the goal which sank Scotland at Hampden Park in February 1987 and sent the Republic on their way to the 1988 European Championships in Germany.

In his final international, against Israel in November 1987, Mark captained the national side. He departed in true style, leading Ireland to a resounding 5–0 home victory over Israel.

The capping of Third Division Lawrenson opened a few clubs' eyes to his ability and in July 1977 Brighton, newly promoted to Division Two, snapped him up for £100,000.

He didn't want to leave Preston but the club needed the money and were thus forced to cash in their most valuable asset. At the time the deal went through, he was on holiday and agreed the transfer in a café on the sea front in Benidorm. Liverpool reportedly just failed with a £70,000 bid for the player.

Lawrenson spent four years on the south coast with Brighton, mainly in a pivotal midfield role. During this time he became a First Division player, for the Seagulls won promotion from the Second Division in 1978–79, earning a place among the elite for the first time in the club's history. Lawrenson played a total of 152 League games for Brighton before, in August 1981, at the second time of asking, Liverpool got their man – only

Mark Lawrenson

this time it took them a record-breaking £900,000 fee.

The Liverpool story of the '80s is well known. Suffice to say that Lawrenson reached the pinnacle of his career on Merseyside. He remained a regular in the side in various positions throughout the decade and in doing so picked up League Championship and League Cup winners medals in successive seasons in 1981–82, 1982–83 and 1983–84. He won a European Cup winners medal in 1984 and a runners-up medal in the same competition the following year after the ill-fated clash with Italian champions Juventus at the Heysel Stadium. He was a double winner in 1985–86, when Liverpool won both the League and the FA Cup. Another League Championship medal was added to the collection in his last season at the club, 1987–88.

Mark appeared in a total of 241 League games, netting 11 times. In March 1988, at the age of 30, he was forced into early retirement because of an Achilles tendon injury.

On leaving Merseyside he became manager at Oxford United. Seven months later in October 1988 he was sacked after a disagreement with the club's directors over the sale of Dean Saunders to Derby County. He wasn't out of work long and in October 1989, after a brief spell as player-coach at Tampa Bay Rowdies, he became manager at Peterborough. But again he didn't last long, leaving in November 1990.

After Peterborough he had a short stint with Corby Town, and in October 1992 an attempted comeback with Chesham Town was soon aborted owing to 'business commitments'. He later returned to the game and is now manager of non-League Oxford City.

Michael Leech (CENTRE-FORWARD)

Born: Dublin 6 August 1948
Debut for Eire: v Czechoslovakia May 1969

Gaelic football was Mick Leech's first love; he played his club football with Rialto Gaels and represented Dublin Schools.

Leech played his junior soccer with St Bridgid's from where he graduated to the Leinster Senior League with Ormeau at the age of 16.

He had a four-month trial with Theo Foley's Northampton Town in 1966, but in October of that year Liam Tuohy signed him for Shamrock Rovers.

A player with tremendous tight control and who, for a small man, could lead the line well, Mick was an FAI Cup winner with the Hoops in successive years from 1967 to 1969. With the exception of a 1–1 draw with Cork Celtic in 1969, Mick scored in every final including the replay with Cork.

Described as the Jimmy Greaves of Irish soccer, Mick possessed excellent anticipation and positional sense. He was, in the words of Irish broadcaster Philip Greene, 'the classic example of the poacher – the fox among the chickens'. His record of 56 goals in all competitions in 1968–69 will be hard to beat.

At the beginning of 1973–74 he transferred to Waterford and he stayed there for two and a half seasons before returning to Rovers where he scored the only goal of the tie against Sligo in the 1977 League Cup final. Mick later turned out for Bohemians (1977–78, the Gypsies' League Championship-winning season), Drogheda (1978–79) and St Patrick's Athletic (1980).

He was 33 when he finished at St Pat's and the following term he went to Dundalk as assistant manager to Jim McLaughlin.

Mick was an Irish Youth player, appearing for his country in the UEFA finals in West Germany in 1965. A League of Ireland representative player, he won his first full international honours against Czechoslovakia in May 1969. He won a total of eight full caps and scored two goals, both of which came in the Brazilian Independence Cup in June 1972, against Iran and Portugal.

Denis Lowry (GOALKEEPER)

Born: Dublin 1936
Debut for Eire: v Austria April 1962

Dinny Lowry went to St Patrick's Athletic from local junior club Bulfin United.

Lowry succeeded his coach Jimmy Collins between the posts at Inchicore and helped St Pat's win back-to-back League Championships in 1954–55 and 1955–56. After suffering a loss of form he bounced right back during the 1959 FAI Cup campaign which culminated in St Pat's beating Waterford 2–1 in the replayed final and lifting the trophy for the first time.

A 'brilliant young keeper, who has a steadying influence on his defence', Dinny appeared in two more FAI Cup finals with St Pat's, gaining a winners medal in 1961 and a runners-up medal in 1967.

In March 1969 Lowry, with former Dundalk winger Tony O'Connell, made history by becoming the first professionals to play for Bohemians. Thirteen months later Lowry helped Bohs to their first FAI Cup success since 1935.

A former Schoolboy international and inter-League keeper, Dinny won one full cap, as a 34th-minute substitute for the injured Alan Kelly in the 3–2 defeat by Austria in Dublin in April 1962.

James McAlinden (CENTRE-FORWARD)

Born: Belfast 31 December 1917
Debut for Eire: v Portugal June 1946

Jimmy McAlinden joined Belfast Celtic straight from school and wasted no time in making the grade. His nifty footwork and ball skills were a joy to watch, but his greatest assets were his short passing game and explosive turn of speed. He scored many valuable goals for Celtic including the two that beat Bangor in the replayed Irish Cup final in 1938 and clinched Celtic's second successive League and Cup double.

Jimmy's rapidly developing skills didn't go unnoticed across the water and almost every English manager of repute braved the Irish Sea to check him out. Consequently, in the summer of 1938 Jimmy was on his way to Portsmouth, then a power in the First Division, for £6,000.

He immediately won a first-team place at Pompey and was a good short-term investment as an entertainer and match-winner. In his first season at Fratton Park, he won an FA Cup winners medal after Pompey thrashed Wolverhampton Wanderers 4–1 in the last pre-war Cup final; he scored seven goals in six games in the club's FA Cup campaign that season.

When war was declared in 1939, Jimmy returned to Belfast Celtic and won two more Irish Cup winners medals in 1941 and 1944. He also represented the Irish League, appearing for them against the Army or Combined Services teams.

After the war he returned to Portsmouth where he made 33 League appearances (five goals) before joining Pompey's First Division rivals Stoke City in September 1947. Again he made 33 appearances, netting just twice this time, before transferring to Division Three (South) Southend United as player-coach for £6,000 in September 1948.

Jimmy, who became captain at Southend, gave the club excellent service and ended his League career with 218 League games for them, though he missed 11 games through suspension in 1950 over illegal payments he had allegedly received.

When his playing days ended Jimmy became a successful manager, guiding Lurgan club Glenavon to a famous League and Cup double in 1957 and Belfast club Distillery to success in the 1971 Irish Cup. He later managed Drogheda in the League of Ireland.

One of the Belfast Celtic stars who was honoured by both 'Irelands', Jimmy McAlinden won four Northern Ireland caps: two against Scotland before the war and two versus England after the war.

He won two Eire caps in the Iberian tour of the summer of 1946 when the Republic lost 3–1 to Portugal and then recorded their first away victory over Spain, winning 1–0 in Madrid.

Jimmy McAlinden died in 1994.

Jason McAteer (MIDFIELD)

Born: Liverpool 18 June 1971
Debut for Eire: v Russia March 1994

Jason McAteer had been playing with Parkside in the Birkenhead Sunday League as well as for non-League Marine when he joined Bolton Wanderers in the summer of 1991 for £500. He

Jason McAteer

forfeited the chance to take up a soccer scholarship in America in order to join Bolton.

From a famous Liverpool boxing family, McAteer is a tenacious, hard-running and talented midfielder. He became a regular in Bolton's League side in February 1993 and helped the Trotters win promotion from Division Two in 1992–93.

But it was in the FA Cup the following season that Jason really came to prominence. He played a major role in the First Division's club's FA Cup run, which took them to the quarter-final stages, having seen off Premiership giants Everton, Arsenal and Aston Villa. McAteer's contribution earned him a place in the PFA's First Division XI for that season.

Bolton went one better in 1994–95, for they won promotion to the Premiership and went all the way to Wembley only to lose to Liverpool in the League Cup final.

In September 1994, to the dismay of big spenders Liverpool and Blackburn, McAteer signed a new three-year contract with Bolton, rejecting Liverpool's £2.5 million bid for him. The following summer the chequebooks were

out again and every Premiership club of note was linked with the player. He eventually opted for his boyhood heroes, joining Liverpool in a £4.5 million transfer deal in September 1995 after 115 League appearances for Bolton.

He made 29 appearances for Liverpool in 1995–96 and in May 1996 walked out at Wembley to face Manchester United in the FA Cup final. Five years earlier he had been a League and Cup winner for the Royal Oak pub in the Wallasey Sunday League. There was no happy ending this time, for United ran out 1–0 winners.

McAteer, who was born in Liverpool, has a Welsh mother and paternal grandparents from Ireland, was eligible to play international football for England, Wales, Northern Ireland or the Republic. He opted for the Republic, though it was widely believed that he was on the verge of an England 'B' call-up.

Jason had an outstanding international debut for Eire in the 0–0 draw with Russia in March 1994. He kept his place in the team for the next 10 games and won his 19th cap against Macedonia in October 1996 the game in which he scored his first international goal.

One of only five players who played in all of Ireland's World Cup games in the USA, Jason is an integral part of the Irish set-up.

James McCann (OUTSIDE-RIGHT)

Born: Dublin
Debut for Eire: v West Germany November 1956

The catalyst for Jimmy (or Maxie) McCann's career was an injury to Shamrock Rovers goal machine Paddy Ambrose. Whilst recovering from a broken ankle in 1952–53, Ambrose was 'regraded' to play junior football with Clontarf where he spotted McCann, who was playing on the wing. Ambrose tipped off his sponsor club Shamrock Rovers, and McCann later took his place in the great Rovers side of the 1950s.

McCann, whose speed on the wing and accurate corners and crosses created plenty of openings for his forwards, weighed in with 46 League goals of his own for Rovers. In fact he was top scorer in 1957–58.

In nine seasons with the Hoops, Maxie won three League of Ireland Championship medals, in 1953–54, 1956–57 and 1958–59, and played in four successive FAI Cup finals between 1955 and 1958, collecting winners medals in 1955 and 1956.

During 1961–62 Maxie was transferred to Drumcondra. He was joint top scorer there in 1962–63, and then spent the 1964–65 season with Dundalk.

A former Eire Youth player, Maxie made his international debut without having represented the League of Ireland first. He marked his debut by scoring Ireland's third goal in their 3–0 defeat of West Germany in Dublin in November 1956, helping inflict on the Germans their heaviest defeat since they won the World Cup in 1954. Although it was his only full cap, he represented Ireland again in two 'B' internationals, against Iceland (when he scored the winner in the 3–2 victory) and South Africa in August and October 1958.

Michael McCarthy (DEFENDER)

Born: Barnsley 7 February 1959
Debut for Eire: v Poland May 1984

Mick McCarthy had a rich and varied career in football and provoked a mixed reaction from fans and scribes.

Mick joined his hometown club Barnsley as an apprentice in December 1975. Before that he had cut his teeth in the town's Under-14 side and in the Yorkshire and County Senior League with Wosbrough Bridge Athletic. He also turned out at full-back with Barnsley Boys' club.

He made his League debut for Barnsley in 1977 and was virtually a regular in the club's drive from Division Four to a peak of sixth in Division Two in 1982. Mick's rugged and uncompromising displays at the heart of the Colliers' defence caught the attention of several other clubs, and in December 1983 he joined newly relegated Manchester City for £200,000.

McCarthy gave City the same sterling service that he'd given to his previous club, missing only a handful of League games in his four seasons there and helping City back into Division One in 1985.

In May 1987 McCarthy joined Glasgow Celtic in a £500,000 transfer deal. In just over a season at Parkhead he made 48 League appearances and helped Celtic to the Scottish Cup and Premier League double in 1988 before making an ill-fated move to French club Olympique Lyon in April 1989.

McCarthy experienced a torrid time in France with injuries. Even when he did get a game he was employed as a sweeper, a position he neither enjoyed nor excelled in. In March 1990 Bob Pearson, Millwall's caretaker manager, took him to the Den on loan. Pearson's successor Bruce Rioch signed Mick permanently for £500,000 before the end of the season.

Mick's time as a player at the Den was also disrupted by injuries, which kept him out of the game for long periods. He underwent surgery on his knee for the third time in December 1989 and was later laid low by calf and ligament problems. To the end of 1992–93 he had made just 35 League appearances for the Lions.

In March 1992 he was appointed manager at the Den in place of the recently departed Bruce Rioch. Mick's style of management and the brand of football he has instilled into his team have won him many friends and admirers in the game.

The man who probably more than any other carried Jack Charlton's philosophy on to the field of play, Mick confounded his many critics as Ireland's very own Captain Fantastic, turning in world-class displays in the 1988 European Championships in West Germany and the 1990 World Cup finals in Italy in which he was a regular.

Mick has a proud record as an Ireland captain. He led the Irish team 22 times and finished on the losing side just twice in this role. Both defeats came against Italy: in the quarter-finals of the 1990 World Cup and in the 1992 US Cup.

Mick, who won one Under-23 cap as an over-age player, against Northern Ireland in 1988–89, qualified to wear the green shirt through his father's Waterford birthplace, and no one has worn that shirt with more pride. A slight lack of positional sense and pace was more than compensated for by his highly competitive spirit and his strength in the air, all of which earned Mick 57 caps.

In February 1996 Mick succeeded Jack Charlton as national team manager.

Thomas McConville (CENTRE-HALF)

Born: Dundalk, Co. Louth 1947
Debut for Eire: v Austria October 1971

One of the League of Ireland's most respected players in the '70s and '80s, Tommy McConville enjoyed success aplenty after making the change from amateur to professional status with his hometown club, Dundalk, in June 1969.

A strapping centre-half 'with the Charlie Hurley look', McConville spent three seasons with Dundalk between 1969 and 1972, helping the Lilywhites to success in the 1972 Shield competition.

In 1972–73 he helped Waterford win the League Championship and League Cup, before moving to Shamrock Rovers for a couple of rare barren seasons, and then returning to Dundalk to take part in the most successful era in the Co. Louth club's history. They were

champions three times (1975–76, 1978–79 and 1981–82), FAI Cup winners three times (1977, 1979 and 1981), League Cup winners in 1978 and 1981 and League Cup runners-up in 1983 and 1986.

Tommy, whose brother Brian shared in the club's successes in this period, gave yeoman service to Dundalk and played a major role in Dundalk's promotion to top-club status under the guidance of Jim McLaughlin. He was still holding down his place in the Dundalk side in 1985–86, aged 40, despite the suggestion that he didn't fit into the plans of new boss Turlough O'Connor.

In April 1986 Tommy took up a two-year post at Finn Harps, the first non-Donegal man to manage the Ballybofey outfit since their entry into League football in 1969.

Tommy had a 'brilliant display' in the League of Ireland Golden Jubilee match in 1971 and in September 1971 played for the League of Ireland against the English League, a game in which he had a great battle of brawn and brain with Arsenal's mighty forward John Radford. He displayed 'sound concentration, good positional play and the pluck to keep on the right side of a forward who was strong, mobile and clever'.

That performance earned him his first international cap, against Austria in October 1971. Tommy became a regular in the Irish side between November 1972 and May 1973 when he took his tally to six full caps.

James (Jacko) McDonagh
(CENTRE-HALF)

Born: Dublin 1960
Debut for Eire: v Malta November 1983

A centre-half gifted with defensive skills, Jacko McDonagh saw League and Cup honours slip away from him at the final fence when he was with Bohemians. He was an FAI Cup runner-up with Bohs in 1982 and one of the dominant figures in the Gypsies' side pressing for glory in the League in the early 1980s.

He left Dalymount Park and joined Shamrock Rovers at the start of the 1982–83 season – a time when the Hoops were burgeoning into the most promising side in the League.

In his first season at Rovers he was preferred in midfield, which 'took the shine off the most polished defender in Ireland'. However, when Ireland's most successful manager, Jim McLauglin, arrived at Milltown, he played Jacko in his favoured central defensive role.

McDonagh helped Rovers to successive League Championships in 1983–84 and in 1984–85 (when he scored nine League goals) and to FAI Cup finals in the same seasons. University College Dublin overcame Rovers in 1984 but the Hoops bounced back to beat Galway United 1–0 in the 1985 final to complete the double.

After that successful season Jacko departed for French club Nîmes Olympic.

Honoured by the Republic four times at Under-21 level between February 1981 and June 1983, Jacko reckons he was lucky to get a full cap. David O'Leary cried off injured for Ireland's game against Malta in November 1983, and McDonagh was called up as cover. Kevin Moran went off at half-time and Jacko came on to help Ireland to an emphatic 8–0 victory over the Maltese.

He made a further two substitute appearances for his country, against Poland and Mexico in May and August 1984.

James McDonagh (GOALKEEPER)

Born: Rotherham 6 October 1952
Debut for Eire: v Wales February 1981

The 6ft Jim (Seamus) McDonagh matched height with agility. A former England Youth goalkeeper, he opted for the Republic of Ireland at full international level.

He won his first full cap in the 3–1 home defeat by Wales in February 1981 and over the next four and a half years took his tally to 24 (eight clean sheets) before eventually losing the race for Ireland's number 1 shirt to Packie Bonner and Gerry Peyton.

In a career spanning almost two decades Jim donned the colours of no fewer than 11 clubs and played in every division of the Football League.

He began as an apprentice with his hometown club Rotherham, signing as a professional in October 1970. He made 121 appearances for the Merry Millers and helped them win promotion to Division Three in 1974–75 after two seasons in the Fourth.

McDonagh joined Bolton Wanderers on a month's loan in August 1976 and made such an impression that he was signed permanently for £10,000 as cover for Barry Siddall. After Siddall departed for Sunderland in September 1976, McDonagh was promoted to first-choice keeper. He kept his place in the side for the rest of the season and over the next three seasons at Burnden Park he was a regular, never missing a League game and winning a Second Division Championship medal in 1977–78.

Wanderers were relegated at the end of 1979–80 and during the close season McDonagh was transferred to Everton for £250,000. However, just over a year and 40 First Division games later, he was on his way back to Burnden Park in a player plus cash deal.

In his second spell at Burnden Park Jim took his League appearance total with the club to 242 and even scored a goal, which came in the 3–0 defeat of Burnley in January 1983. At the end of 1982–83 Wanderers dropped into Division Three and in July McDonagh returned to the top flight by joining Notts County.

Jim made 35 League appearances for the Meadow Lane club and had loan spells at Birmingham City (August 1984, one appearance), Gillingham (March 1985, ten appearances) and Sunderland (August 1985, seven appearances). In the summer of 1985 he had a brief spell with Wichita Wings in the

123

USA, before joining Scarborough in November 1987.

He made nine appearances for Scarborough and six on loan to Huddersfield in January 1988.

He didn't get a game at Charlton before the club cancelled his contract during 1988–89. Thereafter he turned out for Galway Rovers in the League of Ireland (1988–89), non-League Spalding United (1989–90) and Grantham Town (1990). He later became reserve team manager at Telford United.

Andrew McEvoy (INSIDE-FORWARD)

Born: Bray, Co. Wicklow 15 July 1938
Debut for Eire: v Scotland May 1961

Former Ireland captain Johnny Carey took Andy McEvoy from junior club Bray Wanderers to Blackburn Rovers in the mid-1950s. But, after a bout of homesickness, Andy returned to Ireland. Carey was well aware of the difficulties experienced by youngsters leaving Ireland for the first time, but he was determined to sign the player. And in October 1956 he succeeded in his mission when he persuaded McEvoy to give the full-time game another go.

Andy was initially regarded as a capable but rather ordinary inside-forward. Carey set about converting his raw recruit into an attacking wing-half. McEvoy had comparatively little success until he moved back to inside-forward where he developed into a poacher supreme, brilliant and deadly in front of goal.

A player with indomitable spirit and excellent turn of speed, Andy spent his entire League career at Ewood Park; he made a total of 183 League appearances and scored 89 goals.

He made his League debut in 1958–59 but his career didn't take off until 1963–64 when he scored 32 League goals in 37 games. Only Jimmy Greaves scored more that season. Indeed McEvoy was christened the Greaves of the north. The following season he shared the top spot with Greaves, scoring 29 goals from 40 appearances.

Rovers were relegated in 1965–66, and Andy spent most of the following campaign in the reserves.

In 1967 he disappeared back to Ireland, as quickly as he had arrived, to drive a tram and play part-time for Limerick in the League of Ireland. He won an FAI Cup winners medal with Limerick after their victory over Drogheda in 1971 and headed the club's scoring charts in four of his five seasons there.

Andy won his first full cap in May 1961 when he replaced his Blackburn team-mate Mick McGrath in the Irish side to face Scotland in the World Cup qualifier in Glasgow. He played regularly for Eire between 1961 and 1967, collecting 17 caps in all and scoring six goals – a creditable total, for his career came at a time when the national side was struggling for results.

Andy McEvoy died in Bray on 7 May 1994.

Paul McGee (FORWARD)

Born: Sligo 19 June 1954
Debut for Eire: v Turkey April 1978

A much-travelled and prolific hitman, Paul McGee was well on his way to soccer stardom even before he left school. He helped his school, Summerhill College, to win the All-Ireland Schools' title in successive seasons, netting a hat-trick in one of the finals.

Local League of Ireland side Sligo Rovers introduced him to senior football when he was 16, and in 1972 he joined Kidderminster Harriers. From there he signed for Hereford but failed to make their first team and returned to Ireland to play for Finn Harps in 1973–74, ending the season with an FAI Cup winners medal. The following season he spent back at

Sligo Rovers where he won a League Championship medal in 1976–77.

During this period McGee spent his summers in Canada, initially with Toronto Mets and then for three seasons with Montreal Castors. He was top scorer in each of his four seasons in Canada and helped Castors win the Canadian League.

In November 1977 Paul got his first taste of English League football when he joined First Division Queen's Park Rangers. Rangers were relegated at the end of 1978–79 and in October 1979, after 40 appearances (seven goals), McGee was sold to Second Division Preston North End.

He spent two seasons at Deepdale, scoring 13 times in 66 League appearances but, when Tommy Docherty – McGee's old QPR boss – arrived at Deepdale as manager in 1981, he sent McGee on loan to Burnley. In March 1982 McGee joined the club permanently for £25,000.

He helped Burnley win the Third Division title in 1981–82 and in March 1983, after nine goals in 34 League outings, he was loaned to Dundalk.

It is difficult to keep track of this wandering footballer thereafter. In 1983 he once again signed for Sligo and in 1984–85 appeared for three League of Ireland clubs: Shamrock Rovers, Waterford and Sligo Rovers. In 1986–87 he was playing for Galway when his career took yet another twist.

His performance for Galway against Dutch side Groningen in 1985 caught the attention of Haarlem who, in an effort to avoid relegation, signed McGee for £12,000. McGee helped the Dutch club avoid the drop and in 1987 went back to Galway. In November 1990 he returned to his hometown club Sligo Rovers and later had brief spells with Derry City (1990–91), Sligo Rovers (November 1990), Athlone Town (1991–92), Sligo Rovers (November 1991), Galway United (September 1992) and in January 1993 returned to Ballybofey to join Finn Harps.

A bubbly, confident character, renowned for his speed off the mark, Paul is a former Republic Youth international and was capped twice at Under-21 level. He graduated to full international level in April 1978, when he made his debut against Turkey, marking the occasion with a goal in Ireland's 4–2 victory. McGee was a regular for the next three seasons, taking his final tally to 15 caps and four goals.

Edward McGoldrick (MIDFIELD)

Born: London 30 April 1965
Debut for Eire: v Switzerland March 1992

The London-born son of a couple from Kimmage, Co. Dublin, Eddie McGoldrick fulfilled a lifetime ambition in February 1992 when he pulled on the green shirt of his parents' country for the first time. The match was a 'B' international against Denmark in Dublin, which Ireland won 2–0.

He won his first full cap the following month in the 2–1 defeat of Switzerland in Dublin. He was taken off with a knee ligament injury just before half-time, but it didn't sour the occasion altogether.

Since then Eddie has been asked to play at left-back and on the left side of midfield and, only occasionally, in his favourite position wide on the right of midfield. Now, with 15 caps, he is very much part of the Ireland set-up and will certainly add to that tally.

Eddie is a versatile and highly talented player who, in addition to his skilled wing play, can operate with equal effectiveness as a full-back, sweeper or tough tackling midfielder. He received a solid grounding with 107 League games for Northampton Town, whom he joined from non-League Nuneaton Borough in August 1986 for £10,000. He left Northampton for Crystal Palace in January 1989 with the Fourth Division Championship medal he'd won in 1986–87 firmly tucked in his pocket.

As a schoolboy, Eddie was rejected by

Nottingham Forest and Peterborough but by the late 1990s he was in demand. In signing McGoldrick for the Eagles, Palace boss Steve Coppell had to see off competition from Newcastle United, Norwich City and Derby County; he got his man for £200,000.

Life at Selhurst Park was a series of ups and downs for McGoldrick, and only in the last few years has he been regarded by the football world as a talent to be reckoned with. Initially he was a regular in the Palace side with a brief – not to mention a panache – for supplying pin-point crosses to Ian Wright and Mark Bright, Palace's celebrated strike force of the period.

In his second season at the club things began to go wrong for him. He missed the 1990 FA Cup final and replay against Manchester United through injury and, in the following two seasons, found himself out of favour and in and out of the side. But when Palace returned to Wembley in 1991 to contest the ZDS Cup with Everton, he was named as substitute. He did get a game, and the Eagles lifted the cup after comprehensively defeating the Merseysiders 4–1.

During this difficult period in his career McGoldrick was on the transfer list, valued at £1.25 million. However, he came of age in a footballing sense in 1991–92 when he excelled in the responsible role of sweeper, and in August 1992, at his own request, he came off the transfer list and signed a new three-year contract with Palace.

To the end of 1991–92 Eddie had made 105 League appearances for Palace. But he had scored only three goals which caused some concern at the club, so much so that Palace Chairman Ron Noades is said to have offered Eddie a financial inducement of some £10,000 for a return of six goals in 1992–93. McGoldrick duly obliged by reaching his target after just 19 games, thereby doubling his career total.

On the final day of the 1992–93 season Palace lost their battle for Premier League survival and thus were resigned to losing Eddie. As one of the game's most versatile performers

there was no shortage of interested parties, and in June 1993 he moved north of the Thames to Arsenal in a £1 million deal, having netted 11 goals in 147 League outings with Palace.

Arsenal manager George Graham, who signed McGoldrick on a four-year deal, had this to say of his new acquisition: 'I tried to look at a certain type of player to bring to the club: talented, good self-motivation, desire, call it what you like, Eddie McGoldrick typifies that.'

To the end of 1994–95 Eddie had made 36 League appearances for the Gunners. He won a European Cup-Winners' Cup winners medal in May 1994 when Arsenal defeated Parma 1–0 in the final. He earned a runners-up medal in the same competition a year later when Arsenal surrendered their trophy to Real Zaragosa at the last hurdle.

1995–96 was a season Eddie would probably prefer to forget. A long-term injury coupled with a transitional period at Highbury which saw George Graham replaced as manager by Bruce Rioch, meant that Eddie got just 14 minutes of Premiership football, against Manchester City in September 1995.

Daniel McGowan (WING-HALF)

Born: Dublin 8 November 1924
Debut for Eire: v Portugal May 1949

Danny McGowan was one of the outstanding players sent from Ireland to West Ham United in the '40s by the Hammers' former Irish player Charlie Walker.

Danny made his debut for hometown club Shelbourne in April 1946. 'McGowan was by no means a failure. He could develop into a useful player and he showed zeal when scoring Shels' only goal.' Danny won a League of Ireland Championship medal with Shelbourne in 1946–47. He also represented the League of Ireland against the English League in May 1947 and had a 'brilliant game'. Almost exactly a year later, in May 1948, he joined West Ham.

An intelligent inside-forward or wing-half, McGowan 'improved beyond recognition' after crossing the channel and won the first of his three full Irish caps a year after arriving in London.

He made his debut for Ireland in the 1–0 home win over Portugal in May 1949, Ireland's first victory in six outings, and was retained for the next two fixtures before losing his place to Middlesbrough's Peter Desmond.

Danny spent six years at West Ham – his one and only League club – and made 81 Second Division appearances, scoring eight goals.

In May 1954 he was placed on West Ham's transfer list. Hammers manager Ted Fenton said at the time: 'It wasn't easy. Danny's been such a fine club man that he will give any team first-class service.' He finished his playing career with Chelmsford City in the Southern League.

Danny McGowan died in Plaistow, east London, in March 1994, aged 69.

John McGowan (DEFENDER)

Born: Cork 8 June 1920
Debut for Eire: v Spain March 1947

John McGowan was a member of Cork United's brilliant team which dominated League of Ireland football in the 1940s, collecting honours galore.

A fine versatile player, John joined Cork from Cobh Wanderers and starred as a right-back, right-half and centre-half. He won five League Championship medals: three in successive seasons between 1940–41 and 1942–43 and two back-to-back in 1944–45 and 1945–46. He also played in four FAI Cup finals in 1941, 1942, 1943 and 1947, emerging with winners medals in 1941 and 1947.

With his Cork colleague Tommy Moroney, McGowan was transferred to West Ham United in August 1947. He arrived at the club bereft of boots and had to break in a new pair, which caused his feet to blister; and therefore he missed his planned League debut. He then suffered a knee injury and later had two cartilages removed. Having failed to get his career off the ground at Upton Park, John returned to Ireland in 1952 where he coached Cork Hibs for a spell before drifting out of the game.

John, who played at right-back and centre-half for the inter-League team, was capped at right-back (with Johnny Carey at left-back) in a 3–2 home win over Spain in 1947.

Michael McGrath (WING-HALF)

Born: Dublin 7 April 1936
Debut for Eire: v Austria May 1958

Mick McGrath was one of Johnny Carey's early protégés after the former Manchester United and Eire captain became manager of Blackburn Rovers in 1953.

Carey had watched McGrath and left-half Charlie Wade play for an Irish Youth XI against Liverpool FA in 1953. He had been suitably impressed and, after keeping an eye on them for a year, he signed both players from his old club Home Farm in August 1954.

The 5ft 7in, 10st 11lb McGrath was a 'fine, consistent performer who always gave 100 per cent'. He got his opportunity to play in Rovers' first team when Ken Clayton broke his leg and he went on to make 268 League appearances (eight goals).

He was a regular in the team which won promotion from Division Two in 1957–58. And in 1959–60 he was described as 'The Man with the Golden Boot', for he shot his way to the position of the club's top scorer during Rovers' 1960 FA Cup run. Unfortunately he lost his golden footwear in the final, scoring an

Paul McGrath

Paul McGrath (CENTRE-HALF)

Born: Ealing 4 December 1959
Debut for Eire: v Italy February 1985

The crowning of Paul McGrath as 'Players' Player of the Year' for 1992–93, surely the ultimate accolade in any professional footballer's career, was the culmination of five magnificent seasons after his controversial transfer from Manchester United to Aston Villa. Since then 'The Black Pearl of Inchicore' has gone from strength to strength and is now widely regarded as one of the world's foremost central defenders.

The rise in stature of McGrath and the simultaneous rise in stature of Aston Villa and Ireland is no coincidence. Described as a colossus, he is composure itself on the ball, completely unruffled. His tackling is fearless, impeccably timed and executed with the minimum of fuss, repeatedly stifling danger where others would need a crushing tackle.

Paul has been an outstanding player for club and country for years. In 1985–86 he was runner-up to Gary Lineker in the PFA 'Player of the Year' poll. He was voted Villa's 'Player of the Year' for 1989–90, 1990–91, 1991–92 and 1992–93; the Opel/FAI 'Player of the Year' in 1989–90 and 1990–91; Ireland's 'Player of the Tournament' in the 1988 European Championships in West Germany and the 1990 World Cup in Italy, and runner-up to Gary Lineker and Chris Waddle for the Football Writers' 'Footballer of the Year' in 1992 and 1993. Not bad for a player who, when he arrived at Villa Park for a mere £450,000 in July 1989, was regarded as a clapped-out old banger with something like 200,000 miles on the clock and no MOT certificate.

Born in Ealing, west London, Paul's Irish mother took him to live in Monkstown when he was just two months old. He played his junior football in Dublin with Pearse Rovers before moving to Leinster Senior League side Dalkey United.

own goal in the 3–0 defeat by Wolverhampton Wanderers.

In March 1966 McGrath moved to Fourth Division Bradford Park Avenue. The transfer earned him a 'nice little nest egg': as a reward for 'long and loyal service' Rovers waived any fee, and McGrath was thus able to arrange a suitable signing-on fee.

Mick had the unhappy distinction of scoring an own goal on his debut for Bradford. However, he went on to play 50 League games for the club and managed two goals – into the right net.

Capped once at 'B' level for Ireland, against Romania in October 1957, Mick McGrath was selected to represent his country every season between 1958 and 1966, accumulating a grand total of 22 full caps.

Irish talent-spotter Charlie Walker took him to League of Ireland club St Patrick's Athletic for whom he made his League debut in September 1981. United's Irish scout, the late Billy Behan, liked what he saw and seven months later McGrath was on his way to Old Trafford for £35,000 plus extra payments for international and first-team appearances. The deal included a friendly between St Pat's and United. The whole package was described by United boss Ron Atkinson as an 'absolute bargain'.

An immaculate defender with an excellent footballing brain, it took McGrath two seasons to claim a regular first-team place at Old Trafford. He was well settled at the club when in 1988–89 the bone-flaking condition which has plagued his career first appeared. And when Alex Ferguson replaced Ron Atkinson as United manager in November 1987, McGrath's troubles mounted. Player and manager enjoyed an uneasy relationship, with McGrath being fined £8,500 by the FA for criticising Ferguson. To make matters worse, Paul's knees required eight operations, which kept him out of the side for long periods towards the end of his United career.

Whenever McGrath was out of the side, rumours were rife that he had requested a transfer and, with his reputation as a defender with the composure and timing of Franco Baresi at his most elegant, AC Milan immediately set aside £1 million in the event of him making a full recovery. As it happened, Ferguson and McGrath made up their differences and in September 1988 agreed new terms. The truce was short-lived, however. A report from a top specialist said that the player's knees would only hold out for another year. He was advised to quit the game and take the insurance payout – he declined the offer and in July 1989 moved to Villa Park.

Despite their differences McGrath, who purrs around the field like a Rolls-Royce, was described by Alex Ferguson as the most naturally talented player he had at Old Trafford and in seven seasons there Paul made 163 League appearances (12 goals). The high

point of his United career was the 1985 FA Cup final in which United, down to ten men, defeated Everton 1–0 after extra time. McGrath was voted 'Man of the Match'.

At Villa Park McGrath linked up once again with his Old Trafford mentor Ron Atkinson, who had replaced Graham Taylor in the summer of 1991. Atkinson's reaction was predictable: 'Paul is the best defender in the world, I've always thought so and blimey was I delighted when I came down here from Sheffield to find him here.'

McGrath, despite his well-documented knee problems, has hardly missed a game since his arrival at Villa Park and to the end of 1995–96 had made 253 League appearances. He became the rock around which Villa's confidence flourished in their brave battle to land the inaugural Premier League title in 1992–93, which ironically was won by Manchester United with Villa runners-up. Medical consensus is that he will pay a physical price for fuelling Villa's title fervour.

In 1994 he was a member of the Villa side which defeated Manchester United 3–1 to win the League Cup. Two years later Villa again won the League Cup, this time beating Leeds United 3–0 in the final tie. He lost his place in the Villa side at the start of the season 1996–97 and in October 1996 was transferred to Derby County for £200,000, where he immediately claimed a first-team place.

Capped a record 82 times by the Republic, Paul (who was one of only five Irish players to play in all four of Ireland's World Cup games in 1994) wasn't a regular in the Irish side until Jack Charlton took over the managership in 1986. Charlton offered McGrath the captaincy of the team, which the player refused because he felt he wasn't cut out for it.

Be that as it may, he still became the jewel in Charlton's crown, a splendid example of an all-round footballer; classy and clean, he is solid, quick, exceptionally strong, technically gifted, with excellent anticipation and distribution, great powers in the air, and a marvellous competitor with the knack of scoring goals when they're needed. His versatility in midfield or defence is but an addition to his full repertoire of skills: the majestic Paul McGrath is undoubtedly head and shoulders the best centre-half in the country.

Alan McLoughlin (MIDFIELD)

Born: Manchester 20 April 1967
Debut for Eire: v Malta June 1990

Alan McLoughlin – the man who scored the multi-million-dollar goal – secured his place in the annals of Irish football folklore with his second-half equaliser against Northern Ireland in Belfast in November 1993, which sent the Republic to their second successive World Cup finals.

With a Galway father and Limerick mother, 'there was no other international choice' for McLoughlin. Capped twice by the Republic at 'B' level, he scored in the 'B' team's 4–1 victory over their England counterparts at Turners Cross in March 1990. He made his full debut in a friendly against Malta in June 1990 and got a dramatic late call-up to the Italia '90 World Cup squad as a replacement for the injured Gary Waddock, though he didn't get a game in Italy. Indeed his last competitive match for Ireland, before coming on as a second-half substitute for his 14th cap on that memorable night in Belfast, was a European Championship qualifying game against England almost exactly three years earlier.

When Mick McCarthy became national team manager in February 1996, he brought McLoughlin back into the squad. He has blossomed under McCarthy and in August 1996 started his first competitive game for Ireland – all his previous appearances had been as a substitute – in the 5–0 defeat of Liechtenstein. It was his 24th cap.

He had joined Manchester United in April

1985, but when he left for newly promoted Swindon Town in August 1986, he had yet to experience the cut and thrust of League football.

In 1986–87 he made nine League appearances for Swindon plus 16 on loan to Torquay United in March 1987. Swindon won promotion to Division Two that season, whereas Torquay finished just one place off the bottom of the Football League.

Alan made a further eight appearances for Torquay at the beginning of the next campaign, before returning to Swindon's County Ground where he developed under the watchful eye of Ossie Ardiles. By 1989–90 he was well established as a first-teamer.

That season he was one of only a handful of Swindon players to appear in all 46 of the club's League fixtures. Player and club enjoyed a bountiful season. McLoughlin came to be regarded as one of the most talented midfielders in British football. His excellent vision, driving energy and passing ability earned him an international call-up. Swindon finished in fourth place in Division Two and a McLoughlin goal saw off Sunderland in the Second Division play-offs at Wembley in May. Little Swindon had shot themselves into the top flight for the first time in their history and just four seasons previously had been a Fourth Division club!

The celebrations were short-lived, however. Swindon were denied their place among the élite for alleged financial irregularities and started the 1990–91 season once again as a Second Division club.

To make matters worse the overall financial position of the club was somewhat precarious. In December 1990 Ardiles was forced to sell his star midfielder to Southampton for £1 million. The sale of McLoughlin actually halved the debt of the Wiltshire club.

The move to Southampton wasn't a success. Alan scored just once in 24 games compared with 18 in 108 at Swindon; and when Saints' new manager Ian Brantfoot replaced Chris Nicholl – who'd bought

McLoughlin – Alan was immediately transfer-listed. He moved to Portsmouth for £400,000 in February 1992.

To the end of 1995–96 McLoughlin had netted 33 times in 176 League games for Pompey.

William McMillan (RIGHT-BACK)

Born: Carrickfergus
Debut for Eire: v Portugal June 1946

Billy McMillan was an outstanding full-back in an equally outstanding Belfast Celtic side of the 1930s and 1940s. He had signed for Celtic as a junior in 1933–34 at a time when the west Belfast club were the dominant force in Irish League football. He won successive Irish League Championship medals with the club between 1937 and 1940, and added another after the war in 1948. As well as a host of winners medals in the City and Gold Cups, Irish Cup winners medals made their way to the McMillan household in 1942, 1943, 1944 and 1947.

The Irish League closed down for the duration of the 1939–45 war. During that time Billy played for the North Regional League on nine occasions, against the League of Ireland, the British Army and Combined Services.

McMillan was an ever-present at right-back in the Celtic team which toured the USA in 1949 and which defeated Scotland – 'the wonder team of 1949' – 2–0 at the Triborough Stadium in New York. The *New York Times* observed: 'This trio of McAlinden, McMillan and Aherne combined to turn in one of the most outstanding defensive performances here in years.'

He was also in the Celtic team which drew 1–1 with Linfield on 27 December 1948, when Celtic's Jimmy Jones had his leg broken when attacked by spectators. That incident all but spelt the end of Belfast Celtic in Irish League football.

When the club withdrew from football, Billy was appointed player-manager of Ballymena United but remained there for only two seasons before drifting out of football.

A first-class defender, Billy played against the Football League in 1947 and 1948 and played for the IFA in Victory internationals against England, Scotland and Wales in 1946.

In June 1946 McMillan was chosed to replace Cork United's unfit Billy Hayes for Ireland's Iberian tour. He had originally been down to travel as a reserve. He joined Belfast colleagues Bud Aherne and Jackie Vernon in the side which lost 3–1 to Portugal on 16 June.

A week later he won his second Eire cap in what was described as the 'greatest-ever soccer team to play on the continent' after the 1–0 victory over Spain in Seville in front of General Franco.

Billy McMillan died in Carrickfergus in the early 1990s.

Brendan McNally (FULL-BACK)

Born: Dublin 22 January 1935
Debut for Eire: v Czechoslovakia April 1959

Ireland was a fertile recruiting ground for Luton Town in the 1950s: when they signed Shelbourne defender Brendan McNally in May 1956, they brought to three the number of Irish full-backs on the club's books – the others being Seamus Dunne and stalwart Bud Aherne.

McNally began in Dublin junior football and was Shelbourne's most consistent player in the 1955–56 season, at the end of which he was invited to Kenilworth Road for a trial. That trial turned out to be the Hatters' League duel with Fulham in April 1956, and McNally did well enough for Luton to sign him immediately. A considerable achievement for the Dubliner insofar as he had met his new team-mates just 45 minutes before the game.

A well-built, two-footed player who tackled hard and used the ball intelligently, Brendan made great strides at right-back in Luton's reserves and soon found himself in the first XI. In 1959 Luton reached the final of the FA Cup for the first time in their history. McNally was the right-back in the Hatters' team which went down 2–1 to Nottingham Forest in the Wembley showdown.

The following season, 1959–60, Luton were relegated to Division Two and in September 1961 McNally was placed on the transfer list at his own request. He subsequently dropped out of League football, having made 134 League appearances for the Hatters.

Cool, confident and quick in recovery, McNally was honoured once by Ireland at 'B' level, against Romania in 1957–58. The following year, in April 1959, in the absence of club colleague Seamus Dunne, he graduated to full international level, winning his first cap against Czechoslovakia in April 1959.

There followed a gap of two years before Brendan represented Ireland again, against Scotland in May 1961. His third and final cap came in the 1–1 draw with Iceland in September 1962.

Anthony Macken (MIDFIELD/DEFENDER)

Born: 1950
Debut for Eire: v Spain February 1977

Former Home Farm player Tony Macken left Irish League club Glentoran in Belfast at the start of the 1972–73 season to play for Waterford in the League of Ireland and ended the season with a Championship medal.

A year later, in August 1974, Derby County supremo Dave Mackay paid Waterford £30,000 to take the 24-year-old to the Baseball Ground.

Macken was used as cover in the Rams' engine-room and in three seasons at Derby he made just 23 League appearances. Derby farmed him out on loan to Portsmouth in (November 1975 and February 1976, ten appearances), Washington Diplomats (April

1976 and May 1977) and then to Dallas Tornado (July 1977).

Macken's old boss at Derby, Dave Mackay, took over the managerial reins at Third Division Walsall in 1977 and in October of that year signed Macken for a second time, paying Derby a fee of £10,000. In five seasons at Fellows Park Tony made 190 League appearances, almost exclusively in the right-back position, and all in Division Three with the exception of 1979–80 which was spent in Division Four.

In 1982 Macken returned to Ireland and had spells in the League of Ireland with Drogheda, Waterford United and Home Farm. He is now assistant manager at Shamrock Rovers.

Capped once by the Republic at Under-23 level, against France in 1972–73, Tony won one full cap in the 1–0 home defeat by Spain in February 1977.

Gerard Mackey (DEFENDER)

Born: Dublin 10 June 1933
Debut for Eire: v Denmark October 1956

Gerry Mackey's League of Ireland career may appear brief in comparison to that of others, but in eight years as a Shamrock Rovers player he achieved more than most.

Like so many of his contemporaries, Mackey began his playing days with Johnville in the Dublin Schoolboy League (1945–51). Just six years later, he was fulfilling his boyhood ambition of turning out for Shamrock Rovers.

A strong and versatile defender, he played with style and panache in both full-back positions and at centre-half. He captained Rovers, won League Championship medals in 1953–54, 1956–57 and 1958–59, and played in four successive FAI Cup finals between 1955 and 1958, collecting winners medals in 1955 and 1956. He also won a fistful of medals in the Shield Competition, the Dublin City Cup, the Leinster Cup and the President's Cup.

Between 1959 and 1963 (when he retired to concentrate on family and business), Gerry turned out for King's Lynn in the Southern League where he was said to have played 'some of the best football in his career'.

A former Schoolboy and Youth international captain, Gerry also gained international honours at Amateur level and, as captain of the League of Ireland XI, he led the inter-League team to 'great heights' in 1956–57.

After two caps at 'B' international level, Gerry won his first full cap against Denmark in October 1956. The following month, he was honoured with the captaincy of the side (one of the few home-based players to achieve that distinction), leading Ireland to a 3–0 victory over West Germany. He won his third cap, against England, the following May.

Gerry, whose eldest son David followed in his footsteps to Shamrock Rovers and beyond, for four years in the early 1970s coached the Irish Youth side which contained future stars David O'Leary, Frank Stapleton, Tony Grealish, Dave Langan and Packie Bonner.

Gerard Malone (OUTSIDE-LEFT)

Born: Dublin
Debut for Eire: v Belgium April 1949

Gerry Malone's best seasons were with Shelbourne in the League of Ireland between 1944 and 1956.

Gerry was often described as slow, but he was in fact a skilful dribbler who 'could be dangerous and often showed enterprise'. He also possessed a 'scoring shot in either foot' and was Shels' top scorer in 1945–46 and 1955–56. In a dozen seasons with Shelbourne he netted 68 League goals.

Malone helped the Reds win the League of Ireland Championship in 1946–47 and in

1955–56. He also played in two FAI Cup finals for the club: in 1949 when they lost to Dundalk and two years later when they were beaten by Cork Athletic 1–0 in the replayed final.

Gerry was a 'surprise selection' for Ireland's game against Belgium in Dublin in April 1949 – a game in which his striking partner at Shelbourne, Brendan Carroll, also made his international debut. It was Gerry's only cap and the visitors won 2–0.

Terry Mancini (CENTRE-HALF)

Born: London 4 October 1942
Debut for Eire: v Poland October 1973

Of an Italian father and an Irish mother – with a cockney accent – from a family more renowned for their prowess in the boxing ring than on the football field, Terry Mancini was perhaps one of the more unlikely players to turn out for the Republic of Ireland; and yet in the mid-1970s he won five full caps.

He made his full debut in Johnny Giles's first game in charge of the national side, in which Ireland defeated Poland 1–0 in Dublin in October 1973. He played in Ireland's next four games and scored his only international goal in the 2–1 defeat by Brazil in Rio in May 1974. Mancini was ordered off after 'flooring' Soviet defender Vladimir Kaplichny in the 3–0 home victory over the USSR in October 1974 – he never played for Ireland again.

Armed with a quip and a ready smile, Terry was one of the most colourful and popular characters on the domestic scene in the '60s and '70s. He was a junior at Watford before signing professional terms with the Third Division club in July 1961.

Terry had four seasons at Vicarage Road, making 67 League appearances before leaving England to join South African club Port Elizabeth in 1965.

He returned to the Football League in November 1967, joining Leyton Orient for

133

whom he made 167 League appearances (16 goals) and won a Third Division Championship medal in 1969–70.

After Orient, Terry spent three years with Queen's Park Rangers, whom he joined in October 1971. He helped Rangers win promotion from Division Two in 1972–73 and had made 94 League appearances when, in October 1974, Arsenal manager Bertie Mee paid Rangers £20,000 to take the 32-year-old Mancini to Highbury.

Terry took over from Jeff Blockley in the centre of the Gunners' defence. He became a great favourite at Highbury and became club captain. In two seasons with Arsenal he made 52 League appearances and scored one, very important, goal. It came in his penultimate League game for the club in the relegation dogfight with Wolves in April 1975. Mancini's goal was enough for Arsenal to take the points, thus keeping them in the top flight and condemning Wolves to the drop.

A resolute defender with a wealth of experience, Mancini joined Aldershot in October 1976 having been freed by Arsenal. He ended his League career with 21 Fourth Division appearances with Shots before they cancelled his contract in April 1977.

He later had a spell as assistant manager with Fulham, a post he resigned from in June 1985.

Cornelius Martin

(DEFENDER/GOALKEEPER)

Born: Dublin 20 March 1923
Debut for Eire: v Portugal June 1946

One of the select band of players to play for both 'Irelands'. Con Martin opened his international account by becoming the Republic's first–ever substitute. That was in June 1946 when, as a player with Belfast club Glentoran, he came on as a deputy goalkeeper for the injured captain Ned Courtney of Cork United, in the friendly against Portugal in Lisbon. He went on to win a further 29 caps for Eire and, as the best utility player of the era, popped up in no fewer than five different positions for his country: goalkeeper, right- and left-back, right-half and in his more usual position of centre-half. In addition he captained the Republic five times and netted six international goals.

Between 1946 and 1950 he also collected six Northern Ireland caps, making his debut at right-half against Scotland in November 1946.

Father of Eire international Mick Martin of Manchester United and Newcastle United, Con was a fine all-round athlete, excelling in Gaelic football, basketball and soccer in the Irish Air Corps.

Martin began with Drumcondra before moving to Irish League club Glentoran. In January 1947 he left the Oval for Leeds United in an £8,000 transfer deal but arrived at Elland Road too late to save the club from relegation to Division Two.

Con had made just 47 League appearances for the Yorkshire club when, completely out of character, he suffered a loss of form and was subsequently dropped from the side. Aston Villa manager Alex Massie immediately stepped in and on 1 October 1948 secured the player's signature for an 'undisclosed big fee'.

In his first two seasons at Villa Park, Con played at left-back but began the 1951–52 First Division campaign as the club's goalkeeper.

A 'capable and daring keeper', Con did not consider keeping goal all that difficult. He played in goal 26 times for Villa. In total Con gave Aston Villa eight seasons of sterling service during which he made 194 First Division appearances.

Michael Martin (MIDFIELD)

Born: Dublin 9 July 1951
Debut for Eire: v Austria October 1971

Mick Martin is the son of Con Martin, the

former Eire international who won caps as a goalkeeper, defender and midfielder in the '40s and '50s. Like his father, Mick was a versatile player. Although regarded as one of the finest defenders in the Irish game, he made his name in the Football League as a classy midfielder.

Martin began in Ireland with Home Farm and Bohemians and was already an Irish international when Manchester United took him to Old Trafford in January 1973 – a position reflected in the £20,000 transfer fee, a record receipt for a League of Ireland club at the time.

Mick walked straight into United's League side and kept his place for the remainder of that 1972–73 season. But he was only an occasional player in 1973–74, a season which ended in relegation to Division Two for United. Despite his undoubted ability, Mick failed to hold down a regular first-team place at Old Trafford and in September 1975, after just 40 League outings, he was sold to Second Division West Bromwich Albion.

He walked straight into Albion's first team and didn't miss a match for the rest of that 1975–76 promotion-winning season. However, when they returned to the top flight the following season, manager John Giles was replaced by Ron Atkinson, and Martin found himself out in the cold. The crunch came in December 1978 when, after 89 games and 11 goals for West Brom, Mick was sold to newly relegated Newcastle United for £100,000.

Martin became captain at St James' Park and in six years there made 147 Second Division appearances (five goals). In September 1983 he went on trial to Wolverhampton Wanderers but was released after just two weeks to play in the North American Soccer League with Vancouver Whitecaps.

He returned to the Football League in November 1984 and over the next ten months donned the colours of four different clubs. The first of those clubs was Second Division Cardiff City. He made five appearances for the Welsh club before transferring to Peterborough in January 1985. A dozen outings for the Posh were followed by a transfer to Rotherham United in August 1985. Four months and five games later Martin signed for his final League club, Preston North End, with whom he ended his League career with 35 games.

When Liam Brady became manager of Glasgow Celtic in June 1991, he appointed Martin, his former international colleague, as coach at the club.

A former Irish Amateur international, Mick represented the League of Ireland during his Bohemians days and was a member of the historic All-Ireland side which entertained world champions Brazil in Dublin in 1973.

Capped once by the Republic at Under-23 level, against France in November 1972, Mick won his first cap against Austria in October

Michael Martin

1971. He became a regular in the Irish set-up in the '70s and took his final tally to 51 caps when he captained the side to a 1–0 away victory over Malta in March 1983.

In a somewhat chequered international career Mick led Ireland five times, scored four goals and was dismissed on two occasions, against Turkey in 1975 and Bulgaria two years later.

Michael Meagan (DEFENDER)

Born: Dublin 29 May 1934
Debut for Eire: v Scotland May 1961

Mick 'Chick' Meagan joined Second Division Everton from Dublin junior side Johnville in September 1952. Eighteen months later he became a full professional at the Merseyside club.

By the time Chick broke into the first team at Goodison in 1957, Everton were firmly re-established as a force in Division One. The Goodison revival continued unabated and reached a climax in 1962–63 when, for the sixth time in their history, the Toffeemen were crowned League champions.

A resourceful, whole-hearted player whose commitment never waned, Meagan's whole approach and attitude epitomised the spirit within the club during this era and contributed in no small way to the upturn in the club's fortunes.

In July 1964, after 165 League appearances, Mick left Everton to join Second Division Huddersfield Town in a player exchange deal which brought England World Cup winner Ray Wilson to Goodison Park. Soon after his arrival at Leeds Road, Chick was appointed club captain. He donned the colours of Town 121 times in League encounters before transferring his services to Fourth Division Halifax Town in July 1968.

At Halifax he was also made club captain. However, although he joined the Shaymen on

a three-year contract, he turned out for them on just 23 occasions before returning to Ireland to become player-manager at Drogheda United.

Mick, whose son Mark played for Shamrock Rovers and Waterford, began his League career as an inside-forward and later played at wing-half before eventually finding his most successful niche at half-back.

A former Eire Schoolboy international, he was capped once at 'B' level, against Romania in October 1957, and made his full debut in the World Cup qualifier against Scotland in May 1961. He ended his international career against the same opposition in September 1969 when he won his 17th cap. That game, in which he captained his country for the only time, also marked the beginning of his 12-match stint as national team manager.

Michael Milligan (MIDFIELD)

Born: Manchester 20 February 1967
Debut for Eire: v USA May 1992

Mike Milligan began his career as an Associate schoolboy with Manchester City but took up Oldham Athletic's offer of a traineeship. In February 1985 he signed professional terms with Second Division Oldham.

A tenacious tackler who never stops running, Mike combines superb vision with great passing skills. He was introduced to the Latics' first team a year after signing and settled quickly, impressing the Irish selectors who capped him once at Under-21 level, once at Under-23 level and once at 'B' level.

Milligan's rapidly developing talent made him a magnet for the big guns in the north-west, and in August 1990 he joined Everton in a £1 million deal – the biggest fee Oldham had ever received for a player.

After moving to Goodison, Mike was plagued by injuries and struggled to regain the form that had made him one of the most talked-about players in the League the previous season. As a result, in his one season at the club he made just 17 League appearances.

Meanwhile his former colleagues at Oldham were claiming the Second Division title in dramatic fashion on the final day of the 1990–91 campaign. During the close season Milligan was reunited with them, with Everton losing £400,000 in another record deal. It was the biggest fee Oldham had ever paid for a player.

Mike recovered his earlier form and was made captain of the Boundary Park club. In May 1992 he won his only full cap, as a substitute, against the USA. The following year he helped the Latics perform 'the great escape' when they just avoided relegation from the Premier League owing to a cliff-hanging 4–3 victory over Southampton on the last day of the season. Mike was voted Oldham's 'Player of the Year' in that 1992–93 campaign.

The next season, 1993–94, the pull of relegation was finally too strong for Oldham, and after finishing in 21st place, they were relegated. In his two spells with the club Milligan netted 23 goals in 279 League games

During the close season Milligan was once again transferred, this time to Norwich City. And once again he was involved in an unsuccessful relegation battle, for the Canaries lost their Premier League status at the end of 1994–95. In two seasons to date at Carrow Road he has made 54 League appearances (four goals).

Michael Milligan

John (Jackie) Mooney (INSIDE-RIGHT)

Born: Dublin 1938
Debut for Eire: v Poland October 1964

Jackie Mooney had spells with Home Farm, Manchester United, Bangor in Wales and Cork Hibernians before joining Shamrock Rovers in 1962. He won the League and Cup double with the Hoops in 1963–64 and an FAI Cup winners medal the following season.

In 1969, following a three-year absence through injury, Jackie made a comeback to League of Ireland football with Athlone, who had been re-elected to the League that year after a 40-year absence. He made an immediate impact at Athlone. His hat-trick in the 1969 Leinster Senior Cup final was largely responsible for winning the club's first senior trophy in 45 years.

Jackie Mooney was not fast, but he excelled as a striker. Using his head more than his feet, he was Cork's top scorer in 1960–61 and 1961–62; Rovers' top marksman in 1962–63; and the League's top scorer in 1964–65, with 16 goals. He also topped Bohemians' scoring charts in 1971–72.

A former Youth international and inter-League player, Jackie 'made a wonderful international debut at centre-forward' against Poland in Dublin in October 1964, linking up well with the hero of that game, Andy McEvoy. Ireland had been trailing 2–0 after 22 minutes when Mooney scored one of the goals in the fightback to win 3–2.

Jackie, who worked at the Cargo Department at Dublin airport, won his second cap in Ireland's next fixture, a 2–0 defeat by Belgium in March 1965.

Alan Moore (MIDFIELD)

Born: Dublin 25 November 1974
Debut for Eire: v Czech Republic April 1996

The FAI/Opel 'Youth Player of the Year' in 1993, Alan Moore joined Middlesbrough from Finglas junior club Rivermount Boys. There was no shortage of Irish Company for Moore at Boro. Seasoned Eire internationals Alan Kernaghan and Chris Morris were already there, as were Dubliners Curtis Fleming and Graham Cavanagh.

Alan made his League debut for the club against Everton in April 1993. The dazzling left-winger was a fixture in the side the following season and in 1994–95 when Boro were crowned First Division champions.

Moore found himself out in the cold for much of the 1995–96 season as Boro boss Bryan Robson reverted to a 5–3–2 formation in the Premiership. Towards the end of that season, he got his place back, playing just behind the two front-runners, and taking his League appearance tally to 92 games (17 goals) by the end of that term.

A player with loads of ability, Moore scored on his first match for Ireland's Under-18s and on his Under-21 debut, against Latvia in Riga, in September 1994. He won his first full cap in the 2–0 defeat by the Czech Republic in April 1996, and had taken his tally to seven by the 3–0 defeat of Bolivia the following June.

Kevin Moran (CENTRE-HALF)

Born: Dublin 29 April 1956
Debut for Eire: v Switzerland April 1980

Kevin Moran is one of the most physically combative and committed players in the game's history. A solid, upright centre-back in the old-fashioned mould, his strengths are most apparent in aerial battle and when confronted with powerful aggressive strikers – an archetypal product of the Gaelic game in which he achieved almost legendary status in his native land.

Moran was one of Ireland's top exponents of the national game and won an All-Ireland medal with Dublin. When Manchester United scout Billy Behan recommended him to his employers, Moran, who at the time was playing his soccer with University College Dublin club Pegasus, had only the flimsiest of soccer backgrounds.

Nevertheless his transfer to Old Trafford, for a nominal fee, went through in February 1978 and caused considerable consternation in Irish Gaelic football circles. There were those who felt Moran would have difficulty making the full transition to Association rules – they were wrong.

Kevin progressed through United's ranks under Dave Sexton, who preferred him in midfield. But when Ron Atkinson arrived at the club in 1981, followed soon after by Bryan Robson, Kevin was switched to central defence.

In seven seasons as a United player he made 231 League appearances and scored 21 goals, many of them coming from set pieces when he attacked powerfully hit crosses to rocket the ball goalwards.

As one of the game's most battle-scarred players, Moran's bravery became legendary at Old Trafford; he literally gave blood in the cause of the club, collecting over 100 stitches in what were mostly facial injuries.

As a United player he won two FA Cup winners medals in 1983 and 1985. In the latter final tie, against Everton, he wrote himself into the annals of soccer history by becoming the first player to be sent off in a major final at Wembley when he was harshly dismissed for a tackle on Peter Reid.

In August 1988 Kevin joined Spanish club Sporting Gijon on a free transfer. He returned to the Football League in January 1990 to join up-and-coming Blackburn Rovers, after turning down his former boss at Old Trafford, Ron Atkinson, who had taken over at Sheffield Wednesday, and Jim Smith at Newcastle.

He helped Rovers win their place in the Premier League by beating Leicester City in the Division Two play-off final in May 1992.

In June 1994 Moran, who had become Rovers' captain, announced his retirement from the game having played 147 League games and scored ten goals for the Ewood Park club.

Clean and hard, Moran was a diplomat both on and off the field. He was an Irish international for almost 14 years, winning his first cap against Switzerland the day after his 24th birthday in April 1980. He scored six international goals, opening his account with a couple against Czechoslovakia on his 25th birthday.

Moran was something of a footballing Lazarus at international level: his career seemed to have ended several times but he always returned, taking his final tally to 70 caps.

He played in all of Ireland's games in the 1988 European Championships, when he captained the national side, and in the 1990 World Cup finals in Italy. At 38 Kevin was the oldest member of the Republic's USA '94 squad, although he didn't get a game at the finals.

Thomas Moroney (WING-HALF)

Born: Cork 10 November 1923
Debut for Eire: v Spain May 1948

Zealous and constructive Tommy Moroney

was an excellent reader of the game. A member of the great Cork United side which swept all before them in the 1940s, he won League of Ireland Championship medals in 1944–45 and 1945–46 and an FAI Cup winners medal in 1947, scoring one of the two goals in the defeat of Bohemians in the replayed final.

A fine all-round athlete, Tommy played rugby for Cork Constitution and Munster, and would have been capped at rugby but for the cancellation of internationals during the war years.

Leeds United, West Ham and several other English clubs were interested in signing Moroney during the summer of 1949. It was the Hammers who won the day.

There was a touch of farce in the transfer deal which took Moroney and his Cork colleague, full-back John McGowan, to Upton Park that summer. They arrived in the East End a week after the other players had begun training because of 'passage and passport delays' and came without their boots: the Cork club refused to part with them. They had to break in new ones – every footballer's nightmare.

Nevertheless Tommy was a hit in his trial game. The expert assessment was that 'although he showed a great deal of stiffness he displayed the fact that he is a footballer. His ground passes to forwards were evidence of this and proof of the fact that when he "loosens up" properly the Hammers will have in him a fine wing-half.'

Tommy claimed a first-team place almost immediately and spent his entire Football League career at Upton Park. In six seasons there he made 148 Second Division appearances and scored eight goals before returning to Ireland in 1953 to join Evergreen United. He later managed Cork Celtic.

Tommy played the game with easy nonchalance. He made good use of the ball and was always in position to support the attack, while his defensive play was also 'excellent'.

He played for Munster against the RAF in

May 1947 and represented the League of Ireland during his Cork days. A former international Amateur half-back, Tommy marked his full international debut with Ireland's goal in the 2–1 defeat by Spain in Barcelona in May 1948.

He earned his second cap the following May and from then until October 1951 he was a regular in the Irish defence. His 11th cap came in the 3–2 defeat of West Germany in October 1951.

Tom waited two years for another call from the Irish selectors. As an Evergreen United player, he was recalled for the World Cup qualifier with France in October 1953. The 5–3 defeat by the French, in which Tom played most of the game at outside-right, was his last for his country.

Tommy Moroney died in Cork in May 1981.

Christopher Morris (FULL-BACK)

Born: Newquay 24 December 1963
Debut for Eire: v Israel November 1987

The son of a Co. Mayo-born mother, Chris Morris was born in the Cornish seaside resort of Newquay. A natural sportsman, had fate not taken a hand, he might have played for England against Ireland in rugby, soccer or even cricket.

Chris represented the South West Counties at rugby union, Cornwall Schools at cricket and was an England Under-18 player. He didn't neglect his studies either, leaving school with ten 'O' Levels and three 'A' Levels. He was set for a career as a PE teacher when he tagged along with a mate to Sheffield Wednesday for a trial. Chris spent a month at Hillsborough before persuading Wednesday boss Jack Charlton to sign him, which he did in October 1982.

In 1983–84 Morris broke into the Owls' first XI, but as a right-winger. He remained on the flank for most of the season until the club became top heavy with wingers, which meant a switch in position if he wanted to stay in the side. Initially he moved to midfield, and then he found his niche at right-back.

Chris spent five years at Hillsborough and made 74 League appearances. In the summer of 1987 Billy McNeill took him north of the border to Glasgow Celtic in a £125,000 transfer deal.

Quick and crisp in the tackle, Chris immediately laid claim to the right-back position at Parkhead. Never losing his attacking instinct from his early days as a winger, he helped Celtic to a Scottish League and Cup double in his first season, 1987–88; that season he was one of only two Celtic players who didn't miss a game. A fine season was crowned by his full international call-up. Irish manager Jack Charlton hadn't forgotten the youngster he signed for Wednesday in 1982 and in November 1987 awarded him his first full cap in the record 5–0 defeat of Israel.

Chris became a regular in the Irish set-up, playing mostly at right-back but occasionally turning up in midfield. He played in all of Ireland's games in the 1988 European Championships in West Germany and in the 1990 World Cup finals in Italy two years later. He collected a total of 35 caps; when competition for the full-back positions became fierce with the arrival of Denis Irwin, Stephen Staunton and Terry Phelan on the scene, Morris found himself out in the cold.

Meanwhile he continued his winning ways at Parkhead, helping Celtic win the 1989 Scottish Cup with a 1–0 win over Rangers in the final. Two years later Chris was a substitute when Rangers exacted revenge by beating their rivals 2–1 in the final of the Scottish League (Skol) Cup.

In five seasons Chris had made 163 League appearances in the famous green and white hoops before his transfer to Middlesbrough at the end of 1991–92.

In November 1993 he damaged a cruciate ligament, an injury which required surgery and kept him out for the rest of the 1993–94 season.

Chris returned to the fray the following season, 1994–95, and made 16 appearances in Boro's First Division Championship-winning season. To the end of 1995–96 he had made 78 League appearances for Boro.

George Moulson (GOALKEEPER)

Born: Clogheen, Co. Tipperary 6 August 1914
Debut for Eire: v Portugal May 1948

George Moulson, whose family had moved from Tipperary to Grimsby in the 1920s, was bought out of the Army by Grimsby Town to sign for them in July 1936.

A 'finely built keeper', George's first-team chances at Grimsby were limited owing to the presence of England international keeper George Tweedy. But when Tweedy went down with flu, the way was clear for George to make his senior debut in the ill-fated 1939 FA Cup semi-final against Wolves. He had hardly touched the ball when he collided with Wolves' forward Dick Dorsett. George suffered concussion and took no further part in the game; and the ten-man Mariners went down 5–0.

During the war years George played regularly for Grimsby (103 appearances) and made 102 guest appearances for Lincoln City. He did not make his League debut for Grimsby until April 1947, more than ten years after signing. It was his only League game for the club. In June that year he joined Lincoln City.

In 1947–48 he was a regular as Lincoln won the Division Three (North) Championship. He had made 60 League appearances when he lost his place in the team to Arthur Jepson and in the summer of 1949 George left for Midland League club Peterborough United.

George was Ireland's goalminder for three consecutive games between May and December 1948. The games – against Portugal, Spain and Switzerland – all ended in defeat for the Irish.

George, who settled in Grimsby when he retired, is the younger brother of Con Moulson who won five Eire caps in the '30s while on the books of Lincoln City and Notts County.

Cathal Muckian (FORWARD)

Born: Dundalk, Co. Louth 1952
Debut for Eire: v Poland April 1978

A self-assured front man, Cathal Muckian spent six seasons with Drogheda, where he was an FAI Cup runner-up in 1976, before his transfer to their Co. Louth rivals Dundalk in 1978. Cathal had been working at the Bank of Ireland in Drogheda for some years and was transferred on his promotion to assistant manager at the Bank's regional office in Dundalk.

Dundalk had good reason to be enthusiastic about their new acquisition, because Muckian had topped Drogheda's scoring charts with 21 League goals the previous campaign.

In his first season at Oriel Park, 1978–79, Cathal helped his new club to the double of League of Ireland Championship and FAI Cup, and won critical acclaim in the local press for his contribution to the Lilywhites' success: 'No single player has come on as well from early season as Cathal Muckian, who only needed patience and a return of confidence to produce the sort of form we expected from him. He has been playing with mounting assurance, very fast on the ball, shields it well and moves it well and with intelligence.'

In 1980 Muckian was again transferred by the Bank, this time to Dublin where in 1980–81 he turned out for Shamrock Rovers and Shelbourne.

Cathal was brought into the Irish side at the last minute to face Poland in April 1978. He joined his former colleague at Drogheda, Jerome Clarke, in the side which lost 3–0 in Lodz. It was both players' only cap.

Patrick Mulligan (RIGHT-BACK)

Born: Dublin 17 March 1945
Debut for Eire: v Czechoslovakia May 1969

Paddy Mulligan joined Shamrock Rovers in February 1964 from Bohemians, with whom he had had two games after leaving Home Farm.

A strong, rugged and talented defender with bundles of enthusiasm and indomitable energy, he combined playing part-time with Rovers and working as an office furniture salesman.

An FAI Minor Cup winner, Paddy won FAI Cup winners medals with Rovers in 1965, 1966, 1967 and 1969. In October 1969 he was transferred to Chelsea for a League of Ireland record £17,500.

Although his overlapping skills and turn of speed were greatly admired among the Chelsea

Patrick Mulligan

faithful, Paddy took some time to break into the first XI at the Bridge. A long-term injury to Eddie McCreadie eventually allowed him to establish himself in the side.

An injury sustained against CSKA Sofia in the second round of the European Cup-Winners' Cup in 1970 sidelined Mulligan for two months, and although he got another sustained run in the side in 1971–72, he ended up in the reserve team.

Paddy collected a League Cup runners-up medal in 1972, after Chelsea lost 2–1 to Stoke City in the final. An injury in the game compelled him to leave the fray at half-time. His absence is said to have contributed to Chelsea's defeat.

In three seasons at Chelsea Paddy made just 58 League appearances; and in September 1972, he was sold to Chelsea's First Division rivals Crystal Palace for £80,000.

Mulligan's three seasons at Palace, during which he made 57 League appearances, witnessed a steady decline in the fortunes of the south London club: they dropped from the First to the Third Division in successive seasons.

In September 1975 Paddy left Selhurst Park to link up with his Republic of Ireland colleague, Johnny Giles, who had just taken over as manager of West Bromwich Albion. He made 109 League appearances with West Brom and helped them win promotion to Division One in 1975–76, his first season at the club.

Paddy returned to Ireland and Shamrock Rovers in 1977 and later had a spell as player-manager at Galway.

Paddy won a Schoolboy cap in 1960 and a Youth cap three years later. Although standing just 5ft 7in, Mulligan was surprisingly good in the air and soon broke onto the Irish international scene. He played in the Under-23 game against France in June 1966 and won his first full cap, while a Shamrock Rovers player, in the 2–1 defeat by Czechoslovakia in a World Cup qualifier in May 1969.

Despite the relative indifference of his domestic career, Paddy was a regular in the Republic's defence throughout the '70s. He was capped at every club he played for and captained his country 13 times. He earned his 50th and final full cap, while again on the books of Shamrock Rovers, against the USA in October 1979.

Liam Munroe (FORWARD)

Born: Dublin
Debut for Eire: v Luxembourg October 1953

'A determined player who carries a useful shot', Liam 'Mousie' Munroe was a League Championship winner with Shamrock Rovers in 1953–54.

An inter-League player, he played so well against the Welsh League in 1953 that his elevation to full international status seemed a mere formality.

Nevertheless his call-up, in preference to the experienced Sheffield Wednesday player Alf Ringstead, for the team to face Luxembourg in October 1953 raised a few eyebrows. Luton Town's George Cummins and West Ham's Noel Cantwell also made their international debuts in this game; they would last longer.

On his debut Liam was 'a glutton for work and tried to play centre-forward from the right wing in the first half and showed his best form when shifted to centre-forward in place of Gibbons 15 minutes from time. Then the attack gathered new power.'

Ireland won 4–0. However, a perceptive Seamus Devlin wrote in the *Irish Press* after the game that: 'Liam Munroe's lack of height will deprive him of a second cap even though he tried very hard against Wagner, the best defender of the Luxembourg team.'

Albert Murphy (RIGHT HALF-BACK)

Born: Dublin November 1930
Debut for Eire: v Yugoslavia October 1955

One of the most promising right half-backs to play in the League of Ireland, Albert 'Albie' Murphy was transferred from Dublin club Transport to Scottich club Clyde in November 1949, just a couple of weeks after playing for the League of Ireland against the Scottish League. At the end of that season he returned to Ireland and played for one season with Shamrock Rovers before settling down in Glasgow.

During his second stint with the Bully Wee, Albie developed into one of the most consistent and skilful right-backs in Scotland. During his time at the club he won two Division Two Championship medals in 1951–52 and 1956–57, and played in two Scottish Cup finals: in 1955 when Celtic were defeated 1–0 after a replay, and in 1958 when Hibs were overcome by a single goal.

It was reported in 1955–56 that Murphy was playing 'brilliantly'. The news was not lost on the Irish selectors who, in October 1955, awarded the player his only cap, thereby displacing experienced internationals Seamus Dunne and Don Donovan, for the game against Yugoslavia.

Barry Murphy (CENTRE-HALF)

Born: Dublin 1 April 1959
Debut for Eire: v Uruguay April 1986

Barry Murphy was a double runner-up in 1979–80, for St Patrick's Athletic lost the FAI Cup and League Cup finals to Waterford and Athlone Town. Two seasons later, manager Billy Young signed him for Bohemians.

Murphy missed Bohs' FAI Cup final defeat by Limerick in 1982 through injury. He scored a rare goal against Sligo in the following year's final, but it was a consolation strike as the Dubliners went down 2–1. In the summer of 1988, having seen Bohs finish in the top four in each of his ten seasons there, including several runners-up spots, Barry moved to Shamrock Rovers.

In 1991 he collected his third FAI Cup runners-up medal as a member of the Hoops team beaten 1–0 by Galway United in the final. Later that year he departed for Kilkenny City and two years later signed for Athlone Town.

Barry, who was a gas converter by trade, realised a cherished dream in April 1986 when he was called up to the Irish squad to face Uruguay. He had thought that any chance of playing for his country had passed him by: he was 27 years old and he had been in the last League of Ireland squad before the Uruguay match but hadn't got on the field. However, injuries to Paul McGrath and David O'Leary, allied to a recommendation to new boss Jack Charlton (who had never seen him 'in or out of action') by physio Mick Byrne, saw him called up.

It was Barry's only cap, and his sudden and belated elevation to the international stage agreed with him, because he had a 'disciplined and sensible display' alongside Mick McCarthy in the heart of the Irish defence in the 1–1 draw with the South Americans.

Jeremy Murphy (MIDFIELD)

Born: Stepney, London 23 September 1959
Debut for Eire: v Wales September 1979

Born in east London, Jerry Murphy joined Crystal Palace as an apprentice in October 1976. The following year he was a member of Palace's famous 'Team of the Eighties' youth team, which defeated Everton 1–0 to lift the FA Youth Cup for the first time in the club's history; they repeated the feat the following season with another 1–0 victory, this time over Aston Villa.

Murphy broke into the first team soon after and in nine years as a professional at Selhurst Park he made 229 League appearances (20 goals) and won a Second Division

Championship medal in 1978–79. A creative left-sided midfielder who held nothing back in the tackle, Jerry was given a free transfer in August 1985 and subsequently joined Chelsea.

Although he became part of Chelsea's first-team set-up almost immediately his early days at Stamford Bridge were punctuated by injuries, which hampered his progress in the team. In May 1988, after just 34 League outings in a Chelsea shirt, the club cancelled Jerry's registration.

In March 1991 he returned to the game, joining non-League Basingstoke.

A former England Schoolboy international, Jerry came into the international side for the game against Wales in September 1979 because of a hamstring injury to Gerry Daly. He won a further two caps in that 1979–80 season.

Terence Murray (INSIDE-FORWARD)

Born: Dublin 22 May 1928
Debut for Eire: v Belgium May 1950

Terry Murray began his professional career with League of Ireland club Dundalk in 1948. A former clerk with the Irish Transport Company, he was transferred to Hull City for a £6,000 fee in October 1951.

Terry appeared at inside-left in the Tigers' reserves but mostly at inside-right and occasionally as a right-winger in the 32 Second Division games (six goals) he played for the club.

In March 1954 he went to Bournemouth as a replacement for Len Gaynor, who had departed for Southampton. Bournemouth manager Jack Bruton had watched Murray several times before inviting him to Dean Court: 'He's a very useful player, one of those who gives everything he has and runs himself into the ground . . . he should be well groomed with his new chums next season and bring extra experience to the team.'

But it wasn't to be. Murray managed just 13 League appearances and one goal with the Cherries before he was released at the end of 1954–55.

At 5ft 8in and 11st 7lb, Terry had a strong physique and could be match-winner on his day. He had represented the League of Ireland on seven occasions by the time he arrived in Hull and was a member of the FAI team which played Glasgow Celtic at Dalymount Park in April 1953.

Terry was one of four League of Ireland players who made their international debut against Belgium in Brussels in May 1950. Ireland lost 5–1 and only one of the debutants (Martin Colfer) played for Ireland again.

William Newman (MIDFIELD)

Born: Dublin 1947
Debut for Eire: v Denmark May 1969

After a dozen goals in two seasons with Bohemians, whom he signed for in 1966, midfielder Billy Newman joined Bohs' Dublin rivals Shelbourne. In 1973 he was an FAI Cup runner-up with Shels after they lost the replayed final 1–0 to Cork Hibs.

'One of the most underrated midfielders in the League, Billy quietly and unobtrusively does the right thing in the simple way and is very effective.'

A former Eire Youth and Amateur international, Newman was called up as a replacement for the unavailable Tony Dunne of Manchester United for the World Cup qualifier against Denmark in Copenhagen in May 1969. He described his elevation to the international arena as 'the best news he ever had, especially as he'd been surprised to find himself in the original panel'. Billy came into the side at left-half. But he had been on the field for only 55 minutes when he was replaced by Frank O'Neill of Shamrock Rovers.

Ronald Nolan (RIGHT HALF-BACK)

Born: Dublin 1935
Debut for Eire: v Denmark October 1956

A former Johnville junior, Ronnie Nolan spent the lion's share of his senior career with Shamrock Rovers.

He was a League Championship winner with the Hoops on four occasions: 1953–54, 1956–57, 1958–59 and 1963–64. But Nolan's biggest success was in the FAI Cup competition: he played in an amazing eight finals between 1955 and 1966, collecting winners medals six times.

The 1956 showdown against Cork Athletic, however, is the one which will stand out from the rest in Nolan's mind. Rovers trailed 2–0 with just 13 minutes left on the clock. They clawed their way back to level terms; then, with a minute to go, Nolan came up from left-back to head home the winning goal from a corner kick.

Ronnie later played for Rovers' Dublin rivals Bohemians, with whom he won another FAI Cup winners medal in 1970 after Bohs eventually overcame Sligo Rovers 2–1 in a second replay.

Ronnie played as a right-winger for the Irish Schoolboys, was a regular League of Ireland representative player in the '50s and '60s and was a member of the Dublin City select which played Arsenal in 1964.

He played in three winning Irish 'B' international sides in 1958–59 and 1960–61, scoring his only international goal in the 3–2 defeat of Iceland in Reykjavik in August 1958.

Ronnie's full international career spanned six years, between October 1956 and September 1962. In his first six international games Ireland were undefeated, recording memorable home and away victories over West Germany. He won his tenth and final cap in a 1–1 draw with Iceland in Reykjavik.

Francis O'Brien (FULL-BACK)

Born: Dublin 1955
Debut for Eire: v Czechoslovakia
September 1979

Fran O'Brien shared in the Bohemians' successes of the mid-1970s: he was in the side that won the Leinster Cup, the President's Cup in three successive seasons and, in 1976, the FAI Cup.

However, in March 1978 – just as the Gypsies were about to clinch the League title – Fran left the club, with his Bohs colleagues Eddie and Pat Byrne, to join Philadelphia Fury in the North American Soccer League.

While in the USA O'Brien made history by becoming the first player permanently attached to an American club to be called up by the Republic; he made his international debut against Czechoslovakia in Prague in September 1979. Three other players made their debuts in that game and two more new caps came on as substitutes, as the under-strength Irish side went down 4–1.

Although regarded as a full-back, O'Brien played on the left side of midfield against the Czechs, the position he had held for most of the previous summer in America. 'Fran took time to settle in but caught the eye after the interval with a stream of good runs.'

Fran, whose older brother Ray was also an Ireland full-back, won two more full caps, against England and Cyprus in February and March 1980, whilst still a Fury player.

Liam O'Brien (MIDFIELD)

Born: Dublin 5 September 1964
Debut for Eire: v Uruguay April 1986

Not many players turn their back on the offer of a new contract with Manchester United. But that's exactly what Liam O'Brien did in the summer of 1988.

Throughout his career, O'Brien has been compared favourably with many greats of the game. A creative midfielder who takes no prisoners, he was hailed as the new Johnny Giles when he arrived at Old Trafford from Shamrock Rovers. His knack of scoring spectacular goals with ferocious shots from dead ball situations and open play drew comparisons with the Brazilian showman Zico, while his vision is said to be in the class of Glenn Hoddle. 'There is much of Trevor Brooking in his ability to run with the ball and withstand challenges that one feels sure will nobble him. In his passing too there is the similar ability to broaden the geometry and shape of attack.'

Liam arrived at Old Trafford in October 1986 on the back of a trio of consecutive League of Ireland Championship successes with Shamrock Rovers. To secure his signature, United had to see off a host of other bidders. They paid Rovers £50,000 and agreed to two challenge matches with the Hoops, in which O'Brien captained his new club against his old.

At Rovers Liam had acquired a form of superstar status but at United he was reduced to the role of stand-in behind Whiteside, Robson and Moses and made 15 of his 31 League appearances for the club as a substitute.

In November 1988 Liam left Old Trafford for Newcastle's St James' Park as Geordies boss Colin Suggett's first signing. The £275,000 deal was struck in somewhat controversial circumstances. Liam was frustrated at his lack of first-team duty but United, although wanting him to stay, couldn't guarantee him a regular place. Consequently the offer of a new contract was rejected in preference to signing for Newcastle.

On Tyneside a broken leg followed by ligament problems carved out more than a year from his career. But he recovered full fitness and claimed his regular place in the Magpies' engine-room. When Newcastle became the first club to win the new Division One Championship in 1992–93, Liam was one of the principal rallying forces behind the success, though again he missed the last third of the season through injury.

Liam had made 151 League appearances for Newcastle (19 goals) when he was transferred to Tranmere Rovers for £250,000 in January 1994. To the end of 1995–96 he had made 77 League appearances for Rovers.

Dublin-born Liam, like many other Irish international stars, began his career with local junior club Stella Maris. He later had a spell in the League of Ireland with Bohemians and in the North American Soccer League with Cleveland Ohio before joining Shamrock Rovers in 1983.

Capped once at Under-23 level, Liam was still on Rovers' books when he won his first full cap against Uruguay in April 1986. Due to the unprecedented strength of the Republic's midfield in the '80s and '90s, O'Brien found himself playing a bit-part role at international level. He was a surprise exclusion from the USA '94 squad and won his 11th cap against Russia in March 1994.

After being out of the international reckoning for over two years, he was brought back in by new boss Mick McCarthy in the summer of 1996 and now has 16 full caps.

Raymond O'Brien (LEFT-BACK)

Born: Dublin 21 May 1951
Debut for Eire: v Norway March 1976

The son of former Drumcondra left-half Frank O'Brien, Ray wasn't the only one of Frank O'Brien's sons to play the game. His brothers Fran and Derek played for Philadelphia Fury and Boston United respectively in the late 1970s – and both of them, like Ray, were left-backs.

Ray signed for Manchester United from Shelbourne for £40,000 in May 1973 just after playing in Shels' FAI Cup final defeat by Cork Hibs. He failed to make United's first team and

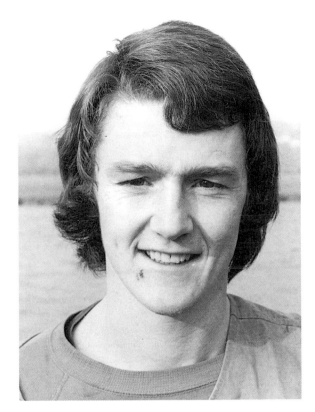

Raymond O'Brien

less than a year later, in March 1974, he was sold to Notts County for what turned out to be a bargain £45,000.

A decided asset to any side, O'Brien was a teak-tough but honest and solid defender whose commitment soon won over the Meadow Lane faithful. He became a regular in the side and in nine seasons at the club made 323 League appearances (30 goals). In 1979–80 he created a club record at County when, with ten goals, he ended the season as the club's top scorer, thereby becoming the first full-back to achieve that distinction. The following season, 1980–81, he helped them win promotion to Division One, after an absence of some 55 years.

In September 1983 Ray made four appearances on loan to Derby County and in July 1984 joined non-League Boston United, taking over the managerial reins there in

January 1986. In November 1987 he was appointed manager of Corby Town.

During his time at Old Trafford Ray represented Ireland's Under-23 side twice in games against France in 1972–73. In a 13-month period between March 1976 and April 1977, he made four appearances for the senior side.

He made his debut, on the same day as Mick Walsh and Tony Grealish launched their international careers, in the 3–0 defeat of Norway in March 1976 and played his last game for Ireland in the goalless draw with Poland in April 1977.

Lar O'Byrne (LEFT-BACK)

Born: Dublin
Debut for Eire: v Belgium April 1949

Former Shamrock Rovers defender Lar O'Byrne made the giant leap from Leinster League football to international competition in just one season.

O'Byrne made his full international debut, with four other League of Ireland debutants, in the 2–0 defeat by Belgium in Dublin in April 1949. It was Ireland's first-ever defeat at the hands of the Belgians. Although 'lacking the polish of the cross-channel players [Lar] had a really promising international debut, clearing cleanly he showed an excellent sense of position and made two goal-line clearances'.

It was, however, his only full international. Lar, who was a former inter-League left-back, turned out for St Patrick's Athletic and Transport in the early 1950s.

Brendan O'Callaghan

(FORWARD/CENTRE-HALF)

Born: Bradford 23 July 1955
Debut for Eire: v West Germany May 1979

Brendan O'Callaghan joined Fourth Division Doncaster Rovers as a junior, signing professionally when he was 18 in July 1973. He spent almost five years at the Belle Vue Ground, scoring a respectable 65 goals in 187 League games.

O'Callaghan's scoring feats at Doncaster tempted Alan Durban to make his first signing after taking over as manager of Stoke City: he landed the player for the Second Division club for a fee of £40,000 in March 1978.

Brendan had a sensational debut for Stoke. He scored the only goal of the game within ten seconds of coming on as a substitute against Hull in March 1978. The following season, 1978–79, he headed Stoke's scoring charts with 17 goals, which helped shoot the club back into the top flight.

He was normally used as a big target man. But O'Callaghan's frame and build – he stood 6ft 2in and weighed 13st – lent itself also to a central defensive role. When Dave Watson was signed from Southampton in January 1982, O'Callaghan was moved to central defence. It was in this position that he played out the last of his 245 League games (45 goals) for the Potteries club.

His performances in central defence persuaded relegation-threatened Oldham Athletic to part with £45,000 to take him to Boundary Park in February 1985. Brendan was pitched straight into the Latics' Second Division relegation battle. He played in nine of the remaining League games of 1984–85 and helped Oldham avoid the drop.

After just ten minutes of the first game of the 1985–86 season, against Norwich City, O'Callaghan was forced to withdraw owing to a recurring groin injury and in January 1986 he announced his retirement from the game.

Between May 1979 and May 1982 Brendan won six full caps for the Republic, the last one coming almost exactly three years after the first, when he opened his international account as a substitute against West Germany in 1979. He finished on the winning side on just one occasion, when Eire beat the USA 3–2 in October 1979.

Kevin O'Callaghan (FORWARD)

Born: Dagenham 19 October 1961
Debut for Eire: v Czechoslovakia April 1981

Since joining Millwall as an apprentice in 1977, Kevin O'Callaghan has appeared for four League clubs. But, undoubtedly, the most famous side he has appeared in was the one which included Pele, Ossie Ardiles, John Wark, Bobby Moore and . . . Sylvester Stallone – in the box office hit *Escape to Victory*.

Kevin agreed professional terms with Millwall in November 1978 and the following year was a member of the Lions' FA Youth Cup-winning side. He made his League debut in that 1978–79 season, a season which ended with the club's relegation to Division Three.

He had played just 20 League games for Millwall when, in January 1980, he was transferred to Ipswich Town for a club record £250,000. In exactly five years at Portman Road O'Callaghan made 115 First Division appearances (43 of which started from the dug-out) and equalled his Millwall scoring tally of three goals.

In January 1985 he joined Portsmouth on a month's loan. The temporary transfer became a permanent one in March when Portsmouth paid Ipswich £90,000 for the player.

Kevin played 87 Second Division games (16 goals) for the Fratton Park club and in his final season there, 1986–87, helped the club complete a remarkable decade by winning promotion to Division One that season, having been in Division Four in 1979–80.

He returned to the Lions' Den during the close season. His second stint there got off to a bright start but the remainder of his time there was blighted by injury and discord.

In a side which included Teddy Sheringham and Tony Cascarino he scored only once from open play and added a further half a dozen from the penalty spot in his first season (1987–88) and ended the campaign with a Second Division Championship medal.

Plagued by long-term injuries, he spent the whole of 1989–90 trying to shake off a mystery knee problem. He finally forced his way back into the team in October 1990 but in February 1991 a bust-up with manager Bruce Rioch prompted him to request a transfer.

Kevin had scored 14 goals in 76 League outings for Millwall when he joined Southend United in July 1991. He made 21 appearances for the Roots Hall club prior to being released by the club in November 1992.

Capped by the Republic of Ireland at Youth level, Kevin won five caps at Under-21 level. He won his first full cap in the 3–1 defeat of Czechoslovakia in April 1981 and scored his only goal at this level in the record 8–0 defeat of Malta in November 1983.

Kevin won a total of 20 full caps, 11 of which were as a substitute, all during Eoin Hand's reign as national team manager.

Anthony O'Connell (OUTSIDE-LEFT)

Born: Dublin 1941
Debut for Eire: v Spain October 1966

Like many of his fellow-citizens, Tony O'Connell started playing soccer with Dublin junior club Stella Maris. In 1959 he joined Shamrock Rovers as a minor.

Lightly built, Tony was skilled at working the ball at speed on the wings and was capable of creating brilliant openings, though he was often criticised for being over-elaborate.

O'Connell was an FAI Cup winner with the Hoops in 1962. He left Dublin to play in Canada and America in 1963–64 – the season that Rovers won the double. After he returned to Rovers at the start of 1964–65, with Liam Tuohy holding down the left-wing position most of the time, Tony was switched to various positions, including centre-forward.

He won back-to-back FAI Cup winners medals in 1965 (after Rovers defeated Limerick in the replay) and 1966. He retained his place in the side for the 1966 final only because Liam Tuohy was injured; but he certainly justified his selection by scoring one of Rovers' goals in the 2–0 defeat of Limerick.

Soon after that final Tony joined Dundalk and in his first season, 1966–67, helped the Lilywhites win the League title. In March 1969 he 'obtained his release' from Dundalk for a substantial fee to become Bohemians' first professional player.

'Always a threat and rises to the big occasion', O'Connell was Bohs' top scorer in 1969–70 and that season won his fourth FAI Cup winners medal after Bohs defeated Sligo Rovers 2–1 in a second replay in which Tony netted the winner. He is currently president of Bohemians.

A former inter-League player, Tony was the hero of the sensational 2–1 defeat of the English League at Dalymount Park in October 1963 when he gave seasoned international captain Jimmy Armfield a 'nightmare 90 minutes'. He won his first full cap in the 0–0 European Championship game with Spain in October 1966. Almost exactly four years later he was a half-time replacement for Mick Lawlor in the Ireland side which lost 2–0 to Poland in Dublin.

his earlier form and had difficulty holding down a first-team place at Rovers.

Nevertheless, he was selected for the Irish XI to face Finland in September 1949. He turned out to be the surprise packet in the 3–0 defeat of the Finns in the World Cup qualifier. 'Although a trifle slow in getting the ball across in the first quarter hour,' reported one newspaper, 'O'Connor subsequently played with great confidence and was about the most enterprising forward.'

He retained his outside-left position, the selectors preferring him over Eglington and John O'Driscoll, for Ireland's visit to Goodison Park to face England a fortnight later: 'He may not be stylish but he's a hard worker and direct and has regained his confidence; the bigger the match, the better he plays.' On that memorable occasion O'Connor played his part by providing the passes which led to both goals in the visitors' 2–0 victory, the first home defeat suffered by England by a 'foreign' team.

One of the only two home-based players on the victorious side (the other being Shamrock Rovers keeper Tommy Godwin), Tommy subsequently played most of his football in the Leinster Senior League.

He did win two more full caps to add to his inter-League honours, playing in World Cup games against Sweden and Finland in October and November 1949.

Thomas O'Connor (WINGER)

Born: Dublin
Debut for Eire: v Finland September 1949

Tommy O'Connor first attracted attention as a promising outside-left for Shamrock Rovers in the early part of 1948–49. Unfortunately an injury just before Christmas 1948 kept him out of the game for a few months, and caused him to lose a certain amount of confidence in himself – on his return he failed to recapture

Turlough O'Connor

(CENTRE-FORWARD)

Born: Athlone, Co. Westmeath 22 July 1946
Debut for Eire: v Czechoslovakia November 1967

One of eight children of an Irish Army tuba player, Turlough O'Connor's rare ability to hit the target regularly first became apparent when at local junior side Gentex in his native

Athlone. His performances with Gentex won him two Youth caps and attracted the attention of several League of Ireland clubs. Initially he joined Limerick and later had a brief spell with Athlone Town before joining Bohemians in February 1965. In May 1966, with Bohs colleague Jimmy Conway, O'Connor transferred to Fulham.

Turlough spent two seasons at Craven Cottage but two hernia operations, one in the middle of each season, proved setbacks from which he could not recover. He was consigned to the reserves where, despite playing at below full capacity, he ended each season as top scorer. When he finally gave up the English game and returned to Ireland in 1968, he had just one full League appearance to his credit.

Although Fulham were reluctant to part company with the player, O'Connor refused to budge from his Athlone home and eventually the Londoners grudgingly accepted £4,000 from Dundalk for his services.

Over the next decade in the League of Ireland Turlough's class really shone through. In four seasons with Dundalk he scored 54 goals and in six seasons with Bohemians he notched up an incredible 106 goals and picked up two League Championship medals.

In 1979 he became player-manager of Athlone Town, bringing unprecedented success to the Midlands club in the form of their first League Championships in 1980–81 and 1982–83. They also won the League Cup three times, the Leinster Cup, the President's Cup and the Tyler Cup under his guidance. In May 1985 he was appointed manager of Dundalk whom he led to a League Champioship and FAI Cup double in 1987–88. Turlough was appointed manager of Bohemians in December 1993.

In November 1967 O'Connor won his first full cap in the European Cup qualifier against Czechoslovakia in Prague and, true to form, marked the occasion with the winning goal in Ireland's surprise 2–1 victory.

Almost four years later, in October 1971, he won his second cap when he lined up against Austria in Linz. He missed just one of the next six games, taking his caps tally to seven. Turlough scored just one more international goal, which again proved to be a winner. It came in the 3–2 victory over Ecuador in June 1972.

John O'Driscoll (WINGER)

Born: Cork 20 September 1921
Debut for Eire: v Switzerland December 1948

John 'Jackie' O'Driscoll spent nine successful years in League of Ireland football, starting with Cork City when he was 17, in 1938, before trying his luck in the English Football League.

He spent 1940–41 with Waterford and was a member of the Blues' side which lost the 1941 FAI Cup final to Cork United (Cork City's successor). Jackie spent the following season with Shelbourne before joining his hometown club, Cork United, in 1942.

In five years with United Jackie won three League of Ireland Championship medals, in 1942–43, 1944–45 and 1945–46, and two FAI Cup winners medals, in 1943 and 1947. O'Driscoll was one of three players in that Cup-winning side who secured contracts with Football League clubs in the weeks after the final. John McGowan and Tommy Moroney joined West Ham, and in May 1947 Jackie joined Swansea Town for a 'substantial four figure fee'!

A clever, direct and enterprising winger with blistering pace and a powerful shot, Jackie came to Wales at a time when the Irish influence at the Vetch field was on the increase. Norman Lockhart, Sam McCroy and Jim Feeney were already there and were to be followed by Tom Keane in June 1947. Ernie Jones, Swansea's Welsh international winger, was sold to Tottenham to make way for O'Driscoll who arrived in south Wales as the club were embarking on Third Division football after 25 years in the higher grade.

In Jackie's first season, 1948–49, Swansea won the Third Division (South) title, and in a total of five seasons there he scored 26 goals in 117 games.

Jackie represented a Munster XI against the RAF in May 1947 and was in the League of Ireland side which took on the English League the same month.

Honoured at senior level by both the North and the South, Jackie won his first cap for the Republic in the 1–0 defeat by Switzerland in December 1948. He won two more caps for Eire in defeats by Belgium and Sweden the following year. He was a member of the Northern Ireland team which contested the 1948–49 Home International series. He played in all three games in the series, once at outside-right and twice on the other flank, but finished on the losing side every time.

Sean O'Driscoll (MIDFIELD)

Born: Wolverhampton 1 July 1957
Debut for Eire: v Chile May 1982

Born in Wolverhampton of Irish parents, Sean O'Driscoll was spotted by Fulham playing for non-League Alvechurch and signed by the west London club in November 1979 for £12,000.

A skilful midfielder with a fine repertoire of deft touches, O'Driscoll soon became a regular in the Fulham first XI, playing an important role in the club's promotion from Division Three in 1982–83.

A loss of form in the 1983–84 season cost Sean his place at the Cottage and in February 1984, after three months on loan to Bournemouth, he transferred there permanently for a bargain price of £6,000, having made 148 League appearances (13 goals) for Fulham.

Sean 'fitted into the AFC team with ease, adding speed and thrust to the flanks'. With the south coast side he won an Associate Members' Cup winners medal in 1984 and was a regular

first-teamer in the Cherries' team which clinched the Third Division title in 1986–87.

At the close of 1994–95 Sean was Bournemouth's longest serving campaigner, having appeared in 414 League games (19 goals) in his 12 seasons with the club.

On the international scene, O'Driscoll won three caps at Under-21 level in 1982–83. He won three full caps on the Republic's disastrous tour of Central and South America in 1982 in which they suffered humiliating defeats at the hands of Chile, Brazil and Trinidad and Tobago.

Frank O'Farrell (WING-HALF)

Born: Cork 9 October 1927
Debut for Eire: v Austria May 1952

Frank O'Farrell will probably be remembered more for his achievements as a manager than for his prowess as a player. A graduate of the famous West Ham soccer academy of the '50s – which produced a generation of managers such as fellow Corkonian Noel Cantwell, Malcolm Allison, Malcolm Musgrove, Jimmy Andrews, Ken Brown, Dave Sexton, and John Bond – O'Farrell's teams played exciting, attractive and attacking football in true Upton Park tradition.

His League management career began at Torquay United (1965–68). He took over at Leicester City in December 1968 and took the Filbert Street club to the Second Division title in 1970–71 and to the FA Cup final in 1969. He later managed Manchester United (June 1971–December 1972), followed by a spell as coach to the Iranian national side; Cardiff City (1973–74) before ending his managerial career back at Torquay (1981–82). He continued as general manager at the Plainmoor Ground until 1983.

Frank started his career when he joined West Ham in January 1948, less than six months after his predecessor in the Cork United side, Tommy

Moroney, had joined the Upton Park club.

O'Farrell was drilled in the Upton Park football philosophy in the Football Combination where he played over 50 games before making his League debut in December 1950. A competent, polished wing-half, he kept his place in the Hammers side for six years, making 197 League appearances.

It was during his time in the Hammers' reserves that he came under the international spotlight for the first time. His performance for the Football Combination side which played the Brussels League in 1952 impressed the international selectors and in May of that year he won his first full cap in the 6–0 defeat by Austria in Vienna.

His second cap came less than a year later. The opposition was once again Austria but the outcome was somewhat different as Ireland exacted revenge in the form of a 4–0 victory. Frank played his part in the rout by scoring his first international goal. He also scored in his next outing, in a 5–3 defeat by France. He won a total of nine caps, the last of which came against Czechoslovakia in May 1959.

In November 1956 Frank left east London for First Division Preston North End in a player exchange deal which took Preston's former Manchester United full-back Eddie Lewis to Upton Park. In four seasons at Deepdale O'Farrell made 118 League appearances before joining Southern League club Weymouth as player-manager.

Kevin O'Flanagan (WINGER)

Born: Dublin 10 June 1919
Debut for Eire: v Norway November 1937

Kevin O'Flanagan was an all-round sportsman. He was the Irish sprint champion in 1941, long jump champion on four occasions between 1938 and 1943, an accomplished tennis player and a single-figure handicap golfer!

Amazingly he found time to add team sports to his fantastic repertoire of individual skills. He was captain of Bohemians when they won the Irish Cup in 1945 and, after taking up a medical appointment in Middlesex, he signed as an amateur for First Division Arsenal for whom he made 17 appearances, at outside-right and centre-forward. At the same time he was playing top-class rugby with London Irish.

Not surprisingly Kevin's busy schedule limited his availability for the Gunners and in 1949, after a spell in non-League football with Barnet, he joined Second Division Brentford for whom he made half a dozen League appearances before an ankle injury ended his playing career.

As an international Kevin was doubly honoured, appearing for his country at both rugby and soccer. He scored on his international debut, in the 3–3 draw with Norway in November 1937, and won a total of ten full caps, seven before the war as a Bohemians player and three during his Arsenal days.

Following his premature retirement from the game Kevin returned to medical practice in Ireland. He was also team doctor to the Irish National Olympic side for three years and was a member of the International Olympic Committee for the 1992 Olympic Games in Barcelona.

Michael O'Flanagan (WINGER)

Born: Dublin 29 September 1922
Debut for Eire: v England September 1946

A 'more than useful player, with speed and shooting power', Michael O'Flanagan started his soccer career with junior club Kenilworth. From there he had spells at Home Farm, St Patrick's CYMS and Bohemians junior teams.

O'Flanagan signed for Bohemians in 1939, making his way into the first XI in 1941. He became a regular first-team player with the famous amateur club.

Michael won many trophies with Bohs; perhaps their best achievement during that period was winning the Inter-City Cup in 1945. The cup was competed for on a home-and-away basis between clubs from the North and South. But the northern teams were strengthened by some of the best English pros who were stationed in the North during the war. Even so Bohemians defeated the famous Belfast Celtic 3–2 on aggregate to lift the trophy that year.

Michael played on the same Bohemians and Lansdowne rugby sides as his brother Dr Kevin O'Flanagan, later of Arsenal, and in the Bohs select which beat Manchester United 2–1 in May 1948. He was called up by the Republic to face England in place of the injured Davy Walsh in September 1946. It was England's first visit to Dublin and the tie was settled by a Tom Finney goal for the visitors.

Michael joined Lansdowne rugby club in 1947 and won a cap against Scotland two years later in Ireland's Triple Crown-winning season.

In 1949 O'Flanagan was invited by Belfast Celtic to replace the injured Jimmy Jones on Celtic's famous North American tour of that year. He played in all ten of Celtic's games on the tour, including the famous 2–0 defeat of Scotland on 29 May.

Michael retired at the end of 1949.

Kelham O'Hanlon (GOALKEEPER)

Born: Saltburn 16 May 1962
Debut for Eire: v Israel November 1987

A 6ft 1in, 13st goalminder, Kelham O'Hanlon is a former pupil of Southlands Secondary School. As a youngster he had trials with Aston Villa and Derby County but chose to join Middlesbrough. He had been an apprentice with the club before agreeing professional terms in May 1980.

O'Hanlon succeeded Northern Ireland international keeper Jim Platt in Boro's goal in January 1983 and immediately became the club's first-choice keeper. He later lost his place to former Manchester United keeper Stephen Pears and had made 87 Second Division appearances when he was transferred to Rotherham in August 1985.

Kelham walked straight into the Millermen's first XI and won a Fourth Division Championship medal in 1988–89. In six seasons at the club he guarded the Rotherham goal 248 times in League encounters.

In July 1991 O'Hanlon was transferred to Carlisle United for £25,000. Again he took his place between the sticks immediately, this time ousting Jason Priestly from pole position. In his first season at Burnton Park, 1991–92, O'Hanlon was a regular and the PFA voted him the Fourth Division's best keeper. Kelham had made a total of 83 League appearances for Carlisle when he was sold to Preston North End for £25,000 in July 1993.

He had guarded the Lilywhites' goal on 23 occasions when he was transferred to Scottish Premier Division club Dundee United for £30,000 in October 1994. To the end of 1995–96 he had made 35 League appearances for the Terrors.

In September 1996 he returned to Preston in a £12,000 transfer deal. He will act as goalkeeping coach at Deepdale but the club have retained his playing registration.

Kelham won two Under-21 caps for the Republic: in a 1–0 defeat by Argentina and a 5–1 victory over China, both in June 1983. In his only full international he kept a clean sheet when, in November 1987, Ireland thrashed Israel 5–0 in the biggest margin of victory achieved by an Irish team under Jack Charlton – a feat equalled against Turkey in October 1990.

Eamonn O'Keefe (FORWARD/MIDFIELD)

Born: Manchester 13 March 1953
Debut for Eire: v Wales February 1981

Few young players get the opportunity to fulfil their dream of becoming professional footballers, but Eamonn O'Keefe got two bites at the cherry.

In February 1974 Third Division Plymouth Argyle plucked him from non-League Stalybridge Celtic. He failed to impress, however, and soon found himself back in the non-League arena without playing a League game.

Eamonn had a spell with Hyde United, another in Saudia Arabia and was turning out for Mossley in July 1979 when Everton signed him for £22,500.

A small, sharp and nippy player, O'Keefe's three seasons at Goodison were spent mostly in Everton's Central League side. He was occasionally utilised as cover in the Blues' engine-room and managed to get his name on the teamsheet 40 times and on the scoresheet six times, before his £65,000 transfer to Wigan Athletic in January 1982.

In his first season at Springfield Park O'Keefe's goals helped shoot Wigan into Division Three for the first time in their short League history. Revelling in his new striking role, he netted 25 times in 58 League outings for the Latics.

In July 1983 he joined Division Three newcomers Port Vale for £10,000, scoring 17 goals in 59 games before moving to Blackpool for a similar fee in March 1985.

O'Keefe surpassed himself at Blackpool. In 1985–86, despite a long lay-off due to a knee injury, he was Blackpool's leading scorer and, when in September 1986 he announced his retirement from the game because of the injury, he had netted 23 goals in 36 League games for Blackpool.

He later attempted to make a comeback, initially with Cork City in the League of Ireland and later with Chester City, whom he joined in March 1989. However, after four goals in 17 League games for Chester he was finally forced to retire.

Eamonn was eligible to represent Ireland through his grandparents and made his full debut in the 3–1 home defeat by Wales in February 1981.

In 1979 he had played for England's semi-pros against Scotland and Holland. This, according to FIFA, made him ineligible to play for Ireland. He fought FIFA's decision and eventually won his case.

His next taste of international football came in 1982–83 when he represented Ireland's Under-21s four times. In June 1983 he scored a record four goals for the Under-21s in a 5–1 victory over China in Toulon.

Curiously, Eamonn's next senior appearance, in June 1984, came against the Chinese in the semi-final of the Japan Cup in which he scored the only goal of the game. Eamonn won his fifth and final cap in the 2–1 defeat by England at Wembley in March 1985.

David O'Leary (CENTRE-HALF)

Born: London 2 May 1958
Debut for Eire: v England September 1976

David O'Leary of Leeds United has an unfamiliar ring to it; the man whose name became synonymous with Arsenal after spending most of his adult life at Highbury reluctantly departed the famous marble halls in the summer of 1993 to join the Yorkshire club on a free transfer.

A player of great temperament, good judgement and pace, O'Leary became the bedrock around which Arsenal defences were built for almost two decades. Known as 'The Boss' during the autumn of his Highbury career, David won every honour the domestic game has to offer – in duplicate. He was an FA Cup winner in 1979 and 1993; a League Cup winner in 1987 and 1993; and a League

David O'Leary

Championship winner in 1988–89 and 1990–91.

On the other side of the coin he played in losing FA Cup finals in 1978 and 1980; and missed Arsenal's League Cup final defeat by Luton in 1988 through injury. In the 1980 European Cup-Winners' Cup final against Valencia he marked the great Argentinian Mario Kempes out of game, but Arsenal lost the game on penalties. That particular defeat was described by O'Leary as the lowest point in his career.

Born in Stoke Newington, London, David returned to Dublin with his family as an infant. He joined Shelbourne's Under-13 team, progressing through the various junior teams at the Dublin club until 1973 when Arsenal's Irish scout Bill Darby sent him to Highbury for

trials, thus setting in motion the beginning of the most enduring relationship between player and club in English football. Within three years of arriving in north London David was in the first team via the youths and reserves.

In a career remarkably free from injury, he went on to make a record 558 League appearances for the club by 1989–90, breaking the previous record of 500 held by George Armstrong.

The departure of Liam Brady to Juventus and Frank Stapleton to Manchester United in the early '80s witnessed the disintegration of Arsenal's famous Irish spine. O'Leary could have gone also. He had talks with Torino in 1980, and offers from Bayern Munich and Cologne reflected his status as one of Europe's finest ball-playing defenders. He turned down the money-making moves, electing to stay loyal to Arsenal. Now he's rich beyond his wildest dreams in memories that money couldn't buy.

A magnificent centre-back, O'Leary's elegant strides from defence, searching for the right target and stroking a pin-point pass to his chosen colleague became his hallmark. He was captain at Highbury for a period at the beginning of 1980–81.

The only blot on David's Highbury career was his demotion to the reserves after turning up late for pre-season training following his World Cup endeavours with Ireland in Italy in 1990. Several top clubs began hovering around Highbury, waiting for an announcement of his release, but he was labelled as 'not for sale' by Arsenal.

Towards the end of his days at Arsenal David became a utility player, turning up at full-back and as a sweeper. His adaptability earned him a place in the Gunners' double whammy over Sheffield Wednesday in the League Cup and FA Cup finals of 1993. Injuries and suspensions in the Arsenal camp meant O'Leary could bring the curtain down on a glorious Arsenal career in the grandest of fashions – with two Wembley appearances.

Arguably one the greatest tributes of David's career came when Leeds United boss

Howard Wilkinson signed the 35-year-old on a three-year contract in July 1993.

Injury kept David out of the Leeds side for most of 1993–94, a season in which he made just ten League appearances. To make matters worse, he was surprisingly left out of the Republic's squad for the World Cup finals in the USA in 1994. In October 1995 an Achilles tendon injury forced him to announce his retirement. When George Graham took over as Leeds boss in August 1996 he appointed O'Leary as his number two at Elland Road.

A former captain of Ireland's Youth and Schoolboy teams, his penalty against Romania in 1990 took Ireland to the quarter-finals of the World Cup. It was his first penalty at any level and with it he became a national hero.

A model professional, David has collected a total of 67 full caps; a tally which would have been much greater had he not been left in the international wilderness for three years when he missed out on 30 caps.

Pierce O'Leary (CENTRE-HALF)

Born: Dublin 5 November 1959
Debut for Eire: v Czechoslovakia September 1979

Pierce O'Leary became a Shamrock Rovers player in 1977 when he was 17. The following year he won an FAI Cup winners medal after Rovers beat Sligo 1–0 in the final. A week later O'Leary left to play in America with Philadelphia Fury. He later spent four seasons (1981–84) playing for Vancouver Whitecaps, and in November 1984 joined Glasgow Celtic.

Centre-half O'Leary made 39 League appearances for the Bhoys. He won a Scottish FA Cup winners medal in 1985, replacing the injured Paul McStay after 74 minutes in the 2–1 victory over Dundee United. And he played 13 games in Celtic's 1985–86 Championship winning-season, a season which ended in the most dramatic fashion.

Hearts had led the table since before Christmas and went into their last game two points ahead of Celtic. But their unbeaten run of 27 games came to an end at Dundee, whilst Celtic thrashed St Mirren 5–0 and snatched the title on goal difference.

Pierce's unhurried style and calming influence in defence was similar to that of his more famous brother David O'Leary. Pierce captained Celtic against Arsenal in brother David's testimonial game in 1986, and was also forced to retire through injury, in his case in 1988 as a result of recurring pelvic trouble.

Capped five times by the Republic at Under-21 level, Pierce won seven full caps. He partnered his brother three times in the heart of the Irish defence against Bulgaria and Northern Ireland in 1979 and Holland in 1980. Ireland won each time the brothers played together.

With Celtic goalkeeper Packie Bonner, O'Leary runs a successful cleaning company in Rutherglen, Scotland.

Frank O'Neill (OUTSIDE-RIGHT)

Born: Dublin 13 April 1940
Debut for Eire: v Czechoslovakia October 1961

Regarded as a wing-half of 'considerable ability', Frank O'Neill joined Arsenal from Dublin junior club Home Farm as an amateur in December 1958, signing professional terms in April 1959.

Frank spent his brief Highbury career in the youth and reserve teams and was a member of the 1960–61 reserve side which swept all before them. That season they won the Metropolitan League Championship, the Metropolitan League Challenge Cup and the Metropolitan League Professional Cup. By the time O'Neill returned to his native Dublin to join Shamrock Rovers in the summer of 1961, he had made just two League appearances for the Gunners.

An 'extremely clever player', O'Neill was a match-winner in League of Ireland football. In 13 glittering years at Glenmalure Park he won a host of honours, including a League of Ireland Championship medal in 1963–64 and seven FAI Cup winners medals. The first Cup medal came in 1962 and was followed by an incredible run of six consecutive successes in the competition between 1964 and 1969.

Frank, who scored 87 League goals for Rovers, was appointed player-manager of the Hoops in 1970 and remained in that post for four seasons before his transfer to Waterford in 1974.

He was a member of the Waterford side which won Ireland's inaugural League Cup in October 1973 when they beat Donegal side Finn Harps 2–1 in the final tie.

A former inter-League player, Frank was capped by the Republic at Youth, Minor and Schoolboy levels. He was called up for his first full cap for the World Cup qualifier with Czechoslovakia in Dublin in October 1961.

Ten years, almost to the day, later Frank won his 20th and final cap in Liam Tuohy's first game as manager when a team consisting of half a dozen League of Ireland players and seven new caps lost 6–0 to Austria in Linz.

Frank scored one goal whilst on international duty. It came in the 2–1 European Championship defeat of Turkey in November 1966.

James A. O'Neill (GOALKEEPER)

Born: Dublin 13 October 1931
Debut for Eire: v Spain June 1952

The son of a leading golf professional, Jimmy O'Neill was spotted playing for local junior club Bulfin United by scouts from Everton and taken to Goodison Park for trials. In May 1949 he was offered full professional status by the club.

A goalminder with safe hands who excelled at intercepting crosses, Jimmy became one of the country's foremost keepers after working his way through Everton's junior sides and making his senior debut in August 1950.

In 1953–54, three seasons after Everton had been relegated, Jimmy helped the Toffees battle their way back to the top flight. He made 201 League appearances for the club, and then in 1959–60 he lost his number 1 shirt to Albert Dunlop. He was transferred to Stoke City for £5,000 in July 1960.

Jimmy became an automatic choice at Stoke, maintaining the high standards which made him Eire's first-choice keeper in the '50s, despite having a disastrous international debut when he had to pick the ball out of the net six times in the thrashing by Spain in Madrid in June 1952.

In a 17-match international career he conceded 33 goals and kept four clean sheets.

In four seasons with Stoke Jimmy made 130 League appearances and was one of only two players not to miss a game in the club's Second Division Championship-winning season in 1962–63. In March 1964 he departed for Fourth Division Darlington.

Jimmy made 32 appearances for the Quakers before ending his League career with 42 appearances for Third Divison Port Vale, whom he joined in February 1965.

John N. O'Neill (DEFENDER)

Born: Dublin 8 September 1935
Debut for Eire: v Wales September 1960

John O'Neill joined First Division Preston North End from League of Ireland champions Drumcondra in April 1958.

O'Neill had played regularly at centre-half for Drumcondra and had represented the League of Ireland in that position. However, upon his arrival in Lancashire he was immediately switched to full-back, the position in which he made most of his 50 first-team appearances for the club. In July 1967 he left Preston for Barrow and was immediately shunted back to centre-half.

In one season with Barrow, John made 42 League appearances before returning to Drumcondra in 1964. In his first season back in Ireland, O'Neill helped the Dubliners to League Championship success. The following season, 1965–66, he joined the Drums' League of Ireland rivals Waterford and immediately set about putting together one of the most impressive arrays of medals of any player in the Irish game.

His first season with Waterford ended with a League Championship medal and over the next decade he added a further five League Championship medals to his collection. He was a League Cup winner in 1974 and collected FAI Cup runners-up medals in 1968 and 1972 to add to the winners medal he had won in the same competition with Drumcondra in 1957.

John also discovered his shooting boots at Waterford, scoring 60 times in League football including 16 in 1968–69, which confirmed him as the Blues' leading marksman that season.

John won one full Eire cap, against Wales in September 1960, the occasion of Ireland's first home defeat since Yugoslavia's 4–1 victory five years earlier.

culminated in his League debut against Southampton in November 1994. However, any hopes of an extended run in the first team were dashed when he broke his ankle in a reserve match soon after. To the end of 1995–96 O'Neill had made 20 first-team appearances.

Tall and powerfully built, O'Neill is a skilful individual; he can ease past opponents, using either pace or guile, and has the ability to deliver subtle or powerful service for his colleagues. Almost totally left-footed, he is not dissimilar in style to Chris Waddle, with the almost arrogant ease with which he goes past opponents and the variety of his crosses.

A former Youth international, he made his full international debut against Portugal in May 1996 as a 62nd-minute substitute for another young debutant, David Connolly. He was on the field from the start against Croatia the following week and scored the first goal under Mick McCarthy's new regime in the 2–2 draw.

He won plaudits galore for his performance against the Croats. His pace, instincts and reactions around goal had some observers hailing the arrival of Ireland's new John Aldridge. He scored twice against Bolivia in June 1996, helping Ireland to a 3–0 victory – the first victory of Mick McCarthy's eight-match reign. In August 1996 he scored his fourth goal in just seven international appearances in the 5–0 win over Liechtenstein and also played in the Republic's win over Macedonia.

Keith O'Neill (MIDFIELD)

Born: Dublin 16 February 1976
Debut for Eire: v Portugal May 1996

A pacey and direct left-sided midfield player, Keith O'Neill signed professionally for Norwich City in July 1994, having previously been a trainee at the club. From the Dublin suburb of Finglas, Keith was a Home Farm junior and the Canaries beat off several top clubs in the race for his signature.

O'Neill's rapid progress at Carrow Road

Kieran O'Regan (DEFENDER/MIDFIELD)

Born: Cork 9 November 1963
Debut for Eire: v Malta November 1983

From Capwell Road in Cork, Kieran O'Regan played his junior football in the Munster League with Tramore Athletic.

He joined Brighton and Hove Albion on trial in September 1982, landing a professional contract the following April after making 'tremendous progress' in the club's reserves. Kieran had played both in midfield and as a sweeper for Tramore, but Brighton boss Jimmy Melia used him as an attacking full-back.

He made his League debut for Brighton on the final day of the 1982–83 season and became the club's regular right-back the following term. In four seasons at the Goldstone ground he made a total of 86 League appearances before transferring to Swindon Town in August 1987.

O'Regan made just 26 Second Division appearances for the Wiltshire club before moving to Huddersfield Town in August 1988. In five years at Leeds Road, where he was employed as a midfielder, O'Regan played in 199 League games and scored 25 goals.

In June 1993 he moved to West Bromwich Albion, the £25,000 fee being set by a tribunal. In two seasons at the club to date, Kieran has made 45 First Division appearances. At the end of 1994–95 he was one of eight players given free transfers in manager Alan Buckley's end-of-season clear-out.

A former Irish Youth player, Kieran scored a hat-trick against Wales in Cardiff on his Youth debut in 1982. He collected four Under-21 caps in the Toulon Tournament in June 1983 and won his fifth cap at that level against England in March 1985.

In November 1983 O'Regan came into the senior side for the first time at right-back in the record 8–0 victory over Malta. He won three more caps over the next 18 months: against Poland, Mexico and Spain – all of which ended in scoreless stalemates.

John (Jackie) O'Reilly (WINGER)

Born: Cobh, Co. Cork 7 May 1914
Debut for Eire: v Portugal June 1946

A dashing and tireless right-winger, Jackie O'Reilly was part of the brilliant Cork United side which dominated League of Ireland football in the 1940s.

An all-round athlete, Jackie was a Cork County Cup winner at rugby and only missed out on a place in Ireland's Olympic swimming team because of an allergy.

O'Reilly played his junior football with Cork Bohemians, Cobh Wanderers, and Cobh Ramblers and joined League of Ireland club Cork in 1935. He was an FAI Cup runner-up in 1936 when Cork lost the final 2–1 to Shamrock Rovers. Soon after the final he left to join Norwich City.

Although he netted a couple on his debut for the Canaries, O'Reilly was destined to play second fiddle to Billy Warnes. Relegated to the reserves, he scored 17 goals in a dozen games and by the time he returned to Ireland in 1939 to join Cork United he had scored 11 goals in 33 first-team appearances.

Jackie won five League Championship medals with Cork United (1940–41, 1941–42, 1942–43, 1944–45 and 1945–46) and one in 1949–50 with the renamed Cork Athletic. He also played in a further five FAI Cup finals in the post-war era, scoring a record seven Cup final goals. He was a winner with Cork United in 1941 and 1947 and a runner-up in 1942 and 1943, and a runner-up with Cork Athletic in 1950.

Jackie also won eight Munster Cup medals and between 1941 and 1948 he represented the League of Ireland five times.

He was capped when internationals were resumed after the war, with the FAI travelling to Portugal and Spain in June 1946; he scored Ireland's first post-war goal against Portugal on 16 June 1946.

After he retired from the game Jackie emigrated to Mississauga in the Canadian province of Ontario.

Gerard Peyton (GOALKEEPER)

Born: Birmingham 20 May 1956
Debut for Eire: v Spain February 1977

If anyone deserves a medal for loyalty and

persistence, it is Peyton – the amiable goalkeeping giant. 'Always the bridesmaid, seldom the bride', Gerry Peyton has been a very capable deputy to Mick Kearns, Jim McDonagh and latterly Packie Bonner, for Ireland's number 1 shirt.

Capped once by the Republic at 'B' level, against Denmark in February 1992, Gerry won two Under-21 caps, against France and the USSR in June 1983. He travelled with Ireland to the European Championship finals in West Germany in 1988 and to the World Cup finals in Italy in 1990, turning up time and again over some 16 years and answering the call when required, gradually to notch up 33 full caps.

It could have been so different, however. In 1976 he was given the opportunity to appear in an England Under-21 game against Wales but gave it up in the hope of an Ireland call-up. Gerry, whose mother hails from Galway and father from Mayo, answered the call for the first time in February 1977 when he made his debut as a half-time substitute for Mick Kearns in the 1–0 defeat by Spain in Dublin.

He is one of the few players who can claim to have played under four different Irish managers: Alan Kelly, Johnny Giles, Eoin Hand and Jack Charlton. Peyton, who kept clean sheets in 13 internationals, earned his last cap, standing in for the suspended Packie Bonner, in the 2–0 victory over Portugal in Boston in June 1992.

As a teenager Gerry joined Aston Villa, but his apprenticeship ended when, at the age of 17, he required a cartilage operation. From Villa Park he move to Southern League club Atherstone Town. First Division Burnley, spotting his potential, signed him for £15,000 in May 1975.

At Burnley he was groomed by former England keeper Gil Merrick. But after less than two seasons and 30 League games at Turf Moor, Gerry lost his place to regular keeper Peter Mellor and was transferred to Fulham for £40,000 in December 1976.

An agile and consistently good custodian with immense confidence in his own ability,

Gerard Peyton

Gerry gave ten years of excellent service to the west London club. Fulham were relegated to Division Three in 1979–80, but Peyton was on hand two seasons later to help the club haul itself back to Division Two. He clocked up 345 League appearances for Fulham, (plus ten on loan to Third Division Southend in September 1983), earning a well-deserved testimonial in 1986.

In July 1986 Gerry joined Bournemouth on a free transfer. He got off to a flying start with his new club, missing just one League game and ending his first season with a Third Division Championship medal as the Cherries moved into Division Two for the first time in their 88-year history.

Gerry gained an abundance of experience in the lower divisions. His anticipation, safe handling and long, accurate throws convinced Everton manager Howard Kendall that Peyton was the right man to understudy Wales keeper

Neville Southall in the Everton goal. Consequently, after 202 League appearances and exactly five years after arriving, Gerry left Dean Court for Goodison Park in an £80,000 deal.

In the two years he was on Everton's books Peyton was never called upon to do serious battle and, following periods on loan to Bolton (one appearance), Norwich, Chelsea (one appearance), and Brentford, he joined Brentford permanently, on a free transfer, in March 1993.

After just 19 appearances for the Bees in the new First Division Gerry was once again freed and in June 1993 joined West Ham. He walked away from Upton Park under a cloud of controversy in January 1994 because the club didn't want to let him go to take up a coaching contract in Japan.

Noel Peyton (INSIDE-FORWARD)

Born: Dublin 4 December 1935
Debut for Eire: v West Germany November 1956

Noel Peyton was halfway through his fourth season with Shamrock Rovers in January 1958 when he transferred to First Division Leeds United.

A speedy, snipe-like and skilful inside-forward, Peyton, who had joined Rovers from junior club East Wall, appeared in two FAI Cup finals with the Hoops, earning a winners medal in 1956 and a runners-up medal the following year. He also won a League of Ireland Championship medal in 1956–57.

By the time he joined Leeds, Peyton had already represented the League of Ireland and had been capped once at 'B' level and once at full international level.

In just over four years at Elland Road, Noel made 104 League appearances, scored 17 goals and won five of his six full caps. At the close of 1962–63 – Leeds' third season in Division

Two after their relegation at the end of 1959–60 – Noel moved to Fourth Division York City.

A series of injuries severely limited his appearances for York and, by the time he moved to non-League Barnstaple Town as player-manager in the summer of 1965, he had made just 37 and scored four goals.

Terence Phelan (DEFENDER)

Born: Manchester 16 March 1967
Debut for Eire: v Hungary September 1991

As a youngster growing up in Salford, Greater Manchester, Terry Phelan was on Manchester City's books as an Associate Schoolboy. City released him and in August 1984 he joined Leeds United as a youth trainee. Eight years later, in September 1992, Phelan became the world's most expensive defender when City paid Wimbledon £2.5 million to bring him home.

When he was at Leeds, Elland Road supremo Billy Bremner was of the opinion that Terry wouldn't make the grade. Thus after just 14 appearances in Division Two, Phelan was released by the Yorkshire club.

In July 1986 he joined Fourth Division Swansea City, for whom he made 45 League appearances before a £100,000 move to Wimbledon in July 1987.

A diminutive, tenacious left-sided full-back, Terry came of age in five seasons in south London. Swift in the tackle, with uncommonly electrifying pace for a defender, Terry played in 159 League games for the Wombles.

A year after joining Wimbledon, Phelan was walking out at Wembley to face Liverpool in a David and Goliath FA Cup final. Wimbledon were in just their second season in the top flight and only their tenth as a League club. No one gave the club from SW19 a chance against the League champions; a headed winner from Northern Ireland's Lawrie Sanchez made for one of the biggest upsets in the Cup's history.

Phelan's consistently efficient performances for Wimbledon made him one of the most sought-after players in the League in 1991–92. A combination of transfer talk and homesickness increasingly unsettled the player and problems arose between Phelan and Wimbledon chairman Sam Hamman, which at one stage saw the player briefly walk out on the club.

Hamman slapped a £3 million price tag on Phelan, which inevitably frightened off a seemingly endless list of interested clubs which included Chelsea, Crystal Palace, Celtic, Blackburn, Everton, Spurs, Arsenal, Manchester United, Newcastle and Leeds.

Terry was elated when Manchester City's Peter Reid brought the episode to a successful conclusion in September 1992 when he agreed to pay £2.5 million to take him to Maine Road. Reid regarded Phelan as the best left-back in the business and was prepared to pay to get his man.

Phelan's time back home in Manchester was fraught with difficulties. He was actually released by City at the end of 1993–94 after clashing with manager Brian Horton and new chairman Francis Lee over contractual difficulties.

In November 1995, having made 103 League appearances for the Maine Road outfit, Phelan was the subject of a £700,000 transfer to Chelsea, for whom he made a dozen League appearances in 1995–96.

Phelan, whose mother hails from Tubbercurry in Co. Sligo, has represented Ireland at Youth level and was capped once at Under-21, Under-23 and 'B' levels.

He made his full debut in the 2–1 defeat of Hungary in Gyor in September 1991 and went on to become the Republic's regular left-back where he used his famous pace to full advantage in defence and attack. Although he played in the 1994 World Cup finals in the USA, Terry has recently become

Terry Phelan

a victim of Ireland's embarrassment of riches in the form of versatile full-backs such as Manchester United's Denis Irwin, Leeds United's Gary Kelly, Jeff Kenna of Blackburn Rovers, not to mention Aston Villa's Stephen Staunton.

Terry was Ireland skipper for the first time against Bolivia in June 1996, taking the captain's armband from the substituted Alan Kernaghan. Terry won his 35th cap in that game which was also Ireland's first victory under Mick McCarthy.

Niall Quinn (CENTRE-FORWARD)

Born: Dublin 6 October 1966
Debut for Eire: v Iceland May 1986

Niall Quinn, a 6ft 5in tower of power from Perrystown in south Dublin, was an all-round sportsman before deciding on a full-time career in soccer.

A former Dublin hurler, he played for Dublin Minors in the 1993 All-Ireland Minor Gaelic football final and was captain of the Dublin Colleges GAA team which toured Australia. During his time Down Under, Niall was offered a £100,000 annual contract to switch to Aussie rules football, an offer which he refused.

Another Bill Darby discovery, Quinn joined Arsenal straight from school in November 1983 and, although he had almost seven

Niall Quinn

seasons at Highbury, he enjoyed just one full season in the first team: 1986–87.

That same season he won a League Cup winners medal after the Gunners' 2–1 defeat of Liverpool in the final.

Thereafter he fell out of favour and spent the next three years on the sidelines as his team-mates marched to League Championship success. Quinn's frustration was exacerbated by the club's rejection of numerous transfer requests during his wilderness years.

Niall had scored only 14 goals in 67 League games for Arsenal when, in March 1990, Manchester City manager Howard Kendall ended his Highbury hell by paying £700,000 to take him to Maine Road.

Quinn was immediately thrown in at the deep end and played a major role in City's successful battle against relegation in his first season.

Since then he has gone from strength to strength. An indispensable leader of the line, he has been showing an encouraging deftness of touch on the ground to complement his renowned aerial prowess, and to the end of 1995–96 had scored 66 goals in 203 League games.

The move north revitalised the big man's career and his goalscoring, not to mention goal-stopping feats won the hearts of the City fans, who voted him their 'Player of the Season' in 1990–91.

In April 1991 the poacher briefly turned gamekeeper. City were leading Derby County by a Quinn goal when City's keeper Tony Coton was sent off. Quinn, who fancies himself as a goalkeeper, took Coton's place between the sticks and had hardly donned the green jersey before he was flinging his beanpole frame across the goal to palm away a Dean Saunders penalty.

City were relegated to Division One at the end of 1995–96 and Quinn was transferred to Premiership new boys Sunderland for £1.3 million at the start of the following season.

A former Irish Youth, Under-21, Under-23 and 'B' player, Niall holds an incredible hoodoo over England. He has lined up against them eight times at different levels and has never finished on the losing side. His two goals in Ireland B's 4–1 defeat of their English counterparts in Cork in 1990 ensured him of a place in the Irish squad for Italia '90.

In Italy he became one of the stars of Ireland's first World Cup finals by scoring the equaliser against Holland which ensured Ireland's place in the second phase of the tournament.

In November 1993 he was ruled out for the rest of that season and the following summer's World Cup finals after an exploratory operation revealed he had severed cruciate ligaments in his knee. The injury, sustained against Sheffield Wednesday, is similar to those which nearly wrecked the careers of Paul Gascoigne and John Salako.

Niall returned to the international arena in September 1994 and soon re-established himself as Ireland's first-choice centre-forward. He captained the Republic for the first time against Croatia in 1996 and celebrated the occasion with a last-minute equaliser, his 14th international goal. Despite being on the substitutes bench for the game against Mexico a fortnight later, Quinn managed to get himself 'sent off' after running on to the pitch to remonstrate with a Mexican player. He netted twice against Liechtenstein in August 1996 to bring his goal tally to 16.

Damien claimed a first-team place soon after joining Gillingham and over the next nine seasons he figured in 323 League games for the club. He helped the Gills win promotion to Division Three at the end of 1973–74 and in 1974–75 was voted the club's 'Player of the Year'. The club's 'penalty expert' in the '70s, Damien scored 91 goals during his career at the Priestfield Stadium.

In 1981 Damien was released by Gillingham. But seven years later, after spells with Gravesend, Folkestone, Faversham and Chatham, he returned to Priestfield as youth team coach and a year later, in May 1989, he succeeded Keith Burkinshaw as manager.

In October 1992, after a poor start to the season, Damien again parted company with Gillingham. The following July he became manager of League of Ireland club Cork City but left soon after to become manager of Cobh Ramblers. In the summer of 1995 he became manager of Shelbourne.

Damien won his first Irish cap against Austria in October 1971 whilst a Shamrock Rovers player. When he won his second cap, against Norway in June 1973, he became the first Gillingham player for 48 years to appear in a full international. He won his third and final cap over six years later, against Czechoslovakia in September 1979.

Damien Richardson (FORWARD)

Born: Dublin 2 August 1947
Debut for Eire: v Austria October 1971

At Shamrock Rovers Damien Richardson developed into a skilful striker who found the net with increasing regularity. He scored 33 times and won two FAI Cup winners medals in 1968 and 1969. He was just beginning his seventh season with Shamrock Rovers in October 1972 when he signed for Fourth Division Gillingham.

Alfred Ringstead (OUTSIDE-LEFT)

Born: Dublin 14 October 1927
Debut for Eire: v Argentina May 1951

A goal poacher of the highest order, Alf Ringstead signed for Second Division Sheffield United from non-League Northwich Victoria in November 1950.

In nine seasons with the Blades, Ringstead proved himself a fine all-round craftsman. A master of the half-chance, he demonstrated uncanny anticipation in and around the penalty area, combining a powerful shot with exceptional prowess in the air.

United, who had been relegated at the end of 1948–49, were crowned Second Division champions in 1952–53 and owed their return to the élite in no small part to the celebrated predatory skills and intelligent play of Alf Ringstead. By the time he left Bramall Lane for Mansfield in July 1959, he had scored 101 times in 247 League games.

His obvious talent did not go unnoticed by the selectors. He won his first full Eire cap just six months after arriving in Sheffield. Thereafter he was a regular in the Irish side and between 1951 and 1959 represented his country on 20 occasions and scored seven goals.

Alf ended his League career with 27 games for Mansfield in the 1959–60 season. The Stags were in their first season in the new Division Three, having previously played in the old Division Three (North). Unfortunately Alf must have left his scoring boots in Yorkshire, because he managed to find the net just three times, and the following season Mansfield were experiencing life in the new Division Four.

Michael Robinson (CENTRE-FORWARD)

Born: Leicester 12 July 1958
Debut for Eire: v France October 1980

An aggressive, hard-working player, Michael Robinson was involved in four transfer deals totalling almost £1.5 million during his League career.

Robinson joined Preston North End as an apprentice in July 1974 after being spotted playing for Dolphinholme Youth team. He turned professional in July 1976 and in three seasons with the club he managed 15 goals in 48 outings and helped them into Division Two in 1977–78.

Manchester City were suitably impressed and in July 1979 made him one of England's most expensive young players when they forked out £756,000 to take him to Maine Road.

He failed to make any impact on a struggling City side and, with the added burden of his big price tag, he became depressed, spending up to ten hours a day locked in a room brooding. His £400,000 transfer to Brighton a year later, after just eight goals in 30 League games, put an end to his agony.

Robinson enjoyed the best spell of his career with the Seagulls, appearing in 113 League games, scoring 37 goals and picking up an FA Cup runners-up medal in 1983 after their 4–0 defeat by Manchester United in the replayed final. That season he was Brighton's top scorer with just seven goals, as the club forfeited their First Division status. But during the close season Michael was involved in one of the most surprising transfers of the decade when mighty Liverpool took him back to the north-west in a £200,000 deal.

Robinson spent just over a season at Anfield. But, at Liverpool in the '80s, it was enough for him to pick up a few medals. He won a League Championship medal, as Liverpool claimed their third successive title; a European Cup winners medal as a substitute for Kenny Dalglish in the penalties victory over AS Roma in the final; and a League Cup winners medal again as a substitute, this time for Craig Johnston, in the final against Everton. The final was drawn, but although Robinson didn't play in the subsequent 1–0 victory at Maine Road, his appearance in the first game was enough to secure his medal.

Robinson's last League club, before joining Osasuna of Spain in 1987, was Queen's Park Rangers whom he joined for £100,000 in December 1984, having scored six goals in 30 League games for Liverpool.

He made 48 appearances and scored six goals for Rangers and in 1986 collected a League Cup runners-up medal after losing 3–0 to Oxford in the final.

Injury forced Michael to retire from the game after two years with Osasuna, but he remained in Spain and became a media star as the co-host of the award-winning TV football programme *El Dia Despues* (The Day After).

Robinson's grandmother was born in Ireland and in 1980 he made it known that he would like to wear the green shirt. However, at that time this was insufficient grounds for eligibility. Whereupon his mother – citing her own mother – took out Irish citizenship, thus enabling Michael to obtain an Irish passport.

The one-time boot-boy for Ray Treacy won 23 full caps for his adopted country, partnering Manchester United's Frank Stapleton in the Irish attack.

He scored only four international goals, however, and with the arrival of Jack Charlton, John Aldridge, Niall Quinn et al in the mid-1980s, Robinson found himself surplus to requirements.

Patrick Roche (GOALKEEPER)

Born: Dublin 4 January 1951
Debut for Eire: v Austria October 1971

Paddy Roche joined Manchester United from League of Ireland club Shelbourne in October 1973 for £15,000. Although he had almost nine seasons at Old Trafford, he didn't make it to first-choice keeper: he was initially understudy to United's veteran keeper Alex Stepney, and then had to queue up behind the up-and-coming Gary Bailey. In August 1982 Roche was given a free transfer and joined Brentford.

An agile and daring custodian, Paddy doubled his League appearance record in his first season at Griffin Park. He was a regular in the Bees' Third Division side in that 1982–83 season, playing in 46 games – the same number he had played in his nine years at Old Trafford. After 71 League games for Brentford, Roche lost his place to Trevor Swinburne and left Griffin Park for Halifax Town in July 1984.

Paddy became first-choice keeper at the Shay Ground and in January 1985 the club's board rejected a bid from Burnley for him. He had five seasons at Halifax, continuing to play into his 38th year, which had manager Billy Ayre commenting: 'Paddy Roche is just incredible . . . the man is like good wine, he gets better with age.' At the end of 1988–89, after 184 Fourth Division appearances, Roche retired to concentrate on his duties as Halifax's Football in the Community Officer.

As in his early days at club level, Paddy had to settle for second-choice goalminder at international level: Mick Kearns stood between him and Ireland's number 1 shirt. After a disastrous debut against Austria in 1971 – whilst still a Shelbourne player – when he was beaten six times, he was called upon just seven more times over the next five years to guard the Irish goal.

Paddy's final international record reads: eight caps, 11 goals conceded and three clean sheets. He also won two Under-23 caps, against France in 1972–73, both games ending in goalless draws.

Eamonn Rogers (WINGER)

Born: Dublin 16 April 1947
Debut for Eire: v Czechoslovakia November 1967

A dynamic and creative winger, Eamonn Rogers joined Blackburn Rovers as an apprentice, signing professional terms in May 1965. His six seasons at Ewood Park witnessed a steady decline in the fortunes of the once great Lancashire club.

In 1965–66 Rovers reached the quarter-finals of the FA Cup but finished bottom of Division One and were relegated. There was worse to come. The team continued to struggle in the lower division and in 1970–71 lost their grip on their Second Division status. Thus in just six seasons Rogers had appeared for the same club in three out of the four divisions.

Eamonn Rogers

The decline in the club's fortunes coincided with a decline in the fortunes of the player. An alleged refusal to switch position to right-back – peculiar, in that in 1967–68 the versatile Rogers had turned up in no fewer than seven positions in the side – earned him a severe reprimand and a place in the reserves. He became unsettled and was transfer-listed. In October 1971, after netting 30 goals in 165 League games for Blackburn, Eamonn joined Second Division Charlton Athletic.

In one season at the Valley, Eamonn made 37 League appearances, but once again suffered the ignominy of playing in a side doomed to be relegated at the end of the season. In November 1972 he transferred to Fourth Division Northampton Town where he ended his League career with four appearances for the Cobblers.

Described as 'fickle but brilliant', Eamonn was capped once at Under-23 level, against

France in June 1966, and, despite his difficulties at club level, kept his place in the international set-up for five years between November 1967 and October 1972. He scored a total of five international goals and won his 19th and final cap in the World Cup qualifier against the USSR in October 1972.

Gerard Ryan (WINGER)

Born: Dublin 4 October 1955
Debut for Eire: v Turkey April 1978

An outside-right with flair, Gerry Ryan had that rare ability to get spectators on the edge of their seats. He had a fine burst of speed and great control and at times bore a striking resemblance to another Ireland winger, Liverpool's Steve Heighway, with his darts to the byline and dangerous crosses.

Ryan had played more than 80 games for his hometown club Bohemians when, in September 1977, the irrepressible Tommy Docherty paid Bohs £50,000 to take Ryan to Derby County. Ryan settled in well at the Baseball Ground. In his one season there he scored four times in 30 First Division outings and collected the first of his 16 Republic of Ireland caps.

In September 1978 Gerry was transferred to Second Division Brighton for £80,000. In 1978–79 he helped the Seagulls win promotion to the top flight and in 1983 he came on as a substitute for Chris Ramsey in Brighton's drawn FA Cup final with Manchester United. As if defeat by a four-goal margin in the Cup final replay wasn't enough, the Seagulls also had to contend with relegation to Division Two at the end of that 1982–83 season.

On 2 April 1985 Gerry Ryan played his 172nd and final League game for Brighton, against Crystal Palace. During the game he broke his leg, and the injury was so serious that it brought an abrupt and premature end to his League career.

Capped once at Under-21 level, against England in March 1985, Gerry scored once in his 16 full outings, when he gave the Republic a surprise lead against West Germany in Dublin in 1979. Unfortunately the Germans scored three in reply.

Reginald Ryan (INSIDE-FORWARD)

Born: Dublin 30 October 1925
Debut for Eire: v Sweden November 1949

A player who represented his school at Gaelic football, Reg Ryan left Dublin at the age of eight and kicked off his soccer career with Nuneaton Borough. In March 1943 he joined Coventry City, still retaining his amateur status.

In April 1945 Ryan was snapped up by Second Division West Bromwich Albion. He spent a decade at the Hawthorns during which he earned the respect and admiration of fans and fellow pros.

In 1949 Albion regained the First Division status they had lost in 1938 and by the mid-1950s were once again a force to be reckoned with. In 1953–54 they finished runners-up in the League, four points behind Wolverhampton Wanderers, and won the FA Cup after a thrilling encounter with Tom Finney's Preston North End. Albion finished 3–2 victors and Ryan was the star of the show.

At the other end of the League, events at Derby County were to have a profound effect on Reg's career. The once great Rams were languishing in Division Three (North) and in 1955 replaced Jack Barker with Harry Storer as manager. Although Ryan was approaching his 30th birthday, Storer viewed him as the man to inject life into a dispirited team. Consequently, in July 1955, after 234 League games and 28 goals for the Baggies, Ryan moved to Derby for a fee of £3,000.

The move was a complete success. Ryan was appointed team captain and set about thrashing the team into a solid unit and putting his boss's ideas into action on the field. In his second season Ryan led his team back into the Second Division. His leadership even drew comparison with another Derby great, former England international Raich Carter. Indeed it has been said that Ryan's role in Derby's promotion success in 1956–57 cannot be overestimated.

In just over three seasons at Derby Ryan made 133 League appearances and scored 30 goals. His 14 goals in 1957–58 made him the club's top scorer that year. In September 1958 he joined Fourth Division Coventry City, making 65 appearances in just over two years and helping City win promotion in his first season.

In November 1960 Reg retired from the game and took up a post organising Coventry's pools. He took up a similar position with West Brom a year later, before being appointed the club's chief scout in 1962, a position he held for 14 years.

One of the élite band of players who were selected for both the North and the South, Reg played for the North against Wales in March 1950. He would have won his first Eire cap against Finland in Helsinki in October 1949 but his club, West Brom, refused to release him. He didn't have long to wait: the following month he replaced the injured Tommy Moroney in the Irish side to face Sweden.

Reg won a total of 16 caps for Eire and scored three goals, one of which – a penalty against Luxembourg in October 1953 – was the Republic's 100th goal in international competition.

David Savage (RIGHT WINGER)

Born: Dublin 30 July 1973
Debut for Eire: v Portugal May 1996

A player with a bright future, Dave Savage made his debut in the League of Ireland with

Kilkenny City at 17 in October 1990. He had a spell with Brighton in January 1991 but returned to Ireland to play for Longford Town.

Current Ireland boss and then Millwall supremo Mick McCarthy took him back to England to sign for the Lions in May 1994.

His ability to run at defenders and provide accurate crosses for the front men has offered Millwall an exciting edge to their play. He made his League debut for the Lions against Southend United in the first game of 1994–95 and kept his place for most of the season. Injury problems and a dip in form meant that he spent most of the 1995–96 season playing reserve team football. To the end of that season (when Millwall were relegated to Division Two) he had made 64 League appearances for the Lions.

His former colleague at the Den, current Liverpool and Ireland winger Mark Kennedy, was obviously impressed with his fellow Dubliner: 'Dave's a star in the making, there's no doubt about it. If he carries on the way he started here he's got every chance of going all the way and playing for the Republic. I'm convinced of that.' Prophetic words indeed from a mere 20-year-old.

In May 1996 Mick McCarthy gave the former Under-21 player his first full cap as a substitute in the friendly against Portugal at Lansdowne Road. Dave took his cap tally to five, against Bolivia in June 1996.

Patrick Saward (LEFT-HALF)

Born: Cobh, Co. Cork 17 August 1928
Debut for Eire: v Luxembourg March 1954

Born in Co. Cork but raised in south London, Pat Saward turned out for Crystal Palace on amateur forms as a youngster. He got his break in 1950 when he was spotted by Millwall whilst playing for Beckenham Town; he was signed by the Division Three (South) club in July 1951.

A tall, well-built and talented left-half or inside-left, Saward nevertheless suffered from

barracking from parts of the crowd at the Den. Lions' manager Charlie Hewitt made several appeals in his column in the matchday programme for the player to be given a fair chance, as he believed Pat had the ability to make the grade. Hewitt was right, but his pleas fell on deaf ears. After 120 League games and 14 goals for the Lions, Saward was sold to Aston Villa for £16,000 in August 1955.

In six seasons at Villa Park, Pat made 152 League appearances. He was an FA Cup winner in 1957 after Villa's 2–1 defeat of Manchester United in the final, and captained Villa to the Second Division Championship in 1959–60 following their relegation the previous season.

In March 1961 Pat was transferred to Second Division Huddersfield Town for whom he made 59 League appearances before hanging up his playing boots to join Coventry City as their coach in October 1963.

Pat was manager of Brighton from 1970 to 1973, taking them into Division Two at the end of 1971–72. He later coached the Saudi Arabian club AL-NASR, and then ran a holiday business in Minorca.

In an international career spanning some eight years, Pat wore the green shirt on 18 occasions. His finest moment came in May 1960 when he captained the Republic to a historic 1–0 win over West Germany in Dusseldorf.

Thomas Scannell (GOALKEEPER)

Born: Youghal, Co. Cork 3 June 1925
Debut for Eire: v Luxembourg March 1954

Tommy Scannell was signed as an amateur by Division Three (South) Southend United in November 1949 after starring for Tilbury against Barking in a cup-tie.

A 6ft 2in, 13½ st goalkeeper, Tommy played his first game for Blues' Colts that November and from the Colts' team he progressed to the reserves the following January where he was 'playing well, but in need of a great deal of polishing'. The same month he was fined by the FA as a result of enquiries into the affairs of his former club Grays Athletic.

Scannell was behind the long-serving Bert Hankey and Frank Nash for the number 1 shirt at Southend. The situation became more urgent in June 1950 when the club signed yet another keeper, Bristol City's Frank Coombs.

It was Coombs who was ousted from pole position when Tommy took his place between the sticks in December 1950. He became the club's regular keeper for five seasons, making a total of 98 League appearances, including the club's last ever fixture at the Greyhound Stadium in May 1955. Various injuries forced him to retire from League football at the end of that season.

Tommy played for an FAI XI against Glasgow Celtic in 1953 and in March 1954 became the second Southend keeper to represent Ireland – after George McKenzie, the club's most capped player – when he won his only full cap in place of Everton's Jimmy O'Neill in the 1–0 defeat of Luxembourg in a World Cup qualifier.

Tommy Scannell, who is the father of actor Tony Scannell of the TV series *The Bill*, died in 1994.

Patrick Scully (CENTRE-HALF)

Born: Dublin 23 June 1970
Debut for Eire: v Tunisia October 1988

Pat Scully was sent to Highbury by Arsenal's celebrated Irish scout Bill Darby as a youngster, joining initially as a youth trainee and then signing professionally in September 1987.

Pat spent over three years as a professional at Highbury but, because of a plethora of experienced central defenders at the club, failed to break into the first team.

A strong defender who likes to attack the ball and always gets his tackle in, Scully was farmed out on loan to other clubs three times during his Arsenal career. In September 1989 he made 13 Third Division appearances for Preston North End and at the beginning of 1990–91 he made 15 appearances for Theo Foley's Northampton Town.

In January 1991 Pat joined Southend United for what was initially a ten-week loan period. However, at the end of the spell Southend were suitably enough impressed by what they'd seen to offer Arsenal £100,000 for Scully on a permanent basis.

Pat immediately claimed a regular first-team place at the heart of the Shrimpers' defence, joining the club just in time to make a telling contribution in their historic promotion-winning season, 1990–91, which shot the club into Division Two for the first time in their 81-year history.

In March 1994, after 115 League appearances (six goals) for Southend, Scully was transferred to Huddersfield Town for a £100,000 fee. The following month Pat was a member of the Huddersfield side beaten in a penalty shoot-out in the final of the Autoglass Trophy at Wembley. To the end of 1995–96 he had clocked up 74 League appearances for The Terriers.

Capped by the Republic of Ireland at Under-19 level, Pat won nine caps at Under-21 level, one at Under-23 level and two at 'B' level. He won one full cap in the 4–0 defeat of Tunisia in October 1988.

Kevin Sheedy (MIDFIELD)

Born: Builth Wells, Powys 21 October 1959
Debut for Eire: v Holland October 1983

Kevin Sheedy is one of the few players to have the distinction of turning out for both Merseyside clubs – Liverpool and Everton.

Sheedy's career began at lowly Hereford United whom he joined as an apprentice from school and signed as a professional in October

1976. He made 51 League appearances for United before moving to Anfield in an £80,000 deal in July 1978.

Despite his outstanding form in Liverpool's reserves, the wealth of talent at the club prevented him from showing what he was capable of in the top flight and, although Liverpool boss Bob Paisley recognised his immense potential, he was restricted to just three League games in four years at the club.

In August 1982 an unwritten rule, stretching back almost two decades, which prevented players from moving between the two Merseyside clubs, was broken when Sheedy crossed Stanley Park to join Everton. Mr Paisley was reluctant to lose the player, but Kevin was fed up waiting in the wings and the deal went through, with a tribunal setting the fee at £100,000.

Arguably one of the best left-sided midfielders in the 1980s, Sheedy was famed for his 'cultured' left foot from which he combined accurate passing with deadly shooting either from free kicks or open play.

He enjoyed ten good seasons at Goodison Park, and his craft and graceful presence were major contributing factors to Everton's successes in the '80s.

In 1982–83 Kevin was voted Everton 'Player of the Year', having picked up 11 'Man of the Match' awards during the season.

He played in three Everton losing FA Cup sides: 1985 v Manchester United, 1–0; 1986 v Liverpool, 3–1 and 1989 v Liverpool, 3–2. On the plus side he scored the Blues' third goal in the 3–1 victory over Rapid Vienna in the 1985 European Cup-Winners' Cup final and won League Championship medals in 1985 and 1987.

Towards the end of his career at Everton, Kevin found it difficult to hold his place in the side through injuries and inconsistent form. In February 1992, after 274 League games and 67 goals, he accepted a pay cut and then gave up the chance of a testimonial by moving to Newcastle United on a free transfer. Geordie boss Kevin Keegan declared himself to be 'delighted' at having signed such a 'class player'.

In just over a season at St James' Park, Sheedy made 37 League appearances and in 1992–93 won a First Division Championship medal. The 33-year-old's reward for helping the Magpies book their place in the Premier League was a free transfer; at the close of the campaign he joined newly promoted Cardiff City. His stay in Wales was a brief one – just weeks after arriving he was on his way to Second Division Blackpool.

He made 26 League appearances for the Seasiders in 1993–94 and at the end of the following season, in which he didn't feature, he was granted a free transfer.

Kevin later became youth team manager at Blackburn Rovers and in June 1996 he was appointed reserve team manager at Tranmere Rovers by his former Ireland colleague, Tranmere player-manager John Aldridge.

A highly skilled player rarely guilty of losing possession, Kevin qualified to play for Eire through his father, who was born in Co. Clare. A former Republic Youth player, he won five caps at Under-21 level before winning his first full cap in 1983. A regular in the World Cup finals in Italy in 1990, he has scored nine international goals, including Ireland's first in a World Cup finals when he equalised against England in Cagliari in June 1990.

Kevin won his 45th cap against Wales in February 1993.

John Sheridan (MIDFIELD)

Born: Manchester 1 October 1964
Debut for Eire: v Romania March 1988

John Sheridan was hailed as the new Johnny Giles when he broke into the Leeds United first XI in November 1982. A creative midfield playmaker with the rare ability to dictate the course of a game, John was held in such high esteem at Elland Road that his boss at the time, Billy Bremner, threatened to resign if ever he was sold.

Of Dublin-born parents, John began his

career as a junior with Manchester City, joining Leeds, who had just lost their battle for First Division survival, in March 1982. Soon after moving to Yorkshire, he was capped by the Republic at Youth and Under-21 levels.

John kept his place in the Leeds' engine-room for seven seasons, making 230 League appearances (47 goals). This total would have been much greater had he not broken his leg in October 1983, which kept him out of action for the rest of that season.

In July 1989 Nottingham Forest paid £650,000 to take him to the City Ground as a replacement for Manchester United-bound Neill Webb.

The deal which took Sheridan to Forest was agreed when manager Brian Clough was on holiday and on his return Clough simply ignored him, making it very clear that the player didn't figure in his plans. During his four months at the club John didn't play a League game.

In November 1989 Sheffield Wednesday boss Ron Atkinson ended John's nightmare by taking him off Forest's hands at a cut-price £500,000.

Sheridan got back into the groove at Hillsborough, becoming the corner-stone of Atkinson's new-look side. He had the added pleasure of helping the Owls take three points off Nottingham Forest in his first game for the club. Wednesday were relegated to Division Two at the end of 1989–90 but bounced back immediately the following season (1990–91) with Sheridan the only player who didn't miss a game. Player and club capped a fine season by beating Manchester United in the final of the League Cup, with John scoring the only goal of the game – an unstoppable piledriver which has become one of his hallmarks.

Wednesday, now under the managership of Trevor Francis, went from strength to strength in 1991–92. They finished third in Division One to book their place in the inaugural Premier League the following season.

In that 1992–93 season, with Sheridan adding hard graft to his usual repertoire of invention and accuracy, the Owls battled all the way to Wembley in the two major Cup finals. Unfortunately they were blown from their nests in both the FA Cup and League Cup finals by a solid and determined Arsenal. Earlier in January 1993, Sheridan had signed a new three-year contract with the club.

To the end of 1995–96 Sheridan had scored 25 goals in 195 League games for Wednesday. He spent part of that season on loan to Birmingham City for whom he made two appearances.

Capped twice by the Republic at Under-21 level and twice at Under-23 level, John is regarded as one of the sweetest passers of the ball in the English game, arguably the most skilful Irish player since Liam Brady. Yet it took him all of six years to establish himself in Ireland's first XI. He made his debut in the 2–0 home win over Romania in March 1988 but collected just 16 caps over the next six years.

He saw just 13 minutes of World Cup action in Italy in 1990 and when he replaced John Aldridge for the last 15 minutes of the World Cup qualifier against Latvia in Riga in June 1993 it was his first competitive international for three years. John's lack of international duty in this period was due to a series of injury problems and to Ireland's star-studded midfield which includes Roy Keane, Andy Townsend and Ray Houghton.

It was a different story by the time of the 1994 World Cup finals in the USA, however. John became a regular just before the finals and in the USA he was one of only five Irish players to appear in all four of the Republic's games.

John, who has scored five goals for Ireland, won his 34th cap against Holland in December 1995.

Bernard Slaven (FORWARD)

Born: Paisley 13 November 1960
Debut for Eire: v Wales March 1990

Scotland and Ireland fought for the services of

Bernard Slaven

Bernie Slaven. The striker who was born in Scotland and had grandparents from Donegal and Tyrone, ended the battle in 1990 when he opted for the country of his forefathers.

Slaven began his career in Scotland with Morton but, along with most of the staff, he was released after the club was relegated from the Premiership at the end of 1982–83. He had made just 22 League appearances for the club.

He was out of the game for most of the next season, playing a couple of games for Airdrie at the start of the season, a couple for Queen of the South in the middle of the season and three for Albion Rovers at the end.

The following season, 1984–85, Bernie proved what a difference regular football makes to a player. He appeared in all of Albion Rovers, fixtures that season and ended the campaign as the club's top scorer, with 27 goals from 39 games. Middlesbrough boss Bruce Rioch had watched him and in September 1985 took him south of the border for a mere £25,000.

Slaven paid Rioch back in full and with interest. During his seven seasons at Ayresome Park he maintained a high scoring-rate. The club's top scorer for six consecutive seasons, his total haul was 118 in 307 League games.

If Slaven's goalscoring exploits were the epitome of consistency then the overall performance of the team was the exact opposite as they yo-yoed between the divisions. In 1985–86 they were relegated to Division Three and then, in successive seasons, went into the Second and the First Divisions. They spent just one season (1988–89) among the élite before being relegated again. They bounced back again when in 1991–92 they won a place in the inaugural FA Premier League. But when Boro were fighting a losing relegation dogfight at the end of the season, their star attraction had gone.

Slaven had joined Port Vale in March 1993 amid rumours of disagreement with Bruce Rioch, who had granted him a free transfer 'in lieu of eight years loyal service'. Vale's gain was Boro's loss.

Soon after arriving at Vale Park Bernie was at Wembley inspiring Port Vale to success in the Autoglass Trophy – the club's first trophy in their 113-year history. He left the club 'by mutual consent' in February 1994 and joined Darlington on a free transfer.

Slaven had scored seven times in 37 games for the Quakers when, in June 1995, he was forced to retire from the game.

A player with good close control and an eye for goal, his hard work off the ball fitted well into the Republic's scheme of things. Be that as it may, he has played a somewhat peripheral role at international level and won just seven full caps, six of which came in friendly internationals.

Joshua Sloan

(INSIDE-FORWARD/WING-HALF)

Born: Lurgan 30 April 1920
Debut for Eire: v Portugal June 1946

Better known as 'Paddy', Joshua Sloan was the original football gypsy. In a career spanning four decades, he played for no fewer than 14 clubs in five countries, including some of the greatest names in Europe.

Paddy started in the Irish League with Glenavon, from whom he joined Manchester United in September 1937. Two years later and without having made his League debut, he left Old Trafford to join Tranmere Rovers.

He returned to Glenavon on loan when war broke out, and when Glenavon resigned from the Regional League he had a short spell with Glentoran before joining the air force. Sloan served in Europe during the war and spent the 1944–45 season with Fulham before returning to Prenton Park for the first post-war season, 1945–46. In May 1946 he joined Arsenal and for the first time in his career tasted League football. He made 33 First Division appearances for the Gunners before departing for Sheffield United in February 1948.

In the summer of 1948, after just a dozen appearances for the Blades, Sloan became one of the first players to be transferred to the Italian League. In three years in Italy he turned

out for Milan, Torino, Udinese and Brescia. In December 1951 he was transferred from Brescia to Norwich City. He played six League games for the Canaries and later signed for Peterborough.

In July 1954 he became player-coach at Maltese club Rabat FC and later held similar positions with Hastings United (September 1955), Leamington Lockheed (March 1956) and Bath City (August 1956). He emigrated to Australia in 1963 and became coach at Melbourne club Juventus. He later became Chairman of the National Coaches Association.

Appropriately enough, Paddy was one of the handful of players to play for both 'Irelands'. He won two caps for the Republic in 1946, against Portugal and Spain, scoring Ireland's winner in their 1–0 victory over the latter in Madrid. He collected his only Northern Ireland cap in the 2–1 defeat of Wales the following April.

Paddy Sloan died in Australia in January 1993, aged 72. His ashes were returned to Britain to be scattered at Arsenal's Highbury Stadium.

Michael Smyth (GOALKEEPER)

Born: Dublin 13 May 1940
Debut for Eire: v Poland October 1968

A genial giant of a goalkeeper, Mick 'Smudger' Smyth started out with St Patrick's CYMS. From there he joined Drumcondra with whom he won an FAI Cup runners-up medal in 1961 after losing 2–1 to St Pat's in the final.

In August 1962 Smyth was transferred to Fourth Division Barrow. He made eight League appearances for the club before moving to non-League Altrincham. Smyth returned to Dublin in December 1964 to join Shamrock Rovers.

He won five FAI Cup winners medals with Rovers in successive seasons from 1965 to

1969. He collected a sixth winners medal with Bohemians in 1976 and after the final presented his medal to Bohs boss Mick Byrne.

The 6ft 3in, blond Dubliner, who was 'a great comfort to have behind a defence, possessing assurance, intelligence and no little ability', was a League Championship winner with Bohemians in 1974–75 and 1977–78, and won four League Cup winners medals, with Bohemians in 1975 and 1979 and with Athlone in 1980 and 1982 – the last one coming just four months before his 42nd birthday.

A former League of Ireland keeper, Smudger won one cap, as a substitute for the injured Alan Kelly, in the 1–0 defeat by Poland in Katowice in October 1968.

Francis (Frank) Stapleton (FORWARD)

Born: Dublin 10 July 1956
Debut for Eire: v Turkey October 1976

Frank Stapleton had almost 20 years as a professional in the Football League, donning the colours of seven clubs. But he will probably be best remembered for his exploits with two of England's most illustrious clubs – Arsenal and Manchester United.

From Harmonstown in north Dublin, Stapleton played Gaelic football as a youngster and played his junior soccer with St Martins and Bolton Athletic in his native Dublin.

He had trials with Manchester United when he was 16, in 1972, but while United procrastinated over a decision on whether or not to sign him, Arsenal stepped in, taking him on as an apprentice in June 1972 and as a professional 15 months later.

Frank's eight seasons at Highbury were a mixture of despondency and joy. He appeared in three successive FA Cup finals for the Gunners, collecting runners-up medals in 1978 and 1980 after 1–0 defeats by Ipswich and West Ham, and a winners medal in 1979 following

the 3–2 victory over Manchester United. He also had to settle for a runners-up medal in the 1980 European Cup-Winners' Cup final, which Arsenal lost on penalties to Valencia.

It took Stapleton a few seasons to find his scoring touch at Highbury, but in his last three seasons there, 1978–79, 1979–80 and 1980–81, he was the club's top marksman. By the time he left Highbury for Old Trafford in a protracted £900,000 transfer deal in August 1981, he had netted 75 times in 225 League games and was regarded by many, including Manchester United boss Ron Atkinson, as one of the best strikers in the League.

Creative and sharp, Frank had few peers in aerial battle, and many of his goals came from powerfully propelled headers. He was Arsenal's 'Player of the Year' in 1977 and again in 1980. There was understandable anxiety among the Highbury faithful when he was allowed to join one of the club's biggest rivals. The club did attempt to persuade him to stay, but the player, who was out of contract at the time, felt the time was right for a change of scenery.

Frank continued at Old Trafford where he'd left off at Highbury. He was United's leading scorer in his first three seasons there and he continued his regular visits to the national stadium to contest major cup finals.

He was in the United side which lost the 1983 League Cup final 2–1 to Liverpool and which faced Brighton in that year's FA Cup final and replay, which United won 4–0. The first game against Brighton ended in a 2–2 draw, but when Frank scored United's first goal, he wrote himself into the history books by becoming the first player to score in the final for two different FA Cup winning teams – having scored for Arsenal against United in 1979. He picked up his third FA Cup winners medal when United beat Everton 1–0 in the 1985 showdown.

In March 1986, after 60 goals in 223 League games, Stapleton was freed by United as a reward for 'long and loyal service' and subsequently joined Ajax Amsterdam. An unhappy eight months in Holland followed. He required a back operation for the removal of a disc and when Ajax manager Johan Cruyff moved to Barcelona, Stapleton found himself out of favour. In November 1988, after ten games on loan to Derby County in March 1988, he signed a two-year contract with French club Le Havre.

He failed to settle in France and in July 1989 returned to the Football League to join up-and-coming Blackburn Rovers. In two seasons at Ewood Park he scored 13 times in 81 games and was the club's top scorer in 1990–91. At the end of the season he was given a free transfer.

After three months without a game, he joined Huddersfield Town on a short-term basis in October 1991. He played five Third Division games for the Terriers before being appointed player-manager of Bradford City in December 1991.

Stapleton, who holds an FA coaching badge, was still turning out for the Bantams at the age of 37. Limited resources meant that sometimes he had to dust down his boots and turn out for the team. In May 1994 he was sacked after failing to steer Bradford to the Second Division play-offs. He had made 68 League appearances for the club.

In November 1994 he joined Liam Brady's Brighton on a non-contract basis but left after two weeks, having played two games, to become reserve team coach at QPR. He left QPR in February 1995 for family reasons, having failed to sell his house in Manchester, and in January 1996 took up the post of manager of New England Revolution in the new American Soccer League. Stapleton resigned in September 1996 just days after the club failed to qualify for the US major league play-offs.

A former Eire Schoolboy and Youth international, Frank won 70 full caps. He captained the senior side a record 30 times, including the 1988 European Championships in West Germany.

He scored his first goal on his international debut against Turkey in 1976 and surpassed Don Givens' scoring record set in 1980 by recording his 20th international goal against Malta in May 1990.

Stephen Staunton

(FULL-BACK/MIDFIELD)

Born: Drogheda, Co. Louth 19 January 1969
Debut for Eire: v Tunisia October 1988

The elegant Stephen Staunton is the epitome of calmness and assurance while under pressure. An excellent left-sided player, he is equally comfortable on the wing or at the back.

Liverpool signed Staunton from League of Ireland club Dundalk in September 1986; however, he made his League debut not at Anfield but at Second Division Bradford whilst on loan in November 1987.

Steve broke into Liverpool's first team in 1988–89, a season which he ended with probably the most emotionally and physically demanding period of his young life. In April 1989 he witnessed the Hillsborough disaster in which 90 Liverpool fans died before the FA Cup semi-final with Nottingham Forest.

On 20 May he won an FA Cup winners medal after Liverpool overcame neighbours Everton 3–2 after extra time in the final. Six days later he saw a League Championship medal snatched from his grasp by Michael Thomas's injury-time goal for Arsenal in the final game of the season at Anfield, which gave the Londoners the title on goal difference. Staunton had little time to brood, for two days later he was running out at Lansdowne Road in an Irish shirt to face Malta in a crucial World Cup qualifying game, followed by another qualifier against Hungary a week later.

Stephen had a further two seasons at Anfield, helping them to the League title in 1989–90 and to second place, runners-up to Arsenal for the second time in three years, the following season. Towards the end of Kenny Dalglish's managerial reign at Anfield, Staunton found himself in and out of the side and in August 1991, four months after Graeme Souness replaced Dalglish, Steve was transferred to Aston Villa for £1.1 million, having made 65 League appearances for Liverpool. The fee earned his old club Dundalk a £70,000 bonus.

Stephen immediately established himself as the regular left-back at Villa Park and was a key member of the team who were runners-up to Manchester United in the inaugural Premier League season in 1992–93. He was also a member of the Villa side which defeated Manchester United 3–1 to win the 1994 League Cup final and a non-playing sub when Villa won the trophy again, in 1996. To the end of 1995–96, Staunton had appeared 151 times in League encounters for Villa and scored 13 goals.

Capped four times for the Republic at Under-21 level, Stephen was the FAI/Opel 'Under-23 Player of the Year' in 1989 and was runner-up for the PFA's 'Young Player of the Year' in 1990–91. In 1992–93 he was named as Ireland's 'Player of the Year'.

Now a fixture in the Irish side, Staunton was a regular in the 1990 World Cup finals and took part in the 1994 finals in the USA. The youngest player to reach the 25-caps mark, he has scored six goals and won his 64th cap against Macedonia in October 1996.

Preferred on the left side of midfield since Terry Phelan's arrival on the Irish scene, Steve revels in the opportunity of getting forward more and has scored some crucial and spectacular goals with his excellent left foot from open play and set pieces, including directly from corners.

Alexander Stevenson

(INSIDE-FORWARD)

Born: Dublin 9 August 1912
Debut for Eire: v Holland May 1932

Hailed as one of the finest entertainers of his generation, Alex Stevenson was endowed with all the ingredients of a top-class player.

Described as possessing a sharp footballing brain and intricate close control, he was 'capable of beating a man on the space of a sixpence' and 'bamboozling opponents with a feint of the body'. In addition he had the strength and physique to withstand the sometimes ferocious challenges that players of his style and calibre regard as an occupational hazard.

Stevenson was 'discovered' by Glasgow Rangers' coach Arthur Dixon playing junior football with the Dolphin club in Dublin and signed for the Ibrox club in 1931. Alex became something of a superstar at Rangers, scoring 90 goals in 271 games for the club. In January 1934, however, after a lot of coaxing, he was persuaded to cross the border to join Everton.

At Goodison he struck up an awe-inspiring partnership with fellow countryman Jackie Coulter; the duo became the bane of many a defence and delighted the Goodison faithful with their quick-fire interplay and telepathic understanding.

Between 1933 and 1949 Alex made 255 First Division appearances for Everton and, despite being employed chiefly as a provider, he registered a respectable 82 goals and picked up a League Championship medal in the last pre-war season, 1938–39.

Alex left Goodison in 1949 to join local non-League club Bootle. He later returned to Ireland and in 1953–54, when he was 41 years old, was turning out for St Patrick's Athletic in the League of Ireland.

Alex's 'two Ireland' international career, like his Everton career, straddled the war. He made his Northern Ireland debut in the 2–1 win over Scotland in Glasgow in September 1933 and played his final game for the North almost exactly 14 years later against the same opposition. He won a total of 17 caps for the North.

Alex won seven caps for Eire and holds the record for the longest gap between winning first and second caps. He made his debut for Eire, when playing with Dolphin, in the 2–0 defeat of Holland in Amsterdam in May 1932. He didn't play for Eire again until they met England in Dublin in September 1946, a gap of over 14 years!

Alex Stevenson died in 1985.

Frederick Strahan (CENTRE-HALF)

Born: Dublin
Debut for Eire: v Poland May 1964

Freddie Strahan was a 'mobile' centre-half whose trenchant tackling and industry played a major role in Shelbourne's successes in the 1960s. For much of that decade he captained the Reds.

He was the Reds' skipper when they beat Cork Hibs 2–0 in April 1960 to win the FAI Cup. He led them to success in the League Championship in 1961–62, missing out on the double by going down 4–1 to Shamrock Rovers in the 1962 FAI Cup final. A year later, however, Fred once again held aloft the FAI Cup after Shelbourne for the second time in three years defeated Cork Hibs 2–0.

By 1963–64 Strahan was the inter-League's regular centre-half and his brilliant display for the Dublin City select against Arsenal in 1964 obviously impressed the selectors who called him up for the game against Poland in May 1964.

'Amazed at his selection, Strahan was nevertheless "very pleased at being honoured". Despite being played out of position at right-half on his debut, Fred rose to the big occasion, demonstrating a fine big match temperament.'

Strahan had an 'outstanding' game at centre-half against Norway when he won his second cap three days later. He was preferred to Ray Brady at right-half for the home game against England, which came just a fortnight after his debut. He scored his only international goal in that game which Ireland lost 3–1. Fred won his fifth and final cap

against West Germany in May 1966.

In June 1966 an International select played Shelbourne in a benefit match for Strahan. When his League career ended, he carried on playing in the Leinster Senior League with Rialto.

Maurice Swan (GOALKEEPER)

Born: Dublin 27 September 1938
Debut for Eire: v Sweden May 1960

A confident and skilful keeper, Maurice Swan signed for First Division newcomers Cardiff City from Drumcondra in July 1960. He had to share the goalkeeping duties at Ninian Park with Ron Nicholls and Welsh international Graham Vearncombe and had made just 15 League appearances when he departed for Hull City in June 1963.

Agile anticipation, courage and the ability to inspire his colleagues won Swan many admirers at Boothferry Park. He made 103 League appearnces for Hull and in 1965–66 won a Third Division Championship medal.

Maurice left Hull in 1967 and returned to Ireland where he played for Dundalk. By the early '70s he was back guarding Drumcondra's goal.

Maurice, who was once kept out of the game for a year with a damaged collar bone, got 45 minutes of international football when he was a half-time replacement for the injured Noel Dwyer in the game against Sweden in Malmo in May 1960.

The game was already lost when the debutant keeper – described as one of the safest net minders in the country – took the field. Ireland were trailing 3–0, but Swan acquitted himself well, conceding only one goal in the 89th minute; the final score was 4–1.

179

Noel Synnott (CENTRE-HALF)

Born: Dublin 1952
Debut for Eire: v Turkey April 1978

Brought up in Cabra, Co. Dublin, Noel Synnott spent 17 years in London. He played in the same Ealing team as former Spurs player Steve Perryman. He then had a period with Guilford City in the Southern League, where he was utilised as a striker, before returning to Ireland to play for Shamrock Rovers via Sligo Rovers in 1974.

Synnott spent almost ten years at Milltown and was captain under manager Johnny Giles, who was also national team boss between 1973 and '80 and who regarded Synnott as the best centre-half in the League. 'He's strong in the air, quick and tenacious in the tackle, abrasive and is never less than competitive,' said the manager.

Noel was a League Cup winner with Rovers in 1976–77 after beating Sligo Rovers in the final. He held aloft the FAI Cup in 1978 after Rovers overcame the same opposition by the same scoreline.

In March 1983 disaster struck. In a game against Dundalk he suffered a badly broken leg and a dislocated ankle. Long before the doctors told him he wouldn't play again, the pain and anguish had forced the player himself to the same conclusion.

He returned to his work as an Aer Lingus fitter. Then the company's Leinster Senior League side asked him to manage them and the long journey back began.

After leaving the Aer Lingus team, he started training with Bohemians and then signed for Waterford. In 1986 he lined up for Waterford against his former club Shamrock Rovers in the FAI Cup final. It was a sad occasion for Synnott. Rovers won 2–0 and he scored an own goal. After Waterford, Noel became manager of Kilkenny City.

In April 1978 Mark Lawrenson's withdrawal from the Irish squad and the unavailability of Mick Martin and David O'Leary brought Synnott a surprise call-up to face Turkey. He was retained for Ireland's next game, a 3–0 away defeat by Poland, and in September 1978 won his third cap in a goalless draw with Northern Ireland.

Thomas Taylor (GOALKEEPER)

Born: Dublin
Debut for Eire: v Poland October 1958

Perfect timing, excellent positional sense, safe handling of the ball, long, accurate kicking and complete control of his area were attributes which marked Tommy Taylor out as a keeper far above the ordinary.

He joined Waterford United in 1955 following a disinguished career in junior football with Home Farm, with whom he won a Junior cap. From the first day he wore the keeper's jersey at the club, he made it his own. 'There were occasions when his brilliance alone served to illuminate the grey drabness of the ordinary Shield or League game.'

In September 1958 he became the first keeper in a first-class match ever to score from inside his own area, when he netted in a 3–2 Shield victory over Shamrock Rovers.

Tommy's pleasant personality made him a firm favourite with everybody, and he won the hearts of Blues followers as few other outside players have ever done. One of the main reasons for the fans' admiration was the knowledge that he could have had his pick of the clubs at home or across the channel, at the time he joined Waterford.

Taylor had three seasons as Waterford's first-choice keeper, but 1958 will be the year that stands out in his memory. In September news of his departure to take up a building contract in Malta caused dismay among Blues fans. Ironically, just as he was about to leave, the honours began going his way. His first senior honour was a Shield medal won in November. He also won a couple of 'B' caps:

against Ireland in Reykyavik in August (won 3–2) and in the 1–0 defeat of South Africa in October.

That same month, he was called up as a reserve for the full international against Poland. The score stood at 2–2 with 65 minutes on the clock – Ireland having contrived to squander a two-goal advantage – Taylor was called into action after Jimmy O'Neill injured himself in the act of pulling off a brilliant save. 'Judging by his garb the Waterford man was quite unprepared. Through no fault of his own, he presented an odd and most un-international-like spectacle between the posts,' recorded one observer. Nevertheless, Taylor could say that he never conceded a goal in his full international career, as the score remained as it had been when he came on.

Peter Thomas (GOALKEEPER)

Born: Coventry 20 November 1944
Debut for Eire: v Poland October 1973

Peter Thomas joined his local League side Coventry City from Coventry GEC in June 1966. But, as understudy to England Under-23 international Bill Glazier at Highfield Road, Thomas got little opportunity to demonstrate his talents. He managed just one League appearance for the club, a 3–2 victory over Cardiff City, in the Sky Blues' historic Second Division Championship-winning season of 1966–67.

In 1967 he left Coventry to join League of Ireland club Waterford United. In his first game for Waterford he saved a penalty, and over the next 15 years he was elevated to the status of club hero. One local scribe summed up Thomas thus: 'His agility seemed to defy the laws of gravity . . . to stand behind his goal was to receive a lesson in the English language.'

The late '60s and early '70s were halcyon days at Waterford. They won five League of Ireland titles between 1967–68 and 1972–73

and finished third in 1970–71. With Waterford Thomas also appeared in four FAI Cup finals, losing in 1968, 1972 and 1979 before finally winning in 1980 when Waterford defeated St Patrick's Athletic. Although he was 35 at the time of the final, Thomas was still regarded as the best keeper in the country.

In 1969–70 he was voted 'Personality of the Year' by the Irish Soccer Writers' Association – the first Englishman to win the award. At that time he was virtually an automatic choice for the League of Ireland side.

It has been suggested that had Thomas been a few inches over 6ft rather than a few inches under it, he would surely have been one of the best keepers in England. As it was he played for Ireland and won two full caps.

He guarded Ireland's goal in Johnny Giles' first two games in charge of the national side – a 1–0 victory over Poland in Dublin in October 1973 and a 2–1 defeat by Brazil in Rio in May 1974.

Andrew Townsend (MIDFIELD)

Born: Maidstone 23 July 1963
Debut for Eire: v France February 1989

A man who leads by example: fiery and competitive, he'll never be found standing still; always making the crucial challenge; always making dangerous, piercing runs between the boxes. Add good vision, passing ability and a scorching left-foot shot, and you have Andy Townsend – the quintessential football all-rounder.

Andy's hallmark of unflagging effort and commitment have made him hugely popular with the supporters of Aston Villa and Ireland. Captain of the Irish XI, he is the driving force in the Republic's midfield. A regular in the side since 1988, he put together a run of 24 consecutive appearances, including all five of Ireland's World Cup games in 1990.

The son of Don Townsend, the former

Crystal Palace and Charlton full-back, Andy is the only player in the present Irish squad with Kerry connections: Andy's grandmother came from Castleisland in Co. Kerry. Totally committed to the Irish cause, Townsend is the first inheritor of Liam Brady's tradition and has scored seven goals in his 62 appearances for Ireland to date. The current Irish captain, he led Ireland to the 1994 World Cup finals in the USA.

The 1990 World Cup was the turning-point in his career. He returned from the tournament as a million-pound player. That summer he signed for Chelsea in a £1.2 million deal. Ironically he had been on trial with the club in 1982, but the Londoners couldn't come up with a deal to match his computer operator's pay supplemented by playing expenses at non-League Welling.

Townsend's rise to the status of one of the top midfielders in the country came via a rather unorthodox route. He left school at 16 and found work as a bricklayer, having decided he wasn't good enough to make it as a professional snooker player. He became a part-time professional at Welling and then joined Weymouth. Southampton boss Lawrie McMenemy took him to the Dell for £35,000 in January 1985.

He had three 'reasonably successful' seasons with Southampton, but because he was preferred wide on the left, he found his time there somewhat frustrating and, after 83 League appearances for the Saints, he joined Norwich City for £350,000 in August 1988.

During his two seasons at Carrow Road Townsend emerged as one of the country's most coveted and influential midfielders. He had made 71 League appearances for the club when he moved to Chelsea in May 1990.

Andy became captain at Stamford Bridge and had netted 12 times in 110 games by the time of his next big-money transfer, to Aston Villa for £2 million in July 1993.

In three seasons at Villa Park, to the end of 1995–96, Townsend had made 96 League appearances (six goals), and won the first major honour of his career in the form of a League Cup winners medal after the 3–1 defeat of Manchester United in the 1994 final. The feat was repeated two years later as Villa overran Leeds United 3–0 to reclaim the trophy.

Thomas Traynor (LEFT-BACK)

Born: Dundalk 22 July 1933
Debut for Eire: v Luxembourg March 1954

A tough, uncompromising defender with electrifying pace, Tommy Traynor began his playing career in the League of Ireland with Dundalk. Chelsea and Manchester City wanted to take him to England, but Southampton won the day, owing in no small measure to the persuasive powers of the Saints' Eire international goalkeeper of the time, Fred Kiernan.

Tommy joined the ground staff at the Dell in June 1952. He made his first-team debut in 1952–53 (at the end of which the Saints were relegated to Division Three (South) from Division Two), and the following year he became Southampton's regular left-back.

Tommy spent 14 years at the Dell during which he made a record 433 League appearances. During the latter part of his career, he became an influential figure at the club, something of a father-figure. He played an important role in the Saints' Third Division Championship-winning season in 1959–60 and in 1965–66, his final season at the club before his retirement, he helped Southampton into Division One for the first time their history.

As a reward for long and loyal service, Tommy was given a prestigious testimonial in which Southampton entertained Dutch side Twente Enschede. He later became a checker at the docks in his adopted city, but he still maintains his interest in the game by helping in the organisation of the Tyro Junior League.

A former Eire Amateur player, he won his first full cap in the 1–0 defeat of Luxembourg in March 1954. He had to wait eight years for his second call-up, which came against Austria in April 1962. From then until March 1964 Tommy was a regular in the Irish defence, taking his final cap tally to eight.

Raymond Treacy (FORWARD)

Born: Dublin 18 June 1946
Debut for Eire: v West Germany May 1966

Ray Treacy had 13 action-packed seasons in the Football League after joining West Bromwich Albion as an apprentice in August 1961.

Treacy learnt his trade in Dublin Schools football and with Home Farm before joining West Brom as a professional in June 1964. He had made only five First Division appearances for the Baggies in 1966–67 when he was transferred to Second Division Charlton in February 1968 for £17,500.

A shrewd user of the ball, Ray was the type of player who created all sorts of problems for opposition defences. He fitted in well at the Valley and in just over four seasons there he scored 44 goals in 149 League games. The Valiants were relegated at the end of 1971–72 and during the close season Ray transferred to Second Division Swindon Town.

In a season and a half at the County Ground he scored 16 goals in 55 League games before his £30,000 transfer to Preston North End in December 1973. Unfortunately his signing came too late to stave off relegation for the Lilywhites at the end of 1973–74. He scored 11 goals in 58 League games for the Deepdale club and once in three games on loan to Oldham Athletic in March 1975 before returning to the club where he started his career – West Brom.

Albion's new manager Johnny Giles, Treacy's fellow Dublin and Republic of Ireland colleague, took him back to the Hawthorns in August 1976. Ray ended his League career with six goals in 21 First Division games for Albion

Raymond Treacy

before returning to Dublin in May 1977, with Giles and another former Irish international, Eamonn Dunphy, to join Shamrock Rovers.

Ray was the Hoops' leading scorer in two of his three seasons with the club, netting a total of 35. He had a reputation as an ace penalty taker in the Football League, and when Rovers were awarded a spot kick in the 1978 FAI Cup final against Sligo Rovers, Ray was called upon to do the honours. He hit the target and Shamrock Rovers won the trophy.

He played with Toronto Mets in the North American Soccer League in 1978–79 and returned to take up the position of assistant manager at Shamrock Rovers in 1979.

He spent 1980–81 with Drogheda United and he ended the season as the club's top scorer with nine goals. The following season Ray was appointed player-manager at Drogheda.

Ray later managed Home Farm and in

January 1992 succeeded Noel King as manager of Shamrock Rovers.

A former Republic Schoolboy international and League of Ireland representative player, Ray was capped once at Under-23 level, against France in June 1966. He was a full international for over 13 years and was capped at each of his four League clubs. Used mainly as a target man at this level, he scored five times in his 42 international outings.

Liam Tuohy (OUTSIDE-LEFT)

Born: Dublin 27 April 1933
Debut for Eire: v Yugoslavia September 1955

One of the great personalities on the Irish soccer scene over the past four decades, Liam 'The Rasher' Tuohy is a former pupil of St Joseph's, East Wall. He played Gaelic football and hurling as a goalkeeper and played in that position in the local streets league. He then switched to wing-forward for St Mary's, East Wall, which was then a nursery for Shamrock Rovers, before signing for the Hoops in 1951.

A ball-playing winger with an eye for goal, Tuohy won a wealth of medals during his time at Glenmalure Park. He won League Championship medals in 1953–54, 1956–57 and in 1958–59 when he was the Hoops' top scorer with ten goals.

In the same period he played in four FAI Cup finals with Rovers. In 1955 Liam scored the single goal that beat Drumcondra in the final; the following year Rovers beat Cork Athletic 3–2 in the final. Runners-up medals were added to Tuohy's collection in 1957 and 1958 after Cup final defeats by Drumcondra and Dundalk.

In May 1960 Liam was transferred to Newcastle United for £9,500. He made a reasonable start with the Magpies and scored nine goals in 38 League games. However, a 'mixture of circumstances' forced his return to Shamrock Rovers in August 1963 where as player-coach he continued his winning ways.

He added another League of Ireland Championship medal to his collection in 1963–64 and won two more FAI Cup winners medals in 1964 and 1965 after victories in replayed finals over Cork Celtic and Limerick.

Voted the Soccer Writers of Ireland 'Personality of the Year' for 1965–66, Liam took over as coach of Rovers when his playing days ended. He was the national team manager between 1971–73, a post from which he retired to pursue business interests. He managed Shelbourne in the early '80s and was coach to the Irish Youth team until Jack Charlton dispensed with his services in 1986.

Liam represented the League of Ireland on many occasions, was capped three times at 'B' level and won his first full cap in the 4–1 defeat by Yugoslavia in September 1955.

On his next international outing, against Czechoslovakia in Dublin in April 1959, Liam scored Ireland's first-ever goal in the European Nations Cup (the forerunner to today's European Championships), when Ireland beat the Czechs 2–0.

Tuohy scored in consecutive internationals against Austria and Iceland (twice) in 1962, taking his international goal tally to four. He won his eighth and final cap in the 2–0 home defeat by Belgium in March 1965.

Patrick Turner (INSIDE-RIGHT)

Born: Dublin
Debut for Eire: v Scotland June 1963

Motor mechanic Paddy Turner began his senior career in the League of Ireland with Shamrock Rovers. In his first season with the club, 1958–59, he won a League of Ireland Championship medal.

Turner spent the 1960–61 campaign with Rovers' Dublin rivals Shelbourne and in November 1961 was transferred to Scottish club Morton.

A 'cultured inside-forward', Turner was a 'big success' at Cappielow and in May 1963 was transferred to Glasgow Celtic. In his one season at Celtic, Paddy made just seven League appearances, losing out to the up-and-coming Bobby Murdoch.

The fair-haired Turner returned to Ireland in June 1964 to join Belfast club Glentoran in the Irish League where he spent one season before returning south and signing for Dundalk in 1965.

Paddy had seven seasons at Oriel Park. He was the club's top scorer in two seasons, 1965–66 and 1969–70, and won a Championship medal in 1966–67. He spent the 1972–73 season back in Dublin with Bohemians.

Just ten days after signing for Celtic, Paddy was in the Irish side which defeated Scotland 1–0 in Dublin. He won his second cap in the European Nations Cup game against Spain in April 1964.

John (Jackie) Vernon (CENTRE-HALF)

Born: Belfast 26 September 1918
Debut for Eire: v Portugal June 1946

Jackie Vernon, like many Irish soccer stars, learnt his football in the Gaelic code. He first played soccer for Spearmint FC before signing for intermediate club Dundela. In 1938 he rejected the advances of Liverpool and opted to play for local Irish League side Belfast Celtic.

During the war years Jackie won every honour in local football with the legendary Belfast side. In 1940 he was a member of the team which, for the fifth time, won the Irish League and added the City and Gold Cups to their title success. They were regional League champions in 1941 and 1942 and won the Irish Cup in 1941, 1943 and 1944.

The transfer system, which had been in cold storage during hostilities, was restored after the war and in February 1947 Jackie joined his only Football League club, Second Division West Bromwich Albion. In six seasons at the Hawthorns he made 190 League appearances and in 1948–49 helped Albion win promotion to Division One as runners-up to Fulham.

'He seldom wastes a pass, most of which are short and neat.' Jackie was Northern Ireland's team captain in the immediate post-war era. He was the North's automatic choice for the centre-half position from September 1946 to November 1951, a period in which he won 17 caps.

Jackie made two appearances for the Republic, both in the summer of 1946 as a Belfast Celtic player, in an Iberian tour when the Republic lost 3–1 to Portugal and, for the first time, defeated Spain away from home in a 1–0 victory in Madrid.

But probably Jackie's greatest achievement on the international front was his inclusion in the Great Britain side which played the Rest of Europe in a Victory international at Hampden Park in 1947.

Jackie Vernon died in 1981.

Gary Waddock (MIDFIELD)

Born: Kingsbury, London 17 March 1962
Debut for Eire: v Switzerland April 1980

Gary Waddock started out with his local team Kingsbury before joining First Division Queen's Park Rangers as an apprentice in 1977. Gary worked his way through the ranks at Loftus Road, making his first-team debut at 18 in 1978–79.

A tough tackling and inspirational midfield general, Gary became one of the most popular QPR players of all time. He began in the first team in the season that the club lost their grip on the top rung of the Football League; and he went on to play a starring role in Rangers' Second Division Championship-winning side in 1982–83. He was also a member of the side which lost the 1982 FA Cup final replay 1–0 to Tottenham Hotspur.

He played 203 League games for the 'R's. Then, in 1985, a serious knee injury threatened to end his career. In typical style he refused to give in and battled his way back to peak fitness. In 1988 he signed for Belgium club Royal Charleroi.

In August 1989 he returned to England and joined Millwall. He made 58 League appearances for the Lions and earned a surprise international recall on the recommendation from his Millwall colleague and Irish striker Tony Cascarino.

In December 1991 QPR boss Gerry Francis took Waddock back to his spiritual home at Loftus Road. Gary failed to make the first team second time around in west London and in November 1992, after a six-game period on loan to Swindon Town in March 1992, he joined Bristol Rovers in the new Division One.

Gary was voted the Pirates' 'Player of the Year' for 1992–93. He had made 71 League appearances for the club when he moved to Luton Town in August 1994.

He had made 76 Division One appearances for the Hatters to the end of 1995–96, and Luton were relegated at the end of the season.

Gerry qualified to play for Ireland because of his parents' birthplace (his father is from Gorey, Co. Wexford and his mother from Limerick) – and not his St Patrick's Day birthday.

He won one Under-21 cap and one 'B' cap, and made his full debut in the 2–0 defeat of Switzerland in Dublin in April 1980. By October 1985 he had accumulated 19 appearances in the green shirt.

After an absence of almost five years, Gary was recalled to the international arena and played in the 1–0 defeat of the USSR in April 1990, completing his collection of 21 caps against Turkey the following month.

David Walsh (CENTRE-FORWARD)

Born: Waterford 28 April 1923
Debut for Eire: v Portugal June 1946

An 'unorthodox opportunist who could find his way through a web of defences', Dave Walsh first attracted attention as a prolific striker during his junior career in his native Waterford. He started out with local junior clubs St Joseph's, Corinthians, Shelbourne and Glen Rovers and later served Shelbourne and Limerick in the League of Ireland. He was Limerick's top scorer with 13 goals in 1942–43. At the end of that season he moved north to join Belfast club Linfield in the Irish League.

In three years at Windsor Park, Walsh scored 105 goals, including 60 in Linfield's Championship-winning season, 1945–46. He also collected Irish Cup winners and runners-up medals during his stay in Belfast.

In July 1946 Dave was snapped up by West Bromwich Albion for £3,500. He had an immediate and decisive impact at the Hawthorns, scoring in each of his first six matches for the club at the start of the 1946–47 season. In all, Walsh scored 94 League goals in 165 games for the Baggies and in 1948–49 shot the club into Division One.

In October 1950 Albion's neighbours, Aston Villa, who had lost their own star striker Trevor Ford to Sunderland, earmarked Walsh as the Welsh international's successor at Villa Park. Two months later Villa got their man for a hefty £25,000.

In four and a half seasons at Villa Park, Dave netted 37 goals in 108 First Division games. In July 1955 he transferred to Division Three (South) club Walsall where he ended his League career with six goals in 20 games.

In May 1956 Dave joined non-League Worcester City, retiring the following year through injury. After he left the game he ran a sports shop and newsagents at Droitwich before retiring to Torquay in 1984.

A former Irish League representative player, Dave was reserve when Great Britain played the Rest of Europe in 1947 and is one of the handful of players to represent both 'Irelands'.

He was the North's centre-forward in the immediate post-war era and scored five goals in just nine starts. He equalled that goalscoring tally for the Republic, albeit over a longer period: his five for Eire came in 20 games between June 1946 and November 1953.

John Walsh (FORWARD)

Born: Limerick 8 November 1957
Debut for Eire: v Trinidad and Tobago May 1982

Garryowen-born Johnny Walsh was only ten when he signed for local junior club Wembley Rovers. In seven years with the club, until he joined local League of Ireland club Limerick, he won a plethora of under-age honours.

Walsh, who retired from the game in April 1994, spent 18 full seasons with Limerick during which he played under many managers. He refused numerous offers to leave.

But, in names at least, Walsh can claim to have played for many teams. Various trials and tribulations have seen the Shannonsiders change name several times. They began as Limerick, later became Limerick United and then Limerick City, finally reverting back to their original name in 1992.

Walsh, who 'on his day could be brilliant', won a League Championship medal with United in 1979–80 and a First Division winners medal with City in 1991–92; they had been relegated the previous year.

In his first season, 1976–77, he was an FAI Cup runner-up after Limerick lost the final to Dundalk; Walsh was carried off injured after 25 minutes. In 1982 he won a Cup winners medal following Limerick's victory over Bohemians in the final. He was 'Man of the Match', an award which carried with it a cheque for £300. The following day he was due to jet off to New Zealand with the League of

Ireland team but was withdrawn after injuring his ankle in the post-match celebrations.

He was a League Cup runner-up in 1991 and a League Cup winner in 1993. He also won three Munster Cup successes in the '80s and a Shield winners medal in 1984.

Johnny won his first inter-League honours in 1978–79 when the League of Ireland played a Basque selection in front of 75,000 people in Bilbao. There was more to follow. As a member of the League side which toured South America two years later, Johnny lined up in front of 85,000 at the famous River Plate stadium to face world champions Argentina, complete with their 17-year-old starlet Diego Maradona.

In May 1982, after having sat on the subs bench six times, Johnny finally won his only full cap in the Irish side which played Trinidad and Tobago in May 1982.

Michael A. Walsh (FORWARD)

Born: Chorley 13 August 1954
Debut for Eire: v Norway March 1976

Mick Walsh signed professional forms for Blackpool from non-League Chorley in November 1971 as a right winger. It was, however, as centre-forward that he made his mark in League football.

The 1975–76 season was the turning-point in Walsh's career. He established himself as a first-team regular at Bloomfield Road for the first time and was included in the Republic of Ireland squad, making his debut against Norway in March.

Once in Blackpool's League side he consistently topped the club's scoring charts, and his form in front of goal kept the Seasiders riding high at the top of Division Two. In three seasons he scored 72 goals in 180 games.

Many of Walsh's strikes were spectacular efforts. He possessed a penchant for doing the unexpected, conjuring up classic goals from unlikely situations. In 1974–75 he won the

Michael Walsh

BBC's 'Goal of the Season' for his goal against Sunderland in February 1975.

Blackpool were relegated to Division Three at the end of 1977–78, and during the close season Everton, impressed by Walsh's deadly finishing, made him the most expensive player to play for Ireland at the time by splashing out £325,000 for his signature.

Initially he formed a partnership with Bob Latchford, spearheading Everton's attack, but halfway through his first season Mick sustained an injury which kept him out of contention for some time. Upon recovery he couldn't force his way back into the side and in March 1979 he was transferred to Queen's Park Rangers, having scored just once in 21 games for Everton.

Walsh went to Loftus Road in a straight swap deal with Rangers' Peter Eastoe, with both players valued at around the £250,000

mark. Mick made just 18 League appearances (three goals) for Rangers before joining Portuguese giants Porto in September 1980. In 1984 he won a Portuguese Cup winners medal and was one of Porto's playing subs in the final of the European Cup-Winners' Cup competition, which Porto lost 2–1 to Italian giants Juventus.

Mick left Porto in 1985 and later had spells with Sal Gueiros, Espinho and Rio Avenue before returning to England in 1989 to join the backroom staff at non-League Slough Town where he remained for two years.

In February 1995 he was appointed joint manager, with Tony O'Driscoll, of Diadora League Division One club Chertsey Town.

Although Mick scored on his international debut, against Norway in March 1976, he found it difficult to establish himself in the Irish side, for the front positions in the national team at the time were occupied by Ireland's most prolific hitmen, Don Givens and Frank Stapleton. He did manage 21 appearances, however, and scored three goals.

Walsh won his 21st and final Republic of Ireland cap against Denmark in November 1984. He was dropped for Ireland's next fixture against Italy in February 1985. The day that the squad was announced, 29 January 1985, his wife presented him with quads!

Michael T. Walsh (CENTRE-HALF)

Born: Manchester 20 May 1956
Debut for Eire: v Chile May 1982

A product of Bolton Wanderers' youth scheme, Mike Walsh joined the club from school. He signed professionally in July 1974 and spent the next few years being groomed in the reserves in preparation for a first-team place.

Although primarily a central defender – his favourite position – he spent those formative years as an understudy for any of the defensive or midfield positions which became available through injury or suspension.

1977–78 was Walsh's first season as a regular member of the Bolton side; he missed just one League game and ended the campaign with a Second Division Championship medal. The Trotters were relegated after just two seasons in the top flight and the drop of a division frustrated the player who made no secrets of his ambition to play international football for the country of his grandfather – Ireland. Consequently when his contract at Burnden Park expired, he refused the offer of a new one.

Walsh had made 177 League appearances for Bolton when, in August 1981, he returned to the First Division by joining Everton in exchange for Eire international goalkeeper Jim McDonagh (who had left Bolton a year earlier) plus a £90,000 cash adjustment in Bolton's favour.

'A strapping six-footer', Mike was described by new Goodison boss Howard Kendall as 'a good player, who will be a tremendous asset to the squad'. Unfortunately for Walsh, 'squad' was the key word in Kendall's statement. Despite 'looking confident and settling in quickly' in Everton's central defence, Walsh never progressed beyond the role of bit-part player at Goodison.

He made five appearances on loan to Norwich City in October 1982, and then three on loan to Burnley in December. He had managed just 20 First Division games for Everton when, in May 1983, he left England to join North American Soccer League club Fort Lauderdale.

He did, however, fulfil one ambition during his sojourn on Merseyside: he played for Ireland, winning all of his four Irish caps over a six-month period in 1982 whilst he was on Everton's books.

Mike returned to the Football League in October 1983 and had just four League outings for Manchester City before transferring to Blackpool for £6,000 in February 1984. In just over five seasons at Bloomfield Road Mike made 153 League appearances and in 1984–85 helped the Seasiders win promotion to Division Three.

In July 1989 he joined Bury and the following December was appointed manager at the club. He went on to become the longest-serving manager in the Third Division, taking the club to three play-offs in five years, but in September 1995 parted company with the club by 'mutual consent'. He then became manager at Barrow and in October 1996 moved to Swindon to be number two to his former Everton team-mate Steve McMahon.

William Walsh (WING-HALF)

Born: Dublin 31 May 1921
Debut for Eire: v England September 1946

Billy Walsh was seven in 1928 when his family left Dublin to live in England. As a youngster, Billy attended St Gregory's School, Ardwick, and represented Manchester Boys. On leaving school, he landed an office job and in 1935 joined Manchester United as an apprentice. The following year he became an apprentice at Manchester City, signing professional terms in June 1938.

A Second World War veteran, Billy guested for several clubs during the war years. At the end of the war, he was turning out for City on Saturday afternoons and working as a miner for the rest of the week. He clocked up 109 League appearances between 1946 and 1951 and in 1946–47 won a Second Division Championship medal.

In April 1951 Walsh was appointed player-manager at Chelmsford City and in August that year became player-manager at Canterbury. He later had a spell coaching at Xaverian College, Manchester, where one of his young charges was Colin Barlow – City's new Chief Executive.

Billy is the nephew of former Shelbourne keeper Paddy Walsh. Billy's brother Shaun was an amateur at Manchester City and his son Kevin was an apprentice at the club.

Walsh was one of the stars of the famous Irish side which defeated England 2–0 at Goodison Park in 1949, England's first home defeat by a foreign team. 'Billy Walsh was in one of his cheekiest moods, going into tackles with real dash, coming out with the ball, dribbling through and passing with an accuracy that sent shivers through the English defence.'

Unknown to Irish fans before that debut against England, Walsh quickly became popular with the Irish players and supporters.

Billy holds a unique international record in that he was honoured by three countries. He played three times for England Boys, won five Northern Ireland caps in successive internationals between October 1947 and November 1948 and won nine Republic of Ireland caps in the immediate post-war era.

When he ended his playing career, Billy emigrated to Australia.

Joseph Waters (MIDFIELD)

Born: Limerick 20 September 1953
Debut for Eire: v Turkey October 1976

A 5ft 5in, 10st 5lb midfield pocket dynamo, Joe Waters was an apprentice at Leicester City before joining the club as a professional in October 1970.

Although he made just 13 First Division appearances for City, he will be remembered for his two brilliant goals at QPR which sent City into the semi-finals of the 1974 FA Cup. And he was only in the side as an eleventh-hour replacement for Alan Birchenall!

In 1976 Waters moved to Grimsby Town on loan and immediately stole the hearts of the Mariners' faithful. The club were preparing to allow him to return to Leicester at the end of his month's loan, but such was the outcry from the fans that they relented and in February

1976 secured his services permanently in a £8,500 transfer deal, with the Supporters' Club dipping into their own pockets for a quarter of the fee.

The Mariners were relegated to Division Four in 1976–77 soon after he arrived. Joe was an inspirational captain as he skippered the side to promotion in 1978–79 and then, in 1979–80, went one better by leading the Mariners to the Third Division title. He was voted Town's 'Player of the Year' for 1978–79.

One of Grimsby's finest and most popular players, Joe made a record 266 consecutive League appearances between November 1976 and October 1982. When he was freed by the club at the end of 1983–84, he had made a total of 357 League appearances and scored 65 goals, many from the penalty spot.

When his League career ended, he moved to America – where he still lives – and enjoyed a successful spell in the American's Soccer 6s League.

An energetic and astute performer, Joe was capped by the Republic at Schoolboy and Youth levels but was limited to just two full caps, mainly by the competing claims of Johnny Giles and Liam Brady.

Joe won his first cap, playing at right-back, in a pulsating encounter with Turkey in Ankara in October 1976. The Irish were 2–0 up after 14 minutes and 3–2 down after 65 minutes. Debutant Waters intervened with the equalising goal 15 minutes later to spare Irish blushes. Three years later, in November 1979, Joe won his second cap, as a 53rd-minute substitute for Gerry Daly, in the 1–0 defeat by Northern Ireland in Belfast.

Ronald Whelan (INSIDE-FORWARD)

Born: Dublin 17 November 1936
Debut for Eire: v Austria September 1963

The father of former Liverpool captain Ronnie

Whelan, Ronnie Whelan (sen.) was 'discovered' by the wife of former Eire international Paddy Moore. She recommended him to her husband, who was coaching junior club Stella Maris. Ronnie was then invited to join Home Farm from Stella Maris by another neighbour, future Manchester United player, Liam Whelan.

A gifted inside-forward who was difficult to dispossess, Whelan was adept at carving out openings and excelled in aerial duels. He won honours galore with Home Farm, who at the time were a junior club. A three-month trial with Chelsea as a teenager turned sour, and so he returned to Dublin to St Patrick's Athletic in 1956.

From 1957–64 he was the schemer in St Pat's attack and was the club's leading scorer in five of his 12 seasons there, netting a total of 89 League goals.

St Pat's won the League of Ireland title in 1955–56, and in 1959 Whelan played a leading role in the club's first FAI Cup success, a feat repeated two years later.

Following a run of injuries in the mid-1960s Ronnie joined Drogheda where he had six good seasons, helping them to the 1971 FAI Cup final, which they lost 3–0 to Limerick in the replayed final.

Ronnie retired from League of Ireland football in 1973 but continued to play with Aer Lingus – his employers – in the Leinster Senior League for many seasons.

In 1964 Ronnie was a member of the Dublin XI which played Liverpool. He had already represented the League of Ireland against the Irish League in March 1961 and scored the winning goal against the English League in October 1963. A week after that game he won the first of his two full caps in the European Nations Cup qualifier against Austria in 1963.

Ronnie Whelan died in 1993.

Ronald Whelan (MIDFIELD)

Born: Dublin 25 September 1961
Debut for Eire: v Czechoslovakia April 1981

The son of former Irish international striker Ronnie Whelan (sen.), Ronnie (jun.) has been the enduring link between Ireland and Liverpool FC for 14 years and played a starring role in the relentless Liverpool success story of the 1980s.

Finglas-born Ronnie developed in Dublin Schools football and made his debut for League of Ireland club Home Farm on his 16th birthday. Three years later, in October 1979, he joined Liverpool after Manchester United, with

Ronnie Whelan

whom he'd spent three years as a schoolboy, declined to take up an option to sign him.

Whelan's potential in the Football League was quickly spotted and recognised when he won the 'Young Player of the Year' award for 1981–82. He certainly lived up to his early promise, going on to captain Liverpool and collect a wealth of medals. He won First Division Championship medals in 1981–82, 1982–83, 1983–84, 1985–86, 1987–88 and 1989–90; FA Cup winners medals in 1986 and 1989; League Cup winners medals in 1982, 1983, 1984 and a runners-up medal in 1987; a European Cup winners medal in 1984 and a runners-up medal in 1985.

In older days Ronnie would have been described as an attacking left-half. At 5ft 9in and just under 11st, he is ideally equipped for a midfield role. A tireless worker and eye-catching performer, he is quick, intelligent, an excellent distributor of the ball, a tough tackler and he has a penchant for creating spectacular goals out of 'nothing'. His winner against Manchester United in the 1983 League Cup final and the mid-air volley for Ireland against the USSR in the 1988 European Championships are prime examples. Furthermore he scored twice against Spurs in the 1982 League Cup final and also found the net against Sunderland in the 1989 FA Cup final.

Just when Whelan had become accustomed to unbroken success in the '80s, he experienced a sharp contrast in the '90s, as a woeful catalogue of injuries put his career on a stop-go mode.

Whelan was captain of the Ireland team that travelled to Italy for the 1990 World Cup finals. His tournament lasted just 29 minutes as a substitute. Thereafter he suffered a broken foot and a broken leg, underwent a thigh operation and three knee operations.

He spent almost three years in the international wilderness and from the beginning of 1990–91 to the end of 1992–93 he played just 41 League games for Liverpool. His absence from the Liverpool engine-room coincided with a dramatic downturn in the fortunes of the club.

In August 1993 Whelan signed a one-year 'pay as you play' contract with Liverpool. Two months later Liverpool manager Graeme Souness told Whelan that he didn't figure in his plans for the future. After 14 glorious years at Anfield, it was a bitter pill for Ronnie to swallow.

And so in August 1994, after 362 League games and 46 goals for Liverpool, Ronnie joined Division One club Southend United. He made 33 League appearances in 1994–95 and was appointed the club's player-manager at the end of that season. A serious knee injury saw him miss all but one League game of the 1995–96 season.

A former Republic of Ireland Schoolboy, Youth and Under-21 player, Ronnie was unable to command a regular international place under Eoin Hand but blossomed under Jack Charlton to become the manager's number-one player.

A brilliant midfield all-rounder who has performed at left-back for Ireland, Ronnie at his peak was recognised as one of the best players in the League, at best world class.

Whelan has scored three international goals, has captained his country and won his 53rd cap against Austria in June 1995.

William Whelan (INSIDE-FORWARD)

Born: Dublin 1 April 1935
Debut for Eire: v Holland May 1956

A ball-playing inside-forward of the highest calibre, Billy (or Liam) Whelan joined Manchester United from Home Farm as an 18-year-old in May 1953. Two years later he made his first League appearance in a United shirt. Billy went on to represent the club in 79 League encounters in which he averaged a goal in every other game. He had accumulated a total of 43 goals when his young life was tragically ended on a snowbound runway in Munich in 1958.

In his relatively short playing career, Whelan achieved more than most players achieve in a lifetime in the game, picking up League Championship medals in successive seasons, 1955–56 and 1956–57, and an FA Cup runners-up medal in 1957.

An intelligent player who read the game superbly, his overall command of the game's finesse was second to none. As United's top scorer in 1956–57 with an amazing 26 goals in 39 games, Billy had a major say in keeping the title at Old Trafford that season.

United were denied the distinction of becoming the first club this century to pull off the League and Cup double, after losing the 1957 final to Aston Villa in controversial circumstances. United's keeper Ray Wood had to leave the fray with a fractured cheekbone after a challenge by Villa's McParland which resulted in one of Villa's goals in their 2–1 victory.

Billy made his international debut in the 4–1 defeat of Holland in Rotterdam in May 1956 at a time when away victories for Eire were few.

He had made just three more appearances in an Ireland jersey when, in February 1958, after Manchester United's 5–4 aggregate victory over Red Star Belgrade in the quarter-final of the European Cup, the plane carrying the team home crashed on take-off. Billy Whelan was among those killed.

The FA of Ireland Yearbook of 1958–59 paid tribute to their fallen colleague: 'We shall miss the cheerful smile and cheekily efficient football, but we shall not forget him, nor those other Manchester United players so tragically torn from the field on sport's blackest day.'

Richard Whittaker (DEFENDER)

Born: Dublin 10 October 1934
Debut for Eire: v Czechoslovakia May 1959

A compactly built full-back, Richard Whittaker played his junior football with St Mary's Boys'

Club in his native Dublin. He left Ireland to join Chelsea's ground staff and in May 1952 signed professional forms for the club.

For five seasons at Stamford Bridge Whittaker remained on the fringes of regular first-team football, playing second fiddle to the Sillet brothers, John, later of Coventry City and England international Peter. After 48 First Division appearances Richard finally left the Bridge and joined Peterborough United in September 1960.

The Posh had been admitted to the League at the beginning of 1960–61 and proceeded to take the Fourth Division by storm, winning promotion as champions in their first League season. In July 1963, with 82 appearances under his belt, Richard left the London Road Ground to return to west London and QPR where, after 17 games, he ended his League career.

A former Eire 'B' international, Richard won his one full cap in Ireland's second-ever European Nations Cup game, against Czechoslovakia in May 1959.

IRELAND MANAGERS PAST AND PRESENT

Mick Meagan

September 1969–May 1971

In the '50s and '60s Ireland was well down the European pecking order and the team was selected by a five-man committee.

In 1969 Ireland entered a new era when the FAI appointed former Drogheda player-manager Mick Meagan as national team manager. Whereas previous incumbents were confined to coaching, the new manager was given responsibility for team selection, tactics and so on. The new step was counterbalanced by the problem that had bedevilled Irish international football for years: most of the players had played League games the day before.

Meagan took the dual role of captain and manager for his first game in charge, before handing authority on the field to Manchester United's Tony Dunne and concentrating on management.

He started off reasonably well, for a Don Givens goal earned Ireland a 1–1 draw with Scotland in September 1969. But there followed the serious business of World Cup qualifying games for the 1970 World Cup. Ireland had already played three of their Group Two games and had yet to register a point. It didn't get much better.

Meagan, rather than beg, steal or borrow players from English clubs, looked instead to the League of Ireland. Against Czechoslovakia in Prague in October 1969, he gave first caps to Limerick goalkeeper Kevin Fitzpatrick and included four other home-based players in the 12. His 'I'm backing Ireland' policy was in ruins after just 44 minutes of the World Cup qualifying games, as by that time, Adamec had helped himself to a hat-trick.

Ireland did manage to pick up a point against Denmark, but then were humiliated in Budapest, losing 4–0.

Friendlies against Poland and West Germany brought little comfort except for the debut of Liverpool star Steve Heighway. Then it was into the qualifiers for the 1972 European Championships in which Ireland were drawn with Sweden, Italy and Austria.

A Tommy Carroll penalty earned Ireland a point against Sweden in the first game in October 1970. But it was their only point of the campaign. The next four games were defeats.

Austria's 4–1 hammering of Ireland at Dalymount Park in May 1971 was Meagan's swansong. He had been in office for two years, overseen a dozen internationals and failed to record a victory.

Mick Meagan's complete record as national team manager:

	PLAYED	WON	DREW	LOST	F	A
HOME	6	0	3	3	5	11
AWAY	6	0	0	6	2	15
OVERALL	12	0	3	9	7	26

Liam Tuohy

October 1971-May 1973

After Mick Meagan's term of office the torch passed to Liam Tuohy. He had played most of his football in the League of Ireland and had an occasion taken charge of the League of Ireland representative side.

The former Newcastle United and Shamrock Rovers player was given a three-year contract in October 1971. He was very much a players' manager, virtually one of the lads, but also highly respected.

He was aware that his biggest difficulty was the lack of preparation before games, not least due to the difficulty of getting players released by their English clubs in the absence of FIFA regulations.

In his first assignment as sole selector, for Ireland's last qualifying game for the 1972 European Championships against Austria in Linz, Tuohy reacted to the frustrations of trying to get players released from cross-channel clubs by fielding ten League of Ireland players, including six debutants (with a seventh coming on as a substitute), and Chelsea's Paddy Mulligan.

He wanted to lay the foundations of a new Irish soccer era. He was looking at the long term: 'If I'm to contribute anything, I would like to see that, at the end of three years, League of Ireland football would be upgraded both domestically and internationally. I've thrown youngsters in at the deep end.'

His League of Ireland experiment went disastrously wrong, for his young side were swept aside 6–0 by the Austrians. Tuohy, however, was determined to create a team spirit among the English and home-based players. As part of this process, his team took part in the Brazilian Independence Cup in Recife in June 1972. It was a welcome innovation; Ireland had never before participated in close season tours of this sort. The first game, against Iran, started badly: after ten minutes they went 1–0 down when Ghelik Khani scored. Then Mick Leech of Shamrock Rovers scored the equaliser; Don Givens netted another three minutes later; and Ireland had scored their first victory since Prague in November 1967.

Eamonn Rogers, Mick Martin and Miah Dennehy scored the goals in a 3–2 victory over Ecuador, in which Don Givens was sent off with 30 minutes to go. Turlough O'Connor was sent off in the next match, against Chile, with 15 minutes to go when Ireland were trailing 2–0. Eamonn Rogers pulled a goal back before the final whistle. Another 2–1 defeat followed against Portugal; Mick Leech hit Ireland's goal. The games were played in empty grounds and not a single Irish newspaper had a reporter with the squad.

Tuohy's first serious assignment was the qualifiers for the 1974 World Cup finals. The campaign opened with home games against the USSR and France in October and November 1972. The Russian game ended in a 2–1 defeat, but goals from Terry Conroy and Ray Treacy were enough to collect the points against France. More significant were the away performances: Ireland went 1–0 down in Moscow and drew 1–1 in Paris. Before the return match against France in May 1973, Tuohy announced that he would resign after the game. As it happened, it was the best away performance under his control and earned Ireland their first World Cup point on foreign soil for 12 years.

The home defeat by the Soviet Union at the start of the campaign meant that Ireland were not in the running for a place in the finals, but they had won back their pride. For the first time since 1957 Ireland didn't finish bottom of their World Cup group.

Tuohy quit because: 'My family life has been neglected lately – there's a new baby in the house and I would like to spend more time at home.' He also had business commitments and was boss of Shamrock Rovers.

Liam Tuohy's complete record as national team manager:

	PLAYED	WON	DREW	LOST	F	A
HOME	2	1	0	1	3	3
AWAY	8	2	1	5	8	17
OVERALL	10	3	1	6	11	20

Sean Thomas

June 1973

One of the most successful managers in League of Ireland football, Sean Thomas was appointed caretaker manager of the national side in June 1973 for one game between the managerships of Liam Tuohy and Johnny Giles.

Thomas had plenty of managerial experience at domestic level. He was at the helm at Shamrock Rovers between 1961 and '64, winning the FAI Cup twice and the League title once. In 1963–64 Rovers won all the major trophies open to them except the Top 4 trophy.

He then managed Bohemians, where he was credited with transforming the amateur club into the new glamour club of the League of Ireland. He left Bohs in June 1973 for business reasons and was out of the game until April 1976 when he returned to Shamrock Rovers, taking over from Mick Meagan as manager. At that time he was a technical sales adviser to a systems building firm and took the post on a part-time basis. In the late 1970s he was manager of Athlone Town.

At national level Sean was the manager of the League of Ireland select which defeated their English counterparts 2–1 at Dalymount Park in October 1963. He also managed the Under-23 sides which recorded three successive 0–0 draws with France.

Sean's one game as national team boss was a friendly against the amateurs of Norway in Oslo in June 1973. The only new cap in his side was Shamrock Rovers' Eamonn Fagan. The game ended in a 1–1 draw, Miah Dennehy scoring Ireland's goal.

The team comprised: Alan Kelly (Preston); Tommy Carroll (Birmingham); Mick Martin (Man. Utd.); Paddy Mulligan (Crystal Palace); Jimmy Holmes (Coventry City); Gerry Daly (Man. Utd.); Miah Dennehy (Notts. For.); Tony Byrne (Southampton); Terry Conroy (Stoke City); Ray Treacy (Swindon Town); Don Givens (QPR). Subs: Damien Richardson (Gillingham) for Byrne; Eamonn Fagan (Shamrock Rovers) for Treacy after 79 mins.

Johnny Giles

October 1973–March 1980

In October 1973 former Leeds midfielder Johnny Giles succeeded Liam Tuohy as manager of the Irish national team. It was another landmark in the career of the man who left Dublin and Stella Maris at 15 to join Manchester United and won the lot.

After watching his country finish bottom of their group for the 1970 World Cup and the 1972 European Championship, Giles set about reorganising the international set-up. He convinced the FAI that they should play their games midweek and on the same dates as England in order that more Irish players would be available. Previously, England-based players had often played for their League clubs on the Saturday afternoon, taken the ferry to Dublin on the Saturday night and played for Ireland on a Sunday afternoon – hardly the ideal preparation for an international game. But under his managership, Ireland for the first time in its history was regularly able to field its strongest team.

Giles won the respect of the players and gradually established the Republic as a team to be respected, especially in Dublin.

He kicked off his new career against Poland in October 1973 but was faced with an old difficulty. The Poles came fresh from their historic 1–1 draw with England: the Irish players had travelled overnight after playing for their English League clubs on Saturday. It says much for the new manager and his professional approach that this problem did not occur again. Giles himself was injured and unable to play; it was the first of only six games he missed until he retired from playing in 1979.

Giles caused controversy by virtually snubbing League of Ireland players for his first match in charge, although Waterford's Peter Thomas won his first cap in that game at the expense of veteran keeper Alan Kelly, and Thomas's Waterford team-mate Alfie Hale managed 14 minutes as a substitute. A Miah Dennehy goal after 31 minutes got Giles's regime off to a winning start.

Ireland were drawn with the USSR, Turkey and Switzerland in the qualifying Group Six for the 1976 European Nations Cup. The Soviets were clear favourites to win the group. But in the first game they were swept aside in Dublin by a Don Givens hat-trick.

The mistake that eventually cost Ireland qualification for the finals was made in Izmir against Turkey barely a month after the drubbing of the USSR. Terry Conroy headed into his own net in the 56th minute, and although Givens equalised seven minutes later, Ireland lost a costly point. Expectations remained high, however. In the match against Switzerland in May 1975, Mick Martin scored after just two minutes and Ray Treacy added a second goal after 29 minutes for a 2–1 victory. But two defeats in three days in Kiev and Berne added to the Republic's pitiful away record. The Soviets virtually secured the group by winning 1–0 in Switzerland and had a point to spare over Ireland at the end of the qualifying stages. When Ireland returned to Dalymount in October for a largely meaningless 4–0 win over Turkey, Don Givens again scored all of the goals.

Nevertheless Giles had moulded a new skilful and aggressive Ireland. His management was proving the most successful to date, though

only in Dublin. He can be credited with introducing several Irish 'greats' to the international arena. He gave first caps to the Arsenal quartet of Liam Brady, David O'Leary, John Devine and Frank Stapleton – all fellow Dubliners. Ashley Grimes of Manchester United and Liverpool's Mark Lawrenson also came to the fore under Giles' tutelage.

The bad results – not to mention the crazy refereeing decisions – away from Dublin continued for the 1978 World Cup and 1980 European Championship qualifiers when the two 'Irelands' were grouped together for the first time.

The draw for the 1978 World Cup also put Ireland in the same group as France and Bulgaria, and left them with a reasonable chance of qualifying for the finals in Argentina. The team had been boosted by two newcomers: 6ft 3in goalkeeper Mick Kearns and midfielder Gerry Daly, one of the most reliable penalty-takers in the history of the game for both club and country.

Ireland lost 2–0 to the French in their crucial first match in Paris in November 1976. But what Irish fans remember of the game is the first of the three great injustices in Irish soccer in the '70s. After 57 minutes Brady sent in a cross that Stapleton headed into the net. The 3,000 Irish fans went wild, but the Yugoslav linesman had his flag up. Irish fans learnt to look instinctively at the linesman every time Ireland scored away from home. Some of the damage was repaired in the return game in Dublin in March 1977 when a Liam Brady goal after ten minutes secured the points.

On 1 June 1977 Ireland faced Bulgaria in Sofia. A push in the back by Dimitrov tumbled Don Givens as he lined up a shot inside the penalty area in the 43rd minute. No penalty was given. In the 59th minute Giles struck what looked like a superb winning goal. For a minute the linesman's flag stayed down, then it suddenly popped up and the referee disallowed the goal. And the ratio of free kicks was 5:1 in Bulgaria's favour.

In the 80th minute the game erupted into a free-for-all, as six players from each side got involved in a punch-up. Four players were sent off, including Noel Campbell (who had been on the field for only 90 seconds) and Mick Martin. The player who had started the altercation escaped unpunished.

French manager Michel Hidalgo, although 'delighted' with the result, commented that 'Ireland were robbed' and the Bulgarian fans applauded the Greek referee Nicko Zlatanos back to the changing rooms while the 500 Irish in the stadium watched in disbelief. Normally placid sportswriters jumped to their feet in the press-box; the word 'biased' was sent back in match reports.

Qualification was now out of Ireland's reach. Only 25,000 turned up for their home game against Bulgaria in October 1977 and they watched an inept 0–0 draw.

The group draw for the 1980 European Championships pitted the Republic against England, Northern Ireland, Bulgaria and Denmark. The campaign began with a run of three draws, with Denmark in Copenhagen and with the North and England in Dublin. An 80th minute goal by Tzetkov in Sofia in May 1979 inflicted on the Republic their first defeat of the campaign, and although Ireland won the return 3–0 in Dublin, away defeats in Belfast and London saw them finish the campaign in third place, behind England and the North.

Ireland were ranked as fourth seeds when they landed in one of the toughest groups in the draw for the 1982 World Cup – with France, Belgium and the Netherlands. Again they finished in third place, going out on goal difference to eventual semi-finalists France.

In fact, they lost their chance to qualify in the very first match. Giles took his team to Nicosia and beat Cyprus 3–2. 'Points were a priority here, rather than goals,' Giles said after the match. Mark Lawrenson from Brighton, the discovery of the European campaign, ran for 80 yards before interchanging with Brady and scoring the first goal of his career. He put Ireland 2–0 up. They led 3–1 at the start of the second half, but they flagged and Cyprus converted a marginal penalty award after 79 minutes.

Less than a month after the game, Giles resigned as national team boss; the remainder of the campaign was left to Eoin Hand.

Under Giles, Ireland had some good results in Dublin, losing just two of 17 games played in the capital, including five wins in a row. But by the time he stood down as manager, Ireland had won just three games away from home, drawing five and losing 12.

It was Ireland's most successful period prior to Jack Charlton's arrival. For seven years they held their own on the international arena, without quite achieving the breakthrough Giles had promised.

He used 53 players in total and introduced 33 new caps to international football; those debutants included Jeff Chandler, Chris Hughton, Paul McGee, Tony Macken, Jerry Murphy, Ray O'Brien, Brendan O'Callaghan, David O'Leary, Gerry Peyton, Gerry Ryan, Frank Stapleton, Mick Walsh, Liam Brady, Dave Langan, Mark Lawrenson, John Devine and Ashley Grimes.

Giles served Ireland as player and manager for over 20 years and departed having delivered them from the dark ages.

Johnny Giles complete record as a national team manager:

	PLAYED	WON	DREW	LOST	F	A
HOME	17	11	4	2	29	10
AWAY	20	3	5	12	20	35
OVERALL	37	14	9	14	49	45

Alan Kelly

April 1980

Former international goalkeeper Alan Kelly was appointed manager of the Republic after Johnny Giles's resignation. Kelly had been Giles's assistant for two games, both of which ended in Irish victories.

His term of office was a short one; he was forced to resign owing to his commitments to his club, Preston North End.

Goals from Don Givens and Gerry Daly secured victory in Kelly's one match in charge, which was against Switzerland on 30 April 1980.

He gave debuts in this game to QPR's Gary Waddock and Manchester United's Kevin Moran.

The full team was Gerry Peyton (Fulham); Dave Langan (Derby Co.); Kevin Moran (Man. Utd.); Mark Lawrenson (Brighton); Chris Hughton (Spurs); Gerry Daly (Derby Co.); Tony Grealish (Luton Town); Gary Waddock (QPR); Gerry Ryan (Brighton); Don Givens (Birmingham); Paul McGee (Preston).

Eoin Hand

April 1980 – November 1985

Eoin Hand was favourite to succeed Johnny Giles. He took over in April 1980 after Alan Kelly's one game in charge. Like other Republic of Ireland managers BC (Before Charlton), Hand was a 'nearly man', the homeboy who took his country to the edge of the world stage, only to be felled by some cruel twist of fate.

On his appointment at 34, Hand was one of the youngest national team bosses in the world. He had won his 20 Eire caps while at Portsmouth. He returned to Ireland to manage Limerick City in the League of Ireland in 1979. He took the Munster side to the Championship in their first League season, for which he was voted 'Sports Personality of the Year'. They were runners-up a year later and, in his third season, won the FAI Cup. When Giles resigned, Hand was at the forefront of Irish domestic football.

Hand, who had actually played under Giles briefly at Shamrock Rovers, had never tasted top-flight football in England, and before joining Limerick, had been out of the Irish game for a long time.

His first game in charge, before the FAI offered him the job permanently, was against world champions Argentina in May 1980. His appointment was confirmed after the match, which Ireland lost 1–0.

The number of English-born players declaring for Ireland increased during Hand's reign. The relaxation in FIFA's qualification criteria prompted many second-generation Irishmen – whose families had emigrated in the 1950s – to declare for the mother country. Eoin gave first caps to a host of second-generation Irishmen including John Byrne, Tony Cascarino, Tony Galvin, Mick McCarthy, Jim McDonagh, Kevin O'Callaghan, Sean O'Driscoll, Eamonn O'Keefe, Gary Waddock and Mick T. Walsh.

He also uncovered some magnificent home-grown talent, who would go on to serve Ireland brilliantly for years to come; he gave first caps to Paul McGrath, Ronnie Whelan and Packie Bonner.

Few complained about Hand's team selections. His style was a bit more adventurous than his predecessor's, though it was questionable he had a solid game plan. There were times, especially away from Dublin (where Ireland were virtually invincible), when the Irish needed to play a bit tighter as a team. Thus the bad away results, exacerbated by some highly dubious refereeing decisions, kept the Republic on the outside looking in. During the Hand reign, the mythical luck of the Irish failed to extend to the soccer arena.

The 1982 World Cup qualifying stages

were the first test of Hand's mettle as manager. This tense and exciting campaign began well, as Gerry Daly and Mark Lawrenson scored the goals which beat Holland 2–1 in Dublin in September 1980. The following month a home match against Belgium saw Ireland disappointingly drop a point in a 1–1 draw.

Next up were France in Paris. Ireland were trailing 1–0 when Michael Robinson put the ball in the net after latching on to Kevin Moran's knock-down. Incredibly the goal was ruled out for handball against Moran – even though he had clearly headed the ball.

Cyprus were brushed aside 6–0 in Dublin in November, then Ireland were off to Brussels for the return match with Belgium on 25 March 1981. One of the finest Irish performances away from Lansdowne Road was seemingly rewarded when Frank Stapleton's 'goal' on the stroke of half-time gave them the lead. Somehow the official in charge disallowed the goal – despite being unable to explain the reason for doing so – and an even greater wound was inflicted when Jan Cuelemans guided Belgium to the finals with a header. Again, the man in the middle was the target for Ireland's frustrations, having ignored the fact that goalkeeper Jim McDonagh was being trampled into the ground.

Another fine away performance followed, in Rotterdam. A mistimed pass let Franz Thijssen in for a goal, but after 40 minutes Robinson struck an equaliser. David Langan gave away the penalty that put the Netherlands 2–1 up, before Stapleton headed an equaliser with six minutes to go.

But this performance was dwarfed by the game at home against France. Ireland forced an own goal after five minutes, Bellone equalised after nine, Stapleton capped a great display with a goal after 20 minutes and Robinson capitalised on a defensive mistake to make it 3–1 at half-time. Platini scored France's second goal after 82 minutes. The Irish had four close chances of further goals. Many of the 52,000 spectators who applauded the players off the field still rank this 3–2 victory as one of the three great performances by an Irish team, comparable only to the draw with the Soviet Union in the 1988 European Championship finals and the defeat of Italy in the 1994 World Cup finals.

The turning-point in the Hand era came in 1982, when the Republic embarked on a disastrous series of friendlies. First they were beaten 2–0 by Algeria in April. Then came an ill-advised tour of South America the following month, during which Ireland were beaten 1–0 by Chile, 7–0 by Brazil (a record for the FAI), and 2–1 by Trinidad and Tobago.

Hopes of qualifying for the European Championship were quickly dashed. The Republic were to cross swords yet again with Holland; in September 1982 they went down 2–1 to the Netherlands in Rotterdam. The first points of the campaign came at home with a win over Iceland in October. In November they slipped up against Spain in Dublin: they fell 3–1 behind before Frank Stapleton grabbed back two goals to earn a point. Stapleton again came to the rescue when Ireland went to Malta in March 1983, scoring the only goal with a back-heeled shot in the last minute.

Then, in October 1983, came the setback of a home defeat, the first in a competitive match in ten years, when Ireland went down 3–2 to Holland. Thrashing Malta 8–0 the following month was poor consolation as the Spanish and the Dutch fought out the group.

As press and public were baying for his head, Eoin Hand's luck changed. He survived an attempt to install Bob Paisley as manager for the 1986 World Cup campaign. Then, on 12 September 1984, in their first game of that campaign against the Soviet Union, Ireland at last got the rub of the green. Although Ireland won with a 64th-minute Mick Walsh goal, Oganesian had earlier had a 'goal' somewhat harshly disallowed for offside and the Soviets hit the post twice in the dying minutes in what one sportswriter described as 'the most agonising countdown in Irish football since the night John Atyeo's equaliser earned an improbable reprieve for England'.

Just weeks after the Soviet game, Ireland suffered back-to-back defeats in Oslo and Copenhagen. The dream – or what remained of it – had died. The rest of the campaign was a shambles. When Norway earned a 0–0 draw at Lansdowne in May 1985, angry supporters applauded the visitors off the pitch and called for the manager's head. A 3–0 win at home against Switzerland went barely appreciated, and a scoreless draw in Berne was regarded as another disappointment. The announcement of Hand's resignation came after a 2–0 defeat in Moscow, on 16 October 1985. 'I am not in the habit of putting myself in places where I am unwanted and I have no intention of going forward for another term as manager. The job is too demanding and my immediate plans are not relative to international football.'

Hand was close to tears in the press-room of the Lenin Stadium. He described it as the most disappointing night of his life. He vowed the team would go out and attack against Denmark in the final match of the campaign.

Ireland got only their fifth goal of the entire campaign against Denmark that day, Stapleton netting after six minutes. Unfortunately,

Denmark equalised within a minute and went on to win 4–1. It was Ireland's heaviest competitive defeat under Hand and Ireland's biggest home defeat since 1971.

Eoin Hand had come closer than Johnny Giles to taking Ireland to a major championship finals. Unfortunately, he ran into disaster and discredit soon after some great performances. Like Giles, he had two disallowed away goals to blight his record. Nevertheless, it was the abysmal away record that kept Ireland among the also-rans of Europe and the world. Under Hand, the only away wins were against Malta and Iceland. But the legacy to his successor, Jack Charlton, was a side bursting with talent, if little team spirit.

A more pleasant memory of Eoin's time in charge of Ireland was the establishment of record-breaking victories. The first was created in November 1980 when Ireland beat Cyprus 6–0 at Lansdowne Road. Almost exactly three years later that record was surpassed with an 8–0 victory over Malta in a European Championship qualifying game.

Eoin Hand's complete record as a national team manager:

	PLAYED	WON	DREW	LOST	F	A
HOME	19	8	6	5	37	21
AWAY	21	3	3	15	10	38
OVERALL	40	11	9	20	47	59

Jack Charlton

February 1986–December 1995

Born on 8 May 1935, in Ashington, a pit village north of Newcastle, Jack Charlton joined Leeds United in May 1952. Over the next 20 years he made a record 628 appearances (70 goals) for the club.

A hard, uncompromising defender, Charlton went from strength to strength under Don Revie at Elland Road, winning an array

of top domestic honours. He helped them win promotion to Division One in 1957 and again as Division Two champions in 1964. Five years later he was a League Championship winner. He also played in FA Cup finals in 1965, 1970 and 1972, gaining a winners medal in 1972. And he appeared in Fairs Cup finals in 1967, 1968 and 1971, picking up winners medals in 1968 and 1971. In 1968 he was a League Cup winner and in 1967 was voted 'Footballer of the Year'.

Jack won an England place against Scotland in April 1965 at the late age of 30. Younger brother Bobby made his 60th England appearance in that game. Both played a fundamental part in England's World Cup success in 1966. By the time he retired Jack had won 35 caps.

He began his managerial career at Middlesbrough in 1973 and was voted 'Manager of the Year' in 1974 for taking them into the First Division, after they won the Second Division title by a record 15-point margin in his first year in charge. He left Boro in 1977 to become boss at Sheffield Wednesday, earning them promotion to Division Two in 1980. At Hillsborough he linked up with his future Ireland assistant Maurice Setters for the first time.

Jack left Sheffield in 1983 to devote more time to his hobbies of shooting and fishing. But he took over at Newcastle in 1984, just after Arthur Cox had taken the club back into Division One. Much was expected of Charlton and when he didn't deliver and the crowd began to get on his back – the Magpies having just avoided relegation – he upped and left.

In those formative years as a manager, Charlton learnt the importance of making the most of limited resources. At Boro and Wednesday he became known as a Messiah, taking nondescript sides up a division. He left both clubs when he felt he could go no further.

Then came the phenomenon of Charlton's 'sainthood' – his emergence as the greatest and most unlikely hero in the history of Irish sport. It was in February 1986 that he landed the Ireland job. His appointment as Eoin Hand's successor, ahead of former Liverpool manager Bob Paisley, was seen by some as a mistake.

He inherited a team of glorious failures, who played attractive football but lost more matches than they won. The team wasn't short of talent; players like Liam Brady, Ronnie Whelan, Paul McGrath and Mark Lawrenson could have walked into any international XI. But the attitude was wrong – Charlton's first task was to change that.

Within three months of arriving in Ireland, Big Jack had earned the Republic their first senior trophy by winning two games away from home. It may only have been the triangular tournament in Reykjavik, with wins over hosts Iceland and Czechoslovakia in May 1986, but it was a significant start.

Charlton applied much of the simplicity and directness of his own personality into the playing style of the Irish team; abandoning the 'possession game' advocated by his predecessors, he got the Irish to play the game with which they were familiar at club level. It was the beginning of Ireland's long-ball game. It was far from aesthetically pleasing, but it was certainly effective.

He was often criticised for his tactics, but he was a much better tactician than he was often given credit for and when the occasion demanded Ireland could and did play the passing game. It was a case of 'give a dog a bad name'.

Another effective measure he took was to increase the number of second-generation Irishmen in the side. This policy has been described in some quarters as 'the brazen recruitment of tenuously linked mercenaries'. The truth is that the 'granny rule' (i.e. going beyond second generation) was hardly used. Players such as Eddie McGoldrick, Phil Babb, David Kelly, Alan Kelly and many others including the recently capped London-born David Connolly, had harboured childhood ambitions to play for the country of their parents.

Undue importance wasn't placed on the strengths and weaknesses of the opposition, as illustrated in Charlton's habit of naming his team long before deemed necessary by international football law. His teams started and finished games in their own inimitable fashion – as if they were 1–0 down in a cup final with ten minutes on the clock.

Charlton's first major task was qualification for the 1988 European Championships in West Germany. They qualified but, as became the norm under his leadership, they left it late.

Ireland produced many fine performances over the eight-game qualifying rounds. They took three points off Scotland, beat Bulgaria 2–0 in Dublin, were unlucky to lose 2–1 in Sofia, beat Luxembourg twice and drew twice with Belgium. They finished their campaign top of the pile with 11 points. Bulgaria had ten points but had yet to play Scotland, who could not qualify, in Sofia. In November 1987 Gary Mackay's dramatic late strike for Scotland was the goal that took the Republic to the finals of their first major tournament.

The Irish went to West Germany in June 1988 and took the football world by surprise. To many fans, the 1–0 defeat of England – courtesy of Ray Houghton – in the opening game in Stuttgart was their final. But it's generally accepted that the 1–1 draw with the Soviet Union in Hanover was one of their best performances under Jack. And they were unfortunate not to progress to the semi-finals, going out to a late and highly dubious goal from Holland.

Charlton's no-nonsense approach worked again as Ireland qualified for the 1990 World Cup finals for the first time. They began their Group Six campaign with a 2–0 defeat by Spain in Seville. Those were the only goals conceded in the eight-match qualifying series; they went to Italy in 1990 as group runners-up.

Although they didn't actually win a game in normal time in Italy, they made it all the way to the quarter-finals through draws with England, Holland and Egypt and the never-to-be-forgotten penalty shoot-out with Romania, won with a Packie Bonner save from Daniel Timofte and David O'Leary's dramatic spot kick. They faced hosts Italy in Rome, losing 1–0 to a Schillaci goal.

Ireland went World Cup crazy. Ninety per cent of the country watched the Italy game and, when the squad arrived back from Rome, 500,000 people took to the streets of Dublin to welcome back the players – and Jack Charlton. People drove over the central reservation and the wrong way up the motorway to get to the airport. Ireland, after years of trying, had finally arrived as a force on the world stage.

The qualifying tournament for the 1994 World Cup in the USA bore striking similarities to the 1990 campaign. The Spanish again posed the biggest threat and the Republic again suffered just one defeat in their 12-match campaign – again it was the Spanish who were the executioners.

Going into the last set of games, Denmark sat at the top of Group Three on 18 points, with Spain and Ireland on 17 points in second and third place. In order to guarantee qualification, the Republic needed to win against Northern Ireland in Belfast. They managed just a draw, Alan McLoughlin netting the all-important equaliser; he was only playing because of injuries to Houghton and Staunton. Yet they still qualified. Fernando Hierro's goal gave Spain victory over Denmark, and the Republic earned the priceless runners-up place, having scored more goals than Denmark.

On 18 June 1994, in the Giants Stadium, New Jersey, Ireland lined up against the team that had sent them home early from Italy four years previously – Italy.

Ireland had never beaten the Italians. Until now. A Ray Houghton wonder goal proved enough to secure the points. Then they were off to the baking heat of Orlando to face Mexico. Ireland wilted under the fierce midday sun, going down 2–1. The 'one' was vitally important. It was that 84th-minute John Aldridge goal which separated Ireland from Norway, with whom they eked out a 0–0 draw in their final group game.

Next up, for the third time in successive championships, the Dutch masters. Two mistakes in the Irish defence sent Holland through to the quarter-finals. The Irish went back home, with just over eight weeks to go before the qualifiers for the 1996 European Championships in England. It was a Championship too far for Charlton.

They got off to a flying start: they recorded convincing wins over Latvia, Liechtenstein and Northern Ireland, scoring 11 goals without reply. The disappointment of dropping a point against the North in Dublin in March 1995 was offset a month later by a 1–0 victory over

Portugal, the side perceived as the main threat to the Republic's progress. A place in the finals seemed secured.

But there followed a disastrous 0–0 draw with minnows Liechtenstein in Eschen in June 1995 and back-to-back 3–1 defeats by Austria.

The points in the bag gained at the beginning of the campaign kept Ireland's hopes alive right to the death. Although hammered 3–0 by Portugal in Lisbon, the Republic still had a chance of going to England in the summer of 1996 after Northern Ireland's defeat of Austria in Belfast on the same November evening – if they defeated who else but Holland in a play-off at Liverpool's Anfield ground.

That December night was Big Jack's swansong. Ireland were outplayed and, despite a spirited performance, lost 2–0. Weeks later, Jack and his able assistant Maurice Setters parted company with the FAI after almost ten glorious years.

Jack left having forged Ireland into a force in world football. They lost just 17 games out of 94. Under his managership they peaked at sixth place – ahead of Brazil in FIFA's official world ranking order.

The success he brought to the national team revolutionised football in the country. Lansdowne Road, the national stadium, used to be half-full for international fixtures; now tickets sell out weeks before matches. He will always be extremely popular with most of the fans in the Republic.

Jack Charlton complete record as a national team manager:

	PLAYED	WON	DREW	LOST	F	A
HOME	45	28	12	5	75	24
AWAY	49	19	18	12	53	39
OVERALL	94	47	30	17	128	63

Mick McCarthy

February 1996–present

Ten years and one day after Ireland had been defeated 1–0 by Wales in Dublin in front of 15,000 spectators, Mick McCarthy's new Ireland faced Russia in front of a sell-out 42,000 crowd – a measure of how far Jack Charlton had brought Irish football in a decade.

McCarthy was appointed Charlton's successor in February 1996; in order to take up his new post, he had to leave his job at Millwall with two years still to run on his contract. His former number two at Millwall, Ian Evans, was appointed as his second-in-command.

A real motivator, Mick has promised a new order and a new style. A series of eight tough friendlies were arranged, beginning with the visit of Russia to Dublin in March and ending with US Cup games in America in June. McCarthy used these friendlies as a mining operation with the purpose of uncovering 'nuggets' for the 1996 World Cup qualifiers. He capped ten new players in his first four games in charge.

The long-ball game so beloved of Charlton was abandoned in favour of the European style of pass and move. He has also adopted the new approach of wing-backs and a trio of centre-backs.

In his first game in charge, Mick was faced with an age-old problem: a small pool of players depleted further by withdrawals through injury. In that game against Russia he gave a first cap to Co. Donegal goalkeeper Shay Given, one of the finds of the summer. More new caps came – Keith O'Neill, Curtis Fleming, Alan Moore, Ken Cunningham, Gary Breen, Ian Harte, David Connolly, Gareth Farrelly and

David Savage – in the games that followed against Portugal, the Czech Republic and Croatia. Others, such as Alan McLoughlin, Liam Daish and Liam O'Brien, who must have thought their time had passed, were brought back into the fold.

Mick had to wait until his fourth game in charge for his new boys to get a result: in that game against Croatia Ireland registered their first goal under his new régime and it came from one of his youngsters, Norwich City's Keith O'Neill.

O'Neill was one of the 'nuggets' uncovered in the summer of 1996. He scored twice in the Republic's first win under McCarthy, a 3–0 defeat of Bolivia in New Jersey.

Four dismissals cast a cloud over the early days of Mick's reign. Roy Keane was sent off in McCarthy's first game in charge and Liam Daish was sent off against Mexico in June 1996. McCarthy and Niall Quinn, both of whom were on the substitutes' bench, were shown the red card in the same game.

McCarthy declared himself excited and daunted at the prospect of his job and said that his first aim was qualification for the 1998 World Cup finals in France.

He got that campaign off to a thundering start with emphatic wins over Liechtenstein and Macedonia.

APPENDICES

APPENDIX A:
FULL INTERNATIONALS
PLAYED BY EIRE

	DATE	VENUE	OPPONENTS	RESULT (IRISH SCORE FIRST)
	16 June 1946	Lisbon	Portugal	1–3
	23 June 1946	Madrid	Spain	1–0
	30 September 1946	Dublin	England	0–1
	2 March 1947	Dublin	Spain	3–2
	4 May 1947	Dublin	Portugal	0–2
	23 May 1948	Lisbon	Portugal	0–2
	30 May 1948	Barcelona	Spain	1–2
	5 December 1948	Dublin	Switzerland	0–1
	24 April 1949	Dublin	Belgium	0–2
	22 May 1949	Dublin	Portugal	1–0
WC	2 June 1949	Stockholm	Sweden	1–3
	12 June 1949	Dublin	Spain	1–4
WC	8 September 1949	Dublin	Finland	3–0
	21 September 1949	Liverpool	England	2–0
WC	9 October 1949	Helsinki	Finland	1–1
WC	13 November 1949	Dublin	Sweden	1–3
	10 May 1950	Brussels	Belgium	1–5
	26 November 1950	Dublin	Norway	2–2
	13 May 1951	Dublin	Argentina	0–1
	30 May 1951	Oslo	Norway	3–2
	17 October 1951	Dublin	West Germany	3–2
	4 May 1952	Cologne	West Germany	0–3
	7 May 1952	Vienna	Austria	0–6
	1 June 1952	Madrid	Spain	0–6
	16 November 1952	Dublin	France	1–1
	25 March 1953	Dublin	Austria	4–0
WC	4 October 1953	Dublin	France	3–5
WC	28 October 1953	Dublin	Luxembourg	4–0
WC	25 November 1953	Paris	France	0–1

WC	7 March 1954	Luxembourg	Luxembourg	1–0
	8 November 1954	Dublin	Norway	2–1
	1 May 1955	Dublin	Holland	1–0
	25 May 1955	Oslo	Norway	3–1
	28 May 1955	Hamburg	West Germany	1–2
	19 September 1955	Dublin	Yugoslavia	1–4
	27 November 1955	Dublin	Spain	2–2
	10 May 1956	Rotterdam	Holland	4–1
WC	3 October 1956	Dublin	Denmark	2–1
	25 November 1956	Dublin	West Germany	3–0
WC	8 May 1957	London	England	1–5
WC	19 May 1957	Dublin	England	1–1
WC	2 October 1957	Copenhagen	Denmark	2–0
	11 May 1958	Katowice	Poland	2–2
	14 May 1958	Vienna	Austria	1–3
	5 October 1958	Dublin	Poland	2–2
ENC	5 April 1959	Dublin	Czechoslovakia	2–0
ENC	10 May 1959	Bratislava	Czechoslovakia	0–4
	1 November 1959	Dublin	Sweden	3–2
	30 March 1960	Dublin	Chile	2–0
	11 May 1960	Dusseldorf	West Germany	1–0
	18 May 1960	Malmo	Sweden	1–4
	28 September 1960	Dublin	Wales	2–3
	6 November 1960	Dublin	Norway	3–1
WC	3 May 1961	Glasgow	Scotland	1–4
WC	7 May 1961	Dublin	Scotland	0–3
WC	8 October 1961	Dublin	Czechoslovakia	1–3
WC	29 October 1961	Prague	Czechoslovakia	1–7
	8 April 1962	Dublin	Austria	2–3
ENC	12 August 1962	Dublin	Iceland	4–2
ENC	2 September 1962	Reykjavik	Iceland	1–1
	9 June 1963	Dublin	Scotland	1–0
ENC	25 September 1963	Vienna	Austria	0–0
ENC	13 October 1963	Dublin	Austria	3–2
ENC	11 March 1964	Seville	Spain	1–5
ENC	8 April 1964	Dublin	Spain	0–2
	10 May 1964	Cracow	Poland	1–3
	13 May 1964	Oslo	Norway	4–1
	24 May 1964	Dublin	England	1–3
	25 October 1964	Dublin	Poland	3–2
	24 March 1965	Dublin	Belgium	0–2

WC	5 May 1965	Dublin	Spain	1–0
WC	27 October 1965	Seville	Spain	1–4
WC	10 November 1965	Paris	Spain	0–1
	4 May 1966	Dublin	West Germany	0–4
	22 May 1966	Vienna	Austria	0–1
	25 May 1966	Liège	Belgium	3–2
ENC	23 October 1966	Dublin	Spain	0–0
ENC	16 November 1966	Dublin	Turkey	2–1
ENC	7 December 1966	Valencia	Spain	0–2
ENC	22 February 1967	Ankara	Turkey	1–2
ENC	21 May 1967	Dublin	Czechoslovakia	0–2
ENC	22 November 1967	Prague	Czechoslovakia	2–1
	15 May 1968	Dublin	Poland	2–2
	30 October 1968	Katowice	Poland	0–1
	10 November 1968	Dublin	Austria	2–2
WC	4 December 1968	Dublin	Denmark	1–1
WC	4 May 1969	Dublin	Czechoslovakia	1–2
WC	27 May 1969	Copenhagen	Denmark	0–2
WC	8 June 1969	Dublin	Hungary	1–2
	21 September 1969	Dublin	Scotland	1–1
WC	7 October 1969	Prague	Czechoslovakia	0–3
WC	15 October 1969	Dublin	Denmark	1–1
WC	5 November 1969	Budapest	Hungary	0–4
	6 May 1970	Dublin	Poland	1–2
	9 May 1970	Berlin	West Germany	1–2
	23 September 1970	Dublin	Poland	0–2
EC	14 October 1970	Dublin	Sweden	1–1
EC	28 October 1970	Malmo	Sweden	0–1
EC	8 December 1970	Florence	Italy	0–3
EC	10 May 1971	Dublin	Italy	1–2
EC	30 May 1971	Dublin	Austria	1–4
EC	10 October 1971	Linz	Austria	0–6
	11 June 1972	Recife	Iran	2–1
	18 June 1972	Natal (Brazil)	Ecuador	3–2
	21 June 1972	Recife	Chile	1–2
	25 June 1972	Recife	Portugal	1–2
WC	18 October 1972	Dublin	USSR	1–2
WC	15 November 1972	Dublin	France	2–1
WC	13 May 1973	Moscow	USSR	0–1
	16 May 1973	Wroclaw	Poland	0–2
WC	19 May 1973	Paris	France	1–1

	Date	Venue	Opponent	Score
	6 June 1973	Oslo	Norway	1–1
	21 October 1973	Dublin	Poland	1–0
	5 May 1974	Rio de Janeiro	Brazil	1–2
	8 May 1974	Montevideo	Uruguay	0–2
	12 May 1974	Santiago	Chile	2–1
EC	30 October 1974	Dublin	USSR	3–0
EC	20 November 1974	Izmir	Turkey	1–1
	1 March 1975	Dublin	W. Germany 'B'	1–0
EC	10 May 1975	Dublin	Switzerland	2–1
EC	18 May 1975	Kiev	USSR	1–2
EC	21 May 1975	Berne	Switzerland	0–1
EC	29 October 1975	Dublin	Turkey	4–0
	24 March 1976	Dublin	Norway	3–0
	26 May 1976	Poznan	Poland	2–0
	8 September 1976	London	England	1–1
	13 October 1976	Ankara	Turkey	3–3
WC	17 November 1976	Paris	France	0–2
	9 February 1977	Dublin	Spain	0–1
WC	30 March 1977	Dublin	France	1–0
	24 April 1977	Dublin	Poland	0–0
WC	1 June 1977	Sofia	Bulgaria	1–2
WC	12 October 1977	Dublin	Bulgaria	0–0
	5 April 1978	Dublin	Turkey	4–2
	12 April 1978	Lodz	Poland	0–3
	21 May 1978	Oslo	Norway	0–0
EC	24 May 1978	Copenhagen	Denmark	3–3
EC	20 September 1978	Dublin	N. Ireland	0–0
EC	25 October 1978	Dublin	England	1–1
EC	2 May 1979	Dublin	Denmark	2–0
EC	19 May 1979	Sofia	Bulgaria	0–1
	22 May 1979	Dublin	West Germany	1–3
	11 September 1979	Swansea	Wales	1–2
	26 September 1979	Prague	Czechoslovakia	1–4
EC	17 October 1979	Dublin	Bulgaria	3–0
	29 October 1979	Dublin	USA	3–2
EC	21 November 1979	Belfast	N. Ireland	0–1
EC	6 February 1980	London	England	0–2
WC	26 March 1980	Nicosia	Cyprus	3–2
	30 April 1980	Dublin	Switzerland	2–0
	16 May 1980	Dublin	Argentina	0–1
WC	10 September 1980	Dublin	Holland	2–1

WC	15 October 1980	Dublin	Belgium	1–1
WC	28 October 1980	Paris	France	0–2
WC	19 November 1980	Dublin	Cyprus	6–0
	24 February 1981	Dublin	Wales	1–3
WC	25 March 1981	Brussels	Belgium	0–1
	29 April 1981	Dublin	Czechoslovakia	3–1
	21 May 1981	Bremen	W. Germany 'B'	0–3
	24 May 1981	Bydgoszcz	Poland	0–3
WC	9 September 1981	Rotterdam	Holland	2–2
WC	14 October 1981	Dublin	France	3–2
	28 April 1982	Algiers	Algeria	0–2
	22 May 1982	Santiago	Chile	0–1
	27 May 1982	Uberlandia	Brazil	0–7
	30 May 1982	Port of Spain	Trinidad & Tobago	1–2
EC	22 September 1982	Rotterdam	Holland	1–2
EC	13 October 1982	Dublin	Iceland	2–0
EC	17 November 1982	Dublin	Spain	3–3
EC	30 March 1983	Valletta	Malta	1–0
EC	27 April 1983	Zaragoza	Spain	0–2
EC	21 September 1983	ReykjaviK	Iceland	3–0
EC	12 October 1983	Dublin	Holland	2–3
EC	16 November 1983	Dublin	Malta	8–0
	4 April 1984	Tel Aviv	Israel	0–3
	23 May 1984	Dublin	Poland	0–0
	3 June 1984	Sapporo (Japan)	China	1–0
	8 August 1984	Dublin	Mexico	0–0
WC	12 September 1984	Dublin	USSR	1–0
WC	17 October 1984	Oslo	Norway	0–1
WC	14 November 1984	Copenhagen	Denmark	0–3
	5 February 1985	Dublin	Italy	1–2
	27 February 1985	Tel Aviv	Israel	0–0
	26 March 1985	London	England	1–2
WC	1 May 1985	Dublin	Norway	0–0
	26 May 1985	Cork	Spain	0–0
WC	2 June 1985	Dublin	Switzerland	3–0
WC	11 September 1985	Berne	Switzerland	0–0
WC	16 October 1985	Moscow	USSR	0–2
WC	13 November 1985	Dublin	Denmark	1–4
	26 March 1986	Dublin	Wales	0–1
	23 April 1986	Dublin	Uruguay	1–1
	25 May 1986	Reykjavik	Iceland	2–1

	27 May 1986	Reykjavik	Czechoslovakia	1–0
EC	10 September 1986	Brussels	Belgium	2–2
EC	15 October 1986	Dublin	Scotland	0–0
	12 November 1986	Warsaw	Poland	0–1
EC	18 February 1987	Glasgow	Scotland	1–0
EC	1 April 1987	Sofia	Bulgaria	1–2
EC	29 April 1987	Dublin	Belgium	0–0
	23 May 1987	Dublin	Brazil	1–0
EC	28 May 1987	Luxembourg	Luxembourg	2–0
EC	9 September 1987	Dublin	Luxembourg	2–1
EC	14 October 1987	Dublin	Bulgaria	2–0
	10 November 1987	Dublin	Israel	5–0
	23 March 1988	Dublin	Romania	2–0
	27 April 1988	Dublin	Yugoslavia	2–0
	22 May 1988	Dublin	Poland	3–1
	1 June 1988	Oslo	Norway	0–0
EC	12 June 1988	Stuttgart	England	1–0
EC	15 June 1988	Hanover	USSR	1–1
EC	18 June 1988	Gelsenkirchen	Holland	0–1
WC	14 September 1988	Belfast	N. Ireland	0–0
	19 October 1988	Dublin	Tunisia	4–0
WC	16 November 1988	Seville	Spain	0–2
	7 February 1989	Dublin	France	0–0
WC	8 March 1989	Budapest	Hungary	0–0
WC	26 April 1989	Dublin	Spain	1–0
WC	28 May 1989	Dublin	Malta	2–0
WC	4 June 1989	Dublin	Hungary	2–0
	6 September 1989	Dublin	West Germany	1–1
WC	11 October 1989	Dublin	N. Ireland	3–0
WC	15 November 1989	Valletta	Malta	2–0
	28 March 1990	Dublin	Wales	1–0
	25 April 1990	Dublin	USSR	1–0
	16 May 1990	Dublin	Finland	1–1
	27 May 1990	Izmir	Turkey	0–0
	2 June 1990	Valletta	Malta	3–0
WC	11 June 1990	Cagliari	England	1–1
WC	17 June 1990	Palermo	Egypt	0–0
WC	21 June 1990	Palermo	Holland	1–1
WC	25 June 1990	Genoa	Romania	0–0
			(5–4 on pens)	
WC	30 June 1990	Rome	Italy	0–1

214

	Date	Venue	Opponent	Score
	12 September 1990	Dublin	Morocco	1–0
EC	17 October 1990	Dublin	Turkey	5–0
EC	14 November 1990	Dublin	England	1–1
	6 February 1991	Wrexham	Wales	3–0
EC	27 March 1991	London	England	1–1
EC	1 May 1991	Dublin	Poland	0–0
	22 May 1991	Dublin	Chile	1–1
	1 June 1991	Boston	USA	1–1
	11 September 1991	Gyor	Hungary	2–1
EC	16 October 1991	Poznan	Poland	3–3
EC	13 November 1991	Istanbul	Turkey	3–1
	19 February 1992	Dublin	Wales	0–1
	25 March 1992	Dublin	Switzerland	2–1
	29 April 1992	Dublin	USA	4–1
WC	26 May 1992	Dublin	Albania	2–0
	30 May 1992	Washington	USA	1–3
	4 June 1992	Boston	Italy	0–2
	7 June 1992	Boston	Portugal	2–0
WC	9 September 1992	Dublin	Latvia	4–0
WC	14 October 1992	Copenhagen	Denmark	0–0
WC	18 November 1992	Seville	Spain	0–0
	17 February 1993	Dublin	Wales	2–1
WC	31 March 1993	Dublin	N. Ireland	3–0
WC	28 April 1993	Dublin	Denmark	1–1
WC	26 May 1993	Tirana	Albania	2–1
WC	9 June 1993	Riga	Latvia	2–0
WC	16 June 1993	Vilnius	Lithuania	1–0
WC	8 September 1993	Dublin	Lithuania	2–0
WC	13 October 1993	Dublin	Spain	1–3
WC	17 November 1993	Belfast	N. Ireland	1–1
	23 March 1994	Dublin	Russia	0–0
	20 April 1994	Tilburg	Holland	1–0
	24 May 1994	Dublin	Bolivia	1–0
	29 May 1994	Hanover	Germany	2–0
	5 June 1994	Dublin	Czech Republic	1–3
WC	18 June 1994	New York	Italy	1–0
WC	24 June 1994	Orlando	Mexico	1–2
WC	28 June 1994	New York	Norway	0–0
WC	4 July 1994	Orlando	Holland	0–2
EC	7 September 1994	Riga	Latvia	3–0
EC	12 October 1994	Dublin	Liechtenstein	4–0

EC	16 November 1994	Belfast	N. Ireland	4–0
	15 February 1995	Dublin	England	1–0
EC	29 March 1995	Dublin	N. Ireland	1–1
EC	26 April 1995	Dublin	Portugal	1–0
EC	3 June 1995	Eschen	Liechtenstein	0–0
EC	11 June 1995	Dublin	Austria	1–3
EC	16 September 1995	Vienna	Austria	1–3
EC	11 October 1995	Dublin	Latvia	2–1
EC	15 November 1995	Lisbon	Portugal	0–3
EC	13 December 1995	Liverpool	Holland	0–2
	29 March 1996	Dublin	Russia	0–2
	24 April 1996	Prague	Czech Republic	0–2
	29 May 1996	Dublin	Portugal	0–1
	2 June 1996	Dublin	Croatia	2–2
	4 June 1996	Rotterdam	Holland	1–3
	9 June 1996	Boston	USA	1–2
	13 June 1996	New Jersey	Mexico	2–2
	15 June 1996	New Jersey	Bolivia	3–0
WC	31 August 1996	Eschen	Liechtenstein	5–0
WC	9 October 1996	Dublin	Macedonia	3–0

ENC – European Nations Cup games
WC – World Cup games
EC – European Championship games

APPENDIX B:
EIRE INTERNATIONAL APPEARANCE RECORDS

The following are the international career records of all those players who won caps for the Republic of Ireland between 1945 and 1996. The year indicated refers to the season, i.e. 1996 is the 1995–96 season. Substitute appearances appear in brackets.

Aherne, T. (16) 1946 v Portugal, Spain; 1950 v Finland (2), England, Sweden, Belgium; 1951 v Norway (2), Argentina; 1952 v West Germany (2), Austria, Spain; 1953 v France; 1954 v France.

Aldridge, J.W. (69) 1986 v Wales, Uruguay, Iceland, Czechoslovakia; 1987 v Belgium (2), Scotland (2), Poland, Bulgaria, Brazil, Luxembourg; 1988 v Bulgaria, Poland, Norway, England, USSR, Holland; 1989 v N. Ireland, Tunisia, Spain, France, Hungary (2), (Malta); 1990 v West Germany; N. Ireland, Malta, (Finland), Turkey, England, Egypt, Holland, Romania, Italy; 1991 v Turkey, England (2), Poland; 1992 v (Hungary), Turkey, (Wales), (Switzerland), (USA), Albania, Italy, (Portugal); 1993 v Latvia (2), Denmark (2), Spain, Albania, Lithuania; 1994 v Lithuania, N. Ireland, Czech Republic, (Italy), (Mexico), Norway; 1995 v Latvia, N. Ireland, Portugal, Liechtenstein; 1996 v Latvia, Portugal, Holland, Russia: 1997 v Macedonia.

Ambrose, P. (5) 1955 v Norway, Holland; 1964 v Poland, Norway, England.

Anderson, J. (16) 1980 v (Czechoslovakia), (USA); 1982 v Chile, Brazil, Trinidad & Tobago; 1984 v China; 1986 v Wales, Iceland, Czechoslovakia; 1987 v Bulgaria, Belgium, Brazil, Luxembourg; 1988 v (Romania), (Yugoslavia); 1989 v Tunisia.

Babb, P. (20) 1994 v Russia, Holland (2), Bolivia, Germany, (Czech Republic), Italy, Mexico, Norway; 1995 v Latvia, Liechtenstein (2), N. Ireland (2), Portugal, Austria; 1996 v Latvia, Portugal, Holland, Czech Republic.

Bailham, E. (1) 1964 v England.

Barber, E. (2) 1966 v Spain, Belgium.

Beglin, J. (15) 1984 v China; 1985 v Mexico, Denmark, Italy, Israel, England, Norway, Switzerland; 1986 v Switzerland, USSR, Denmark, Wales; 1987 v (Belgium), Scotland, Poland.

Bonner, P. (80) 1981 v Poland; 1982 v Algeria; 1984 v Malta, Israel, China; 1985 v Italy, Israel, England, Norway; 1986 v Uruguay, Iceland; 1987 v Belgium (2), Scotland (2), Poland, Bulgaria, Brazil, Luxembourg; 1988 v Bulgaria, Romania, Yugoslavia, Norway, England, USSR, Holland; 1989 v Spain (2), France, Hungary (2), Malta; 1990 v West Germany, N. Ireland, Malta, Wales, Finland, Turkey, England, Egypt, Holland, Romania, Italy; 1991 v Morocco, Turkey, England (2), Wales, Poland, USA; 1992 v Hungary, Poland, Turkey, Wales, Switzerland, Albania, Italy; 1993 v Latvia (2), Denmark (2), Spain, Wales,

N. Ireland, Albania, Lithuania; 1994 v Lithuania, Spain, N. Ireland, Russia, Holland (2), Bolivia, Czech Republic, Italy, Mexico, Norway; 1995 v Liechtenstein; 1996 v Mexico, (Bolivia).

Braddish, S. (2) 1978 v (Turkey), Poland.

Brady, T.R. (6) 1964 v Austria (2), Spain (2), Poland, Norway.

Brady, W.L. (72) 1975 v USSR (2), Turkey, Switzerland (2); 1976 v Turkey, Norway, Poland; 1977 v England, Turkey, France (2), Spain, Bulgaria; 1978 v Bulgaria, Norway; 1979 v N. Ireland, England, Denmark, Bulgaria, West Germany, Argentina; 1980 v Wales, Bulgaria, England, Cyprus; 1981 v Holland, Belgium (2), France, Cyprus; 1982 v Holland, France, Chile, Brazil, Trinidad & Tobago; 1983 v Holland (2), Spain, Iceland; 1984 v Iceland, Holland, Malta, Israel, Poland; 1985 v USSR, Norway (2), Denmark, Italy, England, Spain, Switzerland; 1986 v Switzerland, USSR, Denmark, Wales; 1987 v Belgium (2), Scotland (2), Poland, Bulgaria, Brazil, Luxembourg; 1988 v Luxembourg, Bulgaria; 1989 v France, (Hungary) (2); 1990 v West Germany, Finland.

Breen, G. (8) 1996 v (Portugal), Croatia, Holland, USA, Mexico, (Bolivia); 1997 v Liechtenstein, Macedonia.

Breen, T. (5) 1937 v Switzerland, France; 1947 v England, Spain, Portugal.

Brennan, F. (1) 1965 v (Belgium).

Brennan, S.A. (19) 1965 v Spain; 1966 v Spain, Austria, Belgium; 1967 v Spain (2), Turkey; 1969 v Czechoslovakia, Denmark, Hungary; 1970 v Scotland, Czechoslovakia, Denmark, Hungary, (Poland), West Germany; 1971 v Poland, Sweden, Italy.

Browne, W. (3) 1964 v Austria, Spain, England.

Buckley, L. (2) 1984 v (Poland); 1985 v Mexico.

Burke, F. (1) 1951 v West Germany.

Byrne, A.B. (14) 1970 v Denmark, Poland, West Germany; 1971 v Poland, Sweden (2), Italy (2), Austria; 1973 v France (2), (USSR), Norway; 1974 v Poland.

Byrne, J. (23) 1985 v Italy, (Israel), (England), (Spain); 1987 v (Scotland), (Belgium), Brazil, (Luxembourg); 1988 v Luxembourg, (Bulgaria), Israel, Romania, (Yugoslavia), (Poland); 1990 v (West Germany), Wales, Finland, (Turkey), Malta; 1991 v Wales; 1992 v Turkey, Wales; 1993 v Wales.

Byrne, P. (8) 1984 v Poland, China; 1985 v Mexico, (Spain); 1986 v (Denmark), (Wales), (Iceland), Czechoslovakia.

Campbell, A. (3) 1985 v (Italy), Israel, Spain.

Campbell, N. (11) 1971 v (Austria); 1972 v Iran, Ecuador, Chile, Portugal; 1973 v USSR, (France); 1975 v West Germany; 1976 v Norway; 1977 v Spain, (Bulgaria).

Cantwell, N. (36) 1954 v Luxembourg; 1956 v Spain, Holland; 1957 v Denmark, West Germany, England (2); 1958 v Denmark, Poland, Austria; 1959 v Poland, Czechoslovakia (2); 1960 v Sweden (2), Chile; 1961 v Norway, Scotland (2); 1962 v Czechoslovakia (2), Austria; 1963 v Iceland (2), Scotland; 1964 v Austria, Spain, England; 1965 v Poland, Spain; 1966 v Spain (2), Austria, Belgium; 1967 v Spain, Turkey.

Carey, B. (3) 1992 v (USA), 1993 v Wales; 1994 v Russia.

Carey, J.J. (29) 1938 v Norway, Czechoslovakia, Poland; 1939 v Switzerland, Poland, Hungary (2), Germany; 1946 v Portugal, Spain; 1947 v England, Spain, Portugal; 1948 v Portugal, Spain; 1949 v Switzerland, Belgium, Portugal, Sweden, Spain; 1950 v Finland (2), England, Sweden; 1951 v Norway (2), Argentina; 1953 v France, Austria.

Carolan, J. (2) 1960 v Sweden, Chile.

Carroll, B. (2) 1949 v Belgium; 1950 v Finland.

Carroll, T.R. (17) 1968 v Poland; 1969 v Poland, Austria, Denmark; 1970 v Czechoslovakia, Poland, West Germany; 1971 v Sweden; 1972 v Iran, Ecuador, Chile, Portugal; 1973 v USSR (2), Poland, France, Norway.

Cascarino, A.G. (65) 1986 v Switzerland, USSR, Denmark; 1988 v Poland, (Norway), (USSR), (Holland); 1989 v N. Ireland, Tunisia, Spain (2), France, Hungary (2), Malta; 1990 v (West Germany), N. Ireland, Malta, Wales, Finland, Turkey, England, Egypt, (Holland), (Romania), (Italy); 1991 v (Morocco), (Turkey), (England) (2), (Poland), (Chile), USA; 1992 v Poland, Turkey, Wales, Switzerland, (USA); 1993 v Wales, (N. Ireland), (Denmark), (Albania), (Latvia); 1994 v (Lithuania), (Spain), (N. Ireland); Russia, (Bolivia), Germany, Czech Republic, (Holland); 1995 v (Latvia), (N. Ireland), (Portugal), (Liechtenstein), (Austria); 1996 v (Austria), (Portugal), Holland (2), (Russia), Portugal, (Croatia); 1997 v (Liechtenstein), Macedonia.

Chandler, J. (2) 1980 v (Czechoslovakia), USA.

Clarke, J. (1) 1978 v (Poland).

Clarke, K. (2) 1948 v Portugal, Spain.

Clarke, M. (1) 1950 v Belgium.

Clinton, T.J. (3) 1951 v Norway; 1954 v France, Luxembourg.

Coad, P. (11) 1947 v England, Spain, Portugal; 1948 v Portugal, Spain; 1949 v Switzerland, Belgium, Portugal, Sweden; 1951 v (Norway); 1952 v Spain.

Coffey, T. (1) 1950 v Finland.

Colfer, M.D. (2) 1950 v Belgium; 1951 v Norway.

Conmy, O.M. (5) 1965 v Belgium; 1967 v Czechoslovakia; 1968 v Czechoslovakia, Poland; 1970 v Czechoslovakia.

Connolly, D. (4) 1996 v Portugal, Holland, USA, Mexico.

Conroy, G.A. (27) 1970 v Czechoslovakia, Denmark, Hungary, Poland, West Germany; 1971 v Poland, Sweden (2), Italy; 1973 v USSR (2), France, Norway; 1974 v Poland, Brazil, Uruguay, Chile; 1975 v Turkey, West Germany(USSR), Switzerland (2), 1976 v (Turkey), Poland; 1977 v England, Turkey, Poland.

Conway, J.P. (20) 1967 v Spain (2), Turkey; 1968 v Czechoslovakia; 1969 v (Austria), Hungary; 1970 v Scotland, Czechoslovakia, Denmark, Hungary, Poland, West Germany; 1971 v Italy, Austria; 1974 v Uruguay, Chile; 1975 v (West Germany); 1976 v Norway, Poland; 1977 v Poland.

Corr, P.J. (4) 1949 v Portugal, Spain; 1950 v England, Sweden.

Courtney, E. (1) 1946 v Portugal.

Coyle, O. (1) 1994 v (Holland).

Coyne, T. (21) 1992 v Switzerland, USA, (Albania), (USA), (Italy), (Portugal); 1993 v (Latvia), (Wales), N. İreland; 1994 v (Russia), Holland (2), Bolivia, (Germany), (Czech Republic), Italy, Mexico; 1995 v Liechtenstein, (N. Ireland), Austria; 1996 v (Russia).

Cummins, G.P. (19) 1954 v Luxembourg (2); 1955 v Norway (2), West Germany; 1956 v Yugoslavia, Spain; 1958 v Denmark, Poland, Austria; 1959 v Poland, Czechoslovakia (2); 1960 v Sweden (2), Chile, West Germany; 1961 v Scotland (2).

Cuneen, T. (1) 1951 v Norway.

Cunningham, K. (6) 1996 v Czech Republic, Portugal, Croatia, (Holland), USA, Bolivia.

Curtis, D.P. (17) 1957 v Denmark, West Germany, England (2); 1958 v Denmark, Poland, Austria; 1959 v Poland; 1960 v Sweden (2), Chile, West Germany; 1961 v Norway, Scotland; 1962 v Austria; 1963 v Iceland; 1964 v Austria.

Cusack, S. (1) 1953 v France.

Daish, L. (4) 1992 v Wales; 1996 v (Czech Republic), Croatia, Mexico.

Daly, G.A. (48) 1973 v (Poland), Norway; 1974 v (Brazil), (Uruguay); 1975 v West Germany, (Switzerland); 1977 v England, Turkey, France (2), Bulgaria; 1978 v Bulgaria, Turkey, Denmark; 1979 v N. Ireland, England, Denmark, Bulgaria; 1980 v N. Ireland, England, Cyprus, Switzerland, Argentina; 1981 v Holland, Belgium (2), Cyprus, Wales, Czechoslovakia, (Poland); 1982 v Algeria, Chile, Brazil, Trinidad & Tobago; 1983 v Holland, (Spain), (Malta); 1984 v Malta, (Israel); 1985 v (Mexico), Norway, Spain, Switzerland; 1986 v Switzerland, Uruguay, (Iceland), (Czechoslovakia); 1987 v (Scotland).

Daly, M. (2) 1978 v Turkey, Poland.

Daly, P. (1) 1950 v (Finland).

Deacy, E. (4) 1982 v (Algeria), Chile, Brazil, Trinidad & Tobago.

De Mange, K.J.P.P. (2) 1987 v (Brazil); 1989 v (Tunisia).

Dempsey, J.T. (19) 1967 v Spain, Czechoslovakia; 1968 v Czechoslovakia, Poland; 1969 v Poland, Austria, Denmark (2), Czechoslovakia; 1970 v Hungary, West Germany; 1971 v Poland, Sweden (2), Italy; 1972 v Iran, Ecuador, Chile, Portugal.

Dennehy, J. (11) 1972 v (Ecuador), Chile; 1973 v (USSR), Poland, France, Norway; 1974 v (Poland); 1975 v (Turkey), (West Germany); 1976 v (Poland); 1977 v (Poland).

Desmond, P. (4) 1950 v Finland (2), England, Sweden.

Devine, J. (12) 1980 v Czechoslovakia, N. Ireland; 1981 v Czechoslovakia; 1982 v Holland, Algeria; 1983 v Spain, Malta; 1984 v Iceland, Holland, Israel; 1985 v USSR, Norway.

Donovan, D.C. (5) 1955 v Norway (2), Holland, West Germany; 1957 v England.

Donovan, T. (1) 1980 v Czechoslovakia.

Doyle, C. (1) 1959 v Czechoslovakia.

Duffy, R. (1) 1950 v Belgium.

Dunne, A.P. (33) 1962 v Austria; 1963 v Iceland, Scotland; 1964 v Austria, Spain, Poland, Norway, England; 1965 v Poland, Spain; 1966 v Spain (2), Austria, Belgium; 1967 v Spain (2), Turkey; 1969 v Poland, Denmark, Hungary; 1970 v Hungary; 1971 v Sweden, Italy, Austria; 1974 v (Brazil), Uruguay, Chile; 1975 v Turkey, West Germany, Switzerland (2), USSR; 1976 v Turkey.

Dunne, J.C. (1) 1971 v Austria.

Dunne, P.A.J. (5) 1965 v Spain; 1966 v Spain (2), West Germany; 1967 v Turkey.

Dunne, S. (15) 1953 v France, Austria; 1954 v France, Luxembourg; 1956 v Spain, Holland; 1957 v Denmark, West Germany, England; 1958 v Denmark, Poland, Austria; 1959 v Poland; 1960 v West Germany, Sweden.

Dunne, T. (3) 1956 v Holland; 1957 v Denmark, West Germany.

Dunning, P. (2) 1971 v Sweden, Italy.

Dunphy, E.M. (23) 1966 v Spain, West Germany; 1967 v Turkey (2), Spain, Czechoslovakia; 1968 v Czechoslovakia, Poland; 1969 v Poland, Austria, Denmark (2), Hungary; 1970 v Denmark, Hungary, Poland, West Germany; 1971 v Poland, Sweden (2), Italy (2), Austria.

Dwyer, N.M. (14) 1960 v Sweden (2), Chile, West Germany; 1961 v Wales, Norway, Scotland (2); 1962 v Czechoslovakia (2); 1964 v (Poland), Norway, England; 1965 v Poland.

Eccles, P. (1) 1986 v (Uruguay).

Eglington, T.J. (24) 1946 v Portugal, Spain; 1947 v England, Spain, Portugal; 1948 v Portugal; 1949 v Switzerland, (Portugal), Sweden; 1951 v Norway, Argentina; 1952 v West Germany (2), Austria, Spain; 1953 v France, Austria; 1954 v France (2), Luxembourg; 1955 v Norway, Holland, West Germany; 1956 v Spain.

Fagan, E. (1) 1973 v (Norway).

Fagan, F. (8) 1955 v Norway; 1960 v Sweden (2), Chile, West Germany; 1961 v Wales, Norway, Scotland.

Fairclough, M. (2) 1982 v (Chile), (Trinidad & Tobago).

Fallon, S. (8) 1951 v Norway; 1952 v West Germany (2), Austria, Spain; 1953 v France; 1955 v Norway, West Germany.

Farrell, P.D. (28) 1946 v Portugal, Spain; 1947 v Spain, Portugal; 1948 v Portugal, Spain; 1949 v Switzerland, (Portugal), Spain; 1950 v England, Finland, Sweden; 1951 v Argentina, Norway; 1952 v West Germany (2), Austria, Spain; 1953 v France, Austria; 1954 v France (2); 1955 v Norway, Holland, West Germany; 1956 v Yugoslavia, Spain; 1957 v England.

Farrelly, G. (3) 1996 v Portugal, USA, Bolivia.

Finucane, A. (11) 1967 v Turkey, Czechoslovakia; 1969 v Czechoslovakia, Denmark,

Hungary; 1970 v Scotland, Czechoslovakia; 1971 v Sweden, Italy (Italy); 1972 v Austria.

Fitzgerald, F.J. (2) 1955 v Holland; 1956 v Holland.

Fitzgerald, P.J. (5) 1961 v Wales, Norway, Scotland; 1962 v Czechoslovakia (2).

Fitzpatrick, K. (1) 1970 v Czechoslovakia.

Fitzsimons, A.G. (26) 1950 v Finland, Belgium; 1952 v West Germany (2), Austria, Spain; 1953 v France, Austria; 1954 v France (2), Luxembourg; 1955 v Holland, Norway, West Germany; 1956 v Yugoslavia, Spain, Holland; 1957 v Denmark, West Germany, England (2); 1958 v Denmark, Poland, Austria; 1959 v Poland, Czechoslovakia.

Fleming, C. (6) 1996 v (Czech Republic), Portugal, (Croatia), (Holland), (USA), Mexico, Bolivia.

Fogarty, A. (11) 1960 v West Germany, Sweden; 1961 v Scotland; 1962 v Czechoslovakia (2); 1963 v Iceland (2), (Scotland); 1964 v Austria (2), Spain.

Foley, T.C. (9) 1964 v Spain, Poland, Norway; 1965 v Poland, Belgium; 1966 v Spain (2), West Germany; 1967 v Czechoslovakia.

Fullam, J. (11) 1961 v Norway; 1964 v Spain, Poland, Norway; 1966 v Austria, Belgium; 1968 v Poland; 1969 v Poland, Austria, Denmark; 1970 v (Czechoslovakia).

Gallagher, C. (2) 1967 v Turkey, Czechoslovakia.

Gallagher, M. (1) 1954 v Luxembourg.

Galvin, A. (29) 1983 v (Holland), Malta; 1984 v (Holland), (Israel); 1985 v Mexico, USSR, Norway (2), Denmark, Italy, Spain; 1986 v Uruguay, Iceland, Czechoslovakia; 1987 v Belgium (2), Scotland, Bulgaria, Luxembourg; 1988 v Luxembourg, Bulgaria, Romania, Poland, Norway, England, USSR, Holland; 1989 v Spain; 1990 v West Germany.

Gannon, E. (14) 1949 v Switzerland, Belgium, Portugal, Sweden, Spain; 1950 v Finland; 1951 v Norway; 1952 v West Germany, Austria; 1954 v Luxembourg, France; 1955 v Norway (2), West Germany.

Gannon, M. (1) 1972 v Austria.

Gavin, J.T. (7) 1950 v Finland (2); 1953 v France; 1954 v Luxembourg; 1955 v Holland, West Germany; 1957 v Denmark.

Gibbons, S. (4) 1952 v West Germany; 1954 v Luxembourg; 1956 v Yugoslavia, Spain.

Gilbert, R. (1) 1966 v West Germany.

Giles, C. (1) 1951 v Norway.

Giles, M.J. (59) 1960 v Sweden, Chile; 1961 v Wales, Norway, Scotland (2); 1962 v Czechoslovakia (2), Austria; 1963 v Iceland, Scotland; 1964 v Austria (2), Spain (2), Poland, Norway, England; 1965 v Spain; 1966 v Spain (2), Austria, Belgium; 1967 v Spain, Turkey (2); 1969 v Austria, Denmark, Czechoslovakia; 1970 v Scotland, Poland, West Germany; 1971 v Italy; 1973 v France, USSR; 1974 v Brazil, Uruguay, Chile; 1975 v USSR (2), Turkey, Switzerland (2); 1976 v Turkey; 1977 v England, Turkey, France (2), Poland, Bulgaria; 1978 v Bulgaria, Turkey, Poland, Norway, Denmark; 1979 v N. Ireland, Denmark, Bulgaria, West Germany.

Given, S. (8) 1996 v Russia, Czech Republic, Portugal, Croatia, Holland, USA, Bolivia; 1997 v Liechtenstein.

Givens, D.J. (56) 1969 v Denmark, Hungary; 1970 v Scotland, Czechoslovakia, Denmark, Hungary, Poland, West Germany; 1971 v Sweden, Italy (2), Austria; 1972 v Iran, Ecuador, Portugal; 1973 v France (2), USSR, Poland, Norway; 1974 v Poland, Brazil, Uruguay, Chile; 1975 v USSR (2), Turkey, West Germany, Switzerland (2); 1976 v Turkey, Norway, Poland; 1977 v England, Turkey, France (2), Spain, Bulgaria; 1978 v Bulgaria, Norway, Denmark; 1979 v (N. Ireland), England, Denmark, Bulgaria, West Germany; 1980 v (USA), (N. Ireland), England, Argentina; 1981 v Holland, Belgium, (Cyprus), Wales; 1982 v (France).

Glynn, D. (2) 1952 v West Germany; 1955 v Norway.

Godwin, T.F. (13) 1949 v Portugal, Sweden, Spain; 1950 v Finland (2), England, Sweden, Belgium; 1951 v Norway; 1956 v Holland; 1957 v England; 1958 v Denmark, Poland.

Gorman, W.C. (13) 1936 v Switzerland, Hungary, Luxembourg; 1937 v Germany, Hungary; 1938 v Norway, Czechoslovakia, Poland; 1939 v Switzerland, Poland, Hungary; 1947 v England, Portugal.

Grealish, A. (45) 1976 v Norway, Poland; 1978 v Norway, Denmark; 1979 v N. Ireland, England, West Germany; 1980 v Wales, Czechoslovakia, Bulgaria, USA, N. Ireland, England, Cyprus, Switzerland, Argentina; 1981 v Holland, Belgium (2), France, Cyprus, Wales, Poland; 1982 v Holland, Algeria, Chile, Brazil, Trinidad & Tobago; 1983 v Holland, Iceland, Spain (2); 1984 v Iceland, Holland, Poland, China; 1985 v Mexico, USSR, Norway, Denmark, (Spain), Switzerland; 1986 v USSR, Denmark.

Gregg, E. (8) 1978 v Poland, (Denmark); 1979 v (England), Denmark, Bulgaria, West Germany; 1980 v Wales, Czechoslovakia.

Grimes, A.A. (17) 1978 v Turkey, Poland, (Norway); 1980 v Bulgaria, USA, N. Ireland, England, Cyprus; 1981 v Czechoslovakia, Poland; 1982 v Algeria; 1983 v Spain (2); 1984 v Israel, Poland; 1988 v Luxembourg, Romania.

Hale, A. (13) 1962 v Austria; 1963 v Iceland; 1964 v Spain (2); 1967 v Spain; 1968 v (Poland); 1969 v Poland, Austria, Denmark; 1970 v Scotland, Czechoslovakia; 1971 v (Poland); 1972 v (Austria).

Hamilton, T. (2) 1959 v Czechoslovakia (2).

Hand, E.K. (20) 1969 v (Czechoslovakia); 1970 v Poland, West Germany; 1971 v Poland, Austria; 1973 v USSR (2), France (2), Poland; 1974 v Poland, Brazil, Uruguay, Chile; 1975 v Turkey, West Germany, Switzerland (2), USSR; 1976 v Turkey.

Harte, I. (6) 1996 v (Croatia), Holland, Mexico, Bolivia; 1997 v Liechtenstein, Macedonia.

Hartnett, J.B. (2) 1949 v Spain; 1954 v Luxembourg.

Haverty, J. (32) 1956 v Holland; 1957 v Denmark, West Germany, England (2); 1958 v Denmark, Poland, Austria; 1959 v Poland; 1960 v Sweden, Chile; 1961 v Wales, Norway, Scotland (2); 1962 v Czechoslovakia (2); 1963 v Scotland; 1964 v Austria, Spain, Poland, Norway, England; 1965 v Poland, Spain; 1966 v Spain (2), West Germany, Austria, Belgium; 1967 v Turkey, Spain.

Hayes, A.W.P. (1) 1979 v Denmark.

Hayes, W.E. (2) 1947 v England, Portugal.

Hayes, W.J. (1) 1949 v Belgium.

Healey, R. (2) 1977 v Poland; 1980 v (England).

Heighway, S.D. (34) 1971 v Poland, Sweden (2), Italy, Austria; 1973 v USSR; 1975 v USSR (2), Turkey, West Germany; 1976 v Turkey, Norway; 1977 v England, France (2), Spain, Bulgaria; 1978 v Bulgaria, Norway, Denmark; 1979 v N. Ireland, Bulgaria; 1980 v Bulgaria, USA, N. Ireland, England, Cyprus, Argentina; 1981 v Belgium (2), France, Cyprus, Wales; 1982 v Holland.

Henderson, B. (2) 1948 v Portugal, Spain.

Hennessy, J. (5) 1965 v Poland, Belgium, Spain; 1966 v West Germany; 1969 v Austria.

Herrick, J. (3) 1972 v Austria, (Chile); 1973 v (France).

Higgins, J. (1) 1951 v Argentina.

Holmes, J. (30) 1971 v (Austria); 1973 v France (2), USSR, Poland, Norway; 1974 v Poland, Brazil; 1975 v USSR, Switzerland; 1976 v Turkey, Norway, Poland; 1977 v England, Turkey, France (2), Spain, Poland, Bulgaria; 1978 v Bulgaria, Turkey, Poland, Norway, Denmark; 1979 v N. Ireland, England, Denmark, Bulgaria; 1981 v Wales.

Houghton, R.J. (67) 1986 v Wales, Uruguay, Iceland, Czechoslovakia; 1987 v Belgium (2), Scotland (2), Poland, Luxembourg; 1988 v Luxembourg, Bulgaria, Israel, Yugoslavia, Norway, England, USSR, Holland; 1989 v N. Ireland, Tunisia, Spain (2), France, Hungary (2), Malta; 1990 v N. Ireland, Malta, Finland, England, Egypt, Holland, Romania, Italy; 1991 v Morocco, Turkey, England (2), Poland, Chile, USA; 1992 v Hungary, Albania, USA, Italy, Portugal; 1993 v Denmark (2), Spain, N. Ireland, Albania, Latvia, Lithuania; 1994 v Lithuania, Spain, N. Ireland, Bolivia, (Germany), Italy, Mexico, Norway, Holland; 1995 v Portugal, Austria; 1996 v Austria, Czech Republic; 1997 v Liechtenstein.

Howlett, G. (1) 1984 v (China).

Hughton, C. (53) 1980 v USA, England, Switzerland, Argentina; 1981 v Holland, Belgium (2), France, Cyprus, Wales, Poland; 1982 v France; 1983 v Holland, Spain (2), Malta; 1984 v Iceland, Holland, Malta; 1985 v (Mexico), USSR, Norway, Italy, Israel, England, Spain; 1986 v Switzerland, USSR, Uruguay, Iceland; 1987 v Belgium, Bulgaria; 1988 v Israel, Yugoslavia, Poland, Norway, England, USSR, Holland; 1989 v N. Ireland, France, Hungary (2), Spain, Malta; 1990 v (Wales), (USSR), Finland, (Turkey), (Malta); 1991 v Turkey, Chile; 1992 v Turkey.

Hurley, C.J. (40) 1957 v England; 1958 v Denmark, Poland, Austria; 1959 v Czechoslovakia (2); 1960 v Sweden (2), Chile, West Germany; 1961 v Wales, Norway, Scotland (2); 1962 v Czechoslovakia (2), Austria; 1963 v Iceland (2), Scotland; 1964 v Austria (2), Spain (2), Poland, Norway; 1965 v Spain; 1966 v West Germany, Austria, Belgium; 1967 v Turkey (2), Spain, Czechoslovakia; 1968 v Czechoslovakia, Poland; 1969 v Poland, Denmark, Czechoslovakia, Hungary.

Irwin, D. (42) 1991 v Morocco, Turkey, Wales, England, Poland, USA; 1992 v Hungary, Poland, Wales, USA, Albania, (USA), Italy; 1993 v Latvia (2), Denmark (2), Spain, N.

Ireland, Albania, Lithuania; 1994 v Lithuania, Spain, N. Ireland, Bolivia, Germany, Italy, Mexico; 1995 v Latvia, Liechtenstein (2), N. Ireland (2), England, Portugal, Austria; 1996 v Austria, Portugal, Holland, Czech Republic; 1997 v Liechtenstein, Macedonia.

Keane, R.M. (30) 1991 v Chile; 1992 v Hungary, Poland, Wales, Switzerland, Albania, USA; 1993 v Latvia (2), Denmark (2), Spain, Wales, N. Ireland, Albania, Lithuania; 1994 v Lithuania, Spain, N. Ireland, Bolivia, Germany, (Czech Republic), Italy, Mexico, Norway, Holland; 1995 v N. Ireland (2); 1996 v Austria, Russia.

Keane, T.R. (4) 1949 v Switzerland, Portugal, Sweden, Spain.

Kearin, M. (1) 1972 v Austria.

Kearns, F.T. (1) 1954 v Luxembourg.

Kearns, M. (18) 1970 v (Poland); 1974 v (Poland), Uruguay, Chile; 1976 v Norway, Poland; 1977 v England, Turkey, France (2), Spain, Bulgaria; 1978 v Norway, Denmark; 1979 v N. Ireland, England; 1980 v USA, N. Ireland.

Kelly, A.T. (15) 1993 v (Wales); 1994 v (Russia), Germany; 1995 v Latvia, N. Ireland (2), England, Portugal, Liechtenstein, Austria; 1996 v Austria, Latvia, Portugal, Holland; 1997 v Macedonia.

Kelly, D.T. (20) 1988 v Israel, Romania, Yugoslavia; 1989 v (Tunisia); 1990 v USSR, Malta; 1991 v Morocco, (Wales), Chile, USA; 1992 v Hungary, (Italy), Portugal; 1993 v (Spain), Wales; 1994 v Russia, (Norway); 1995 v England, N. Ireland; 1996 v (Latvia).

Kelly, G. (18) 1994 v Russia, Holland (2), (Bolivia), (Germany), Czech Republic, Norway; 1995 v Latvia, Liechtenstein (2), N. Ireland (2), Portugal, Austria; 1996 v Austria, Latvia, Portugal, Holland.

Kelly, J.A. (47) 1957 v West Germany, England; 1962 v Austria; 1963 v Iceland (2), Scotland; 1964 v Austria (2), Spain (2), Poland; 1965 v Belgium; 1966 v Austria, Belgium; 1967 v Spain (2), Turkey, Czechoslovakia; 1968 v Czechoslovakia, Poland; 1969 v Poland, Austria, Denmark (2), Czechoslovakia, Hungary; 1970 v Scotland, Denmark, Hungary, Poland, West Germany; 1971 v Poland, Sweden (2), Italy (2), Austria; 1972 v Iran, Ecuador, Chile, Portugal; 1973 v USSR (2), France (2), Poland, Norway.

Kelly, J.P.V. (5) 1961 v Wales, Norway, Scotland; 1962 v Czechoslovakia (2).

Kelly, M.J. (4) 1988 v Yugoslavia, (Poland); 1989 v Tunisia; 1991 v Morocco.

Kelly, N. (1) 1954 v Luxembourg.

Kenna, J. (14) 1995 v (Portugal), (Liechtenstein), (Austria); 1996 v (Latvia), Portugal (2), Holland (2), (Russia), Czech Republic, Croatia, USA; 1997 v Liechtenstein, Macedonia.

Kennedy, M. (10) 1996 v Austria, (Latvia), Portugal, Russia, (Czech Republic), Croatia, (Holland), (USA), Mexico, (Bolivia).

Kennedy, M.F. (2) 1986 v Iceland, (Czechoslovakia).

Keogh, J. (1) 1966 v (West Germany).

Keogh, S. (1) 1959 v Poland.

Kernaghan, A. (22) 1993 v Latvia (2), Denmark (2), Albania, Lithuania; 1994 v Lithuania,

Spain, N. Ireland, (Bolivia), Czech Republic; 1995 v Liechtenstein, England; 1996 v Austria, (Portugal), (Holland), Russia, Portugal, (Croatia), Holland, USA, Bolivia.

Kiernan, F.W. (5) 1951 v Argentina, Norway; 1952 v West Germany (2), Austria.

Kinnear, J.P. (26) 1967 v Turkey; 1968 v Czechoslovakia, Poland; 1969 v Austria; 1970 v Czechoslovakia, Denmark, Hungary, Poland; 1971 v (Sweden), Italy; 1972 v Iran, Ecuador, Chile, Portugal; 1973 v USSR, France; 1974 v Poland, Brazil, Uruguay, Chile; 1975 v USSR (2), Turkey, West Germany, Switzerland; 1976 v (Turkey).

Langan, D. (25) 1978 v Turkey, Norway; 1980 v Switzerland, Argentina; 1981 v Holland, Belgium (2), France, Cyprus, Wales, Czechoslovakia, Poland; 1982 v Holland, France; 1985 v Norway, Spain, Switzerland; 1986 v Wales, Uruguay; 1987 v Belgium, Scotland, Poland, (Brazil), (Luxembourg); 1988 v Luxembourg.

Lawler, J.F. (8) 1953 v Austria; 1954 v Luxembourg, France; 1955 v Norway (2), Holland, West Germany; 1956 v Yugoslavia.

Lawlor, J.C. (3) 1949 v Belgium; 1951 v Norway, Argentina.

Lawlor, M. (5) 1971 v Poland, Sweden (2), (Italy); 1973 v Poland.

Lawrenson, M. (39) 1977 v Poland; 1978 v Bulgaria, Poland, (Norway), Denmark; 1979 v N. Ireland, England; 1980 v England, Cyprus, Switzerland; 1981 v Holland, Belgium, France, Cyprus, Poland; 1982 v Holland, France; 1983 v Holland, Iceland, Spain (2), Malta; 1984 v Iceland, Holland, Malta, Israel; 1985 v USSR, Norway (2), Denmark, Italy, England; 1986 v Switzerland, USSR, Denmark; 1987 v Belgium, Scotland; 1988 v Bulgaria, Israel.

Leech, M. (8) 1969 v Czechoslovakia, Denmark, Hungary; 1972 v Austria, Iran, Ecuador, Portugal; 1973 v (USSR).

Lowry, D. (1) 1962 v (Austria).

McAlinden, J. (2) 1946 v Portugal, Spain.

McAteer, J. (19) 1994 v Russia, (Holland) (2), (Bolivia), Germany, (Czech Republic), (Italy), (Mexico), Norway; 1995 v Latvia, Liechtenstein (2), (N. Ireland) (2); 1996 v Latvia, Portugal, (Holland), Russia; 1997 v Macedonia.

McCann, J. (1) 1957 v West Germany.

McCarthy, M. (57) 1984 v Poland, China; 1985 v Mexico, Denmark, Italy, Israel, England, Spain, Switzerland; 1986 v Switzerland, USSR, (Wales), Uruguay, Iceland, Czechoslovakia; 1987 v Scotland (2), Poland, Bulgaria, Belgium, Brazil, Luxembourg; 1988 v Bulgaria, Israel, Romania, Yugoslavia, Norway, England, USSR, Holland; 1989 v N. Ireland, Tunisia, Spain (2), France, Hungary; 1990 v West Germany, N. Ireland, Wales, USSR, Finland, Turkey, England, Egypt, Holland, Romania, Italy; 1991 v Morocco, Turkey, England, USA; 1992 v Hungary, Turkey, (Albania), USA, Italy, Portugal.

McConville, T. (6) 1972 v Austria; 1973 v USSR (2), France (2), Poland.

McDonagh, J. (24) 1981 v Wales, Belgium, Czechoslovakia; 1982 v Holland, France, Chile, Brazil; 1983 v Holland, Iceland, Spain (2), Malta; 1984 v Iceland, Holland, Poland; 1985 v Mexico, USSR, Norway, Denmark, Spain, Switzerland; 1986 v Switzerland, USSR,

Denmark.

McDonagh, 'Jacko' (3) 1984 v (Malta), (Poland); 1985 v (Mexico).

McEvoy, M.A. (17) 1961 v Scotland (2); 1963 v Scotland; 1964 v Austria, Spain (2), Poland, Norway, England; 1965 v Poland, Belgium, Spain; 1966 v Spain (2); 1967 v Spain, Turkey, Czechoslovakia.

McGee, P. (15) 1978 v Turkey, (Norway), (Denmark); 1979 v N. Ireland, England, (Denmark), (Bulgaria); 1980 v Czechoslovakia, Bulgaria, USA, N. Ireland, Cyprus, Switzerland, Argentina; 1981 v (Belgium).

McGoldrick, E. (15) 1992 v Switzerland, USA, Italy, (Portugal); 1993 v Denmark (2), Wales, (N. Ireland); 1994 v N. Ireland, Russia, Holland, Czech Republic; 1995 v (Latvia), Liechtenstein, England.

McGowan, D. (3) 1949 v Portugal, Sweden, Spain.

McGowan, J. (1) 1947 v Spain.

McGrath, M. (22) 1958 v Austria; 1959 v Poland, Czechoslovakia (2); 1960 V Sweden (2), West Germany; 1961 v Wales; 1962 v Czechoslovakia (2); 1963 v Scotland; 1964 v Austria (2), England; 1965 v Poland, Belgium, Spain; 1966 v Spain, West Germany, Austria, Belgium; 1967 v Turkey.

McGrath, P. (82) 1985 v (Italy), Israel, England, (Norway), (Switzerland); 1986 v (Switzerland), Denmark, Wales, Iceland, Czechoslovakia; 1987 v Belgium (2), Scotland (2), Poland, Bulgaria, Brazil, Luxembourg; 1988 v Luxembourg, Bulgaria, Yugoslavia, Poland, Norway, England, Holland; 1989 v N. Ireland, France, Hungary (2), Spain, Malta; 1990 v West Germany, Malta, USSR, Finland, Turkey, England, Egypt, Holland, Romania, Italy; 1991 v England (2), Wales, Poland, (Chile), USA; 1992 v Poland, Turkey, Switzerland, USA, Albania, USA, Italy, Portugal; 1993 v Latvia (2), Spain, N. Ireland, Denmark, Lithuania; 1994 v Spain, N. Ireland, Germany, Czech Republic, Italy, Mexico, Norway, Holland; 1995 v Latvia, N. Ireland (2), England, Portugal, Liechtenstein, Austria; 1996 v Austria, Latvia, Portugal, Holland, Russia, Czech Republic.

McLoughlin, A. (25) 1990 v Malta, (England), (Egypt); 1991 v (Morocco), (England), Wales, (Chile); 1992 v (Hungary), (Wales), USA, (Italy), Portugal; 1993 v Wales; 1994 v (N. Ireland), Russia, (Holland); 1995 v (Liechtenstein); 1996 v Portugal, Croatia, Holland, USA, Mexico, (Bolivia); 1997 v Liechtenstein, Macedonia.

McMillan, W. (2) 1946 v Portugal, Spain.

McNally, J.B. (3) 1959 v Czechoslovakia; 1961 v Scotland; 1963 v Iceland.

Macken, A. (1) 1977 v Spain.

Mackey, G. (3) 1957 v Denmark, West Germany, England.

Malone, G. (1) 1949 v Belgium.

Mancini, T.J. (5) 1974 v Poland, Brazil, Uruguay, Chile; 1975 v USSR.

Martin, C.J. (30) 1946 v (Portugal), Spain; 1947 v England, Spain; 1948 v Portugal, Spain; 1949 v Switzerland, Belgium, Portugal, Sweden, Spain; 1950 v Finland (2), England, Sweden, Belgium; 1951 v Argentina; 1952 v West Germany, Austria, Spain; 1954 v France

(2), Luxembourg; 1955 v Norway (2), Holland, West Germany; 1956 v Yugoslavia, Spain, Holland.

Martin, M.P. (51) 1972 v Austria, Iran, Ecuador, Chile, Portugal; 1973 v USSR (2), Poland, France, Norway; 1974 v Poland, Brazil, Uruguay, Chile; 1975 v USSR (2), Turkey, Switzerland (2); 1976 v Turkey, Norway, Poland; 1977 v England, Turkey, France (2), Spain, Poland, Bulgaria; 1979 v Denmark, Bulgaria, West Germany, Argentina; 1980 v Wales, Czechoslovakia, Bulgaria, USA, N. Ireland; 1981 v France, Belgium, Czechoslovakia; 1982 v Holland, France, Algeria, Chile, Brazil, Trinidad & Tobago; 1983 v Holland, Spain (2), Malta.

Meagan, M.K. (17) 1961 v Scotland; 1962 v Austria; 1963 v Iceland; 1964 v Spain; 1965 v Belgium; 1966 v Spain (2), Austria, Belgium; 1967 v Spain (2), Turkey (2), Czechoslovakia; 1968 v Czechoslovakia, Poland; 1970 v Scotland.

Milligan, M. (1) 1992 v (USA).

Mooney, J. (2) 1965 v Poland, Belgium.

Moore, A. (7) 1996 v Czech Republic, (Croatia), Holland, Mexico, Bolivia; 1997 v (Liechtenstein), (Macedonia).

Moran, K. (70) 1980 v Switzerland, Argentina; 1981 v Belgium (2), France, Cyprus, (Wales), Czechoslovakia, Poland; 1982 v France, Algeria; 1983 v Iceland; 1984 v Iceland, Holland, Malta, Israel; 1985 v Mexico; 1986 v Denmark, Iceland, Czechoslovakia; 1987 v Belgium (2), Scotland (2), Poland, Bulgaria, Brazil, Luxembourg; 1988 v Luxembourg, Bulgaria, Israel, Romania, Yugoslavia, Poland, Norway, England, USSR, Holland; 1989 v N. Ireland, Spain (2), Hungary (2), Malta; 1990 v N. Ireland, Malta (2), Wales, (USSR), England, Egypt, Holland, Romania, Italy; 1991 v (Turkey), Wales, England, Poland, Chile, USA; 1992 v Poland, USA; 1993 v Denmark, Spain, N. Ireland, Albania; 1994 v Lithuania, Spain, Holland, Bolivia.

Moroney, T. (12) 1948 v Spain, 1949 v Portugal, Sweden, Spain; 1950 v Finland (2), England, Belgium; 1951 v Norway (2); 1952 v West Germany; 1954 v France.

Morris, C.B. (35) 1988 v Israel, Romania, Yugoslavia, Poland, Norway, England, USSR, Holland; 1989 v N. Ireland, Tunisia, Spain, France, Hungary, (Hungary); 1990 v West Germany, N. Ireland, (Malta), Wales, USSR, (Finland), Turkey, England, Egypt, Holland, Romania, Italy; 1991 v England; 1992 v (Hungary), Poland, Wales Switzerland, USA (2), Portugal; 1993 v Wales.

Moulson, G.B. (3) 1948 v Portugal, Spain; 1949 v Sweden.

Muckian, C. (1) 1978 v Poland.

Mulligan, P.M. (50) 1969 v Czechoslovakia, Denmark, Hungary; 1970 v Scotland, Czechoslovakia, Denmark, Hungary, Poland, West Germany; 1971 v Poland, Sweden, Italy; 1972 v Austria, Iran, Ecuador, Chile, Portugal; 1973 v France (2), USSR, Poland, Norway; 1974 v Poland, Brazil, Uruguay, Chile; 1975 v USSR (2), Turkey, Switzerland (2); 1976 v Turkey, Poland; 1977 v England, Turkey, France (2), Poland, Bulgaria; 1978 v Bulgaria, Norway, Denmark; 1979 v England, Denmark, (Bulgaria), West Germany; 1980 v Wales, Czechoslovakia, Bulgaria, (USA).

Munroe, L. (1) 1954 v Luxembourg.

Murphy, A. (1) 1956 v Yugoslavia.

Murphy, B. (1) 1986 v Uruguay.

Murphy, J. (3) 1980 v Wales, USA, Cyprus.

Murray, T. (1) 1950 v Belgium.

Newman, W. (1) 1969 v Denmark.

Nolan, R. (10) 1957 v Denmark, West Germany, England; 1958 v Poland; 1960 v Chile, West Germany, Sweden; 1962 v Czechoslovakia (2); 1963 v Iceland.

O'Brien, F. (3) 1980 v Czechoslovakia, England, (Cyprus).

O'Brien, L. (16) 1986 v Uruguay; 1987 v Brazil; 1988 v (Israel), (Romania), (Yugoslavia), (Poland); 1989 v Tunisia, (Spain); 1992 v (Switzerland); 1993 v Wales; 1994 v Russia; 1996 v Croatia, Holland, USA, Bolivia; 1997 v (Macedonia).

O'Brien, R. (4) 1976 v Norway, Poland; 1977 v Spain, Poland.

O'Byrne, L.B. (1) 1949 v Belgium.

O'Callaghan, B.R. (6) 1979 v (West Germany); 1980 v Wales, USA; 1981 v Wales; 1982 v Brazil, Trinidad & Tobago.

O'Callaghan, K. (20) 1981 v Czechoslovakia, Poland; 1982 v Algeria, Chile, Brazil, (Trinidad & Tobago); 1983 v (Iceland), Spain, (Spain), (Malta), 1984 v Iceland, Holland, Malta; 1985 v (Mexico), (Norway), (Denmark), (England); 1986 v (Switzerland), (USSR); 1987 v (Brazil).

O'Connell, A. (2) 1967 v Spain; 1971 v (Poland).

O'Connor, T. (4) 1950 v Finland (2), England, Sweden.

O'Connor, T. (7) 1968 v Czechoslovakia; 1972 v Austria, (Iran), (Ecuador), Chile; 1973 v (France), (Poland).

O'Driscoll, J.F. (3) 1949 v Switzerland, Belgium, Sweden.

O'Driscoll, S. (3) 1982 v Chile, Brazil, (Trinidad & Tobago).

O'Farrell, F. (9) 1952 v Austria; 1953 v Austria; 1954 v France; 1955 v Holland, Norway; 1956 v Yugoslavia, Holland; 1958 v Denmark; 1959 v Czechoslovakia.

O'Flanagan, K.P. (10) 1938 v Norway, Czechoslovakia, Poland; 1939 v Poland, Hungary (2), Germany; 1947 v England, Spain, Portugal.

O'Flanagan, M. (1) 1947 v England.

O'Hanlon, K.G. (1) 1988 v Israel.

O'Keefe, E. (5) 1981 v Wales; 1984 v China; 1985 v Mexico, (USSR), England.

O'Leary, D. (67) 1977 v England, France (2), Spain, Bulgaria; 1978 v Bulgaria, Norway, Denmark; 1979 v England, Bulgaria, West Germany; 1980 v Wales, Bulgaria, N. Ireland, England, Cyprus; 1981 v Holland, Czechoslovakia, Poland; 1982 v Holland, France; 1983 v Holland, Iceland, Spain; 1984 v Israel, Poland, China; 1985 v USSR, Norway (2), Denmark, Israel, (England), Spain, Switzerland; 1986 v Switzerland, USSR, Denmark,

Wales; 1989 v Spain, Malta, Hungary, 1990 v West Germany, (N. Ireland), Malta (2), (Wales), USSR, Finland, Turkey, (Romania); 1991 v Morocco, Turkey, England (2), Poland, Chile; 1992 v Hungary, Poland, Turkey, Wales, Switzerland, USA, Albania, Italy, Portugal; 1993 v Wales.

O'Leary, P. (7) 1980 v Czechoslovakia, Bulgaria, USA, N. Ireland, (England), Argentina; 1981 v Holland.

O'Neill, F.S. (20) 1962 v Czechoslovakia (2); 1965 v Poland, Belgium, Spain; 1966 v Spain (2), West Germany, Austria; 1967 v Spain (2), Turkey (2); 1969 v Poland, Austria, Denmark, (Denmark), Czechoslovakia, (Hungary); 1972 v Austria.

O'Neill, J.A. (17) 1952 v Spain; 1953 v France, Austria; 1954 v France (2), Luxembourg; 1955 v Norway (2), Holland, West Germany; 1956 v Yugoslavia, Spain; 1957 v Denmark; 1958 v Poland; 1959 v Poland, Czechoslovakia (2).

O'Neill, J.N. (1) 1961 v Wales.

O'Neill, K. (8) 1996 v (Portugal), Croatia, (Holland), (USA), Mexico, Bolivia; 1997 v Liechtenstein, Macedonia.

O'Regan, K. (4) 1984 v Malta, Poland; 1985 v Mexico, (Spain).

O'Reilly, J. (2) 1946 v Portugal, Spain.

Peyton, G. (33) 1977 v (Spain); 1978 v Bulgaria, Turkey, Poland; 1979 v Denmark, Bulgaria, West Germany; 1980 v Wales, Czechoslovakia, Bulgaria, England, Cyprus, Switzerland, Argentina; 1981 v Holland, Belgium, France, Cyprus; 1982 v Trinidad & Tobago; 1985 v (Mexico); 1986 v Wales, Czechoslovakia; 1988 v Luxembourg, Poland; 1989 v N. Ireland, Tunisia; 1990 v USSR, Malta; 1991 v Chile; 1992 v USA (2), (Italy), Portugal.

Peyton, N. (6) 1957 v West Germany; 1960 v West Germany, (Sweden); 1961 v Wales; 1963 v Iceland, Scotland.

Phelan, T. (35) 1992 v Hungary, (Poland), Turkey, Wales, Switzerland, USA, (Italy), Portugal; 1993 v (Latvia), Denmark, Spain, N. Ireland, Albania, Latvia, Lithuania; 1994 v Lithuania, Spain, N. Ireland, Holland (2), Bolivia, Germany, Czech Republic, Italy, Mexico; 1995 v England; 1996 v Latvia, Holland (2), Russia, Portugal, Croatia, USA, (Mexico), Bolivia.

Quinn, N.J. (60) 1986 v (Iceland), Czechoslovakia; 1987 v (Bulgaria); 1988 v (Luxembourg), (Bulgaria), Israel, (Romania), (Poland), (England); 1989 v (Tunisia), (Spain), (Hungary); 1990 v USSR, Malta, Egypt, Holland, Romania, Italy; 1991 v Morocco, Turkey, England (2), Wales, Poland; 1992 v Hungary, (Wales), USA (2), Albania, Italy, Portugal; 1993 v Latvia (2), Denmark (2), Spain, N. Ireland, Albania, Lithuania; 1994 v Lithuania, Spain, N. Ireland; 1995 v Latvia, Liechtenstein (2), N. Ireland (2), England, Portugal, Austria; 1996 v Austria, Latvia, Portugal, Russia, Czech Republic, (Portugal), Croatia, (Holland), USA; 1997 v Liechtenstein.

Richardson, D.J. (3) 1972 v (Austria); 1973 v (Norway); 1980 v Czechoslovakia.

Ringstead, A. (20) 1951 v Argentina, Norway; 1952 v West Germany (2), Austria, Spain; 1953 v Austria; 1954 v France; 1955 v Norway; 1956 v Yugoslavia, Spain, Holland; 1957 v England (2); 1958 v Denmark, Poland, Austria; 1959 v Poland, Czechoslovakia (2).

Robinson, M. (23) 1981 v France, Cyprus, Belgium, Poland; 1982 v Holland, France, Algeria, Chile; 1983 v Holland, Iceland, Spain, Malta; 1984 v Iceland, Holland, Israel; 1985 v USSR, Norway (2), Spain, Switzerland; 1986 v (Denmark), Wales, Czechoslovakia.

Roche, P.J. (8) 1972 v Austria; 1975 v USSR (2), Turkey, West Germany, Switzerland (2); 1976 v Turkey.

Rogers, E. (19) 1968 v Czechoslovakia, Poland; 1969 v Poland, Austria, Denmark (2), Czechoslovakia, Hungary; 1970 v Scotland, Denmark, Hungary; 1971 v Italy (2), Austria; 1972 v Iran, Ecuador, Chile, Portugal; 1973 v USSR.

Ryan, G. (16) 1978 v Turkey; 1979 v England, West Germany; 1980 v Wales, (Cyprus), Switzerland, (Argentina); 1981 v (France), (Poland); 1982 v (Holland), (Algeria), (Chile), Trinidad & Tobago; 1984 v Poland, China; 1985 v Mexico.

Ryan, R.A. (16) 1950 v Sweden, Belgium; 1951 v Norway (2), Argentina; 1952 v West Germany (2), Austria, Spain; 1953 v France, Austria; 1954 v France (2), Luxembourg; 1955 v Norway; 1956 v Spain.

Savage, D. (5) 1996 v (Portugal), (Croatia), (USA), Mexico, Bolivia.

Saward, P. (18) 1954 v Luxembourg; 1957 v England (2); 1958 v Denmark, Poland, Austria; 1959 v Poland, Czechoslovakia; 1960 v Sweden (2), Chile, West Germany; 1961 v Wales, Norway, Scotland; 1962 v Austria; 1963 v Iceland (2).

Scannell, T. (1) 1954 v Luxembourg.

Scully, P.J. (1) 1989 v (Tunisia).

Sheedy, K. (45) 1984 v (Holland), Malta; 1985 v Denmark, Italy, Israel, Switzerland; 1986 v Switzerland, Denmark; 1987 v Scotland, Poland; 1988 v Israel, Romania, Poland, (England), USSR; 1989 v N. Ireland, Tunisia, Hungary (2), Spain, Malta; 1990 v N. Ireland, Malta, (Wales), USSR, (Finland), Turkey, England, Egypt, Holland, Romania, Italy; 1991 v Wales, England, Poland, Chile, USA; 1992 v Hungary, Poland, Turkey, Wales, (Switzerland), Albania; 1993 v Latvia, (Wales).

Sheridan, J. (34) 1988 v Romania, Yugoslavia, Poland, (Norway); 1989 v Spain; 1990 v Wales, (Turkey), Malta, (Italy); 1991 v (Morocco), Turkey, Chile, (USA); 1992 v Hungary; 1993 v (Latvia); 1994 v (Spain), Holland (2), Bolivia, Germany, Czech Republic, Italy, Mexico, Norway; 1995 v Latvia, Liechtenstein (2), N. Ireland (2), England, Portugal, Austria; 1996 v Austria, Holland.

Slaven, B. (7) 1990 v Wales, Finland, (Turkey), Malta, 1991 v Wales, (Poland); 1993 v (Wales).

Sloan, J.W. (2) 1946 v Portugal, Spain.

Smyth, M. (1) 1969 v (Poland).

Stapleton, F. (70) 1977 v Turkey, France, Spain, Bulgaria; 1978 v Bulgaria, Norway, Denmark; 1979 v N. Ireland, (England), Denmark, West Germany; 1980 v Wales, Bulgaria, N. Ireland, England, Cyprus; 1981 v Holland, Belgium (2), France, Cyprus, Czechoslovakia, Poland; 1982 v Holland, France, Algeria; 1983 v Holland, Iceland, Spain

(2), Malta; 1984 v Iceland, Holland, Malta, Israel, Poland, China; 1985 v Norway (2), Denmark, Italy, Israel, England, Switzerland; 1986 v Switzerland, USSR, Denmark, Uruguay, Iceland, (Czechoslovakia); 1987 v Belgium (2), Scotland (2), Poland, Bulgaria, Luxembourg; 1988 v Luxembourg, Bulgaria, Romania, Yugoslavia, Norway, England, USSR, Holland; 1989 v France, Spain, Malta; 1990 v West Germany, (Malta).

Staunton, S. (64) 1989 v Tunisia, Spain (2), Malta, Hungary; 1990 v West Germany, N. Ireland, Malta (2), Wales, USSR, Finland, Turkey, England, Egypt, Holland, Romania, Italy; 1991 v Morocco, Turkey, England (2), Wales, Poland, Chile, USA; 1992 v Poland, Turkey, Switzerland, USA (2), Albania, Italy, Portugal; 1993 v Latvia (2), Spain, N. Ireland, Denmark, Albania, Lithuania; 1994 v Lithuania, Spain, Holland (2), Bolivia, Germany, Czech Republic, Italy, Mexico, Norway; 1995 v Latvia, Liechtenstein (2), N. Ireland (2), England, Portugal, Austria; 1996 v Latvia, Portugal, Russia; 1997 v Liechtenstein, Macedonia.

Stevenson, A.E. (7) 1932 v Holland; 1947 v England, Spain, Portugal; 1948 v Portugal, Spain; 1949 v Switzerland.

Strahan, F. (5) 1964 v Poland, Norway, England; 1965 v Poland; 1966 v West Germany.

Swan, M.M.G. (1) 1960 v (Sweden).

Synnott, N. (3) 1978 v Turkey, Poland; 1979 v N. Ireland.

Taylor, T. (1) 1959 v (Poland)

Thomas, P. (2) 1974 v Poland, Brazil.

Townsend, A.D. (62) 1989 v France, (Spain), (Malta), Hungary; 1990 v (West Germany), N. Ireland, Malta, (Malta), Wales, USSR, (Finland), Turkey, England, Egypt, Holland, Romania, Italy; 1991 v Morocco, Turkey, England (2), Wales, Poland, Chile, USA; 1992 v Poland, Wales, USA (2), Albania, Italy; 1993 v Latvia (2), Denmark (2), Spain, N. Ireland, Albania, Lithuania; 1994 v Lithuania, N. Ireland, Holland (2), Bolivia, Germany, Czech Republic, Italy, Mexico, Norway; 1995 v Latvia, N. Ireland (2), England, Portugal; 1996 v Austria, Latvia, Holland, Russia, Czech Republic, Portugal; 1997 v Liechtenstein, Macedonia.

Traynor, T.J. (8) 1954 v Luxembourg; 1962 v Austria; 1963 v Iceland (2), Scotland; 1964 v Austria (2), Spain.

Treacy, R.C.P. (42) 1966 v West Germany; 1967 v Spain, Czechoslovakia; 1968 v Czechoslovakia, Poland; 1969 v Poland, Czechoslovakia, Denmark; 1970 v Scotland, Denmark, (Hungary), (Poland), (West Germany); 1971 v Poland, Sweden, (Sweden), Italy, Austria; 1972 v Iran, Ecuador, Chile, Portugal; 1973 v USSR (2), France (2), Poland, Norway; 1974 v Poland, Brazil; 1975 v USSR, West Germany, Switzerland (2); 1976 v Turkey, (Norway), (Poland); 1977 v France, Poland; 1978 v Turkey, Poland; 1980 v (Czechoslovakia).

Tuohy, L. (8) 1956 v Yugoslavia; 1959 v Czechoslovakia (2); 1962 v Austria; 1963 v Iceland (2); 1964 v Austria; 1965 v Belgium.

Turner, A. (2) 1963 v Scotland; 1964 v Spain.

Vernon, J. (2) 1946 v Portugal, Spain.

Waddock, G. (21) 1980 v Switzerland, Argentina; 1981 v Wales, (Poland); 1982 v Algeria; 1983 v (Holland), Iceland, Malta, Spain, (Holland); 1984 v Iceland, Holland, Israel; 1985 v Italy, Israel, England, Norway, Spain; 1986 v USSR; 1990 v USSR, Turkey.

Walsh, D.J. (20) 1946 v Portugal, Spain; 1947 v Spain, Portugal; 1948 v Portugal, Spain; 1949 v Switzerland, Portugal, Sweden, Spain; 1950 v England, Finland, Sweden; 1951 v Norway (2), Argentina; 1952 v Spain; 1953 v Austria; 1954 v France (2).

Walsh, J. (1) 1982 v Trinidad & Tobago.

Walsh, M.A. (21) 1976 v Norway, Poland; 1977 v (France), Poland; 1979 v (N. Ireland), (Denmark), Bulgaria, (West Germany); 1981 v (Belgium), Czechoslovakia; 1982 v (Algeria); 1983 v (Holland), Spain, (Spain); 1984 v (Iceland), Malta, Poland, China; 1985 v USSR, (Norway), Denmark.

Walsh, M.T. (4) 1982 v Chile, Brazil, Trinidad & Tobago; 1983 v Iceland.

Walsh, W. (9) 1947 v England, Spain, Portugal; 1948 v Portugal, Spain; 1949 v Belgium; 1950 v England, Sweden, Belgium.

Waters, J. (2) 1977 v Turkey; 1980 v (N. Ireland).

Whelan, R. (2) 1964 v Austria, (England).

Whelan, R. (53) 1981 v (Czechoslovakia); 1982 v (Holland), France; 1983 v Iceland, Malta, Spain; 1984 v Israel; 1985 v USSR, Norway (Norway), (Italy), Israel, England, (Switzerland); 1986 v (USSR), Wales; 1987 v Belgium, (Belgium), Scotland, Bulgaria, Brazil, Luxembourg; 1988 v Luxembourg, Bulgaria, Poland, Norway, England, USSR, Holland; 1989 v N. Ireland, France, Hungary, Spain, Malta; 1990 v West Germany, N. Ireland, Malta, Wales, (Holland); 1991 v Morocco, England; 1992 v Switzerland, 1993 v Latvia, (Wales), (Lithuania); 1994 v (Lithuania), Spain, Russia, Holland, (Germany), (Norway); 1995 v (Liechtenstein), Austria.

Whelan, W. (4) 1956 v Holland; 1957 v Denmark, England (2).

Whittaker, R. (1) 1959 v Czechoslovakia.

APPENDIX C:
EIRE GOALSCORERS
1945–96

Aldridge, J.	19	Ambrose, P.	1
Anderson, J.	1	Brady, L.	9
Breen, G.	1	Byrne, J.	4
Cantwell, N.	14	Carey, J.	3
Carroll, T.	1	Cascarino, T.	14
Coad, P.	3	Connolly, D.	2
Conroy, T.	2	Conway, J.	3
Coyne, T.	6	Cummins, G.	5
Curtis, D.	8	Daly, G.	13
Dempsey, J.	1	Dennehy, M.	2
Duffy, B.	1	Eglington, T.	2
Fagan, F.	5	Fallon, S.	2
Farrell, P.	3	Fitzgerald, P.	2
Fitzgerald, J.	1	Fitzsimons, A.	7
Fogarty, A.	3	Fullam, J.	1
Galvin, A.	1	Gavin, J.	2
Giles, J.	5	Givens, D.	19
Glynn, D.	1	Grealish, T.	8
Grimes, A.	1	Hale, A.	2
Hand, E.	2	Harte, I.	2
Haverty, J.	3	Holmes, J.	1
Houghton, R.	5	Hughton, C.	1
Hurley, C.	2	Irwin, D.	1
Keane, R.	1	Kelly, D.	8
Kelly, G.	1	Kernaghan, A.	1
Lawrenson, M.	5	Leech, M.	2
McAteer, J.	1	McCann, J.	1
McCarthy, M.	2	McEvoy, A.	6
McGee, P.	4	McGrath, P.	6
McLoughlin, A.	1	Mancini, T.	1
Martin, C.	6	Martin, M.	4
Mooney, J.	1	Moran, K.	6

Moroney, T.	1	Mulligan, P.	1
O'Callaghan, K.	1	O'Connor, T.	2
O'Farrell, F.	2	O'Flanagan, K.	3
O'Keefe, E.	1	O'Leary, D.	1
O'Neill, F.	1	O'Neill, K.	4
O'Reilly, J.	1	Quinn, N.	16
Ringstead, A.	7	Robinson M.	4
Rogers, E.	5	Ryan, G.	1
Ryan, R.	3	Sheedy, K.	9
Sheridan, J.	5	Slaven, B.	1
Sloan, J.	1	Stapleton, F.	20
Staunton, S.	6	Strahan, F.	1
Townsend, A.	7	Treacy, R.	5
Tuohy, L.	4	Waddock, G.	3
Walsh, D.	5	Walsh, M.A.	3
Waters, J.	1	Whelan, R. (jun.)	3

APPENDIX D:
EIRE INTERNATIONALS WHO HOLD THE CAPS RECORD AT THEIR CLUBS

CLUB	CAPS WON WITH CLUB	TOTAL CAPS	PLAYER
ASTON VILLA	51	(82)	Paul McGrath
BOURNEMOUTH	7	(33)	Gerry Peyton
BURY	11	(13)	Bill Gorman
EXETER CITY	1	(17)	Dermot Curtis
GILLINGHAM	3	(65)	Tony Cascarino
HARTLEPOOL	1	(11)	Ambrose Fogarty
LINCOLN CITY	3	(3)	George Moulson*
MILLWALL	22	(23)	Eamonn Dunphy
TRANMERE ROVERS	29	(68)	John Aldridge
WALSALL	15	(18)	Mick Kearns
WIMBLEDON	8	(35)	Terry Phelan
MOTHERWELL	12	(21)	Tommy Coyne**

* Shares the record with David Pugh (Wales).
** Shares the record with George Stevenson (Scotland).

NOTE: George McKenzie, who won nine Eire caps in 1938 and 1939, holds the record at Southend United.